PATRICK PEARSE

Collected Plays

Drámaí an Phiarsaigh

PATRICK PEARSE

Collected Plays

Drámaí an Phiarsaigh

Róisín Ní Ghairbhí

Eugene McNulty

IRISH ACADEMIC PRESS

First published in 2013 by Irish Academic Press

8 Chapel Lane
Sallins
Co. Kildare, Ireland

British Library Cataloguing in Publication Data
Pearse, Padraic, 1879-1916.
Patrick Pearse : collected plays.
I. Title II. Ní Ghairbhí, Róisín. III. McNulty, Eugene.
822.9'12-dc23
ISBN-13: 9780716531555

ISBN: 978 0 7165 3155 5 (cloth)
ISBN: 978 0 7165 3166 1 (paper)
ISBN: 978 0 7165 3214 9 (ebook)

Library of Congress Cataloging-in-Publication Data
An entry can be found on request

Printed in Ireland by
SPRINT-print

CONTENTS

v

Treatments of 'scriptless' plays:

ACKNOWLEDGEMENTS

The Editors would like to express their appreciation to Lisa Hyde and everyone at Irish Academic Press for their patience and assistance with this project. The archival nature of this work has meant we have relied on the knowledge and goodwill of many librarians and archivists, in particular those of the National Library of Ireland, Trinity College Dublin, University College Dublin, the Allen Library and St. Patrick's College, Drumcondra. A very special word of thanks is due to Brian Crowley (Pearse Museum and Kilmainham Museum), without whose knowledge, patience, generosity and guidance this book would not have seen the light of day. The Research Committee at St. Patrick's College also did much to help this project come to fruition; likewise, all our colleagues at St. Patrick's have been unfailing in their support and encouragement. Buíochas ó chroí le Alf and Fionnuala Mac Lochlainn for a stimulating afternoon's conversation that brought the Pearse and MacLochlainn families to life. Sincere thanks to Mr Dave Kenny, journalist, for information about his Walker relations.

Ba mhaith le Róisín buíochas mór a ghabháil le Aidan Lee agus le muintir Uí Ghairbhí as a dtacaíocht agus í ag obair ar an leabhar seo. Saolaíodh Sadhbh Ní Laoi díreach agus an obair á cur i gcrích; b'fhéidir go léifidh sí lá éigin é.

Eugene McNulty would like to thank his family for all their usual support and kindnesses – and in particular young Laura who missed out on the last acknowledgements. Moya and Michael were always interested in the world of Pearse and he hopes they like the end result.

NOTE FROM THE EDITORS

In putting together this new edition of Pearse's plays we have returned to the original sources where possible; in some cases this was the manuscript, in others the first published source. Where variant forms of plays exist this is indicated and material from the alternative version appended. This return to the archive has resulted in the publication here for the first time of *Eoghan Gabha*, and we have provided a translation of this 'lost' play for the interest of readers without Irish.

With the momentum building towards the centenary year of 2016, it seems an opportune moment to return to the work that so occupied Pearse in the years before he became an icon of rebellion. His plays have largely been out of print for a number of years, and with this new edition we hope to introduce or re-introduce these fascinating performance pieces to those readers and theatre practitioners interested in Pearse's contribution to the world of Irish drama. As well as the plays themselves, we have been keen to provide as much contextual material as possible, and so we have provided a substantial selection of Pearse's writings on the theatre (see Appendices) as well as detailed descriptive treatments of those performance pieces for which no script remains extant.

In all of this our approach has been deliberately inter-disciplinary and bilingual: a false dichotomy has too often been drawn between Revivalists who worked mainly in Irish and those who worked in English. Our hope is to have provided an edition that is as accessible and comprehensive as possible – and to this end we have endeavoured to gloss many of the major names and terms encountered when reading about this period of Irish history.

In the build up to 2016 we hope that these plays will draw a new generation of readers and that interested theatre practitioners may find in them a source for innovative and imaginative new productions. Perhaps too these plays will provide some ground on which to explore Pearse's wish that 'the old truths will find new mouths, the old sorrows and ecstasies new interpretation'.[1]

Nóta faoin eagarthóireacht do léitheoirí Gaeilge

Maidir le gach dráma dá bhfuil anseo baineadh leas as an bhfoinse is túisce dar foilsíodh agus an script á réiteach; baineadh leas as an mbunscríbhinn i gcás *Eoghan Gabha*. Chuathas siar go dtí bunscríbhinní agus seiceáladh aistriúcháin an Phiarsaigh féin sa chás go raibh aon amhras faoi bhrí aon fhocail ar leith. Tá mionfhaisnéis faoi na foinsí sin tugtha i dteannta na ndrámaí féin. Sa chás go raibh leaganacha malartacha den script ar fáil (dhein an Piarsach forleathnú ar a bhunscript do léiriú in Amharclann na Mainistreach i gcás *Íosagán*, mar shampla) tugadh é sin le fios sna nótaí faoin dráma féin agus deineadh eolas a sholáthar i dtaobh ábhair bhreise i dteannta na scripte.

Chleacht Pádraig Mac Piarais dhá shaghas friotail ina shaothar drámaíochta. Shaothraigh sé gnáthchaint na Gaeltachta i ndrámaí a bhí suite faoin tuath (*Íosagán*, mar shampla) agus bhain leas as réim ard fhoirmeálta sna drámaí dá chuid a bhí fréamhaithe san ardlitríocht (*Macghníomhartha Chúchulainn*) nó a bhí suite i suíomh a mheabhródh an ardlitríocht sin (*An Rí*). Ó tharla gur aithris ar an saol beo an drámaíocht síleadh gur chóir an canúnachas a chleacht an Piarsach d'aon ghnó i ndrámaí áirithe a aithint san eagrán seo, go háirithe nuair a thug sé féin le fios gur d'aon ghnó a bhain sé leas as leaganacha canúnacha agus as Béarlachas sna drámaí sin:

I have as religiously followed the phraseology of the children and old men in Iar-Connacht from whom I have learned the Irish I speak. I have put no word, no speech, into the mouths of my little boys which the real little boys of the parish I have in mind boys whom I know as well as my pupils at Sgoil Eanna would not use in the same circumstances. I have given their daily conversation, anglicisms, 'vulgarisms' and all: if I gave anything else my picture would be a false one.[2]

Mar sin, cé gur deineadh caighdeánú áirithe, go háirithe ar an litriú, fágadh mar a bhí foirmeacha áirithe de bhriathra ar léir iad a bheith in úsáid d'aon ghnó ag an bPiarsach chun canúint áite ar leith a thabhairt le fios sa dráma *Íosagán*. Cás spéisiúil ar leith ab ea *Eoghan Gabha*, dráma stairiúil a bhain leas as gnáthchaint na Gaeltachta, cé nach Gaeilge Chonamara tríd síos a bhí ann.

Maidir le *Macghníomhartha Chúchulainn* is féidir a rá gur cóiriú é ar ábhar ón *Táin*. Bhí ceist úsáid na gnáthchainte i gcóiriú é ar mhórshaothair na Gaeilge ar cheann de dhíospóireachtaí coitianta lucht Athbheochan na litríochta Gaeilge. Bhí an cheist tarraingte anuas chomh luath leis an mbliain 1910 ag W. B. Yeats agus é ag fáil lochta ar an leagan drámata a bhí déanta ag an Athair Peadar Ó Laoghaire ar an Táin '(a) long rambling drama-tisation'…'in which I hear in the midst of the exuberant Gaelic dialogue the worn-out conventions of English poetic drama'.[3] Fuair moltóirí Oireachtas na bliana 1910, agus Thomas Mac Donagh mar cheann orthu, locht ar an easpa dílseachta do bhunréim na Tána ('modern phrases in the mouths of Red Branch Warriors') maidir le hiarrachtaí na bliana sin.[4] Faoi mar is léir ach comparáid thapaidh a dhéanamh idir eagrán Windisch den Táin agus *Macghníomhartha*, dhein an Piarsach aithris chinnte ar réim ard na litríochta in *Macghníomhartha Chúchulainn* agus dúirt sé féin gur thábhachtach leis an dílseacht seo do theanga na mbunscríbhinní ('religiously followed the phraseology of the Táin').[5] Tugadh aitheantas do mhian seo an Phiarsaigh san eagrán seo. Fágadh 'go bheith inchomhraic do na macaibh beaga seo' leagan *An Macaomh* san áit gur 'go mbeadh na mic bheaga seo inchomhraic' atá ag Ó Buachalla agus coimeádadh na foirmeacha táite sna hamhráin (cloíodh le 'buaileam' in áit 'buailimis' Uí Bhuachalla, mar shampla.)[6] Bheartaigh Mac Piarais 'do' a úsáid in áit 'a' roimh an ainmbhriathar sna treoracha stáitse – is léir go raibh súil aige go léifí an script mar scéal chomh maith agus chloígh sé le stíl chlasaiceach tríd síos. Cloíodh le stíl sin an Phiarsaigh – seo, mar shampla, na treoracha a fhaightear ag tús *Macghníomhartha*: 'Ceol do sheinm. An cór do theacht ar an láthair agus do ghluaiseacht ar fud na páirce'. Cé go bhfágann an cinneadh cloí le mian an Phiarsaigh bheith dílis do *pharole* agus do stíl an bhunábhair Rúraíochta go mbeidh dúshlán beag ann do chompántas a thabharfadh faoin script dílis seo, creideadh go gcaillfí sainmhianach na ceolréime mar ar shamhlaigh an Piarsach é dá gcuirfí nuachaighdeán i bhfeidhm scun scan.

Níl script chlóscríofa *Eoghan Gabha* de réir na scripte lámhscríofa ar fad ar fad cé gur miondifríochtaí a bhíonn i gceist. Ó tharla gur léir gur míléamha cuid de na difríochtaí seo, agus ós rud é nach bhfuilimid cinnte gurb é an Piarsach a dhein an clóscríobh, tugadh tús áite don script lámhscríofa, a bhfuilimid cinnte gur leis an bPiarsach é. Cé gur tugadh a ceart don chanúint in *Íosagán*, tugadh úsáid idirmhalartach do/de mar 'do' chun caighdeáin. Maidir leis an litriú tugadh focail a mbeadh cuma aisteach orthu do léitheoirí nó aisteoirí an lae inniu chun caighdeáin ('inniu' in áit 'indiu') ach fágadh leaganacha canúnacha a bhfuil tuiscint fhorleathan orthu ('nár dhúirt' mar shampla) ar an gcúis gur cuid den dráma cruthú an tsuímh trí úsáid canúna.

Cé gur bunsaothar é *An Rí*, ós cosúil go bhfuil sé suite i ré na Meán-Ghaeilge agus ós léir iarracht ar leith a bheith déanta ag an bPiarsach úsáid a bhaint as réim fhoirmeálta liteartha beartaíodh gur cheart an réim sin a fhágaint mar a bhí. Mar sin, fágadh leaganacha a thuigtear go coitianta agus ar cuid den réim fhoirmeálta sin iad: cloíodh le 'do labhairt' in áit 'a labhairt', mar shampla. Is focail don bhéal agus don chluas a bhíonn i scríbhinn dráma. Mar sin, deineadh caighdeánú ar an litriú tríd síos: 'ó'n mainistir' mar 'ón mainistir' munar chuir sé isteach ar an bhfuaim.

Maidir leis na drámaí seo go léir tá caighdeánú déanta maidir le húsáid fleiscíní (bhí nósmhaireacht an-ait ag an bPiarsach maidir le húsáid fleiscíní) agus deineadh caighdeánú ar litriú focal, ach amháin nuair ba dhlúthchuid den stíl nó den rithim leaganacha ar leith nó má theastaigh siad don cheol. Ar an ábhar seo, agus mar bharr ar na cúiseanna a luadh thuas, fágadh an seanleagan den tuiseal tabharthach ('in irisibh') mar a bhí sna ranna a chuireann tús le gach gníomh in *Macghníomhartha Chúchulainn*. Cloíodh le litriú ainmneacha na gcarachtar faoi mar a bhí ag an bPiarsach (Conchubhar, Follamhan): ba iad na leaganacha céanna sin a bhí ag Mac Piarais is é ag scríobh i mBéarla chomh maith.

NOTE ON THE TRANSLATION OF *EOGHAN GABHA*

While the events depicted in *Eoghan Gabha* are set at the close of the seventeenth century, the language in the original Irish language version of the play is colloquial rather than the formal literary language of *Macghníomhartha Chúchulainn*. As such, the translator follows Pearse's own style when translating ordinary dialogue, according to the exemplar of his own use of everyday Hiberno-English in *The Singer*. This style is not a direct 'foreignising' translation of Irish, such as Synge or Lady Gregory practised but rather an approximation of the Hibernicised style of English still spoken by many people in Ireland. Holloway recalled Pearse's disapproval of Lady Gregory's Kiltartan dialect: 'Lady Gregory's dialect is spoken by no Irish people – it is a sort of free translation of the Gaelic of thought. It distracts the listener from the play & anything that does that on the stage is not good'.[7] Again following a similar usage in *The Singer*, and in his programme summaries for various plays some Gaelicisms in common use are left in place in this translation of *Eoghan Gabha* ('mar dhea' and 'mí-ádh', for example). The verses sung by Muircheartach na mBan are translated in verse that approximates to the original rhythm, which results in some slight deviations from the exact sense of the original in the song translation. While the word 'people' features in the English translation of *Eoghan Gabha* it should be noted that the phrase translates different words in the original Irish 'ginealach mo shinsear' ('the genealogy of my forebears/my ancestors') and 'treibh' ('tribe'). Indeed the nuances of the Irish words approximating to 'people' which are used by Colm in the context of his preoccupation with his father's story help to throw light on Pearse's very particular use of this word in his creative and political writing, where it signifies a hereditary sense of identity. While *Eoghan Gabha* is a lightweight piece and is unfinished it is included here for completion's sake and for the interest of its subject matter.

NOTES

1 'By Way of Comment', *An Macaomh*, May, 1913, p.8.
2 'By Way of Comment', *An Macaomh*, Nollaig, 1909, lch.42.
3 W.B. Yeats, Windlestraws, *Samhain*, October 1901, pp.3–10, 7.
4 'The Oireachtas', *An Claidheamh Soluis*, 21 May 1910.
5 'By Way of Comment', *An Macaomh*, Nollaig, 1910, lch. 42.
6 Féach Séamus Ó Buachalla, (eag.) *Pádraig Mac Piarais: Scríbhinní* (Dublin: Mercier Press, 1979).
7 Joseph Holloway, diary entry in January 1911, transcription courtesy of Brian Crowley.

LIST OF ILLUSTRATIONS

Back row, left to right: Éamonn Bulfin, Conor McGinley, Desmond Ryan, Fintan Murphy, Peter Slattery. Front row, left to right: Brian Joyce, Frank Burke, Eunan McGinley, Joseph Sweeney. Bulfin, Murphy, and the two McGinleys would later take part in the 1917 production of *The Singer*. Iarscoláirí agus múinteoirí ó Scoil Éanna an lá roimh Éirí Amach na Cásca: Éamonn Bulfin, Conor McGinley, Desmond Ryan, Fintan Murphy, Peter Slattery ar cúl, clé go deas. Brian Joyce, Frank Burke, Eunan McGinley, Joseph Sweeney chun tosaigh. Ghlac Bulfin, Murphy agus an bheirt Mhac Fhionnlaoich páirt i léiriú *The Singer* sa bhliain 1917.

INTRODUCTION
PATRICK PEARSE AND THE THEATRE

There is something innately theatrical about the images of Patrick Pearse inscribed in the Irish collective psyche. The most powerful of these imaginative snapshots is undoubtedly that of Pearse standing on the steps of the GPO proclaiming the Irish Republic on that Easter Monday of 1916. It is a moment that can now never escape its own future: this is the act that launches not just another rebellion but Ireland's journey towards independent statehood. But there is something slightly awry in this classic tableau of one man speaking against the might of an empire – there are no steps at the front of the General Post Office. This slight slip between event and remembrance is telling. The collective mis-remembrance suggests a desire to raise Pearse up a little, removed from the crowd around him, to invest in him an extra quantum of authority and perspective – a desire, in other words, to re-create the event as if on a stage, to imbue it with the quality of theatre.[1] One can only think that Pearse would have been pleased with this transformative act of memory; as his sister Mary Brigid would later remember, her brother's 'love for, and interest in, everything relating to "Stageland"' was 'evident from a very early age'.[2] There seems little doubt, moreover, that Pearse envisaged his act of rebellion in terms of the dramatic: the GPO may have been a flawed base militarily but was inspired as a public staging, enabling the rebellion to be powerfully performative. By enunciating the Republic by way of symbolic proclamation, Pearse saw himself as drawing it into existence, performing its reality. For Pearse, politics *was* theatre:

1

after all, this was the man who had electrified Dublin with the rhetoric of his oration at the graveside of O'Donovan Rossa, who had taken the title for the first of his political pamphlets, *Ghosts*, from an Ibsen play, and who spent his final weeks not only planning a revolution but writing a play on that very topic.[3]

While Cathal Ó hÁinle's excellent *Gearrscéalta an Phiarsaigh* (1979) brought Pearse's short stories to renewed public attention and restored their place in the literary canon, Pearse's status as a dramatist is less secure and his dramatic works remain relatively unknown. It was not always so. At the time of their first performance Pearse's plays were viewed by a *who's who* of the Dublin literati and were reported on and discussed widely and positively in the press. While Patrick Pearse is now not generally thought of as a playwright, he was the author and producer of ten plays and pageants, ranging from the 1909 production of the pageant *Macghníomhartha Chúchulainn* to the quasi-autobiographical *The Singer* which was completed shortly before the 1916 Rising. Pearse wrote two miracle plays, *Íosagán* and *An Rí/The King*. Two more plays deal with the politics of rebellion: the short and simple *Owen* and the more nuanced *The Master*. There are four 'scriptless' plays or pageants: *An Pháis/The Passion Play*, *Fionn: A Dramatic Spectacle*, *The Defence of the Ford* and *The Fianna of Fionn*.[4] In addition to these ten works there exists a hitherto unpublished play, *Eoghan Gabha*. Pearse acted in some of his own productions and he produced them all, excepting the unfinished *Eoghan Gabha*. His work in the theatre also involved attempts to reclaim a native dramatic tradition – such as his staging of *Dúnlaing Óg agus an Leannán Sí*. This edition is the first to draw all these works together and to present them fully in the context of Pearse's ideas on theatre practice.[5]

Pearse's belief in the power of theatre to inform and transform was far from unique to him (although his commitment to the performative in the political realm does mark him out as exceptional in other ways). If there was a single unifying drive behind the cultural-nationalist project that is generally termed the 'Revival', or 'An Athbheochan' in Irish, it was the ambition to perform identity in newly empowering ways. Examining Pearse in the context of his commitment to cultural nationalism reveals a thinker and activist who had a deep understanding of not just the power but also the mechanics of theatre. In putting together this new edition of his plays, we have been interested to rewind from that iconic moment in 1916, to draw Pearse out from the shadow of his future self, and future iconic status, and in so doing to rediscover aspects of Pearse the cultural activist, the literary enthusiast and, most importantly, the theatre obsessive.

Critics familiar with the Irish language have long interested themselves in Pearse's pioneering role as a literary theorist and innovator.[6] But by and large, though with notable exceptions, commentators working solely in English have tended to deal with his literary writings in a cursory fashion or in a simplistic reading as biographical sources.[7] In particular, Pearse's writings on and work in the theatre are too often seen as mere adjuncts to an ideological journey from educationalist and language enthusiast to political revolutionary. The idea that Pearse's earlier work was merely a playful or propagandistic preparation for the 'real action' ahead is a damaging over-simplification of a much more subtle career and life. A return to his play scripts (and we hope their fresh publication will encourage their staging) reveals a more complex picture, one in which Pearse emerges as a dedicated theatre practitioner concerned with exploring the limits of dramatic art and its relationship to wider society. Our focus here is on Pearse's dramatic *oeuvre* as literature and on his practice as a man of the theatre – not merely as a cipher for a psyche or an agenda. In order to understand the reasons for the remarkable impact that his dramatic works had when first performed, Pearse's plays will be examined in their original context, as scripts and performances which had their genesis in his involvement in networks of radical, pioneering and cosmopolitan cultural activists.

In this regard the years either side of the twentieth-century's turn was a time when the idea of a specifically Irish theatre began to take shape. This was to be a theatre that would reveal Ireland back to itself, a theatre that would strip away the layers of distortion and caricature that had characterised represent-ation of the Irish on stage for much of the nineteenth century.

The founding of the Irish Literary Theatre in 1897, the inauguration of the first Oireachtas literary and cultural festival that same year and the *Tableaux Vivants* of the newly founded Inghinidhe na hÉireann all helped to create an impetus for a widespread desire for imagining a new identity through performance. An audience was also being cultivated: thousands attended performances of native art performed by their own communities at Feiseanna and Aeraíochtaí all around the country, and cultural-nationalist theatre groups such as Belfast's Ulster Literary Theatre (1904) began to be established in the major cities. The nature of this emerging Irish theatre was debated in newspapers and in specialist magazines such as Alice Milligan's *Shan Van Vocht*, Yeats's *Bealtaine* and *Samhain,* and *The Irish Review*. Rejecting the melodramatic and the formulaic, some (if not all) Irish writers sought to reposition the theatre as a space for debate, for exploration and experimentation, for the taking up of positions and the deconstruction of perceived notions of what it meant to be Irish. These were formative years for Pearse and the role of theatre in creating a new independent Ireland was something that much occupied him. Indeed, along with the Revival in language and literature, and the development of a native education system, the formation of a properly 'Irish theatre' is the issue to which Pearse devoted much of his intellectual energy in the first decade of the twentieth century. Crucially, moreover, these issues were not separate projects in Pearse's eyes – rather they were interlinked elements of the nationalist mission. The Irish language, a native Irish theatre, and an education system built round the specificities of Irish history, culture and temperament were all in a sense external significations of a much deeper-set desire to re-perform a truly independent Irish identity.

Much recent Irish theatre historiography has sought to reappraise the Revival period and in so doing has drawn attention to a number of 'alternative' histories.[8] One of the consequences of this work has been to reveal the depth and scope of Patrick Pearse's involvement in the idea and practice of a distinctly Irish mode of theatre at the beginning of the twentieth century. Mary Trotter's study, for example, locates

Pearse's work as part of a matrix of performative practice that reveals a counter-history to the Abbey-centric narratives that dominated Irish theatre history for so long. Elaine Sisson's *Pearse's Patriots: St. Enda's and the Cult of Boyhood* is equally a rich source of information on Pearse's plays. The focus suggested by its subtitle does, however, at times limit its interpretative range. The discussion of the choice of Frank Dowling for Cúchulainn, for instance, notes his good looks but does not note that Dowling came from a Fenian family.[9] We would argue that Pearse's work has too often been subject to a rather narrow critical gaze of one sort or another.

The question of professional versus amateur endeavour has been another limiting focus in studies of the Revival period. While critics, understandably perhaps, tend to concentrate on professional companies and productions, the reality is that during the Revival very many important productions were by amateur groups or professional productions aided or instigated by amateurs. To cite just some examples from Pearse's work: *An Rí* was staged along with an Abbey production of The Post Office where three of the actors were St. Enda's boys[10], the *Passion Play* was staged by School staff and pupils in the Abbey and *The Master* and *Íosagán* were staged in the Irish Theatre. The way in which the *Passion Play* in particular 'created something of a minor sensation in Dublin' suggests that for contemporary theatregoers the delineation of amateur and professional was of much less import than would be the case today.[11] For Pearse, then, the theatre was not a career. Rather it was a space in which to express ideas and ideals in a time when the very idea of what it was to be Irish was being explored and reinvented and in a city where the lines between performance and reality were at times permeable and shifting.

PERFORMING IDENTITY

Much of Pearse's writing is haunted by the shade of an authentic and uninhibited Irish identity that had been trapped and critically injured by the imposed constrictions of imperial modernity, the English language, and British education methodologies. Rather than the direct politicality with which his name is usually associated, indeed, much of the young Pearse's energies were devoted to addressing the cultural condition of this captive psyche. Writing about the ideals and vision that drove him to establish his own school, for example, Pearse focuses in on the nature of the individual and the struggle to set free each unique selfhood:

> In point of fact, man is not primarily a member of a State, but a human individuality – that is, a human soul imprisoned in a human body; a shivering human soul with its own awful problems, its own august identity, lonelier in its house of clay than any prisoner in any Bastille in the world.[12]

This relationship between self and world is clearly something that much occupied Pearse. His unfinished memoir begins with a moment of reflection on this very question of the relationship between one's deepest self and the world in which it operates:

> I am not sure whether it is a good thing for a man to possess, as fully as I have possessed it, the faculty of getting, as it were, outside of himself and contemplating himself as if from a little distance.[13]

It is a telling moment of self-interrogation, and its enunciation reveals an understanding of identity as intrinsically performative in nature. In a remarkable open 'letter' to himself written in 1912, moreover, Pearse once again works through this fascination with the dialogue between inner self and its external performance in the world:

> I imagine that there are two Pearses, one a cheerless, wintry person and the other pleasant, calm and serene. The calm serene person is seen all too seldom. On public platforms and in Sgoil Éanna he is most often seen. The dull cheerless person is frequently to be seen. He is not a pleasant type. I do not like him. I grow chill when I see him. The funny aspect of this is that I am not sure which is the real Pearse, the gloomy or the bright one.[14]

Such sensitivities to the boundaries between public and private selves, between internal character and external perception, between multiple performative versions of selfhood, reveal an intellect perfectly attuned to the nature of theatre and its role in the re-articulation of personal and collective identity.

EARLY INTEREST IN THEATRE

It is of little surprise, then, that Pearse was attracted to the practice of theatre from a very young age. In her *Home Life of Pádraig Pearse* his sister Mary Brigid would recall that: 'All his life he was a devoted disciple of the dramatic art. When he was a mere child he began to write plays and to teach us how to act them'.[15] It would seem that Pearse began to write plays at the age of 'nine or thereabouts'.[16] These performances clearly made a lasting impact on Mary Brigid, who could recall in great detail the plays that Patrick had composed, directed and acted in during his childhood. These included a melodramatic romance, *The Rival Lovers*, performed with his siblings and cousin Mary Kate and a verse play called *The Pride of Finisterre*. Mary Brigid quotes at length from this latter play in her memoir, which may indicate that the script survived, at least at the time of her writing in the mid 1920s.[17] Another of these early theatrical attempts was a verse play called *The Crusaders* which was never produced, but whose verse poetry was admired by Pearse's father. Other plays written by the young Pearse were for performance with cardboard figures and scenery that Patrick and his brother Willie drew and that Willie set up. One of these plays, written for Willie, told a story set around the Battle of Clontarf. The text quoted in her memoir by Mary Brigid shows that while the young Pearse might have had a precocious interest in Irish history, his view of that history was still filtered through the bombastic and clichéd rhetoric of nationalist ballads and needed a little fine tuning: the closing lament in the Brian Boru play tells the men of Erin to weep as their 'monarch has been slain'.[18] The play also featured a romantic plot about love across enemy lines. The busy young Pearse also wrote a dramatic version of *Uncle Tom's Cabin* for Mary Brigid to perform with the cardboard theatre; a piece that Mary Brigid identifies as revealing her brother's early interest in the dangers of power and the idea of liberty. Indeed the message and tenor of the lines from the play recalled by Mary Brigid anticipate the message and tenor of the adult Pearse's late poem 'The Rebel':

> We stand upon the soil of God and tell you we are free;
> We'll die before we'll wear again the chains of liberty.[19]

The use of verse was a notable aspect of Pearse's early plays: he had a life-long love of Shakespeare and balladry. The whole family was drawn into enactments of *Macbeth* and Patrick and Willie often acted out the quarrel scene from *Julius Caesar*, Patrick playing Brutus and Willie Cassius.[20]

Such memories paint a picture of the young Pearse as having a precocious interest in theatre and performance. The fact that he continued to pursue that interest as a grown man is not surprising. After all, as Máire Nic Shiubhlaigh would recall, Pearse came of age in a city that was 'theatre-mad', where 'the most unexpected people in Dublin, poets, writers, artists were interested in the theatre; everyone was ready to discuss a new play or the work of a player'.[21] Pearse's involvement in this cultural scene intensified when he joined the Gaelic League in October 1896 at the age of seventeen. Pearse quickly became one of the League's most energetic and committed activists; he would also be one of the major proponents of the League's engagement with theatre and new writing for Irish language dramas. The Gaelic League's interest in theatre as a space for cultural resistance can be seen most clearly in its promotion of competitions for newly written plays that gradually came to form an important part of the annual Oireachtas festival.[22] While many of the early plays in Irish, even the prizewinning plays presented during the Oireachtas, were often unsophisticated, propagandistic or wordy, some nonetheless enjoyed huge audiences: the room where the Oireachtas plays were staged at the Rotunda held an audience of several thousand.

The Gaelic League played an increasingly dominant role in Pearse's life in the years from 1896 until the founding of St. Enda's in 1908. During this period Pearse would take on a punishing schedule of writing, lecturing and organising for the League, a schedule that intensified when he took on editorship of its newspaper *An Claidheamh Soluis* in 1903. As Secretary of Coiste na gClónna, the publishing committee of the League, Pearse was also immediately *au fait* with the latest editions of Gaelic literary texts and with all new plays in Gaelic. Pearse's attitude to literature and culture during this period is often presented as one dimensional and profoundly conservative – his youthful dismissal of the English-language literary revival and infamous caricature of W.B. Yeats as 'a mere English poet of the third or fourth rank' is often produced as evidence.[23] In reality Pearse's intellectual engagement with culture was more dynamic and open- minded. His interest in acting, for example, continued and was not limited to the theatre. A curiosity about poverty led him to embark on undercover expeditions with his nephew Alf McGloughlin:

> … just before he founded St. Enda's in fact, he used to masquerade as a poor man. His object was to find out by experience, how to beg. (…) He and Alfred went out more than once around the roads in Donnybrook, where we were living at the time and asked for alms.[24]

While such exploits might seem like uncharacteristic behaviour for a qualified barrister and putative schoolmaster, we should recall that Pearse mixed in bohemian circles and he himself came from a home where independence of thought was valued and artists were frequent visitors.

Philip O'Leary identifies Pearse, along with Pádraic Ó Conaire as being of the 'progressive' rather than 'nativist' strand of Gaelic writers and theorists.[25] While he may have begun his career with the Gaelic League by adopting fixed conservative positions – perhaps to prove his trustworthiness in roles of responsibility – he soon developed a more personal and complex set of ideas and ideals. As Joost Augusteijn puts it:

'When he began to form his own ideas he became more confident and increasingly critical of the narrow-minded insular attitude which led some members to form vigilante committees against evil foreign literature. Patrick began to warn against fanaticism and attacked such nativist philistinism masquerading as moral fervour'.[26] While Pearse would always celebrate 'old Irish literature and prose like the nativists ... unlike them he ... also believed it was necessary to develop a modern literature in Irish which would use contemporary forms and thus lead Ireland away from what he saw as the Anglicised backwaters into the European mainstream'.[27]

The subtle complexity of Pearse's thinking about literary politics is nicely encapsulated in a series of editorials for *An Claidheamh Soluis* published during May 1906. In the first of these articles, entitled 'Folklore and the Zeitgeist', Pearse is at pains to make it clear that the folkloric imagination is a key element in any authentic rendering of Irishness, that it is the imaginative well-spring of collective and personal identity:

> The folktale speaks the same language as the bird which sings in the blue, as the kine[28] which low in the buaile[29], as the streamlet which babbles by the roadside, as the sparks which fly upward from a fire. The man from whom an old tale has no appeal is to be feared and pitied even as the man who is irritated by the prattle of children or repelled by the caress of a dumb animal. He is one apart; he is landless and kindless.[30]

Just a week later, under the title 'About Literature', Pearse was equally intent on opening out the possibilities offered by modern literature – lest too strong a focus on folklore would produce a culture overly insular in outlook:

> Last week we wrote a glorification of the folktale. But it must be distinctly understood that we hold the folktale to be a beautiful and graceful thing only in its own time and place, – and its time and place are the winter fireside, or the spring sowing-time, or the summer hay-making, or the autumn harvesting, or the country road at any season. This

week we lay down the proposition that a living modern literature *cannot* (and if it could, should not) be built up on the folktale. The folktale is an echo of old mythologies, an unconscious stringing together of old memories and fancies: literature is a deliberate criticism of actual life.[31]

What Ireland needed, Pearse argues in this piece, was a literature properly modern in outlook and sensibility. While the recovery of old texts and oral histories has been crucial, it is now time for Irish writers (and his audience is really Irish-language writers) to turn their energies to giving voice to the contemporary moment:

> Will the ancients suffice as exemplars? Frankly, we are afraid not. We must get into touch also with our contemporaries, – in France, in Russia, in Norway, in Finland, in Bohemia, in Hungary, wherever, in short, vital literature is being produced on the face of the globe. Two influences go to the making of every artist, apart from his own personality, – if, indeed, personality is not, in the main, only the sum of these influences: the influence of his ancestors and that of his contemporaries. Irish literature, if to live and grow, must get into contact on the one hand with its own past and on the other with the mind of contemporary Europe. It must draw the sap of its life from the soil of Ireland; but it must be open on every side to the free air of heaven.[32]

What Pearse ends up proposing for the Irish writer is a form of literary hybridity whereby writers would not only draw from the ancient texts as a well-spring of inspiration but would reveal the roots of an authentic native modernity in these same texts. 'Has it ever occurred to anyone that Gráinne is a prototype of Hedda Gabler?' Pearse asks in this same article.[33] Pearse was also open to the myriad fields of influence to be found in European literatures – in the field of drama, for example, he was particularly drawn to Maeterlinck and Ibsen. His aims for Irish language literature were ambitious and pioneering:

> We should have our literature modern not only in the sense of freely borrowing every modern form which it does not

11

possess and which it is capable of assimilating, but also in texture, tone, and outlook. This is the twentieth century: and no literature can take root in the twentieth century which is not of the twentieth century. We want no Gothic revival. We would have the problems of today fearlessly dealt with in Irish: the loves and hates and desires and doubts of modern men and women.[34]

The 1906 editorials also reveal a thinker deeply convinced of the transformative potential of literature. Pearse's thinking in this regard is important in terms of our understanding of his work for the theatre, for what we find here is a suspicion of the straightforwardly realist and a call for writers to imaginatively recreate the world through their work:

Now we hold that it is time for our Irish writers to make a brave effort to express *themselves*, – to tell us what they think, or at any rate (if they do not yet think) what they *feel*. So far for the most part they have not been doing so. They have simply been giving us photographic reproductions of everyday conversations in Irish-speaking districts. Their work in this direction has been useful from certain points of view. It has been invaluable in introducing students to the idioms of the living Irish language. But it is no more literature than would be a verbatim report of the daily conversation which goes on, say in the case-room of our printing-office. And it is as impossible as the foundation of a national literature as a series of photographs of Irish physiognomies and scenery taken by Messrs. Lawrence would be as the foundation of a national art.[35]

Interestingly this series of editorials in *An Claidheamh Soluis* came in the same year that Pearse had his first formal affiliation with a theatrical company (outside of his social interaction with the *ad hoc* companies of the Gaelic League). The Theatre of Ireland was formed in 1906 following the withdrawal of many of the original player-founders from the Irish National Theatre Society the previous year. The rift mirrored an ideological fault. Máire Nic Shiubhlaigh believed that the reason for the secession of the founder members was their unhappiness at the lack of independence that would result from accepting a proposed subsidy from Miss Annie Horniman. Nic Shiubhlaigh understood that the independence of the original group as a national movement 'was to be secured only through the efforts of its members'.[36] Pearse was among those who spoke at the first meeting held by the defectors and others and, at a meeting a few weeks later, was elected to the first committee of the newly constituted Theatre of Ireland, also known as Cluicheoirí na hÉireann. The committee included Edward Martyn (as President) and Padraic Colum, Thomas Keohler, George Nesbitt, Dermot Trench, James Cousins, Helen Laird and Thomas Kettle.[37] Cousins would later be a part-time teacher at St. Enda's. Stephen Gwynn, whose son Denis would later play Conchubhar in *Macghníomhartha*, was also involved, as were A.E., who had written about the dramatic treatment of heroic literature and Eoin Mac Néill, a founder member of the Gaelic League.[38] Countess Markievicz, who had also been active in Inighnidhe na hÉireann, was an early member and Willie Pearse participated as an actor. In 1907 Jack and Fred Morrow of Belfast became involved with the company, Fred as stage manager and Jack as a designer of scenery and the standard of productions improved immensely.[39] Despite their differences, the Theatre of Ireland often worked in cooperation with the Abbey Theatre; they would also often work in collaboration with the Gaelic League. Through his participation in the Theatre of Ireland, Pearse was associating with A.E. and Martyn, both of whom had already been active in the promotion of an Irish theatre and whose essays in *Samhain* he would have read.[40] Such connections meant that he was now associating with those whose interest in Irish language theatre was more considered than many in the Gaelic League, where enthusiasm was not always matched with an understanding of dramaturgy. The Theatre of Ireland's productions were very successful and attracted large audiences. In practical terms they drew larger audiences than the Abbey, especially in the period following the *Playboy* controversy. The group also drew Pearse and his brother into closer contact with radical and bohemian families like the Walkers: Annie, Patricia, Mary (Máire) and

Frank (Proinsias) Walker all acted with the company.[41] Pearse would have known Mary Walker/Máire Nic Shiubhlaigh, who would later be with Cumann na mBan in Jacobs during the Rising, from February 1900 when she joined the Ard-Chraobh of Conradh na Gaeilge.[42] Patricia 'Gypsy' Walker took part with Willie and Mary Brigid in their Leinster Stage Society. Matthew Walker, Máire's father, was involved in the printing of Pearse's *Irish War News* and delivered Pearse's farewell letter to his mother.[43]

What we see emerging here is a vibrant and committed network of cultural practitioners into which Pearse was increasingly connecting. It is clear from his writings for *An Claidheamh Soluis* that during 1906 he became increasingly focused on the role of literature in the articulation of an independent Irish selfhood. His involvement with the Theatre of Ireland would seem to have focused his attention further on the possibilities held by theatre in this regard. In plotting his vision for an Irish language theatre at this time, for example, Pearse urged readers 'first to study the art of the Irish traditional reciter; and secondly to pay an occasional visit to the Abbey theatre – the one puts the student in touch with Ireland while the other puts him in touch with the best contemporary ideas'.[44] Tellingly, he also bemoaned the imaginative torpor he detected in Gaelic novels and dramas, declaring it time to 'move out from the dungheap and the turf-rick'.[45] In the years ahead Pearse would prove himself to be an expert in marketing and public relations, and it seems clear that his writings for *An Claidheamh Soluis* were a way of broadcasting the theories he was intent on putting into practice. There is little doubt that they reveal much about his approach to theatre and the important role that performance would play at his school St. Enda's which he was to found in 1908.

THEATRE AT ST. ENDA'S

The founding of St. Enda's provided Pearse with a space in which to convert his theories about education, the Irish language and history, and self-reliant identity into real-world practice. The school annals, published in *An Macaomh*, show that theatre played a very important role in wider school life from the beginning. As well as attending plays at the Abbey and elsewhere, the pupils were to be involved in producing theatre . The formal study of drama at St. Enda's, moreover, included classics from the English canon: scenes from *Julius Caesar* and *The Merchant of Venice* were enacted at private school gatherings.[46] These performances took place as part of the fortnightly ceilís organised by Willie Pearse and were very convivial occasions, generally taking place around a stove in the refectory and forming part of an evening which Desmond Ryan recalled as being part concert, part debating society.[47]

An Macaomh also records Pearse's developing critical vision on the emerging Irish drama. On the 15th October 1908, having attended Thomas MacDonagh's *When the Dawn is Come* the younger pupils came away 'yearning for rifles' and Pearse expressed interest in MacDonagh's medium, which he deemed 'neither prose nor poetry'. The following month the students were present by invitation at The Theatre of Ireland's productions of *The Flame on the Heath* and *The Turn of the Road*: Pearse deemed the latter 'like a bit of real life'. In March 1909 Pearse's connections (through his brother Willie and nephew Alf) with the Metropolitan School of Art, saw him give a lecture on the 'Fionn saga' in the Metropolitan School of Art, where the Students Union presented Alice Milligan's *The Last Feast of the Fianna*.[48] Rosie Sheppard, the wife of the sculptor Oliver, took part: both she and her husband attended social events at St. Enda's. The input of the Metropolitan School of Art into the Gaelic Revival is often ignored but teachers like Richard Willis and Oliver Sheppard brought themes from epic Gaelic literature to public attention. Pearse was very often inspired by art and works like Beatrice Elvery's 'Íosagán' and Sheppard's 1911 'Cúchulainn' remind us that the themes and motifs in Pearse's plays were embraced also in the Irish art world.

Meanwhile, Willie and Mary Brigid Pearse, along with their nephew Alf McGloughlin, had founded their own theatre company, The Leinster Stage Society, which would provide another strong link with theatre for St. Enda's (they regularly performed sketches for the pupils at the school). Pearse was not alone in getting children to perform the drama that would encapsulate and explore the newly confident sense of Irish identity. Searloit Ní Dhúnlaing (the sister of Frank Dowling), for example, wrote plays which were performed by children learning Irish in Monasterevin and also by the pupils of the Gaelic class in the Marlborough St. schools.[49] In February 1909 the first St. Enda's dramatic productions were staged. Pearse was not the author of these initial productions. Instead he produced plays by two of Ireland's leading scholars. Standish O'Grady's *The Coming of Fionn* and Douglas Hyde's *An Naomh ar Iarraidh* had already been staged with some success; Hyde's *An Naomh ar Iarraidh* had been published in *Samhain*. The plays put on by the boys of St. Enda's were never merely a private operation but rather served as an artistic channel between St. Enda's and the movers and shakers of the emerging world of Irish theatre and of Irish Ireland in general. Douglas Hyde was a co-founder of the Gaelic League and his collections of folktales and folk poetry had been a seminal source of inspiration for Pearse. Standish O'Grady had attended some of the rehearsals for *The Coming of Fionn* and both he and Hyde were frequent attendees at St. Enda's productions. Máire Nic Shiubhlaigh recalled having come out to St. Enda's at Cullenswood with others from The Theatre of Ireland to assist with plays.[50]

The miracle play *Íosagán*, produced at St. Enda's in February 1910, was the first drama penned by Pearse himself.[51] It was staged along with Padraic Colum's *The Destruction of the Hostel*. Colum taught English composition in the school.[52] Pearse had long been interested in the epic Irish literary cycles of Fiannaíocht and Rúraíocht and had lately been much influenced by the scholar and medical doctor George Sigerson's imaginative re-readings of that literature. The chivalry which Sigerson detected in the Ulster Literary Cycle informed Pearse's *Macghníomhartha Chúchulainn* which was given a staging in June 1909. The performances at St. Enda's were major events on the Dublin cultural calendar – in addition to the drama presented, these were occasions that facilitated energetic debate and the exchange of views between competing cultural camps. While tensions existed between many of these public intellectuals and artists (Pearse was highly skeptical of much that went on in the early Abbey for example), the environs of St. Enda's appear to have provided an atmosphere of openness and cooperation across differences.[53] Indeed on returning from just such an occasion in 1909 Yeats remarked to Lady Gregory that St. Enda's was 'one of the few places where we have friends'.[54]

Joseph Holloway's description of the mingling surrounding the staging of *The Coming of Fionn* evokes this important social aspect to the plays produced by Pearse (it also evokes a Pearse who is far from the socially inept aesthete that is often presented):

> Wm Pierce presided over the tea and Mr. Pierce made himself generally useful in making everyone at home, in a beautiful room newly decorated by the Morrows of Ulster Literary Theatre and Theatre of Ireland fame. After tea the company strolled about the College grounds for a little while and I noted what a distinguished company had come – Stephen Gwynn (who by the way has his son at St. Enda's), Edward Martyn, P Colum, John McNeill, Mary Hayden, Mr. and Mrs. Donn Piatt, The Count and Countess, Mr. and Mrs. Standish O'Grady, Miss Agnes O'Farrelly and her brothers and sisters (...) and WB Yeats who had a great chat with O'Grady who was seated just before him at the plays ...[55]

Pearse stated proudly that for *Macghníomhartha Chúchulainn*, 'we had over five hundred guests in our playing-field, including most of the people in Dublin who are interested in art and literature'.[56] When four plays were staged by St. Enda's in the Abbey in April 1910 the audience included Padraic Colum, Seamus O'Kelly and the playwright Rutherford Mayne (Samuel Wadell). The audience for the production of *An Rí* and Tagore's *The Post Office* on 17 May 1913 included Thomas Mac Donagh, Pádraic Colum, Joseph Plunkett, Sara Allgood and Micheál Mac Ruaidhrí, the gardener at St. Enda's, storyteller and occasional actor.[57]

While the political message of the plays was often radical the genteel visitors among the attendees were well catered for. The invited guests for the St. Enda's production of *An Rí* in 1912 enjoyed a garden party before the play was produced.[58] Afternoon tea was served on the lawn and the school pipers played a selection of Irish airs before the 1914 production of *Fionn* in the grounds.[59] The production formed part of the day-long events of the St. Enda's annual reunion – Pearse was always keen to retain the interest (and support) of past pupils.[60]

It is a measure of Pearse's remarkable skills at publicising that the first productions at St. Enda's were reported on by the *Irish Independent,* the *London Sphere,* the *Freeman's Journal,* the *Leader,* the *Nation* and *Sinn Féin.*[61] Pearse knew that his plays were making quite an impact in Dublin and was never one to miss an opportunity to proselytise. The St. Enda's productions were invariably framed by speeches by him and others. Music also played an important role in scene-setting – perhaps also serving as a sweetener for those who did not understand Irish. When *Íosagán* was revived for an Abbey theatre selection Pearse made speeches in Irish and English. Thomas McDonnell played Irish airs on the violin before and Joseph MacDonagh, the brother of Thomas, and later of the Irish Theatre, played a selection from Verdi on the clarinet during one of the intervals.[62] While the music served to create an atmosphere, the speeches provided an immediate explanation and context-ualisation of Pearse's theatrical aims and also gave a platform to others to voice their ideas about the play's content. Standish O'Grady in one particularly enthusiastic speech extolled the virtue of living like the Fianna.[63] Given Pearse's later emphasis on manliness in his political writings, it is noteworthy that he recalled O'Grady 'counselling a return to the manliness of the antique world and the life of the Fianna'.[64]

What we can see quite clearly here is the ways in which theatre, literature and the language movement brought Pearse into contact with many of the figures who also featured so prominently in his political life. Bulmer Hobson – himself a dramatist – was on the committee that organised the 1913 fête in support of St. Enda's.[65] James Larkin, whose sons were at

St. Enda's, helped out at the fête itself.[66] Thomas MacDonagh and Joseph Plunkett ran the Irish Theatre, where *The Master* and a revival of *Íosagán* were staged in 1915. As the Easter Rising approached, indeed, theatre and reality would merge ever closer: Pearse must have drawn on his knowledge of performance as he pretended that life was continuing as normal in the weeks before the Rising. The ex-pupils who had been cast in the aborted production of *The Singer* were to be photographed with rifles outside the school as they headed off to fight in the Rising, and Liam Mellows hid out at St. Enda's disguised as a priest in the week before the Rising.

DESIGN, STAGING AND ACTING

Pearse would seem to have been involved in almost every element of the production of his plays staged at St. Enda's. His responsibility certainly extended well beyond that of author. Mary Brigid refers to 'the beautiful plays which he wrote for his boys, and which he taught them to act so finely', suggesting Pearse as director and producer.[67] Despite bearing much of the workload Pearse appears to have been a relaxed presence in rehearsals. Mary Bulfin recalled Pearse's hands-off approach to directing his actors in the *Passion Play*:

> Mr. Pearse didn't seem to worry too much about rehearsals. He told us simply and clearly what he wanted done; and once he was sure that each one really knew what he or she had to do, he was satisfied. He seemed to have a divine belief that everyone would rise to the occasion and perform their individual parts adequately at the actual performance, no matter how woodenly they behaved at the rehearsals.[68]

Indeed, the productions at St. Enda's were very much collaborative ventures rather than autocratic ones. Many people contributed to the preparation and staging of the plays. As P.J. Matthews and others have noted, a sense of common purpose and mutual cooperation was a salient aspect of the Revival in general, and such a spirit characterised Pearse's theatrical practice.[69] In the programme for the first St. Enda's productions, *An Naomh ar Iarraidh* by Douglas Hyde and *The Coming of Fionn* by Standish O'Grady, Pearse had expressed his specific pride in the cooperative spirit which informed the production:

> Our present attempt is a modest one but it gives us pleasure to think that it is entirely our own. Every detail of the production, from the building of the stage to the designing and making of the costumes, is due to the friendly and fruitful co-operation of the School staff and the pupils, no tradespeople having being summoned to our aid, except indeed the printers of this Programme. We owe the colour scheme and general mounting of the plays to my brother; who also modelled for us the head in the centre of the proscenium; while our friend Mr. Albert Power helped us to paint the scenery. The design on the first page of the Clár is by Pádraig Ó Tuathaigh, one of our pupils.[70]

Pearse always went out of his way to acknowledge the input of others into his plays. He credited his brother Willie and nephew Alf McGloughlin with 'the costumes, grouping and general production' of the pageant *Macghníomhartha Chúchulainn*, for example, while he also acknowledged the input of Thomas McDonnell into the music used during the pageant and the advice given by Tadhg Mac Donnacha regarding the use of the rannaíocht bheag metre for the opening. McGloughlin had made Cúchulainn's chariot,[71] Éamonn Bulfin made the spears and Pádraic (Óg) Ó Conaire and Colm Ó Neachtain cut out shoes.[72] Pearse could always draw on the energetic artistic circle of Willie and Alf for help with design and choreography. The list of those who had contributed to the preparations for *Macghníomhartha Chúchulainn* included the sculptor Albert Power (a close friend of Willie) and the young artist Patrick Tuohy, a pupil at St. Enda's. As well as his input into arranging the plays and pageants, Willie also designed the scenery and 'discussed every detail with Pádraic in the course of long nightly talks'.[73] The Thomas McDonnell/Tomás Mac Domhnaill (1885–1937) who composed the music for *Macghníomhartha* was a teacher in St. Enda's and was himself much involved in drama; he translated Synge's *Riders to the Sea* and his play *Áine agus Caoimhín* was produced at the 1910 Oireachtas. He was also a radical and along with Pearse, Ceannt and others, he formed Cumann na Saoirse in 1912.[74]

While Joseph Holloway would report on the humble nature of the 'theatre' used in the first St. Enda's performances at Cullenswood House – the plays being 'enacted in a little corrugated iron shed in the grounds (…) when the company squeezed in they certainly were a tight fit' – he was clearly impressed by the stage itself:

> The proscenium was excellently and ingeniously worked into the shape of the hall and the opening was of semi-circular shape, with a head forming the key and festooned curtains falling in graceful folds from the centre and on each side. The drop curtains were divided in centre and pulled to either side to disclose the stage.[75]

Although, as the extract above confirms, Pearse was no stranger to the standard presentation of the proscenium arch, he was also a regular exponent of more 'experimental' theatrical modes. One of the most interesting aspects of Pearse's theatre work, indeed, is his use of outdoor staging. Pearse was not necessarily a pioneer here – plays and dramatic dialogues took place outdoors at feiseanna, Standish O'Grady had staged *The Coming of Fionn* outdoors on a previous occasion, and the painterly nature of *tableaux vivants* produced by Inghinidhe na hÉireann and others had an enduring influence on many Revivalist productions. But Pearse does appear to have been a particularly enthusiastic and energetic proponent of breaking the confines of the traditional stage and its fourth-wall conventions. He outlined a discussion he had had with a 'Saldánach' (Sultan) on the importance of moving beyond the regular auditorium in a short but fascinating account entitled 'Na hIndiacha Thoir' published in *An Claidheamh Soluis* in 1906.[76] *The Irish Times* review of *An Rí* (performed in the grounds of St. Enda's in 1912) drew attention to the appropriateness of the outdoor staging:

No more fitting locale could be imagined for the performances of an historical episode, for the grounds of St. Enda's have been specially favoured by nature. In a secluded spot, sheltered by tall elms, the play was enacted, an ivied archway forming a perfect background to a natural stage. The youthful performers, in their traditional Gaelic dress, fitted into the scene as perfectly as if they were part of it.[77]

Unfortunately the success or otherwise of these outdoor productions was weather dependant and the week-long events at the fête in 1913 (held at Jones' Road to raise funds for the school) fell foul of ceaseless rain. Audiences were poor and during the enactment of *The Defence of the Ford*, Cúchulainn's assailant was chased off the field and not slain, as it was too wet for the death scene on the pass and the boys might catch cold.[78] Despite the occasional comic outcome, Pearse's outdoor performance pieces undoubtedly had a major impact on those who saw them. Reviews and remembrances reveal Pearse and his colleagues as theatre practitioners with a sound understanding of the mechanics of performance and the effects that could be produced. For the February 1910 productions of Pádraic Colum's *The Destruction of the Hostel* and Pearse's own *Íosagán* at Cullenswood House Chinese lanterns lighted the way and musicians were led to the 'theatre' by torches.[79] There were other innovative approaches that played with convention: Pearse stated that 'the grand barbaric march' with which these same first productions opened 'took the audience by storm'.[80] Those works performed in a traditional theatre setting – such as the 1911 performances of the *Passion Play* at the Abbey – were equally enlivened by innovative uses of sound and lighting (Joseph Holloway recorded the evocative use of the sounds of hammering and thunder and the striking creation of lightning flashes[81]). For Frank Walker, too, the lighting and the setting of the Passion Play were more effective than anything the Abbey had ever done.[82]

Such memories reveal just how thoroughly networked Pearse was in Dublin's cultural scene. The names we encounter time and again also reveal the ways in which this network would go on to be central to the events of 1916. To take but one example: the 1917 premiere of *The Singer* featured Éamonn Bulfin, David Sears, Fintan Murphy and Conor and Eunan McGinley – all of whom had been involved in the Rising, as had Máire Nic Shiubhlaigh, who played Máire Ní Fhiannachta, the mother of MacDara. Bulfin, who was cast as MacDara in *The Singer* had raised the green 'Irish Republic' flag over the GPO.[83] But that is to skip forward a little too quickly, before his iconic moment at the GPO Pearse would have inscribed himself on the theatrical landscape of a city in which such things truly mattered.

THE PLAYS

Macghníomhartha Chúchulainn (1909)

Pearse's first original dramatic work, the 1909 *Macghníomhartha Chúchulainn*, had a long gestation. From his early youth Pearse had a deep interest in the heroic literature of the Gaelic tradition, both Fiannaíocht and Rúraíocht. His imagination had been fired first of all at home, by the stories and poems of his elderly Aunt Margaret, and later at school where he studied material from the Fiannaíocht in the form of *Laoi Oisín ar Thír na nÓg* and *Diarmuid agus Gráinne*.[84] As early as 1897 he was extolling the heroes of such tales as exemplars in a lecture:

> Fearghus, Conchubhar, Cúchulainn, Fionn, Oisín, Oscar – these were more to the Gael than mere names of great champions and warriors of a former time: they represented to him men who had gone before, who had fought the good fight ...[85]

The next ten years would give Pearse ample opportunity to deepen his knowledge of both cycles as various scholarly editions and popular adaptations brought what could be viewed as an occluded literature to the notice of the metropolitan public.[86] While his initial focus was on Fiannaíocht – he himself edited material – by the time St. Enda's was founded Pearse was much occupied with the Ulster Cycle. He owned a copy of Ernst Windisch's edition of the Book of Leinster's *Táin* which is still in the library of St. Enda's. It would appear that Pearse's own reading of the material was much influenced by a lecture given in 1908 by George Sigerson who believed that one of the main themes of the Rúraíocht literature was chivalry.[87] In his 1907 book *Bards of the Gael and Gall* Sigerson had explored the dramatic potential he detected in both Fiannaíocht and Rúraíocht.[88] Philip O'Leary also detects an influence of Standish O'Grady's *The Coming of Cúchulainn* on Pearse's ideas about the Boy Corps and education.[89] The figure of Cúchulainn was to prove a seminal influence on Pearse. Inspired by Sigerson's lecture Pearse organised a decorative frieze made by the Morrows to be hung in St. Enda's. It proclaimed the motto associated with Cúchulainn, that 'I care not though I were to live but one day and one night provided my fame and my deeds live after me.' For Pádraic Óg Ó Conaire, who attended St. Enda's, Pearse aimed to make every student a 'Cúchulainn'.[90] All this focus on Cúchulainn and chivalry had to find an outlet.

Macghníomhartha Chúchulainn ('The boyhood deeds of Cúchulainn') was written in May 1909 and was first produced in the afternoon of 22nd June in St. Enda's at Cullenswood House. It was the first of two pageants which Pearse based on material from the Rúraíocht; the second, *The Defence of the Ford*, was produced in 1913. From the early years of the twentieth century there had been much discussion about the potential for drama in Early Irish literature in essays by A.E. and Yeats in *Samhain* and a robust debate had taken place in newspapers like *An Claidheamh Soluis* as to the form such drama would take. Pearse was certainly not alone in drawing on early Irish literature for his dramatic muse – there were many others – but his effort was particularly ambitious. *Macghníomhartha Chúchulainn* featured a huge cast, including six pupils of St. Ita's who played the Bantracht or Women. Denis Gwynn, the son of the Irish MP Stephen Gwynn, played Conchubhar Mac

Neasa, the King of Ulster, while Frank Dowling played Cúchulainn. Pádraic Óg Ó Conaire played a Smith.[91]The pageant tells the story of how Seatanta became Cúchulainn. The opening act has the young Seatanta arrive at Eamhain Macha where he joins a hurling game which ends in argument. Seatanta asserts his status. The second act tells a story that a modern audience would be familiar with – the tale of how Seatanta got the name Cúchulainn by killing the hound of Culann ('CúChulainn') and then taking his place. The closing act tells how Cúchulainn demands the king's own arms and chariot and goes into battle to prove his manhood and status. It ends, as school plays tend not to do, with a chariot circling a field three times. Thomas McDonnell put music to the verses (composed by Pearse) that introduced each act; there was also a Smith song taken from the Petrie Collection.

Although many editions of material from the Ulster cycle tended to reach only a specialised audience, there were also popular editions which had a broader appeal. Peadar Ó Laoghaire had drawn on the Ulster Cycle for his rambling play about the *Táin*. Yeats had also drawn (in a very loose way) on the Rúraíocht for creative material. Pearse's adaptation had the advantage of being both (relatively) close to the source material and popular – as usual there was a vast and distinguished audience.

The pageant is remarkable for the formality of its diction, even in the descriptive passages which function as the stage directions. Unlike Ó Laoghaire, who liked making figures from early Irish literature speak Cork Irish, Pearse followed the register and parole of Ernst Windisch's edition closely when he wrote *Macghníomhartha*. Pearse himself stated that he had 'religiously' followed the phraseology of the *Táin*.[92] He had extracted the story and a great part of the dialogue from the *Táin*, merely modernising (but altering as little as possible) the magnificent phrase of the epic:

> I have kept close to the *Táin* even at the risk of missing what some people might call dramatic effect, but in this matter I have greater trust in the instinct of the unknown

shapers of our epic than in the instinct of any modern, merely modernising (but altering as little as possible) the magnificent phrase of the epic.[93]

This was a brave decision, made possible because of Pearse's real understanding of difficult material, and was taken against a backdrop of much debate among Irish Irelanders as to how best to render material from Middle Irish literature into a form which contemporary readers and audiences could understand.[94] While the dialogue was entirely in Irish, guests were given a comprehensive gloss in English as part of the programme notes. While the gloss was a very close reproduction of the Irish original its tone was not immediately reminiscent of Early Irish literature ('wherefore', 'knewest thou'). Pearse leaves certain key words in the original Irish ('geasa', 'léine') in an attempt to ensure that the culture of the original text is not occluded.

Pearse expounded on the inspiration for *Macghníomhartha* in *An Macaomh*. From his very first editorial he hoped for his pupils that the heroic literature would 'stir their hearts or kindle their imaginations to heroic things'.[95] Explaining why he had attempted such an ambitious project so early on in the young school's life he emphasised what he considered the worthiness of the material and its ability to inspire:

> The reason is that we were anxious to crown our first year's work with something worthy and symbolic; anxious to send our boys home with the knightly image of Cúchulainn in their hearts, and his knightly words ringing in their ears. They will leave St. Enda's under the spell of the magic of their most beloved hero, the Macaomh who is, after all, the greatest figure in the epic of their country, indeed, as I think, the greatest in the epic of the world.[96]

The pageant itself was highly visual – that chariot – and hugely successful. In the next issue of *An Macaomh* Pearse recalled its impact:

We had over five hundred guests in our playing-field, including most of the people in Dublin who are interested in art and literature. I think the boyish freshness of our miniature Macradh, and especially the shy and comely grace of Frank Dowling as Cúchulainn, really pleased them. Mr. Colum wrote very generously of us in *Sinn Féin*, Mr. Ryan in the *Irish Nation*, and Mr. Bulfin in *An Claidheamh Soluis*. *The Freeman's Journal*, in addition to giving a special report, honoured us with a leading article from the pen of Mr. Stephen MacKenna.[97]

The pageant was repeated later that summer, again with success, at the Castlebellingham Feis. In bringing the Cúchulainn of the manuscripts and scholarly editions to large and distinguished audiences in such an imaginative production, Pearse had succeeded in establishing a prestigious domain for a literature which had long been sidelined or even derided. The impact he himself had sought in staging the production – to stir the hearts and kindle the imagination of his students to 'heroic things' would take longer to play out.

Íosagán (1910)

Despite his freethinking inclinations, Pearse's father James had a profound interest in religion, and owned multiple copies of the Bible, which in turn found their way to the St. Enda's library.[98] His accomplished sculptural work often featured beautiful Christian images. It is therefore unsurprising that Pearse should turn to Christianity for the subject matter of his second original play. On the third of December 1909 Pearse told his pupils that he had written a 'miracle play' on the subject of 'Íosagán' and that this 'would probably be the Irish play to be staged with Mr. Colum's English play about St. Brigid's Day'.[99] Miracle plays were in vogue: Lady Gregory and Douglas Hyde both authored examples during the Revival. Pearse's short story on which *Íosagán* was based had been published as early as December 1906 in *An Claidheamh Soluis*. The story itself seems to have been partly inspired by Beatrice Elvery's painting of the child Jesus, which hung in St. Enda's and a version of which was published in *An Macaomh*. In both story and play an amusing opening scene of young boys playing is followed by the appearance of one special little boy who turns out to be Íosagán or the child Jesus. The only adult to see Íosagán is Sean Mhaitias/old Maitias who is on the margins of his community and does not attend Mass. At the close of the play Íosagán summons a priest to the old man's deathbed and appears to him in a redemptive vision. The radical message of the play – that those on the margins of their communities, who do not necessarily conform to the accepted rules of the Church, may still be embraced by a loving God – features also in Pearse's short stories 'An Deargadaol' and 'Na Bóithre'. The plot of the play differs slightly from that of the short story, but is essentially the same story. Unlike *Macghníomhartha*, and despite its magical or miraculous plot, *Íosagán* is essentially realistic and contemporary. The characters and place names are typical of the Ros Muc area with which Pearse was familiar and where he had a holiday cottage. While there is no real development in any character except Maitias, there is still much dramatic potential for actors and director. The conversation between the young boys and Maitias, where Maitias's increasing mental confusion wavers between comedy and pathos, allows for a powerful dramatic impact, for example. The dialogue between the young boys is written with humour and empathy. Their chatter is in a rich but colloquial Conamara Irish. Pearse was not precious about Anglicisms and phrases like 'sergeant' and 'peelers' remain in English (in the Irish version), making the dialogue particularly realistic at a time when debates about 'pure' Irish informed much writing. The closing scene, where Maitias has a vision of the child Jesus on his deathbed, might seem simple on a textual reading but it was obviously very carefully staged: Holloway found the final death scene in *Íosagán* to be 'profoundly beautiful'.[100] It is again worth recalling that both Pearse brothers (Willie was usually responsible for the grouping and choreography) would have been very familiar with the pictures created by the Inighindhe's *tableaux* and the imagery of church sculpture. There were other sources: the figure of Íosagán features in a

poem written about Naomh Íde / St. Ita who flourished around
the middle of the sixth century. The poem which dates to c. 900
appears in a commentary accompanying a Féilire or calendar
written in the Leabhar Breac.[101] It is not clear if Pearse was aware
of this poem but he may well have been, given his interest in
early Irish literature: Ita and Íosagán also figure in folklore.

Writing in December 1910 in *An Macaomh*, Pearse outlined
his vision for *Íosagán* and detailed the background to his
inspiration for the plot:

> *Íosagán* is not a play for the ordinary theatres or for the
> ordinary players. It requires a certain atmosphere, and a
> certain attitude of mind on the part of the actors. It has in
> fact been written for performance in a particular place and
> by particular players. I know that in that place and by those
> players it will be treated with the reverence due to a prayer.
> In bringing the Child Jesus into the midst of a group of
> boys disputing about their games, or to the knee of an old
> man who sings nursery rhymes to children, I am imagining
> nothing improbable, nothing outside the bounds of the
> everyday experience of innocent little children and
> reverent-minded old men and women. I know a priest who
> believes that he was summoned to the death-bed of a
> parishioner by Our Lord in person; and there are many
> hundreds of people in the countryside I write of who know
> that on certain nights Mary and her Child walk through the
> villages and if the cottage doors be left open, enter and sit
> awhile at the firesides of the poor.[102]

The first performances of *Íosagán* took place on the 5, 6 and
7 of February 1910 and were preceded by a performance of
Pádraic Colum's *The Destruction of the Hostel*. The atmosphere
had been carefully created. If *Íosagán* was not 'a play for the
ordinary theatres or for the ordinary players' it helped that the
staging was not a commercial operation and attendees were
invited guests, not paying customers. There was tea for some
of the guests in the house, after which the audience entered the
improvised theatre by the light of Chinese lanterns.[103]
Following some music and an address by Pearse the actors for

the Colum play marched in led by a piper.[104] Pearse's vision for the performance of *Íosagán* seems to have been achieved – Joseph Holloway recorded the effect that it produced among many in the audience:

> *Íosagán* (in Gaelic) when we were transported from the heroic age to the present that the spectators were most moved by what they saw as well as heard. Spiritual Ireland was mirrored forth in this 'beautiful little work' which contained the most beautiful and the most terrible thing in the world – children and death, as Mr. Pearse said in his speech.[105]

An expanded version of *Íosagán* was performed again on Saturday 9 April 1910 in the Abbey Theatre on a programme which also featured a revival of the St. Enda's players' productions of Douglas Hyde's *An Naomh ar Iarraidh* (*The Lost Saint*), Padraic Colum's *The Destruction of The Hostel*, and *The Coming of Fionn* by Standish O'Grady.[106] The Abbey provided a prestigious platform for the pupils of a school that was less than two years old and the performance again attracted many of those prominent in the Revival. The dramatic productions were proving to be an impressive vehicle for publicising Pearse's vision of St. Enda's – Joseph Holloway heard the lady behind him in the audience say she wished she were a boy in 'that school'.[107] *Íosagán* was yet again performed in June 1910 at the 'Feis Frankfort' in the grounds of a Mrs. Clarke's residence on Merrion Avenue in Blackrock. This time there were various competitions for children representing the roughly one thousand pupils learning Irish in South County Dublin schools and Douglas Hyde, Agnes Farrelly and Mary Hayden spoke. The presentation of *Íosagán* brought the evening to a close.[108] Again, the pupils of St. Enda's were presented as exemplifying Irish Ireland. *Íosagán* proved to be a favourite play and it was revived again along with *The Master* in 1915 and yet again when *The Singer* premiered in 1917.[109]

An Rí / The King (1912)

Like *Íosagán*, *An Rí* is a short morality play. A handwritten script of *An Rí* survives in a St. Enda's copybook; the script published in *An Macaomh* in May 1913 is an expanded version of this.[110]

An Rí was the chief item in the garden party at St. Enda's on the 15 June 1912 and took place outdoors in the grounds of the Hermitage on the banks of the river. Joseph Holloway noted that the fine afternoon helped to make the students open-air performance a big success. His diary also provides a useful summary of the plot:

> The plot of the play is a simple one and deals with a vanquished king who is a man of sin and cannot for that reason, win any of his battles. An abbot whom he consults tells him that a sinless boy alone could lead the people to victory and a choice is made, Giolla na Naomh, a little lad, who is one of the scholars of the monastic school. The boy is invested with kingship and sets off to battle followed by the soldiers. He wins a glorious victory, but is killed in the final charge. The play ends with a Te Deum in praise of God instead of a keen for the child who by his death has purchased freedom for his people.[111]

Pearse's usual skill in attracting publicity was again an indicator of his expertise in what would now be termed public relations and the school prize-giving ceremony took place alongside the plays.[112] The production was reported on in the *Irish Times*, and in the *Evening Herald*.[113] A professionally taken publicity photograph of Desmond Carney, who played Giolla na Naomh, was later printed in *An Macaomh* and shows that much care was taken with costumes and props. As school productions go, the play was presented with some sophistication. As usual, music played an important part in establishing a solemn tone: there was a trumpet and chanting, a horn and pipes. Some St. Ita's pupils were drafted in to sing the keen over the dead Giolla na Naomh for the 1912 and subsequent 1913 productions.[114]

An Rí is a serious play. The conversation of the young boys at the beginning is formal and repetitive and the ritualistic descriptions of the king (and later of the battle) are reminiscent of the formulaic and quasi-magical runs or *ruthaig* that featured in the epic literature of the manuscripts and learned folk tales:

> Tá claíomh colg-ghéar cinn óir agus craoiseach chrann ramharcheann ghorm agus sciath dhearg dhearscnaithe dhealrach.

> He has a keen-edged gold-hilted sword and a mighty-shafted blue-headed spear and a glorious red-emblazoned shield.

Pearse is deliberately invoking the style of high literature here in order to situate his new work as part of an unbroken tradition. The repetition in some of the simpler dialogue may also owe something to the fact that most of the young actors had only been learning Irish for a few years.

Like Pearse's 1915 play, *The Master*, the setting for *An Rí/The King* is outdoors and the dialogue and action (such as it is) are set in ancient times without either place or time being defined. This sense of timelessness was a characteristic aspect of Fiannaíocht literature, where battles and stories took place in a setting that was 'fadó fadó ar maidin' ('long ago in the morning'), simultaneously ancient and contemporary.[115] As such the literature – like Pearse's play – could function as a safe cipher for radical ideas and feelings. While some of the dialogue in *An Rí* might certainly strike modern audiences or actors as wordy, it nonetheless retains the sense of an 'allagar' or poetic debate. Increasing interest in the work of the nineteenth-century poet Raifteirí/Raftery amongst Gaelic Leaguers and Anglo-Irish dramatists like Yeats and Gregory had raised awareness of the dramatic potential of the poetic debate in Gaelic. The allagar was also the literary form taken by the dramatic lyrics of Fiannaíocht literature:

> AN TREAS MANACH Ar éirí ón mainistir amach do minné, do bhí fear marbh ar imeall na coille. Is uafásach cathanna.

AN DARA MANACH Ní hea, is aoibhinn cathanna! An uair do bhíomar ag déanamh ar Nóna anois[116], a Athair, do chualas tré shalmaireacht na mbráthar glór buabhaill. Do ling mo chroí, agus do b'áil liom éirí ón áit a rabhas agus dul i ndiaidh an cheoil mheanmnaigh úd. Do mba chuma liom dá mba chun mo bháis do gheobhainn.

THIRD MONK As I went out from the monastery yesterday there was a dead man on the verge of the wood. Battle is terrible.

SECOND MONK No, battle is glorious! While we were singing our None but now[117], Father, I heard, through the psalmody[118] of the brethren, the voice of a trumpet. My heart leaped, and I would fain have risen from the place where I was and gone after that gallant music. I should not have cared though it were to my death I went.

The lines cited are also thematically reminiscent of Fiannaíocht literature and in particular of a famous debate between Oisín and St. Patrick, where Oisín argues for the freedom of the adventurous pagan life of the Fianna and St. Patrick argues for the rules and regularity of Christian monastic life. For Oisín, St. Patrick is 'A chléireach na gclog'/ 'cleric of the bells', a person whose imagination and life is limited by rules. This image is deliberately invoked by Pearse when the soldier reports the losing of the battle and chides the monks for their inaction:

Lucht na leabhar agus na gclog, ba bheag bhur gcabhair dúinn sa chomhrac crua!

O ye of the books and the bells, small was your help to us in the hard battle!

In the case of *An Rí/The King*, the debate is about the gloriousness or terribleness of war. This is noteworthy, for the performance took place in summer 1912, well before Pearse became actively involved in the IRB. Meanwhile, although there is much ammunition to be found in *An Rí/The King* for critics detecting a yearning for sacrifice in Pearse's writings, it is important to note that both sides of the argument are presented, almost as though Pearse himself is working out his own views. Following the monks' speeches above, the abbot states sagely that such talk is typical of youth:

Aitheasc ógánaigh an t-aitheasc sin. Fanann gach seanóir leis an mbás agus téann gach óganach ina choinne.

That is the voice of a young man. The old wait for death, but the young go to meet it.

Pearse himself was at this time increasingly impatient with what he viewed as the weak standpoint on Home Rule of the current generation of Irish Party MPs and had published a piece by Eamonn Ceannt which asked young men 'if it was not time to move' in his *Barr Buadh* a few months previously.[119]

In addition to the echoes from Gaelic literature, a Biblical tone runs throughout *An Rí/The King*. This tone adds a sense of gravitas and authority to the various moral pronouncements and helps create the atmosphere that will lead to the dramatic *denouement*. When Giolla na Naomh's death brings about victory for the people the tone is so reminiscent of Christ's sacrifice that it could have been judged almost blasphemous:

AN RÍ Umhlaím duit, a Rí mhairbh agus a leanbh bhuaigh; pógaim thú a gheal cholainn, óir do ghlainese do shaor mo mhuintir.

Clár éadain Ghiolla na Naomh do phógadh dó. Tosnaítear ar an gcaoineadh arís.

AN tAB Ná caointear an leanbh seo, óir do cheannaigh sé saoirse dá chíne.

Déantar libh na gártha maíte agus cantar libh caintic ag moladh Dé.

THE KING I do homage to thee, O dead King, O victorious child! I kiss thee, O white body, since it is thy purity that hath redeemed my people.

He kisses the forehead of Giolla na Naomh. They commence to keen again.

THE ABBOT Do not keen this child, for he hath purchased freedom for his people. Let shouts of exultation be raised and let a canticle be sung in praise of God.[120]

An Rí had perhaps the most interesting afterlife of any of Pearse's plays. Pearse added some speeches for the Abbey production which took place on the 17th May 1913.[121] This production was facilitated by W. B. Yeats who agreed after a meeting with Pearse to stage *An Rí* along with Rabindranath Tagore's *The Post Office* in order to aid in the fundraising efforts for St. Enda's. The choice was well made: a number of critics have discerned clear similarities in tone and theme between Pearse's work and that of Tagore.[122] The play was performed again as part of the week-long events at the St. Enda's fundraising fête in June 1913.[123] The most exotic production of a Pearse play took place in Bengal in 1915 when a version was acted by the pupils of Tagore's school.[124]

Owen (1913)

The extant English-language script for *Owen* is Pearse's own translation of an Irish-language play written to provide a theatrical diversion at Ceilidhes held in St. Enda's and other places around Dublin – it was first performed at a Ceilidhe in the Dublin Mansion House in the winter of 1913. While undoubtedly a slight drama that would last only ten or fifteen minutes in performance, it is noteworthy for its elaboration of a number of themes that would reappear in Pearse's more substantive plays in the years ahead. The year 1913 is also noteworthy as it is the year when Pearse joined the IRB – a fact that provides an added interest to this dramatic expression of rebellion and patriotism.

Owen is set in 1867 in a small country school and reveals the loyalty of a young man to his teacher in the build up to the Fenian rising of that year. As with *The Master* (1915), a play that

Owen in some ways foreshadows, a key theme here is the purity and innate bravery of the child who instinctively knows what is right and wrong in an unjust world. More specifically, and again we can find pre-echoes of *The Master* and *The Singer* (1916) here, *Owen* presented the audience with the special and unbreakable bond that can develop between a teacher and his pupil. This bond, rather chillingly perhaps, is so strong that it leads to the child sacrificing his life to protect the teacher who has been revealed as a Fenian leader.

As with *Íosagán*, the play opens with a playful scene of childhood exuberance – released momentarily from their schoolwork the classroom becomes a site of innocent play and minor rebellion – which soon will provide a counterpoint to the more serious business that shadows much of the action on stage. The intrusion into this childhood space of the adult world of politics and violence is signalled by the arrival of the Ballad Singer:

> *The voice of Ballad Singer singing 'The Wearin o' the Green' is heard. The Master and the boys listen. The singer seems to be at a little distance at first. When he starts the second stanza, 'I met with Napper Tandy', he has apparently come up to the school door, and he sings clearly and loudly.*

Again we can see here the emergence of an idea that will be developed more fully in *The Singer*: folk culture as crucial to the transmission of resistance, folk song as memory, the cultural activist as keeper of knowledge. It soon becomes clear that the Ballad Singer is looking to do more than sell his songs; he has a message for the School Master:

THE MASTER Who is the message from?

THE BALLAD SINGER From them that you know.

THE MASTER Give me a sign.

THE BALLAD SINGER Did you ever hear tell of the Hawk o' the Hill?[125]

THE MASTER I did.

THE BALLAD SINGER I am one of his friends.

Pearse's note at the start of the play prepares the way for this piece of coded dialogue: "'The Hawk of the Hill' was the name given to James Stephens, the Chief Organiser of the Irish Republican Brotherhood. Stephens had left Ireland in 1866, but his name would still be used as a watchword by his followers'. In the moments that follow the School Master is revealed as the local Fenian organizer and the call has been given to start the rebellion. The Master sends the children home from school early (much to their joy) but forgets that he has punished the young Owen by making him stand in the corner. This lapse in memory means that Owen watches on as the Master reveals his gun hidden below the floorboards. In a moment that is pure Pearse, the Master reveals all to his pupil – because to do otherwise would be to tarnish the sacred bond between teacher and pupil:

> Owen, I am your Master, and I must not tell you an untruth. Whisper. I am going to trust you. I am going to let you share a great secret. There are some of us here, there are men in every place in Ireland, that are going to fight tonight. To fight for Ireland. Poor Ireland, Owen that has been down for so long.

The revelation leads Owen to ask whether he can go with his Master and join the rebellion – 'I could carry bullets for ye. I could be your drummer to beat the charge and give ye heart, when ye'd be charging at them' – but the Master refuses him as he is too young and asks instead that he keep what he has seen a secret until the rebels have fully revealed themselves. Having secured Owen's assurance of loyalty the Master escapes the school just as the police arrive to arrest him. In a tragic dénouement – given an added retrospective power by the events that we know will happen in the real world just a few years later – Owen grabs a forgotten gun to make a stand against the police and allow the Master more time to escape their clutches – 'If I fire a bullet at them they'll think the Master is here still, and they won't go after him'. Not knowing that it is only a young boy remaining in the classroom, the police fire a volley of shots through the door and the final stage image is of policemen gathered round the body of a now dead Owen.

While slight, and not often produced, *Owen* is certainly of note for its revelation of the real-life price of rebellion. Although there is certainly a romanticisation of the child and the innate loyalty and patriotism of young boys in particular, Pearse finally leaves his audience with a haunting scene of loss and regret which tempers much of the discourse of rebellion and sacrifice around which the play circles.

The Master (1915)

The Master was the last of his plays that Pearse saw produced on stage, its first production taking place at the Irish Theatre, Hardwicke Street, on 20 May 1915 (just a couple of months later Pearse would make his famous speech at the funeral of O' Donovan Rossa). *The Master* is the most developed theatrical elaboration of Pearse's ideas about education and the almost symbiotic relationship between teacher and pupil that can be brought into existence in the right conditions and with the right pedagogical philosophy. It is also a play about sticking to your principles when confronted by greater force. Most importantly perhaps, the play is a meditation on the nature of belief and faith in the face of doubters and skeptics. As James Moran has noted, in this regard there are clear echoes to be found between *The Master* and W.B. Yeats's *The Hour Glass* (1903) and Rabindranath Tagore's *The Post Office*.

There is something extraordinarily intimate about *The Master*; it is a play in which Pearse bears much of himself as teacher and idealist to the audience. This sense of intimacy can only have been enhanced by the fact that the Master (Ciarán) was played by Willie Pearse – indeed it is a role that seems perfectly designed for Patrick's sensitive and unconditionally loyal brother. *The Master*, perhaps more than any other play, gets us to the heart of the spirit that sustained the loyalty of the St. Enda's boys to each other and their teachers. After all, we now know that 'almost the entire cast of the original production of *The Master* was involved in the 1916 rebellion, with David Sears, Eunan McGinley, Joseph Sweeney, Desmond Ryan, and John Kilgallon all taking part in both the play and the subsequent conflict'.[126]

The Master presents a confrontation between a noble teacher – named Ciarán but partially at least a sublimated version of Pearse' self-image – and a King figure named Daire. The play returns its audience to one of the key turning-points in Irish history, the arrival of Christianity and the subsequent displacement of older druidic religious practices. As with *The King*, its message is the possibility of transformation and the importance of those who are willing to face down entrenched positions of power. Early in the piece three of Ciarán's pupils discuss the King's opposition to his teachings:

ART But why does the King come against Ciarán?

CEALLACH It is the Druids that have incited him. They say that Ciarán is over-turning the ancient law of the people.

MAINE The King has ordered him to leave the country.

Thereafter the play proceeds by way of a Biblical analogue: the Old Testament of Royal power is challenged by the New Testament of an enlightened community represented by the teacher and his pupils. The former stands in for tyranny (the audience is left to decide whether this is the monarchial ancient regime, colonialism, or the more profane aspects of modernity) while the latter presents a form of proto-Republicanism (in which the individual intellect fights for personal sovereignty). As with *The King* and *Owen*, the plot of *The Master* focuses on the ultimate loyalty and faith demonstrated to a teacher by a special pupil – in this case a boy named Iollann Beag. Seduced by the promise of a feast, Ciarán's other pupils leave him rather exposed in his monastery, but the youngest of them, Iollann Beag, foregoes the merriment offered by the King's feast and stays with Ciarán. When the King arrives intent on making

Ciarán renounce his faith with the threat of death as his alternative, it is Iollann Beag who prays for redemption. Earlier we witness Ciarán telling his pupils that in circumstances of ultimate danger the Archangel Michael would respond to prayer and make himself visible to protect those of faith. In this moment of crisis Iollann Beag's prayers are indeed answered and the angelic – but terrible – Michael appears on stage to protect Ciarán from the King's sword. His arrival leaves the King in no doubt as to the validity of the belief so eloquently innunciated by Ciarán and his most loyal pupil:

> MICHAEL I am he that waiteth at the portal. I am he that hasteneth. I am he that rideth before the squadron. I am he that holdeth a shield over the retreat of man's host when Satan cometh in war. I am he that turneth and smiteth. I am he that is Captain of the Host of God (99).

Faced with this divine confirmation that the old order must give way to the new, the King bends to his knee in supplication. Thus *The Master*'s return to a moment when the 'law of the people' was re-imagined and radically translated away from the pagan towards the Christian provides an analogue for nationalist resistance to the impositions of imperial power. As with much of Pearse's other work for the theatre, the costumes may be archaic but the message is extraordinarily modern.

The Singer (1916)

There is a certain amount of confusion regarding the first production of *The Singer*. The play was written in the run up to the Rising and it had been cast – and perhaps had had a run through. It seems clear that the play was to have been produced the week before the rising but Patrick's mother has been cited as stating in a letter that 'on second consideration Padhraic, Willie and MacDonagh thought it better not to produce it as it might give too much away and upset all their arrangements for the coming events of Easter Week'.[127] Interestingly Connolly's similarly nationalist play *Under Which Flag* was produced on the

26 March 1916. Mrs. Pearse later recalled of *The Singer* that 'the very boys in the school who were to take part in it acted in it for the benefit of the school in November or December 1916. I was present on this occasion and I thought it would break my heart it seemed so real'.[128] Nonetheless, a 1938 article seems to suggest that Mrs. Pearse gave permission for a first production organised by a James F. Ford to take place in Liverpool in 1918 – the permission having being given reluctantly as she wished the first staging to be by the St. Enda's students.[129] Despite this confusion, what is beyond doubt is that the play was produced in the school with many of the actors from the original 1916 cast in December 1917. The most likely explanation for the differing details given above is that Mrs. Pearse's later recollection of dates was confused and that the contact from Ford may have taken place in 1917, not 1918 and may even have served to spur on the St. Enda's production in late 1917. The 1917 production was staged on the 13 and 14 December in the Foresters' Hall in Parnell Square, alongside a revival of *Íosagán*. *The Singer* was specifically advertised as 'P.H. Pearse's last play (First production on any stage)'.

From this point onwards the afterlife of *The Singer* is a little easier to trace. It was translated to Irish in 1920, though the translation was not published until 1937,[130] and was produced in the Gate Theatre by Micheál Mac Liammóir in 1932 along with Mac Liammóir's own *Easter 1916*.[131] Interestingly the Micheál Mac Liammóir production took *The Singer*, usually thought of as a relatively realist piece of theatre, to be essentially symbolic and instead of a commonplace conventional cottage evoked a scene where, in the words of Hilton Edwards 'anything was possible and the imagination might soar'.[132] The following year a radio broadcast production was made in April,[133] and the Nic Shiubhlaigh sisters took part in this production.[134]

The Singer is the most obviously political of Pearse's plays. It would be strange, in truth, if this were not the case – Pearse was, after all, writing *The Singer* while heavily involved in plotting the open rebellion that was to be the Easter Rising. In these final months of his life, then, Pearse the theatre practitioner and Pearse the nascent rebel began to merge more closely together. In what seems like an act of thinking aloud, *The Singer* tells the story of preparation for a rebellion. It is a play that reveals something of the fears, anxieties, hopes and desires that must have been consuming Pearse during this time. In the end it has been a play best remembered for the Christ-like declaration of MacDara (the leader of rebellion) on going out to meet the English: 'One man can free a people as one Man redeemed the world. I will take no pike. I will go into the battle with bare hands. I will stand up before the Gall as Christ hung naked before men on the tree!' As dramatic climaxes go it is certainly effective. It has also left a long and fraught critical legacy, with some critics highlighting it as evidence of Pearse's 'messiah-complex'.[135]

Whatever the psychological truth of such claims (and it is hard to imagine how it could be 'proved' one way or another), *The Singer* is certainly a complex play that points towards a relationship between political rebellion and sacred duty. It is also a play that returns to the importance of culture as a transmitter of radical ideas and the keeper of an empowering communal memory. As with *Owen*, a ballad singer stands at the heart of the action in *The Singer*. MacDara is the singer of the title and on returning home he recounts the effect that his songs have had on a downtrodden and hopeless people. On his travels he has also been a teacher, and once again Pearse uses theatre to explore the possibilities held out by a properly imagined education system:

> MacDARA Perhaps that is why I felt it proud and wondrous to be a teacher, for a teacher does that. I gave to the little lad I taught the very flesh and blood and breath that were my life. I fed him on the milk of my kindness; I breathed into him my spirit.

It is only at the end of the play that MacDara is revealed as the leader of political rebellion – his travels and his songs, it turns out, have been in the service of organised revolution. In a moment that is reminiscent of much that underpinned *The Master*, MacDara describes his most powerful revelation, and it is a revelation that translates the republican idea of 'the people' into a powerful discourse of sacredness:

> MACDARA The people, Maoilsheachlainn, the dumb, suffering people: reviled and outcast, yet pure and splendid and faithful. In them I saw, or seemed to see again, the Face of God. Ah, it is a tear-stained face, blood-stained, defiled with ordure, but it is the Holy Face.

What we see again here is Pearse's ability to cloak a very modern ideological position in the costume of more traditional viewpoints. While not as theatrically ambitious as some of his more experimental earlier pieces, there is little doubt that *The Singer* is his most ambitious work in terms of its relationship to real-world action.

Eoghan Gabha

Pearse's unfinished play *Eoghan Gabha* was 'lost' until its discovery among his father's papers by Éamonn Bulfin at Derrinlough, Birr, Co. Offaly.[136] Éamonn Bulfin had been a pupil at St. Enda's and later a member of the Fianna and IRB and a participant in the 1916 Rising. William Bulfin, his father, was a journalist for the Argentine *Southern Star* newspaper. Given that the script was found amid his papers it is pretty certain that *Eoghan Gabha* dates from before 1910, when William Bulfin died. (It is not clear if the typescript which now accompanies the original handwritten script is Pearse's; there are several differences or misreadings and this edition is based on the script in Pearse's hand.) Bulfin Senior had spoken from the steps of St. Enda's following the production of *Mac-ghníomhartha Chúchulainn* at St. Enda's in June 1909.[137] Having shown such enthusiasm perhaps Pearse had given Bulfin the script of *Eoghan Gabha* to read. *Eoghan Gabha* was first produced in 1953 by an amateur group from Tullamore, with the addition of a prologue and epilogue taken from the poem 'A Phádraig

Sairséal, Slán go dtí thú'.[138] Since then scholars have had difficulty locating the script: this to our knowledge is its first publication. The play itself seems to have been pitched as what might now be termed a romantic comedy, with a backdrop of war. It is set in the aftermath of the Battle of the Boyne as some of the soldiers who had fought on the side of King James are regrouping. It is a lighthearted play, rather untypical of Pearse, and was clearly never intended to serve as high literature. Some crowd scenes seem to have been written primarily to provide parts and as an excuse to insert dancing and singing. The folk song sung by Muircheartach shows Pearse's familiarity with this genre; he would later pen a 'folksong' for his short story 'An Bhean Chaointe'. While the crowd scene might be perceived as clumsy or clichéd, the singing of the song *Gráinne Mhaol* is an example of Pearse the scholar inspiring Pearse the playwright.

The opening scene of *Eoghan Gabha* is set in a forge, and introduces some of the main characters – Eoghan, the smith and his seemingly hapless apprentice Colm, who is in reality the son of a raparee. Eoghan is well-drawn character, fond of his own voice and a bit of a bully but nonetheless likeable. There is a romantic subplot, less well executed (though perhaps deliberately simplified for comedic effect), whereby Colm is in love with the smith's daughter, Máire. Their romance is made difficult by an historical enmity between the two families. Meanwhile tension rises as preparations for a move on Limerick begin. The dialogue shows Pearse's deep knowledge of the nuances, cadences and phraseology of native speech. While the dialogue is that of everyday speech and does reproduce some Conamara dialectisms it does not deliberately seek to identify the characters as being from Conamara.[139] The levity in this play is relatively unusual – most of Pearse's plays were quite serious although his sense of humour was evident from writings such as 'The Wandering Hawk' and some of his journalistic pastiche pieces for *An Barr Buadh*. Notwithstanding the comedic element, *Eoghan Gabha* shows quite a sophisticated understanding of history and folk history. The stories of the suffering and heroism of the raparees of the 1640s inherited by Colm are based on historical fact. While the plot is unfinished, it is interesting that the hero, Colm, is several times chastised for not being able to make a proper horseshoe. Folk memory has Sarsfield being saved because a woman belonging to the enemy camp fell behind the rest of her camp because a faulty horseshoe made her horse lame: according to the story, she ended up divulging vital information to Sarsfield's side. Along with the translations Pearse made from Keating, Ferriter etc. for his *Songs of the Irish Rebels*, *Eoghan Gabha* stands as a reminder of Pearse's interest in seventeenth-century political history and his interest in folk literature as an agent of historical memory. As an unfinished play, it is difficult to stage, and does not work, a fact which was acknowledged after its original – and only – staging in 1953.[140]

Note: This is also the first time the play has been translated. The translator (Róisín Ní Ghairbhí) followed the lead given by Pearse in *The Singer* in using Hiberno-English with occasional (common) Gaelicisms left intact.

SCRIPTLESS PLAYS

Note
In addition to those plays with extant scripts we have endeavoured to provide as much material as possible on those performance pieces whose traces are to be found in reviews, programme notes, diary entries etc. There is an added poignancy in the loss of the original scripts for these performance events – *An Pháis/ Passion Play*, *The Defence of the Ford*, *Fionn: A Dramatic Spectacle*, *The Fianna of Fionn* – as the contemporary commentaries that are left to us suggest they were amongst Pearse's greatest and most ambitious achievements as a theatre practitioner. In their different ways each of these pieces was something of a theatrical event in Dublin. The sheer number of people required for their effective production locates these works as the result of major cooperation between many of the revivalist and Irish-Ireland activists in the city. On these occasions, indeed, St. Enda's and St. Ita's were the central fulcrum for much that was most

interesting and dynamic in cultural-nationalist Dublin at the beginning of the twentieth century.

An Pháis / Passion Play (1911)

Pearse's Irish-language rendering of the Passion story – presenting 'the chief incidents in the Passion of Christ as related in the Gospel' – was first performed at the Abbey Theatre during the Easter of 1911.[141] The script does not survive, but the Passion was played in Irish. Pearse had taken the speeches from the Gospel with the exception of certain words in the last act which folk tradition attributed to the holy women.[142] Thomas McDonnell (the teacher at St. Enda's) played the part of Christ and he also composed the music, including a much commented upon *caoine* for the women on Calvary. Willie Pearse played the role of Pilate to much acclaim, while his brother Patrick and Thomas MacDonagh took on the roles of the thieves. The gardener Micheál Mac Ruaidhrí was 'the most ferocious Barrabas one could wish to see'.[143] Mary Bulfin played Christ's mother Mary and both she and Willie featured in the photographic publicity material. As a piece of theatre Pearse's return to the Passion narrative reveals much about his project during this period. Pearse's vision for culture was animated by a desire to bring the Irish language world into contact with the best that European modes of expression had to offer. It is of note, then, that Padraic Colum sensed just this capacity within the piece at the time of its first unveiling: 'This Passion Play takes us back naturally to the origin of modern European drama'. With this return to a source model, Colum goes on to argue, Pearse had presented his audience with the 'first serious theatre piece in Irish. It has root power. Naturally Irish drama begins with the Passion Play, the Miracle Play or the Morality Play. This Passion Play gives the emotion out of which a Gaelic drama may arise. If its production be ever made an annual event it might create a tradition of acting and dramatic writing in Irish'.[144] The use of a *caoineadh* in *An Pháis* was not necessarily pioneering – Synge had already drawn on this tradition in *Riders to the Sea*. There had also been a keen in *An Rí*. But it was certainly a bold move, at a time when the Catholic Mass was said in Latin, to use the Irish language and native Irish cultural forms to represent the Passion and death of Christ. Indeed to represent Christ's Passion on stage at all was a radical move for Pearse: the idea of a people's Catholic church was not to emerge for another fifty years. The production drew some controversy – as Passion Plays in general did at the time – and Pearse was forced to defend the Passion Play before its performance in a letter to *The Irish Times*.[145]

Joseph Holloway's description of the play's opening performance gives a real flavour of the impact that it had for those in attendance:

> I went down to the Abbey to see a Passion Play in 3 acts … Mr. Pearse stepped from behind the curtains and addressed the house first in Irish and then he explained the nature of the piece we were to soon behold and the way he wished us to receive it … soon the wonderful tragedy of the world began with the Garden of Gethsemane and the agony of our blessed Lord and final betrayal by Judas with which the act ends. It was all most impressive and very beautiful to behold. Next came the court of Pilate – a finely presented scene – wherein our Lord was condemned to die and last of all we beheld the mournful procession wend its wearying way up the side of Calvary and our Lord next under the weight of the cross for the last time. Here the grouping was perfect … [T]he lighting of this whole scene from beginning to end could not be more effectively managed and the whole scheme was of unsurpassable beauty. As the people pray on the hillside the ominous sound of hammering is heard and soon after our Lord's voice and those of the thieves who hang on either side of him are heard away in the distance until at last all is still and the stage darkens and the thunder rolls and the lightning flash and in awe we feel all is over and the greatest tragedy of the world consummated and all who had followed the incidents were deeply and wonderfully moved. The students of St. Enda's and St. Ita's had in a simple and

unaffected way re-created the tragedy of the King of the World for us again and we felt all the better for the sight. Never had I seen a more profoundly impressive and beautiful picture than that I had beheld during the Crucifixion. William Pearse was excellent as Pilate, I was greatly struck with by what simple means great effects can be produced and illusion interpreted on the stage. The crucifixion for instance, was far more intensely sorrowful 'off' than ... the picture being really presented to the eye. ... I had a word with Mr. Pierce as I came out. I said to him I had never seen anything quite as lovely or impressive as the final scene in his play: he replied he was pleased to hear that from me.[146]

Holloway's account also highlights just how well Pearse understood the whole gambit of mechanical and technical elements of theatrical production – in this case particularly those connected with sound and lighting effects. *The Irish Times* critic also praised the lighting and the 'pictures of solemn beauty'.[147]

In an interesting aside Holloway also records that he met with some clearly more conservative elements of Dublin society who expressed the wish that the *Passion* had been performed on 'some other stage and not on that where the *Playboy* was being given to the world'.[148] Such specific quibbles aside, Pearse's *Passion Play* was one of the theatrical events of 1911. While Pearse initially intended that it should be staged biennially, it was never repeated and events at an Easter yet to come meant that the *Passion* would only get a limited number of performances.

The Defence of the Ford and *The Fianna of Fionn* (1913)

The pageant *The Defence of the Ford* was first performed from 9 to 14 June 1913 at a week-long outdoor festival held at the Jones Road grounds (now Croke Park) to raise funds for St. Enda's.[149] The pageant was performed late in the evening on the Monday, Wednesday and Saturday and alternated with another pageant entitled *The Fianna of Fionn* and with other displays, including a display by the Fianna Éireann[150]. Holloway did not get to attend the opening night – he attended the fête on another night – but he heard that 'by all accounts' they made 'a delightful spectacle as the shades of night close in and the torches of the marching armies flare (…)'.[151] The summary on the fête programme provides a description of *The Fianna of Fionn* and reveals the painterly and ritualistic nature of the production and the importance of music in the presentation of the various scenes. The final tableau, depicting 'the triumph of the sword drawn at the bidding of the poets' is of note:

> This pageant does not tell any story but is in the nature of a rhythmical march symbolizing the activities of the ancient Fianna. Fianna parade armed with sword and spear. A Hunter enters bearing a slain deer, and a tableau is formed symbolic of the chase. A Smith enters and a sword is forged, the Fianna singing the Song of the Sword. A Warrior enters and a tableau is formed, symbolic of an ancient battle. A Harper enters, and the pageant concludes with a tableau representing the triumph of the sword drawn at the bidding of the poets.[152]

The Fianna of Fionn was performed on the Tuesday and Thursday evenings at 10 p.m, presumably to achieve the utmost effect from the torch-lit parade. *An Rí* was also produced during the week and there were 'al fresco concerts', displays by the Fianna and other amusements.[153]

From the records of it that remain, *The Defence of the Ford* was a quite extraordinarily ambitious undertaking. The narrative staged was that of the *Defence of the Ford* by Cuchulainn and the Boy-Corps of Eamhain Macha against the other provinces as they awaited the rising of the Ulster Chiefs. It was performed on the Monday, Wednesday and Saturday nights of the fête at 9.30 p.m. and it seems Pearse himself acted in the pageant.[154] A comprehensive programme provided summaries of the action for the audience. The programme credited Patrick with the arrangement and Willie with the production of both pageants. (Interestingly, another note credited 'Captain Colbert, of the Fianna Éireann' with the 'military movements' in *The Defence of the Ford*.)[155] The sheer scale of the endeavour tells us much about the cooperative nature of the cultural-nationalist *milieu* in Dublin in the early years of the twentieth century.[156] *The Defence of the Ford* involved over 150 performers and many more 'technical crew' to ensure that all elements (including music, fire, choreography) went off smoothly. The good-will that surrounded St. Enda's at this point is equally demonstrated by the show of support that the week-long festival drew – Sean O'Casey wrote a letter to the *Irish Worker* encouraging its readers to go along, while Jim Larkin had the advertising bills printed up at his own expense (Larkin's children attended St. Enda's). The fête programme lists twenty-nine different groups and individuals who had 'offered their services' for the concerts that took place alongside the pageants. There was a wide spectrum of volunteers, which included numerous bands, piping groups, choirs and dancing groups. They ranged from the National Foresters' Band to the Father Matthew Choir, from traditional singers to Gaelic Glee singers and tenors and baritones.[157]

In the build up to the festival Pearse published a piece in *An Claidheamh Soluis* that outlined his vision for *The Defence of the Ford*:

> In Part I the Boy-Corps are seen at a hurling match on the green of Eamhain. A messenger arrives with tidings that the four provinces under Meadhbh have broken the Ulster border, and that Cuchulainn who has been defending the frontier alone lies wounded and spent. The Boy-Corps volunteer to take the post of danger, and to hold it until Ulster rises. They arm themselves and set out singing a marching song. Part II shows the camp of the men of Ireland on the Ulster border. They are singing by their watchfires. Suddenly they are charged by the Boy-Corps who make three outsets upon them. The boys fall after a gallant fight. Now Cuchulainn rouses himself from his torpor and passes out to avenge the Boy-Corps. Part III shows the camp fires of Feardiadh and Cuchulainn by the Ford. Meadhbh has sent Feardiadh, his bosom friend,

against Cuchulainn and this is the third morning of their fight. After exchanging high courtesies they fall to battle, and Feardiadh is slain. The Ulster hosts have now gathered and arrive at the frontier, which has been held until their coming by Cuchulainn and the boys.[158]

One certainly cannot fault the ambition behind such a grand production. Its scale and the use of a large outdoor space also reveals a fascinating drive to reconnect modern performance with the older social function of carnival and pageant as expressions of collective cohesion and communal identity.

Unfortunately, as Sean O'Casey records in *Drums Under the Window*, the execution did not quite match the grand vision in this case. Not for the first time the Irish weather was to put a dampener on good intentions and potential enjoyment:

> The pageant was held in Jones's Road Park, and the opening night was one of torrential rain, so that all who came crowded into the large hall of the grand-stand, to crouch there, saturated, gloomy, and low in heart as man could be. Pearse sat, the nadir of dejection, his grieving figure telling us that once more the damned weather had betrayed the Gael; with Douglas Hyde, who came to open it, roared out eulogy and boomed out windy joy, all the time the wind shook the sodden walls, and the rain slashed down on the roof above them.[159]

Holloway, visiting on the final evening, described the other entertainments in a disparaging tone, noting that when he arrived there was 'nothing doing' except for swing boats and 'all sorts of showman sideshows'.[160] Noting the relative success of a rival fundraiser, Holloway made the interesting comment that part of the problem may have lain with the fact that the fête was 'only a mere Irish display with no appeal to the fashionable crowd'.[161] He was also unimpressed with the organisation of the fête itself. Having visited on the Saturday (and having spent the duration of the Pageant chatting) he wrote that the fête itself 'lacked dignity' and was 'more on a level with a fair green on a market day'.[162] Such glitches aside, Pearse's imaginative ambition for *The Defence of the Ford* reveals a theatre practitioner undaunted by the scale and complexity of large-scale performance.

Fionn: A Dramatic Spectacle

Pearse's next pageant, *Fionn: A Dramatic Spectacle*, was first performed in June 1914 at St. Enda's (Rathfarnham). As with *The Defence of the Ford*, Pearse once again returned to the mythological for the source of this grand outdoor production. *Fionn* tells the tale of how Fionn came to be leader of the Fianna, and involves an enchanted spear that proves to be the only defence against a mighty enchanter (the Son of Miodhna). Set against the backdrop of a great feast at Tara, Pearse unfolds a narrative in which Fionn's bravery, skill and cleverness mean that he defends Tara while others are defenceless against the magic of the enchanter. His reward is the leadership of the band of heroes. On this occasion the pageant was the centrepiece for a fête at St. Enda's designed to allow parents and those interested in the activities of the school to enjoy the environs of the Rathfarnham campus and experience some of the work being undertaken by the boys and their teachers. It was also the occasion for the ex-pupils reunion.[163] *The Irish Times* recorded the day's events and gives a sense of the atmosphere that surrounded them:

> Saturday was the annual *fête* day, and many past pupils and friends of the present pupils attended to take part in the social pleasures of the occasion. The weather during the afternoon was delightful, and the charming gardens and extensive grounds which adjoin the main building were greatly admired. The earlier part of the programme was devoted to athletic sports, in which both present and past pupils took part. Later on there was an adjournment to the lawn, where afternoon tea was served. While this was going on the school pipers played a programme of Irish airs, varying from the pathetic to the tragic. After tea, the guests were much interested in a dramatic spectacle which was performed in the grounds by the pupils. It was entitled 'Fionn', and was founded on a legend of the Fianna, in which Fionn, the son of Cumhall, with a wondrous spear slays the Son of Miodhna, who had come to burn down

the royal city of Tara. Those who took part in the spectacle were dressed in the picturesque costumes usually associated with the Fianna. The principal part, that of Conn of the Hundred Battles, was admirably played by Mr. William Pearse, while Mr. David Sears as Fionn was also excellent. The boys who took part were Alfred Gaynor, Joseph McGilligan, T. Carleton, E. MacGinley, T. Butler, B. Cooney, W. Kenny, F. Holden, C. MacGinley, Joseph Sweeney, John Hunt, Desmond Murphy, Owen Clarke, John Joyce, and F. O'Docherty. The prizes won at the sports were then distributed by Miss Pearse, and the school prizes by Dr. Douglas Hyde.

Reading back through the records of such occasions at St. Enda's it is clear that these were real events on the Dublin social calendar. There is something very clever indeed about Pearse's use of theatre and performance on such occasions – an atmosphere of cooperation and collegiality was obviously fostered by the range of activities that Pearse and his fellow teachers drew their visitors into. The pageant in the grounds was performative on many levels. Not just a demonstration of theatrical bravura, these events were performative in the sense of putting into action the ethos and ideals of the school and its educational policies, and demonstrating the wider possibilities of nationalist action. As such they encapsulate much that drove Pearse in his work as theatre practitioner and stand as testament to an intellect that was profoundly more dynamic and imaginative than is often presented.

NOTES

1 For a general discussion of the Rising as theatre see James Moran, *Staging the Easter Rising* (Cork: Cork University Press, 2006).
2 Mary Brigid Pearse (ed.), *The Home-Life of Pádraig Pearse* (Dublin: Mercier Press, 1979, 1st pub. 1934), p.64.
3 P.H. Pearse, *Ghosts* (Dublin: Tracts for the Times), 1916.
4 Unfortunately very little record remains of *The Fianna of Fionn*; we have included the brief description of its action that is discernible from the programme of the fête at which it was held.

5 *Íosagán*, *An Rí* and *Macghníomhartha Chúchulainn* were published in
the St. Enda's journal *An Macaomh* in their original Irish language
versions. *The Singer and Other Plays* was published by Maunsell in 1918
and included *The King (An Rí)*, *The Master* and an English language
version of *Íosagán*. The same plays were published in the *Collected
Works* that same year and Irish-language versions of *Íosagán* and *An
Rí (The King)* appeared in the companion volume, *Scríbhinní*. While the
Collected Works in English and Irish were reprinted several times,
Macghníomhartha Chúchulainn was never published outside of *An
Macaomh*. It was not until 1979, with the simultaneous publication of
Séamus Ó Buachalla's excellent *The Literary Writing of Patrick Pearse:
writings in English* and *Na Scríbhinní Liteartha an Phiarsaigh* that a
collection of Pearse's plays was attempted – albeit as part of two
general collections of Pearse's creative writings across various *genres*.
Ó Buachalla's collections have long been out of print and while the
introductory essays provide important initial information on the plays
(with the exception of *Eoghan Gabha*) they do not dwell on them or
on their contexts in any detail. James Moran's excellent *Four Irish Rebel
Plays* includes an annotated edition of *The Master*.
6 See in particular Cathal Ó hÁinle, *Gearrscéalta an Phiarsaigh* (Baile Átha
Cliath: Cló Thalbóid, 1979); Philip O'Leary, *The Prose Literature of the
Gaelic Revival, 1881–1921: ideology and innovation* (University Park, PA:
Pennsylvania State University Press, 1994); Regina Uí Chollatáin, *An
Claidheamh Soluis agus Fáinne an lae 1899–1932: Anailís ar phríomhnuachtán
Gaeilge ré na hAthbheochana* (Baile Átha Cliath: Cois Life Teoranta 2004);
Róisín Ní Ghairbhí, 'A People that did not exist?: Reflections on Some
Sources and Contexts for Patrick Pearse's Militant Nationalism' in Ruan
O'Donnell (ed.), *The Impact of the 1916 Rising: Among the Nations*
(Dublin: Irish Academic Press, 2008), and various authors in Roisín
Higgins and Regina Uí Chollatáin, *The Life and After-life of P.H. Pearse*
(Dublin: Irish Academic Press, 2009).
7 Exceptions include Mary Trotter, *Ireland's National Theaters* (Syracuse,
NY: Syracuse University Press, 2001); Karen Vandevelde, *The
Alternative Dramatic Revival in Ireland* (Cambridge Station, CA:
Academica Press, 2004); Seamus Deane (familiar with Irish) provides
a rare examination of the actual style of Pearse's writings in English
in 'Pearse, Writing and Chivalry' in *Celtic Revivals, Essays in Modern Irish
Literature 1880–1980* (London: Faber & Faber 1985), pp.63–74.
8 See, for example: Mary Trotter, *Ireland's National Theaters* (Syracuse,
NY: Syracuse University Press, 2001); Karen Vandevelde, *The
Alternative Dramatic Revival in Ireland* (Cambridge Station, CA:

Academic Press, 2004); James Moran, *Four Irish Rebel Plays* (Dublin: Irish Academic Press, 2007): Eugene McNulty, *The Ulster Literary Theatre and the Northern Revival* (Cork: Cork University Press, 2008); Nollaig Mac Congail agus Eadaoin Ní Mhuircheartaigh, *Drámaí Thús na hAthbheochana* (Gaillimh: Arlen House, 2008).

9 The editors would like to thank Alf and Fionnuala Mac Lochlainn, Galway, for information about the Dowlings and McGloughlins (interview 17/10/ 2008). Alf Mac Lochlainn of Galway is the son of Pearse's nephew, also Alf McGloughlin, whose stage name for The Leinster Stage Society was 'Morgan O'Friel'. The Dowlings are related to the Mac Lochlainns (Galway). The website www.ainm.ie, based on Breathnach and Ní Mhurchú's magisterial *Beathaisnéis* series, provides information on the Dowlings under the entry for Searloit Ní Dhúnlaing, Frank's sister. The Fenian connection was William Paul Dowling, the Young Irelander who was sent to Tasmania in 1848.

10 See *An Sgoláire* (the student magazine of St. Enda's), Vol. 1, No. 6, 18/5/1913.

11 Máire Nic Shiubhlaigh, *The Splendid Years* (Dublin: James Duffy and Company, 1955), p.146.

12 Padraic Pearse, *The Story of a Success* (Dublin: Maunsel & Co., 1920), p.30.

13 Mary Brigid Pearse (ed.), *The Home-Life of Pádraig Pearse* (Dublin: Mercier Press, 1979, 1st pub. 1934), p.7.

14 Séamus Ó Buachalla (ed.), *The Letters of P.H. Pearse* (Atlantic Highlands, N.J.: Humanities Press, 1980), pp.264–5, dated 11.5.1912. This is a translation of the original 'letter' published as part of the humorous series 'Beart Litreacha do Chuaigh Amú' in Pearse's radical newspaper *An Barr Buadh* in May 1912.

15 Mary Brigid Pearse (ed.), *The Home-Life of Pádraig Pearse* (Dublin: Mercier Press, 1979, 1st pub. 1934), p.45.

16 Ibid., p. 85.

17 The memoir was originally serialised in *Our Boys* in 1926–7.

18 Mary Brigid Pearse (ed.), *The Home-Life of Pádraig Pearse* (Dublin: Mercier Press, 1979, 1st pub. 1934), p.102.

19 Lines quoted from *Uncle Tom's Cabin*, a play by Patrick Pearse, in Mary Brigid Pearse. Ibid., p.103.

20 Ibid., pp.64–5.

21 Máire Nic Shiubhlaigh, *The Splendid Years* (Dublin: James Duffy and Company, 1955), p.141.

22 A selection of early plays in Irish is available in Éadaoin Ní

Mhuircheartaigh agus Nollaig Mac Congail (eag.), *Drámaí Thús na hAthbheochana* (Gaillimh: Arlen House, 2008).

23 Séamus Ó Buachalla (ed.), *The Letters of P.H. Pearse* (Atlantic Highlands, N.J.: Humanities Press, 1980), p. 9, dated 13.05.1899.

24 Mary Brigid Pearse (ed.), *The Home-Life of Pádraig Pearse* (Dublin: Mercier Press, 1979, 1st pub. 1934), p.41.

25 Philip O'Leary, *The Prose Literature of the Gaelic Revival, 1881–1921: Ideology and Innovation* (University Park, PA. : Pennsylvania State University Press, 1994), p.130.

26 Joost Augusteijn, *Patrick Pearse: The Making of a Revolutionary* (Basingstoke: Palgrave Macmillan, 2010), p.84.

27 Ibid.

28 Kine: cattle

29 Buaile: pasture.

30 *An Claidheamh Soluis*, 19 May 1906.

31 *An Claidheamh Soluis*, 26 May 1906.

32 Ibid.

33 Ibid.

34 Ibid.

35 *An Claidheamh Soluis*, June 2nd 1906. Messrs. Lawrence: William and John Lawrence – photographic entrepreneurs who built up an extraordinarily extensive collection of photographic images of the Irish landscape.

36 Máire Nic Shiubhlaigh, *The Splendid Years* (Dublin: James Duffy and Company, 1955), p. 72.

37 Ibid., p. 77.

38 'The Dramatic Treatment of Heroic Literature', *Samhain* 1902, pp.11–13. The source for A.E. and Eoin Mac Néill's involvement is Gearóid Mac Lochlainn, *Ealaín na hAmharclainne*, (BÁC: Clódhanna Teoranta, 1966), lch.444. Mac Lochlainn had a brief involvement with The Theatre of Ireland; his father was a Fenian.

39 Máire Nic Shiubhlaigh, *The Splendid Years* (Dublin: James Duffy and Company, 1955), p.88–90. For more on the Morrows see also McNulty, *The Ulster Literary Theatre and the Northern Revival*.

40 Pearse quoted from *Samhain* in *An Macaomh*; there is also a copy in the St. Enda's library.

41 The editors thank Mr. Dave Kenny for information on his 'bohemian' grandmother Gypsy Walker and her family.

42 See entry for Máire Nic Shiubhlaigh, www.ainm.ie.

43 Thanks are due once again to Mr. Dave Kenny for this information.

44 'Irish Acting', *An Claidheamh Soluis*, July 7th 1906.

45 'Nua-litridheacht', *An Claidheamh Soluis*, May 19th 1906.

46 'A Chronicle', *An Macaomh*, May 1910, p.49.

47 Desmond Ryan, *The Story of a Success* (Dublin: Maunsel & Co., 1920), p. 96.

48 'Annála na Sgoile', *An Macaomh*, Meánsamhradh, 1909, pp.80–9 (School annals).

49 See entry for Searloit Ní Dhúnlaing, www.ainm.ie.

50 Máire Nic Shiubhlaigh, *The Splendid Years* (Dublin: James Duffy and Company, 1955), p. 148.

51 We do not have a date for *Eoghan Gabha*.

52 James Linehin, 'Pearse's School', *Irish Times*, 3 November 1964.

53 Pearse was certainly not an unquestioning admirer of Yeats and Gregory. A diary entry by Holloway on 2 January 1912 provides a glimpse of Pearse's private (and very entertaining) views on Yeats and Lady Gregory and the Abbey – filtered though they were through Holloway, who had strong views on the matter himself. While Holloway notes Pearse's tolerance he also recalls Pearse's sense that the Abbey was not necessarily representative of Irish identity:

> I visited The Hermitage (St. Enda's) and was in town with P. H. Pearse. We spoke of the reception of the Irish Players in America. He is very tolerant of everyone's views and never hisses. The Abbey is a freak theatre and should be treated as such; if you don't like it, stop away (...) Pearse thought the Abbey was run too much on Ascendancy principles. He often saw Lady Gregory enjoying her own pieces and laughing at her own jokes. Yeats does the same. Truly they were both like little children in their ways. It would be fine for someone to burlesque the whole Abbey movement, and get the Abbey theatre and produce the burlesque with someone got up as Yeats to run up and down the stairs, etc. (...) Pearse did not rightly know whether Yeats was a man of self-consciousness or childlike simplicity. Much they thought artistic was eccentricity (...) Pearse did not believe all the Irish were as bad as the Abbey plays would have us believe. He maintained that those who did not hold with the Abbey and its doing should stay away: he believed in freedom for all.

54 As quoted in Joost Augusteijn, *Patrick Pearse: The Making of a Revolutionary* (Basingstoke: Palgrave Macmillan, 2010), p.106.

55 Joseph Holloway, diary entry for 5 February 1910, NLI.

56 'By Way of Comment', *An Macaomh,* December 1909.

57 Joseph Holloway, diary entry for 17 May 1913, NLI.

58 Invitation for Garden Party and *An Rí*, Allen Library.

59 'St. Enda's College, Annual Fête Day', *Irish Times*, 15 June 1914.

60 Invitation to St. Enda's annual reunion, June 1914, Allen Library.

61 *An Macaomh*, p.86.

62 Joseph Holloway, diary entry for 9 April 1910, NLI.

63 Joseph Holloway, diary entry for 22 March 1909 describing the production of *An Naomh ar Iarraidh* and *The Coming of Fionn at St. Enda's.*

64 'Annála na Sgoile', *An Macaomh*, Meánsamhradh 1909, p.86

65 'St. Enda's Fête', *Irish Times*, 15th April 1913.

66 Ibid.

67 Mary Brigid Pearse (ed.), *The Home-Life of Pádraig Pearse* (Dublin: Mercier Press, 1979, 1st pub. 1934), p.85.

68 Mary Bulfin in Mary Brigid Pearse (ed.), *The Home-Life of Pádraig Pearse* (Dublin: Mercier Press, 1979, 1st pub. 1934), pp.120–121.

69 P.J. Matthews, *Revival: the Abbey Theatre, Sinn Féin, the Gaelic League and the Co-operative Movement* (Cork: Cork University Press, 2003).

70 Programme, NLI. Pádraig Ó Tuathaigh was to become well known as the artist Patrick Tuohy.

71 *An Macaomh*, June 1909.

72 'Annála na Sgoile', *An Macaomh*, Meánsamhradh 1909, p.85 (School Annals).

73 Patrick Pearse (Desmond Ryan ed.), *The Story of a Success* (Dublin: Maunsel & Co., 1920), p.95.

74 Source: www.ainm.ie, based on Breathnach/Ní Mhurchú's *Beathaisnéis* series.

75 Joseph Holloway, diary entry for 22 March 1909 describing the production of *An Naomh ar Iarraidh* and *The Coming of Fionn* at St. Enda's. Information on building of stage, Annála na Sgoile, *An Macaomh*, Meánsamhradh, 1909, p.85.

76 'Na hIndiacha Thoir', *An Claidheamh Soluis*, 15 December 1906.

77 'St. Enda's College', *Irish Times*, 17 June 1912.

78 Joseph Holloway, diary entry for 14 June 1913, NLI. The entry refers to the rain on the previous Monday.

79 Joseph Holloway, diary entry for 5 February 1910, NLI.

80 Annála na Sgoile, *An Macaomh*, Meánsamhradh, 1909, p.86.

81 Joseph Holloway, diary entry for 14 April 1911, NLI.

82 Ibid.

83 Statement by Éamonn Bulfin for the Bureau of Military History.

84 Fiannaíocht: Known as Ossianic or Fenian literature in English, these very popular stories and lays are present in both folk and manuscript sources in Ireland and Scotland. The material involves the adventures of Fionn and the Fianna, a legendary band of warriors. The Rúraíocht, known as the Ulster Cycle in English involves a wide range of material and features such figures as Cúchulainn and Queen Maeve. It tends more toward a manuscript tradition. For a discussion of Pearse's exposure to material from these two literary cycles in his childhood and early youth see Róisín Ní Ghairbhí, 'A People that did not Exist? Reflections on some Sources and Contexts for Patrick Pearse's Militant Nationalism', in O'Donnell, Ruán (ed.), *The Impact of the 1916 Rising: Among the Nations* (Dublin: Irish Academic Press, 2008), pp.161–86.

85 'The Intellectual Future of the Gael.' The lecture was later published in *Three Lectures on Gaelic Topics*, (Dublin: M.H. Gill and Son, 1898) p.55.

86 For a detailed overview and discussion of these editions as well as an excellent appraisal of Pearse's expertise in the literature see Philip O'Leary, *The Prose Literature of the Gaelic Revival 1881-1921* (Pennsylvania State University Press, 1994), pp. 223–79.

87 The lecture 'The Celtic Origin of Chivalry' was discussed in the editorial in 'Our Heritage of Chivalry', *An Claidheamh Soluis*, 14 November 1908.

88 See George Sigerson, *Bards of the Gall and Gael examples of the poetic literature of Erinn; done into English after the metres and modes of the Gael by George Sigerson* (London, Dublin: T. Fisher Unwin, 1907).

89 Philip O'Leary, *The Prose Literature of the Gaelic Revival 1881–1921*(Pennsylvania State University Press, 1994), p.255.

90 Pádraic Óg Ó Conaire, 'Cuimhní Scoil Éanna', *Cuimhní na bPiarsach* (Baile Átha Cliath: Coiste Cuimhneachán na bPiarsach, 1958), p.6.

91 See entry on www.ainm.ie on Searloit Ní Dhúnlaing (Frank's sister) for information on the Dowlings.

92 'By Way of Comment', *An Macaomh*, Nollaig, 1909, p.18.

93 'By Way of Comment', *An Macaomh*, Meánsamhradh, 1909, p.15.

94 For an analysis of the extent of Pearse's knowledge of Early Irish literature see Philip O'Leary, pp.253–5.

95 'By Way of Comment', *An Macaomh*, Meánsamhradh, 1909, p.8.

96 'By Way of Comment', *An Macaomh*, Meánsamhradh, 1909, p.8.

97 'By Way of Comment', *An Macaomh*, Nollaig, 1909, p.8.

98 For more on this see Brian Crowley, '"His Father's Son": James and Patrick Pearse', *Folk Life: Journal of Ethnological Studies*, Vol. 43 2004–5, pp.71–88.

99 'Annála na scoile, Fómhar go Nollaig, 1909', *An Macaomh*, Imleabhar 1 Uimhir 2 Nollaig 1909, p.60. (School annals)

100 Joseph Holloway, diary entry for 5 February 1910, NLI.

101 Gerard Murphy, *Early Irish Lyrics* (Dublin: Four Courts Press, 1999), pp.26–29.

102 *An Macaomh*, Christmas 1910.

103 Joseph Holloway, diary entry for 5 February 1910, NLI.

104 Ibid.

105 Ibid.

106 'Scoil Éanna Players', *An Claidheamh Soluis*, 16 April 1910.

107 Joseph Holloway, diary entry for 9 April 1910, NLI.

108 'Dr Douglas Hyde at the Frankfort Feis', *Irish Times*, 11 June 1910.

109 Information from original programme, with thanks to Brian Crowley of the Pearse Museum and OPW.

110 MS 15, 004; *An Rí, An Macaomh*, edited by P. H. Pearse, Imleabhar II, Uimhir 2 Bealtaine , 1913, lgh. 18- 26.

111 Joseph Holloway, diary entry for 15 June 1912, NLI.

112 'St. Enda's School, Rathmines', *Irish Times*, 17 June 1912.

113 'Dublin Happenings', *Evening Herald*, 17 June 1912; 'St. Enda's College', 17 June 1912.

114 Letter from Pearse to Mrs. Bloomer 25 April 1913, Séamus Ó Buachalla (London: Gerrard's Cross/Colin Smythe, 1980), pp. 288–9.

115 The phrase 'fadó fadó ar maidin' was used by the poet Seán Ó Ríordáin while invoking a comparison with Fiannaíocht literature.

116 Nóna: oifig de chuid na hEaglaise a bhíodh ar siúl i dtosach ag an naoú huair.

117 None: One of the daily offices in the Western Church, forming the fifth of the canonical hours of prayer and originally appointed for the ninth hour of the day (OED).

118 Psalmody: the singing of psalms.

119 For a discussion of this and a general discussion of connections between Pearse's creative writings and his militancy see Róisín Ní Ghairbhí, 'A People that did not Exist? Reflections on some Sources and Contexts for Patrick Pearse's Militant Nationalism', in O'Donnell,

Ruán (ed.), *The Impact of the 1916 Rising: Among the Nations* (Dublin: Irish Academic Press, 2008), pp.161–86.

120 Canticle: A song, properly a little song; a hymn (OED).

121 *An Macaomh*, May 1913, pp.8–9.

122 See for example James Moran, Introduction to *Four Irish Rebel Plays* (Dublin: Irish Academic Press, 2007).

123 Information from original programme, courtesy of Allen Library.

124 'A St Enda's Play in Bengal', *Dublin Evening Mail*, 2 September 1915.

125 As Pearse explains in his brief introduction this is a reference to James Stephens (1825–1901), a key leader of the Fenian movement. Pearse also wrote an adventure story for boys entitled 'The Wandering Hawk'.

126 James Moran, Introduction to *Four Irish Rebel Plays* (Dublin: Irish Academic Press, 2007), p.13.

127 *Irish Press*, 27 April 1966.

128 *Irish Press*, 27 April 1966.

129 'A Liverpool Visitor', *Irish Independent*, 19 August 1938.

130 Liam Ó Briain, An tAmhránaidhe, Oifig an tSoláthair, 1937.

131 Between the Acts, Forthcoming Productions, 10 March 1932.

132 'Book of Stage Designs', review of Bulmer Hobson, ed., The Gate Theatre Dublin, *Irish Press*, 30 November 1934.

133 'Weekend Radio Programmes', *Irish Press*, 14 April 1933.

134 'Last of the original Abbey company', 3 May 1967.

135 Most famously Ruth Dudley Edwards in *Patrick Pearse: The Triumph of Failure* (Dublin: Irish Academic Press, 2006 edition).

136 'A Forgotten Play by Patrick Pearse', *Irish Press*, 8 June 1953. See appendix.

137 Joseph Holloway Diaries, 1 February 1910, NLI.

138 'Oireachtas Lá na nÓg, Priest says Ireland needs her youth', *Irish Independent*, 28 October 1953.

139 'Dar príosba' for 'Dar Críost' shows Pearse to have known the dialect very well. Meanwhile the use of the verb 'fuireacht' and not 'fanacht' for 'staying' indicates a flexibility about paróle or perhaps an attempt at echoing classical Irish.

140 'Oireachtas Lá na nÓg, Priest says Ireland needs her youth', *Irish Independent*, 28 October 1953.

141 Mary Bulfin in Mary Brigid Pearse (ed.), *The Home-Life of Pádraig Pearse* (Dublin: Mercier Press, 1979), p.120.

142 'Passion Play in Dublin, This Week's Performance at the Abbey Theatre', *Irish Times*, 3 April 1911.

143 As recalled by Fintan Murphy, former pupil of St. Enda's during an address given to celebrate Pearse's birthday, cited in John Healy, 'The gentle headmaster who was a soldier too', *Irish Press*, 10 November 1955.

144 As quoted in Desmond Ryan, 'A Retrospect', in Patrick Pearse, *The Story of a Success* (Dublin: Maunsel and Co., 1920), pp.101–09.

145 P.H. Pearse, 'The Passion Play in Dublin', *Irish Times*, 7 April 1911.

146 Joseph Holloway's Diaries, 7 April 1911, NLI.

147 'Passion Play at the Abbey Theatre', 8 April 1911.

148 Joseph Holloway's Diaries, 8 April 1911, NLI.

149 Information from original programme, courtesy of the Allen Library.

150 Ibid.

151 Joseph Holloway, diary entry for 14 June 1913.

152 Information from original programme, courtesy of the Allen Library.

153 Ibid.

154 Máire Nic Shiubhlaigh recalls him wearing greasepaint and dressed in character, *The Splendid Years* (Dublin: James Duffy and Company, 1955) p.149.

155 Information from original programme, courtesy of Allen Library.

156 For more on this see P.J. Matthews, *Revival: the Abbey Theatre, Sinn Féin, the Gaelic League and the Co-operative Movement* (Cork: Cork University Press, 2003).

157 Information from original programme, courtesy of Allen Library.

158 *An Claidheamh Soluis*, 31 May 1913, p.9.

159 Sean O'Casey, *Drums Under the Window* (London: Macmillan & Co. Ltd., 1945), p.278.

160 Joseph Holloway, diary entry for 14 June 1913.

161 Ibid.

162 Ibid.

163 Invitation to reunion, courtesy of Allen Library.

SGOIL ÉANNA,

Ceac Feada Cuilinn, Rát Ó Máine.

Dia Máirt, 22 mí an Mheitim, 1909,
an a 3.30 a clog tráčnóna,

léireocaid mic léiginn na sgoile

mac-gníomarta Cúculainn,

.i. Caitréim Trí-Rannač ag n-a Tarraing ar Táin bó Cuailgne
do Pádraic mac Piarais.

An Fuireann annro síor:
An Cóir, .i. Buidean báird agus Manač.
(Chorus : Bards and Monks).

Concubar mac Neasa, Rí Ulad   Donncad Mac Finn,
(Conchubar son of Neasa, King of Ulster)   (Denis Gwynn).

Feargus mac Róig   Peadar Ó Concubair
(Feargus son of Roigh)   (Peter O'Connor).

Conall Cearnač   .i. Laočrad de'n   Eogan Mac Capptaig
(Conall the Triumphant)   Craoib Ruaid   (Eugene MacCarthy).

Laogaire buadač   (Heroes of the Red Branch) Micéal Ó Concubair
(Laoghaire the Victorious)   (Michael O'Connor).

                                  Ailpín Mac Loclainn
                                  (Alfred McGloughlin).

                                  Domnall Ó Concubair
                                  (Donal O'Connor).

Laočrad eile de'n Craoib Ruaid   Pádraic Ó Tuataig
(Other Heroes of the Red Branch)   (Patrick Tuohy).

                                  Seorař Ó Clocartaig
                                  (Joseph Stone).

Catbad Draoi   Éamonn Builtín
(Cathbhadh the Druid)   (Eamonn Bulfin).

Follamán mac Concubair,   Ádamnán Mac Fionnlaoič
.i. Taoireač na Macraide   (Eunan MacGinley).
(Follamhan son of Conchubhar, Chief of the Boy-Corps)

1.1 An chéad leathanach as clár *Macghníomhartha Chúchulainn*. The first page from the programme for *Macghníomhartha Chúchulainn*. (Le caoinchead ó Leabharlann Uí Ailín/Image courtesy of Allen Library)

MACGHNÍOMHARTHA CHÚCHULAINN[1]

.i. *Caithréim Thrírannach*
Arna tharraing ar Táin Bó Cuailgne do Phádraic Mac Piarais
Céadléirithe: 22 Meitheamh 1909, Scoil Éanna, Teach Fheadha
Chuilinn, Ráth Maonais

AN FHOIREANN ANSEO SÍOS:

An cór, .i. buíon bard
agus manach.
Conchubhar Mac Neasa, Rí
Uladh.

Feargus Mac Róigh
Conall Cearnach
Laoghaire Buach .i. laochra
den Chraoibh Rua.

An Chraobh Rua ar cheana.
Cathbhadh Draoi[2]
Follamhan Mac Conchubhair,
.i. Taoiseach na Macraí
Eoghan
Naoise
Ainnle

Ardán
Iollann Fionn
Buinne Rua
Aodh Caomh, .i. mic den
mhacra
An macra ar cheana

Seatanta Mac Sualtaimh, .i.
Cúchulainn
Culann Ceard, .i. ceard uasal
d'Ultaibh
Iubhar Mac Riangabhra .i. ara
Chonchubhair
Fear Faire
Laochra, giollanra, cearda,
aos ceoil agus oirifidigh,
bantracht, srl.

ÁIT DON CHAITHRÉIM SEO
Eamhain Macha
AIMSIR DI
An chéad aois

INCIPIT AN CHAITHRÉIM

[*Ceol do sheinm. An cór do theacht ar an láthair agus do ghluaiseacht ar fud na páirce, ag gabháil na rann seo inár ndiaidh.*]

AN CÓR *(Go mall éirimeach. Tomás Mac Domhnaill do ghléas)*
Scéal linn daoibh, a uaisle Gael,
A ghasra éachtach eolgach,
Scéal nachar fríoth a shárú
In irisibh ársa Fódhla.

Lá dar éirigh Mac Neasa
Rí neartmhar ógbhaidhe Uladh,
Do shuigh ar ard na hEamhna
I dteannta a laoch is a churadh.

Ag imirt ann don mhacra
Ar fhaiche an ríbhaile
Do tháinig chucu an macaomh
Do b'fhearr gaisce is gaile.

Do chuir trí chluiche orthu,
Ghabh dá g
airt is dá dtreascairt,
Gur nascadar air a gcomairc,
'S go mbíodh orthu ina cheannphort.

Fochtas an tArd-Rí scéala
Den tréanmhac go mbuadhghail:
"Is mé mac do dheirbh-shiúrach;
Seatanta Mac Sualtaimh."

AN CHÉAD ROINN

[*Eamhain Macha. Dún Chonchubhair i lár na páirce. Faiche na hEamhna os a chomhair amach. Coill bheag ar thaobh na láimhe clé.*
Conchubhar agus Feargus do theacht ar an bhfaiche, agus laochra ina dtimpeall. Iad do shuí i ndoras an dúin ag imirt fichille. Macra na

hEamhna do theacht ar an láthair, ina rith, um Fhollamhan Mac Conchubhair. A gcamáin ina lámhaibh acu. Iad do sheasamh i lár na faiche. Follamhan do labhairt:]

FOLLAMHAN Buailim ort, a Eoghain!

EOGHAN Leigim leat, a Fhollamhain!

FOLLAMHAN Beidh Naoise agam!

[*Naoise do dhul ar chúl Fhollamhain.*]

EOGHAN Beidh Ainnle agamsa!

[*Ainnle do dhul ar chúl Eoghain.*]

FOLLAMHAN Ardán!

EOGHAN Iollann Fionn!

FOLLAMHAN Buinne Ruadh!

EOGHAN Aodh Caomh!

[*Agus mar sin de go deireadh. Gach macaomh do dhul ar chúl a Thaoisigh de réir mar ghlaotar air. Ansin gach búíon díbh do thriall chum a báire féin, um a Thaoiseach féin. Na Taoisigh do chur na macaomh ina ionadaibh imeartha ar a haithle féin, .i. gach Taoiseach do ghluaiseacht amach óna bháire féin i dtosach a bhuíne; a chamán d'ardú dó agus beirt mhacaomh do sheasamh; a chamán d'ardú dó an dara huair agus an dara bheirt do sheasamh; agus mar sin de go mbeidh gach macaomh ina n-ionadaibh imeartha féin. An dá Thaoiseach do theacht le chéile i lár an mhachaire; a gcamáin d'ardú dóibh; an liathróid do chaitheamh isteach d'Fhollamhan; iad do thosnú ar an gcluiche.*

Leantar don chluiche go ceann tamaill aimsire. Seatanta do theacht ar an láthair, ag déanamh orthu ón gcoill. Ionar dearg deargsnuigthe air; léine ghealchúlphadhach lena chneas; brat caomh corcra uime; a chamán ina láimh aige. É do sheasamh anois is arís d'fhéachain na macraí. Ar theacht go himeall na coille dó, é do sheasamh fá scáth crainn ag a bhféachaint go haireach. Seal dóibh mar sin. Macaomh do bhualadh na liathróide d'ionsaí Sheatanta. Seatanta dá choimhéad lena chois. Follamhan do labhairt de ghuth ardmhór:]

FOLLAMHAN Tá an liathróid agat, a ghiolla! Tiomáin chughainn í!

SEATANTA Aire díbh, a óga Uladh!

[*An liathróid do bhualadh dó le linn é seo do rá; é do leanúint di, ag á bualadh ó cheann ceann an mhachaire in ainneoin na macraí, nó go mbuailidh sé thar bhruach báire í ar an taobh thall. Follamhan do labhairt:*]

FOLLAMHAN Maith, a mhaca, freagraidh le chéile an macaomh seo!

AN MACRA Freagróimid!

[*An liathróid do leagan d'Fhollamhan agus d'Eoghan ar bhéal báire Sheatanta; an macra uile do chosnamh an bháire eile; an liathróid do bhualadh do Sheatanta ó cheann ceann an mhachaire arís agus thar bhruach báire ar an taoibh thall ina n-ainneoin. Follamhan do labhairt:*]

FOLLAMHAN Is náire dúinn ligean don mhac beag seo bua do bhreith orainn ar fhaiche na hEamhna! Freagraidh é, a óga, an turas seo!

AN MACRA Freagróimid!

[*An cluiche do chur do Sheatanta orthu an treas uair mar an gcéanna. Fearg d'éirí don mhacra. Follamhan do labhairt:*]

FOLLAMHAN Maith, a mhaca, tugam faoi le chéile agus díolam air ár ngeasa do bhriseadh; óir is geasa dúinn ligean do mhacamh teacht inar gcluiche gan a choimirce do chur orainn i dtosach. Tugaidh faoi!

AN MACRA Bhéarfaimid!

[*Iad do thabhairt faoi go naimhdeach nimhneach, á bhualadh lena gcamáin. Seatanta dá chosnamh féin orthu lena chamán féin, á leagan ar gach taobh de. An torann do chlos don rí, é d'éirí ina sheasamh agus do theacht dá n-ionsaí agus an laochra ina thimpeall. Conchubhar do bhreith*] *ar láimh ar Sheatanta agus do labhairt de ghlór ríoga:*]

CONCHUBHAR Scoiridh, a óga, den bhruíon seo; agus scoirse, a mhic bhig, den ruathar atá tú do thabhairt ar an macra. Cím nach aon chaoinchluiche atá tú d'imirt leo.

SEATANTA Ní caoinfháilte do fuaras uathu, iar dteacht dom as tíorthaibh imchiana chun cairdeas do dhéanamh leo.

CONCHUBHAR Nárbh eol duit, a leinbh, geasa na macraí, .i. go bhfuil ar gach mac óg dá dtig chucu a choimirce do nascadh orthu?

SEATANTA Níorbh eol; dá mb'eol, do dhéanfainn é.

CONCHUBHAR Maith, a mhaca, gabhaidh anois oraibh féin ligean slán don ghasúr.

AN MACRA Gabhaimid.

SEATANTA Ní ghlacaim leis, a rí! Dar na déithe dá n-adhraim, muna dtigeann said faoi mo choimirce féin, ní choscfad mo lámh díobh.

AN MACRA Gabhaimid faoi do choimirce.

[*A nglúine d'fheacadh agus a gcinn do chromadh dóibh ina fhianaise. Conchubhar do labhairt:*]

CONCHUBHAR Inis dom anois, a mhic bhig, cá haird as a dtángais chughainn, nó cén chonair do gabhadh leat, nó céard is ainm agus is comhainm duit?

SEATANTA Thar Sliabh Fuaid do thángas, ó Mhaigh Mhuirtheimhne. Agus Seatanta Mac Sualtaimh m'ainm, agus is í Deachtaire, do dheirfiúr féin, is máthair dom, a rí Uladh!

CONCHUBHAR Mochean do theacht, a mhic bhig! Mochean an té is máthair duit! Mochean do cheann maiseach agus do lámh láidir luathghonach!

[*É do bhreith ar an mac agus a phógadh agus a fháisceadh lena ucht. Fearghus do labhairt:*]

FEARGUS Mochean do theacht, a mhic bhig!

[*Feargus do bhreith ar an mac agus a ardú ina dhá láimh agus a chur ina shuí ar a ghualainn. An macra agus an laochra do labhairt d'aitheasc aon fhir:*]

AN MACRA AGUS AN LAOCHRA Mochean do theacht! Mochean do theacht!

[*Iad do dhul isteach sa dún, um Chonchubhar agus um Fheargus, agus Seatanta ar ghualainn Fhearguis.*]

INCIPIT An Dara Roinn

[*Ceol do sheinm. An cór do theacht ar an láthair agus do ghluaiseacht ar fud na páirce, ag gabháil na rann seo inár ndiaidh:*]

Scéal linn dhaoibh, a uaisle Gael,
A ghasra éachtach eolgach,
Scéal nachar fríoth a shárú
In irisibh ársa Fódhla.

Lá dá ndeachaigh Mac Neasa
Rí neartmhar ógbhaidhe Uladh,
D'ól fleá agus féasta
Ar éileamh an ríchearda, Culann.

Fágadh i ndiaidh an ríthí,
Mac míleata Sualtaimh,
Go ndeachaigh ar a lorgaibh
Go hoscartha buach.

Do bhí ag Culann rathmhar
Cú chalma chraosach chróga,
Thug fogha faoin mac go feargach
Gur treascradh í sa gcomhrac.

Dúirt an t-óglach: "A Chulainn,
"Beadsa im'choin duit feasta.
"Den ghníomh sin, arsa Cathbhadh,
"A mhacaoimh, Cúchulainn, d'ainmse."

AN DARA ROINN

[*Ceárta Chulainn. Toirt mhór thine inti. Cearda óga ag bualadh ar inneonacha os comhair an dorais. Iad ag tosú ar na ranna seo inár ndiaidh do ghabháil:*]
[*Go mear croíúil. Tomás Mac Domhnaill do ghléas*]

1

NA CEARDA
Ding dong dideró
Buaileam, a óga,
Ding dong dideró,
Ag na hinneonaibh.

Ding dong dideró,
Buaileam go cróga
Ding dong dideró
Le hordaibh móra.

CEARD DÍOBH
Buail sin, a ghabha óig,
Íseal is éadrom.
Buaileam go léir é
Trína chéile.

TRIÚR, Á FHREAGAIRT
Buailimís arís é,
Is buailimís le chéile,
Is buailimís cuaird air,
Go luath is go héasca.

NA CEARDA UILE Ding dong dideró srl.

71

AN CHÉAD CHEARD
Buailidh é, cumaidh é,
A chearda na ceártan
Claíomh claisleathan óir
Do Chonchubhar, don ardrí.

NA CEARDA UILE Ding dong dideró, srl.

[*Culann do theacht agus do sheasamh i ndoras na ceártan. É do labhairt:*]

CULANN Bhfuil sé réidh agaibh?

[*An claíomh d'ardú ina láimh don chéad cheard. É do labhairt ag freagairt Chulainn.*]

AN CHÉAD CHEARD
Féach é, a mháistir
Déanta is cumtha,
Féach in mo láimh é!

AN TRIÚR
Tógam é, creatham é,
Tógam go hard é,
Claíomh claisleathan óir
Do Chonchubhar, don Ard-Rí!

NA CEARDA UILE Ding dong dideró, srl.

[*Culann do labhairt:*]

CULANN Scéala móra agam daoibh, a mhaca!

NA CEARDA Abair, a Chulainn.

CULANN Conchubhar Mac Neasa agus an Chraobh Rua do theacht chughainn d'ól fleá anocht. Scoiridh den bhualadh, óir is clos dom torann na n-óg agus sceimhle na n-arm ag teacht do láthair don rítheaghlach.

[*Na cearda do scor den obair agus do dhul isteach sa gceártain. Conchubhar, Feargus, Conall, Laoghaire, Cathbhadh agus an Chraobh Rua ar cheana, do theacht fán láthair. Culann agus na cearda d'fháiltiú rompu. Iad do shuí ins an gceártain ag ól na fleá. Culann do labhairt iar suí dóibh:]*

CULANN Bhfuil aon duine eile ded' chomhluadar le teacht anocht, a Rí Uladh?

CONCHUBHAR Níl. Céard uime a bhfiafraís?

CULANN Cú chalma chraosfhiaclach atá agam, agus is ar an gcoin sin bhíos an teach d'fhoraire san oíche, agus is mairg an té d'iarrfadh teacht isteach sa teach dá hainneoin, óir do dhéanfadh cosair chró de.

CONCHUBHAR Dúntar an doras agus ligtear amach an chú.

[An doras do dhúnadh do Chulann agus an chú do ligean amach dó. Aos ceoil an rí do ghabháil ceoil agus oirfide. Lena linn seo Seatanta do theacht ar an láthair ag déanamh ar an gceártain; óir tuigtear gur fágadh sa mbaile é agus go dtáinig i ndiaidh Chonchubhair agus na Craoibhe Rua, ag giorrú na slí dó féin lena chamán agus lena liathróid. É do theacht go doras na ceártan (tuigtear gurb ar cúl don doras seo); torann uafar agus gleo gáifeach gráiniúil do chlos don lucht éisteachta. Conchubhar d'éirí ina sheasamh agus do labhairt:]

CONCHUBHAR Is mairg, a óga, go dtángamar ag ól na fleá seo anocht!

ULAIDH Céard uime, a rí?

CONCHUBHAR An giolla beag d'fhágas im' dhiaidh, mac mo dheirféar do thitim leis an gcoin!

[Ulaidh d'éirí ina seasamh agus do bhreith ar a n-airm agus do dhul amach agus Feargus ina dtosach.

Iad do theacht isteach arís agus Seatanta ar ghualainn Fhearguis. Culann do sheasamh sa doras ag féachaint roimhe amach. Conchubhar do labhairt:]

CONCHUBHAR Mochean do theacht, a ghiolla bhig!

[*Culann do theacht agus do sheasamh i bhfianaise Chonchubhair agus Seatanta. É do labhairt:*]

CULANN Mochean do theacht ar son t'athar agus do mháthar, ach ní mochean do theacht ar do shon féin.

CONCHUBHAR Céard atá agat leis an mac?

CULANN Is mairg go ndearnas an fhleá seo duit, a Chonchubhair, óir is maith amú mo mhaithse feasta, agus is beatha amú mo bheatha. Maith an fear muinteartha do thugais uaim, a mhic bhig, fear coimeádta m'éadaigh agus m'eallaigh agus m'fhearainn!

SEATANTA Ná bí i bhfeirg liom, a mháistir, a Chulainn, óir béarfadsa a fhíorbhreith sin.

CONCHUBHAR Cá breith bhéarfairse air, a mhic?

SEATANTA Má tá coileán de shíol na con úd in Éirinn oilfear liom é go mbeidh sé inghníomha mar athair. Agus beadsa im' choin coimeádta a eallaigh agus a fhearainn do Chulann ar feadh na haimsire sin.

CONCHUBHAR Is maith thugais do bhreith, a mhic bhig.

CATHBHADH Ní bhéarfainn féin ní b'fhearr; agus Cú Chulainn bheas mar ainm ortsa feasta dá chionn.

SEATANTA Ní hea. Is fearr liom m'ainm féin, Seatanta Mac Sualtaimh.

CATHBHADH Ná habair sin, a mhic bhig, óir cluinfidh fir Éireann agus Alban an t-ainm sin, agus beidh béil fear nÉireann agus Alban lán den ainm sin.

SEATANTA Más fíor a gcanair, a Chathbhadh, beidh an t-ainm sin orm.

ULAIDH Cúchulainn! Cúchulainn!

[*Conchubhar agus Ulaidh do shuí arís ag ól na fleá. Cúchulainn do shuí ar thairseach an dorais, ina choin choimeádta. An t-aos ceoil do ghabháil ceoil arís. Seal dóibh mar sin. Iar gcaite na fleá dóibh, Conchubhar agus Ulaidh d'éirí agus do cheiliúradh do Chulann, agus d'imeacht rompu, ach Cúchulainn, d'fhanúint ina shuí ar an tairsigh ag cosaint na ceártan.*]

INCIPIT AN TREAS ROINN

[*Ceol do sheinm. An cór do theacht ar an láthair agus do ghluaiseacht ar fud na páirce ag gábháil na rann seo inár ndiaidh:*]

Scéal linn dhaoibh, a uaisle Gael,
A ghasra éachtach eolgach
Scéal nachar fríoth a shárú
In irisibh ársa Fódhla

Lá dar éirigh Mac Neasa
Rí neartmhar ógbhaidhe Uladh
Do tháinig chuige an macaomh
Cú Chalma cróga Chulainn.

D'iarr air airm agus trealamh
D'fhág beannacht ag na hógaibh
Is d'imigh roimhe 'na charbad
Do dhéanamh catha is comhraic.

Níor staon sé dá stárthaibh
Go ráinig boird an chúige
Gur mharbhaigh triúr Mac Neachtain
Cé fearúil na búraigh.

Scéal linn díbh, a uaisle Gael,
A ghasra éachtach eolgach,
Scéal nachar fríoth a shárú
In irisibh ársa Fódhla

AN TREAS ROINN

[*Faiche na hEamhna. Cathbhadh do theacht ar an bhfaiche agus Cúchulainn agus Follamhan agus an macra ar cheana ina thimpeall. Follamhan do labhairt:*]

FOLLAMHAN Inis dúinn, a mháistir, a Chathbhaidh, cén séan atá ar an lá seo thar laethanta na bliana? An séan maith nó séan olc atá air?

CATHBHADH Tá, a mhic, an macaomh gheobhas airm inniu, beidh sé án oirirc, ach beidh sé duthain díomuan.

FOLLAMHAN Conas sin, a Chathbhaidh?

CATHBHADH Déanfaidh gníomharth a áireofar ar ghníomh-artha laochraí an domhain, ach beidh a shaolré gairid.

[*Cathbhadh agus an macra d'imeacht rompu. Cúchulainn d'fhanúint agus do shuí ina aonar. Conchubhar agus Ulaidh do theacht ar an bhfaiche lena gconaibh agus lena gconairt, lena bhfearaibh fiaigh agus lena ngiollanra. Cúchulainn d'éirí agus d'umhlú i bhfianaise Chonchubhair agus é d'agallamh mar leanas:*]

CÚCHULAINN Gach maith duit, a Rí Uladh!

CONCHUBHAR Aitheasc duine atá ag iarraidh athchuinge an t-aitheasc sin. Céard tá uait, a mhic bhig?

CÚCHULAINN Airm do ghabháil.

CONCHUBHAR Cé do ghríosaigh chuige sin tú, a mhic bhig?

CÚCHULAINN Cathbhadh Draoi.

CONCHUBHAR Más ea, ní eiteofar thú. Tugtar airm don mhacaomh seo!

[*Laoch den laochra do thabhairt claímh agus sleá don mhac. Cúchulainn d'fhéachaint na n-arm agus a mbriseadh dó agus é á bhféachain. É do labhairt:*]

CÚCHULAINN Ní maith na hairm seo, a rí.

CONCHUBHAR Tugtar a mhalairt d'armaibh dó.

[*A mhalairt d'armaibh do thabhairt dó agus a mbriseadh dó ar an gcuma chéanna. Cúchulainn do labhairt:*]

CÚCHULAINN Ní maith na hairm seo. Tugtar dom airm mo dhiongbhála.

CONCHUBHAR Bhéarfad duit m'airm féin, a Chú bheag.

[*Airm an rí do thabhairt dó. Cúchulainn dá lúbadh agus dá bhféachain ach gan a mbriseadh. Cúchulainn do labhairt:*]

CÚCHULAINN Is maith na hairm seo: is iad seo airm mo dhiongbhála. Mochean an rí darb airm agus trealamh iad. Mochean an tír as a dtáinig!

[*Cathbhadh do theacht ar an láthair agus do labhairt:*]

CATHBHADH An airm do ghabh sé siúd?

CONCHUBHAR Is ea.

CATHBHADH Ní do mhac do dheirféarsa dob áil liom a ngabháil sin inniu.

CONCHUBHAR Céard uime? Nach tusa do ghríosaigh chuige é?

CATHBHADH Ní mé, go deimhin.

CONCHUBHAR Céard seo, a shíóg shíofraí? An bréag d'insís dom?

CÚCHULAINN Ná bí i bhfeirg liom, a mháistir, a Chonchubhair. Is é go cinnte do ghríosaigh chuige mé, óir ar fhiafraí d'Fhollamhan de cén séan do bhí ar an lá seo dúirt sé, an mac beag do gheobhadh airm inniu, go ndéanfadh sé gníomhartha a d'áireofaí ar ghníomhartha laochra an domhain ach go mbeadh sé féin duthain díomuan.

CATHBHADH Fios dom sin. A Chú bheag, beirse án oirirc ach beirse duthain díomuan.

CÚCHULAINN Beag a bhrí liomsa cé nach mairfinn ach aon lá agus aon oíche amháin ach go mairfeadh mo scéala agus m'imeachta im' dhiaidh.

CONCHUBHAR Maith, a mhic bhig, éirigh id' charbad.

CÚCHULAINN Tugtar chugham do charbad féin a Chonchubhair, óir níl mo dhiongbháil in aon charbad eile.

CONCHUBHAR Cá hairm a bhfuil Iubhar Mac Riangabhra?

IUBHAR Táim anseo, a rí.

CONCHUBHAR Gabh leat mo dhá each féin, agus innill mo charbaid.

[*Iubhar d'imeacht agus do theacht ar an láthair arís agus na heich gafa agus an carbad inneallta aige. Conchubhar do labhairt:*]

CONCHUBHAR Éirigh sa gcarbad, a mhic.

[*Cúchulainn d'éirí sa gcarbad. An carbad do thabhairt cuairte na páirce. Conchubhar agus Ulaidh d'imeacht rompu d'fhiach agus d'fhianchosgairt. Cathbhadh d'imeacht roimhe isteach sa dún. An macra do theacht ar an bhfaiche agus do dhul do leataobh an dúin agus do thosnú ar chleasaibh d'imirt. An carbad do theacht ar ais agus do sheasamh os comhair dhoras an dúin. Iubhar do labhairt:*]

IUBHAR Maith, a mhic bhig, lig dom na heich do scor den charbad.

CÚCHULAINN Is luath liom a scor fós. Tiomáin romhainn go mbeannaí an macra dom ar ghabháil arm dom.

[*Iad do thiomáint rompu gus an áit a bhfuil an macra. Follamhan do labhairt:*]

FOLLAMHAN An airm do ghabhais inniu, a Chúchulainn?

CÚCHULAINN Is ea, go deimhin.

AN MACRA Beir bua catha agus coscartha, a Chú na Ceártan!

IUBHAR Maith, a Chú bheag, lig dom na heich do scor anois.

CÚCHULAINN Is luath liom a scor fós. Cá ngabhann an bóthar seo?

IUBHAR Go hÁth an Fhoraire i Sliabh Fuaid ar imeall-bhordaibh Uladh.

CÚCHULAINN Tiomáin romhainn go dtí an tÁth sin, óir dar déithibh adhartha mo mhuintire, ní fhillfead go hEamhain Macha go bhfeicfead an tÁth sin agus go ndeargód m'airm ar naimhdibh Uladh.

[*Iad d'imeacht rompu., an macra ag céiliúradh dóibh. An macra do thosnú ar a gcleasaibh arís, .i. ar chleas an phoill, ar chleas an rotha agus ar chleasaibh na macra ar cheana. Seal dóibh mar sin.*

Conchubhar agus Ulaidh d'fhilleadh ón bhfianchosgairt. Toirc, fianna, fearbóga, míolta maigh, éanlaith srl., dá n-iomchur ag an ngiollanra. Iad do dhul isteach sa dún. An macra do dhul isteach ina ndiaidh. Conchubhar agus Feargus agus laochra ina dtimpeall do theacht amach agus do shuí i ndoras an dúin ag imirt fichille. Fear faire do dhul i mbéal an bhóthair ag faire. Conchubhar do labhairt iar seal dóibh ina dtost:]

CONCHUBHAR An bhfeicir aon ní?

AN FEAR FAIRE Ní fheicim, a rí.

[*Seal dóibh ina dtost. Conchubhar do labhairt arís:*]

CONCHUBHAR An bhfeicir aon ní?

AN FEAR FAIRE Ní fheicim, ach cluinim torann carbaid dar n-ionsaí.

[*Seal eile dóibh ina dtost. Conchubhar do labhairt den treas uair:*]

CONCHUBHAR An bhfeicir aon ní?

AN FEAR FAIRE Cím an t-aon chairptheach dar n-ionsaí agus is uafar a thig. Carbad caomh clárdaingean faoi. Dhá each luatha lánmhaiseacha faoin gcarbad sin. Tá siúl na gaoithe glanfuaire faoi na heachaibh. Tá an carbad lán de chlaimhte agus de shleánna agus de sciatha curadh.

CONCHUBHAR Tabhair dom tuarascáil an chairpthigh.

AN FEAR FAIRE Mac beag brónach dubh, is áille de mhacaibh Éireann.

CONCHUBHAR Is eol dom an cairptheach sin. Is é an mac beag do ghabh airm inniu atá ann, arna fhilleadh ó imeallbhordaibh an chúige. Is dóigh go bhfuil a airm deargtha aige, agus, a mhaithe Uladh, muna gceannsaítear é, béarfaidh bás dá bhfuil sa dún anocht.

FEARGUS Céard déanfar linn, a rí?

CONCHUBHAR Bantracht na hEamhna do dhul roimhe ar an machaire d'fháiltiú roimhe.

[*Laochra áirithe den laochra do dhul isteach sa dún. Bantracht na hEamhna do theacht amach agus do ghluaiseacht d'fháilitiú roimh Chúchulainn. Cathbhadh, an macra, an laochra, an t-aos ceoil, an giollanra srl., do teacht ar an bhfaiche. Cúchulainn do theacht ar an láthair, agus siúl na gaoithe fán gcarbad. An bhantracht d'fháiltiú roimhe. Cúchulainn do thuirlingt den charbad agus do theacht i láthair an rí, agus claimhte agus sleánna agus sciatha a namhad ina lámha aige. Giollaí den ghiollarna do thabhairt claíomh agus sleá agus sciath eile ar an gcarbad, agus a leagan i bhfianaise an rí. Cúchulainn do labhairt de ghlór ardmhór solasghlan:*]

CÚCHULAINN Claimhte agus sleánna agus sciatha namhad Uladh do thugas chughat, a Chonchubhair!

CONCHUBHAR Mochean do theacht, a Chú Uladh!

FEARGUS Mochean do theacht, a Chú na Ceártan!

CATHBHADH Mochean do theacht, a Chúchulainn!

[*Cúchulainn d'éirí san gcarbad arís. Ulaidh uile, idir laochra, macra, draoithe, aos ceoil, cearda, bantracht, giollanra, srl, srl, do dhéanamh cuairte na páirce fá thrí agus ar a haithle sin do gluaiseacht rompu isteach sa dún. Cúchulainn ina ndeireadh agus an Chraobh Rua ina thimpeall.*]

NOTES

1 Scríofa: Bealtaine 1909. Foilsithe in *An Macaomh*, Iml. 1 Uimh. 1, Meánsamhradh 1909, lgh.34–46.

2 Tugann an Duinníneach 'magician' mar mhíniú ar 'cathbha'.

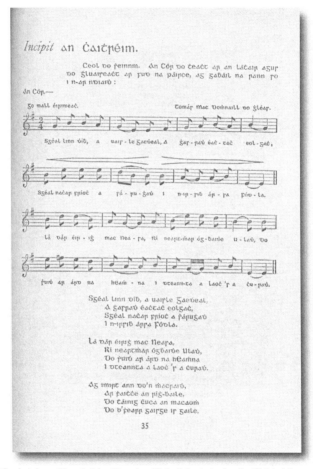

1.2 Ceol a chum Tomás Mac Domhnaill do *Macghníomhartha Chúchulainn* agus a foilsíodh i gcéad imleabhar *An Macaomh*. Original music for *Macghníomhartha Chúchulainn*, composed by Thomas McDonnell, as it appeared with the published script in the first volume of *An Macaomh*. (Le caoinchead ó Mhúsaem na bPiarsach/ Image courtesy of Pearse Museum)

1.3 Photograph of Frank Dowling, who played Seatanta/
Cúchulainn in *Macghníomhartha Chúchulainn* at St. Enda's,
Cullenswood House, in June 1909. Grianghraf de
Phroinnsias Ó Dúnlaing mar Sheatanta/Cúchulainn i
léiriú *Macghníomhartha Chúchulainn*, Scoil Éanna, Teach
Fheá Chuilinn, Meitheamh 1909. (Image courtesy of Pearse
Museum/Íomhá le caoinchead ó Mhúsaem na bPiarsach)

MACGHNÍOMHARTHA CHÚCHULAINN
(Summary from original programme)

PLACE
Eamhain Macha
TIME
The first century

THE STORY

I. On a day that Conchubhar son of Neasa rose in Eamhain Macha of Ulster, he sat with Feargus son of Roigh on the grass-green *faithche* of the royal town, and his chess-board with its company of chess-warriors was brought to him, and he and Feargus played. On to the green, around Follamhan son of Conchubhar, came the Boy Corps of Eamhain, who straight-away fell to hurling. As they hurled, a strange little lad appeared on the verge of the green, issuing from the fringing wood. He was clad in a crimson white-hooded tunic, with a white *léine* next to his skin, and a purple mantle wrapping him about. On his shoulder he bore his hurley of fair white ash. The ball chanced towards the spot where, beneath a tree, the little stranger stood looking at the play of the Boy-Corps. "The ball is with thee, O lad!" quoth Follamhan: "drive it towards us!" "On your guard, O youths of Ulster!" replied the little lad, and into their midst with swift stroke he drove the ball, following it down the field until he had carried into the goal on the opposite

83

side; nor could the Boy-Troop stay his course. "Good now, O lads!" cried Follamhan, "answer this stripling together!" "We will answer!" cried they all, and stood on their defence before him; but again in their despite he carried the ball into the opposing goal. A third time they leagued against him; and a third time down the field he carried the ball and into the far goal. Then, shouldering his hurley, he turned to leave the green; but "Good now O lads!" cried Follamhan, "let us attack him together and avenge on him the violation of our geasa; for it is geasa to us to allow any youth to intrude into our games until he hath first placed himself under our protection. Fall on him!" And forthwith down they came upon him, striking at him with their hurleys; but he, turning on his heel, defended himself gallantly, prostrating them to his right hand and to his left. The din of which affray after reaching the king where he sat at chess, up he rose and, striding across the lawn, placed himself between the combatants. "Hold," he cried, "O boys! And do thou, little fellow, hold too. I see it is no gentle game thou playest with the Boy-Corps." "It is no gentle welcome I received from them," replied the little lad, "after faring towards them from far countries." "Knewest thou not, child, the geasa of the Boy-Corps, namely that every little lad that cometh to them must place himself under their protection?" "I knew it not," replied the boy, "had I known, I would have done so." "Good now, O lads!" said the king, "take this boy under your protection." "We do," said the Boy-Corps. "But I accept it not," cried the little stranger; "by the gods that I adore I swear that unless they come under my protection I will not stay my hand from them!" Then "We accept thy protection," quoth the Boy-Corps with one voice, and straightaway hailed him their leader. "Tell me, now, little lad," said the king, "whence art thou come towards us, and by what path, and what thy name and lineage?" "Across Sliabh Fuaid I have come from the Plain of Muirtheimhne, and Seatanta son of Sualtamh is my name, and Dectire, thine own sister, is my mother, O king of Ulster!" "Dear to me is thy coming, O little lad!" quoth Conchubhar. "Dear to me is she who is thy mother. Dear to me thy comely head and thy strong wolf-wounding hand!" And then, with tumult of welcome, they carried him into the Dún.

II. On a day that Conchubhar went to drink an ale-feast in the house of Culann, the noble smith, all the guests being seated, Culann addressed the king and said: "Doth there remain anyone else of thy train to come tonight, O king of Ulster?" "None," replied the king; "wherefore dost thou ask?" "A gallant but ravenous hound I have, and it is in that hound's charge my house is every night, and woe to anyone who might seek to come into the dwelling in his despite." "Let the door be shut and the hound let loose," said the king. Now Conchubhar did not remember that he had asked the little lad, his sister's son, to accompany him to the feast, and that the boy had lingered behind to finish his game; having finished which, he set out in the wake of the heroes, shortening his road with his hurley and his ball. And now as the heroes sat feasting they heard without the dwelling the ringing cry of a boy's voice and a horrid din of combat. "Alas that we have come to drink this feast tonight!" cried Conchubhar, starting from his seat. "Your meaning, O king?" queried the others. "The little lad, my sister's son, must have perished by the hound." Up the men of Ulster sprang from their seats and burst through the door with Feargus at their head; who presently re-appeared with the little lad on his shoulder, unwounded for he had slain the hound. "Welcome thy coming, o little boy!" cried Conchubhar. But Culann, the noble smith, stood sorrowful on the threshold. "Welcome thy coming for thy mother's sake and for thy father's sake," he said, "but not welcome thy coming for thine own sake." "Why, what hast though against the child?" asked Conchubhar. "Woe is me that I made this feast for thee tonight, O Conchubhar, for henceforward my substance is substance wasted and my life life wasted. Good was the member of my family thous has taken from me, O little boy! – the guardian of my raiment and my cattle and my dwelling." "Be not wroth with me, O my master, Culann," quoth the little lad, "for in this matter I will myself pronounce a just award." "What award wilt thou pronounce?" queried Conchubhar. "If in all Ireland there be a whelp of that dog's breed, he shall be nurtured by me until he be fit for action like his sire. In the meantime O Culann, I myself will do thee a ban-dog's office, in guarding thy cattle and thy substance and thy dwelling." "That is a good award," said Conchubhar. "Not I myself," added Cathbhadh the Druid "could have made a better, and by reason of it thou shalt be known henceforth, O boy, as Cúchulainn, that is Culann's Hound." "Not so," objected the youngster, "I prefer my own name Seatanta son of Sualtamh" "Say not so," said Cathbhadh, "for the men of Éire and of Alba will hear that name and the mouths of the men of Éire and of Alba will be full of that name." "Then that name shall be mine," replied the boy: and the name clave to him henceforward.

III: On a day that Cathbhadh with his pupils was walking on the green of Eamhain, one of them asked him what particular luck or fortune appertained to that day above all others. "This," said Cathbhadh, "the youth that taketh arms today will be famous above all the heroes of Éire but his life will be short and fleeting." Now that prophecy was overheard by Cúchulainn, and, the king chancing to pass on his way out of the Dún on his way to the chase, the boy went straight towards him. "Every good to thee, O king of Ulster!" was his greeting. "That speech is the speech of one who asketh a favour," replied Conchubhar. "What seeketh thou, little boy?" "To take arms." "Who prompted thee to that?" "Cathbhadh the Druid." "Then thou shalt not be denied. Give arms to this boy!" But the arms, when brought, Cúchulainn, when testing them reduced to splinters. And so with every other set of arms that the heroes offered him. "These weapons are not good, O king!" he cried. "Let me given fitting weapons." "I will give thee my own weapons, little Hound," said Conchubhar. And Conchubhar's weapons endured every test to which Cúchulainn subjected them. "These arms are good," he cried, "these are arms worthy of me. Fair fall the king whose arms and armature are these. Fair fall the land from which he sprang." Just then it was that Cathbhadh came on the green. "Is it arms yon boy hath taken?" he asked. "It is indeed," said the king. "It is not thy sister' son I should like to see assuming them today," said the Druid. "How now," said Conchubhar, "was it not thyself that prompted him?" "It was not, indeed." "What meaneth this, thou mysterious elf?" demanded the king of Cúchulainn. "Is it a lie thou hast told me?" "Be not wroth with me, O my master, Conchubhar," pleaded the child, "it is he, indeed, prompted me to it, for I heard him say that the youth who should take arms today would top Erin's heroes in fame, but that his life would be short and fleeting." "True for me it is," said Cathbhadh. "O little Hound thou shalt be noble and famed, indeed but thy life shall pass and fleet quickly." "I care not," replied Cúchulainn, "though I were to live but one day and one night, if only my deeds and my story live after me." "Good now O boy," said Conchubhar, "mount thy chariot." "Let thine own chariot be brought to me, O Conchubhar, for none other is worthy of me." "Where is Iubhar, son of Riangabhra?" asked Conchubhar. "I am here, king," spoke Iubhar from among the charioteers and attendants. "Capture my two horses and yoke my chariot" commanded Conchubhar. Away went Iubhar, returning presently with the chariot yoked. "Mount the chariot, boy," said Conchubhar. So Cúchulainn mounted, and the chariot performed the circuit of the royal green. Conchubhar and the Red Branch fared forth to their hunting. "Good now, O boy," said Iubhar, "let me unyoke the horses." "I deem it too soon to unyoke them yet. Drive forward that the Boy-Corps may salute me on my taking arms." So they drove to where the Boy-Corps were at play. "Is it arms thou hast taken?" queried Follamhan. "It is, indeed." "May victory attend thee in battle O hound of the Forge!" cried the boys saluting him. "Good now, O lad!" spoke Iubhar again, "let me now unyoke the horses." "I deem it too soon to unyoke them yet. Where leadeth yon road?" "To the Watcher's Ford in Sliabh Fuaid on the frontiers of the province," replied Iubhar. "Drive forward then to that Ford, for I swear by the gods my people adore that I will not return to Eamhain Macha until I have seen that Ford and reddened my weapons on the enemies of Ulster." Away then they careered to the frontiers of the province and the Watcher's Ford. The day passed and Conchubhar had returned from his hunting. Towards evening he sat at chess with Feargus on the green of Eamhain. A watchman stood on a little hillock. "Seest thou anything?" asked Conchubhar. "Nought, O king!" "Seest thou anything?" queried the king again, after they had played a space. "Nought I see, but I her the noise of a chariot approaching us." "Seest thou anything now?" asked Conchubhar the third time. "I see a solitary chariot-hero drawing towards us, and terrifically he cometh. Under him a fair firm-boarded chariot. Two swift very handsome steeds beneath the chariot. Their pace is as the pace of the pure cold wind. The chariot is filled with the swords and spears and shields of warriors." "Describe the chariot-hero," commanded Conchubhar. "A small, dark, sad boy, comliest of the boys of Éire." "I know that chariot-hero," cried Conchubhar. "It is the little lad that took arms today, returning from the frontiers of the province. I trow that he hath reddened his weapons, and O chiefs of Ulster, unless we appease his battle-fury he will slay all that are in the Dún tonight!" "What must we do, O Conchubhar?" questioned Feargus. "Let the women of Eamhain come before him on the green to welcome him" (for Cúchulainn was ever shy and modest in company of women-folk). Out then came the women of the Dún, and after them, the heroes and soldiery and Boy-Corps. And the women received Cúchulainn gently, kindly and led him to Conchubhar. "The swords and the shields of the enemies of Ulster I bring thee here, O Conchubhar!" cried Cúchulainn and displayed his trophies. "Dear to me thy coming O Hound of Ulster!" quoth Conchubhar. "Dear to me thy coming O Hound of the Forge!"

said Feargus. And "Dear to me thy coming Ó Cúchulainn," said Cathbhadh; in which cry of welcome the Red Branch and all Ulster joined. Thus did Cúchulainn take arms.

Note: The events narrated in each of the paragraphs above occupy an Act of the Pageant. Each Act is introduced by the Chorus, whose song recounts the incidents that are to follow.

P. Mac P.

Sgoil Éanna,

ceaċ ḟeaḋa Cuilinn, Ráṫ ó máine.

Dia Saṫairn, Dia Domnaiġ, aguṣ Dia Luain,
5, 6, 7 ḟeaḃra, 1910, an a 8 a ċloġ tráċnóna,

léireoċaiḋ mic léiġinn na sgoile

"THE DESTRUCTION OF THE HOSTEL"
(Pádraic Mac Cuilm do sgríoḃ).

aguṣ "Íosaġán"
(Pádraic Mac Piarais do sgríoḃ)

an Clár.

"THE DESTRUCTION OF THE HOSTEL."

An Ḟuireann annṣo ṣíoṣ:

LOMNA DRUTH FERROGAIN FERGABAR	foster-brothers to Conaire, High King of Ireland.	Éamonn Duilḟín (Eamonn Bulfin). Deaṛmuṁa Ó Riain (Desmond Ryan). Muiris Ó Ḟearacair (Maurice Fraher).
INGCEL, a British outlaw.		Saṁairle Mac Ġarḃaiġ (Sorley MacGarvey).
MAINE HONEYMOUTH, son of Meadhbh of Connacht.		Donnċaḋ Mac Ḟinn (Denis Gwynn).
CONALL CERNACH CORMAC CONDLOINGEAS, son of Concobar BRICRIU of the Evil Tongue	Heroes of the Red Branch.	Proinnṣiaṣ Ó Congaile (Frank Connolly). Domnall Ó Conċuḃair (Donal O'Connor). Éamonn Ó Nuallám (Eamonn Nolan).
MAC CECHT, the King's Champion		Uinnṣeann Ó Doċartaiġ (Vincent O'Doherty).
NI-FRI-FLAITH		Riṣteaṣd Ó Raṫġaille (Richard O'Rahilly).
THE THREE RED PIPERS FROM THE ELF-MOUNDS		Fearḋonċa Ó Doċartaiġ (Fredrick O'Doherty). Maolmuire Mag Ṣearraiġ (Milo MacGarry). Eoin Ó Dúnlaing (John Dowling).

1.4 An postaer/clár do léiriú *The Destruction of the Hostel* le Pádraic Colum agus *Íosagán* an Phiarsaigh, Feabhra 1910, Scoil Éanna, Teach Fheá Chuilinn. The poster/programme for the production of Pádraic Colum's *The Destruction of the Hostel* and Pearse's *Íosagán* in February 1910 at St. Enda's, Cullenswood House. (Le caoinchead ó Leabharlann Uí Ailín/Image courtesy of Allen Library)

ÍOSAGÁN[1]

.i. úrchluiche dhárannach
Pádraig Mac Piarais do scríobh.
Céadléirithe 5 Feabhra 1910, Scoil Éanna, Teach Fheadha Chuilinn i
dteannta The Destruction of the Hostel *le Pádraic Colum.*

AN FHOIREANN ANSEO SÍOS

Sean-Mhaitias	Briocán
Fir agus Mná	Máirtín
Malraigh:	Eoghan
Cuimín	Féichín[2]
Cóilín	Íosagán[3]
Pádraic	
Darach	An Sagart

Tuigtear go bhfuil Cuimín, Pádraic agus Darach beagán níos
sine ná na malraigh eile.

ÁIT DON CHLUICHE SEO
Baile in Iar-Chonnacht
AIMSIR DÓ
An aimsir atá i láthair

AN CHÉAD ROINN

[*Teach le hais bóthair i dtaobh tíre uaigneach. Crosbhóthar ar thaobh na
láimhe clé. Giodán féir i lár an chrosbhóthair. Ard sa mbóthar atá ag dul
siar ón gcrosbhóthar.*

*Glór cloig do theacht amach go glé glinn. Osclaítear doras an tí.
Seanfhear .i. Sean-Mhaitias, do theacht amach ar lic an dorais agus ag*

91

seasamh scaitheamh ag breathnú siar an bóthar. É ina shuí ansin ar chathaoir atá taobh amuigh den doras, a dhá lámh i ngreim i maide, a cheann cromtha aige, agus é ag éisteacht go haireach le glór an chloig.

Daoine do thriall thar an doras, ag gabháil an bóthar siar, ina nduine agus ina nduine agus ina miondreamanna. Comhrá ar siúl acu os íseal. Cuid acu ag breathnú ar an seanfhear ach gan beannú dó. Iad d'imeacht suas an t-ard agus siar as amharc. An clog do stad dá bhualadh.

Scata malrach, i. Cuimín, Cóilín, Pádraic, Darach, Briocán, Máirtín, Eoghan agus Féichín, do theacht ar an láthair ina rith. Cuimín do labhairt:]

CUIMÍN Céard a imreos muid inniu?

CÓILÍN Púicín!

PÁDRAIC Ara, bí i do thost, tú féin is do phúicín!

CÓILÍN Geataí arda, mar sin!

PÁDRAIC Ní hea, táimid tuirseach de na geataí arda sin!

DARACH 'bhFalógaíbh![4]

BRIOCÁN Faic!

MÁIRTÍN Sicíní!

CÓILÍN Ní hea! Déanadh muid lúrabóg!

PÁDRAIC Déanfaidh mé lúrabóg díotsa!

CÓILÍN Bíonn tú liom i gcónaí a Phádraic.

PÁDRAIC *(do bhreith air)* Éist liom a deirim leat!

CÓILÍN Labhair tú féin a Phádraic, ó tharla nach dtugann tú cead cainte do dhuine ar bith eile.

PÁDRAIC Caitheadh muid léim mar sin!

EOGHAN Caitheadh muid léim! Caitheadh muid léim!

DARACH Cuirfidh mé geall go mbuailfidh mé thú, a Phádraic.

PÁDRAIC Ag caitheamh léim, an ea?

DARACH Sea.

PÁDRAIC Ar ndóigh, nár bhuail mé arú inné thú ar chreigeán na scoile?

DARACH Mise i mbannaí nach mbuailfidh tú inniu mé. An bhféachfaidh tú leis?

PÁDRAIC Ní fhéachfad. Tá mo chois tinn.

[*Na malraigh eile do thosnú ag gáire; Pádraic do labhairt agus cosúlacht náire air:*]

PÁDRAIC B'fhearr liom cluiche liathróide.

EOGHAN Cluiche liathróide! Cluiche liathróide!

DARACH Bhfuil liathróid ag duine ar bith?

CUIMÍN Agus dá mbeadh féin cá n-imreodh muid?

PÁDRAIC Imreoimid in aghaidh bhinn tí Shean-Mhaitias. Níl áit is deise le fáil.

CÓILÍN Cé aige a bhfuil an liathróid?

CUIMÍN M'anam nach bhfuil sí agamsa.

DARACH Níl, ná agamsa.

PÁDRAIC Agat féin a bhí sí Dé hAoine, a Chóilín.

CÓILÍN Ar ndóigh, nár rug an máistir uirthi san áit a raibh mé dhá hopáil sa scoil i rith an Teagaisc Chríostaí?

FÉICHÍN Is fíor duit, ar mh'anam.

CUIMÍN M'anam muise gur cheap mé go dtabharfadh sé an tslat duit an uair úd.

CÓILÍN Thabharfadh freisin murach go raibh ag súil leis an sagart do teacht isteach.

DARACH 'Sí an liathróid a theastaigh uaidh. Beidh cluiche aige leis na *peelers* inniu tar éis Aifrinn.

PÁDRAIC M'anam muise go mbeidh, agus is é atá in ann na *peelers* a bhualadh freisin.

DARACH Níl sé in ann an *sergeant* a bhualadh. Is é an *sergeant* an fear is fearr acu uilig. Bhuail sé Hoskins agus an fear rua le chéile Dé Domhnaigh seo caite.

BRIOCÁN Ara, stop! Ar bhuail?

DARACH Bhuail, mhuis. Bhí an fear rua ar buile, agus an máistir agus na *peelers* uilig ag gáire faoi.

PÁDRAIC Cuirfidh mé geall go mbuailfeadh an máistir an *sergeant*.

DARACH Cuirfidh mise geall nach mbuailfeadh.

PÁDRAIC An gcluin sibh é?

DARACH Cuirfidh mise geall go bhfuil an *sergeant* in ann fear ar bith sa tír seo a bhualadh.

PÁDRAIC Ara, cá bhfios duitse an bhfuil nó nach bhfuil.

DARACH Tá fhios agam go maith go bhfuil. Nach mbím ag breathnú orthu i gcónaí?

PÁDRAIC Níl fhios agat!

DARACH Tá fhios agam! Is agamsa atá a fhios!

[*Iad do bhagairt ar a chéile. Gleo d'éirí idir na garsúin uile, cuid acu ag rá "Is fearr an* sergeant!" *agus dream eile "Is fearr an máistir!" Sean-Mhaitias d'éirí ina sheasamh ar chlos an torainn sin dó, agus do theacht chucu; é craptha cromtha agus gan tarraingt na gcos ar éigin ann. É do labhairt leo go mín socair ag leagan a láimhe ar chloigeann Dharaigh.*]

MAITIAS Ó! ó! ó! Mo náire sibh!

PÁDRAIC Deir sé seo nach mbuailfeadh an máistir an *sergeant* ag imirt liathróide.

DARACH Ar ndóigh, nach mbuailfeadh an *sergeant* duine ar bith sa tír seo, a Mhaitiais?

MAITIAS Ná bacaigí leis an *sergeant*. Féachaigí an cadhan aonraic sin atá ag déanamh orainn thar Loch Eiliúrach! Breathnaigí!

Na gasúir uile do bhreathnú suas.

PÁDRAIC Feicim é, ar m'anam!

DARACH Cérb as a bhfuil sí sin ag teacht anois, a Mhaitiais?

MAITIAS As an Domhan Thoir. Déarfainn go bhfuil míle míle siúlta aicí ó d'fhág sí a nead ins na críocha ó thuaidh.

CÓILÍN An créatúr! Agus cá luífeas sí?

MAITIAS Isteach go hÁrainn a rachas sí, seans. Féachaigí anois í amach thar farraige! Mo ghrá thú a chadhain aonraic!

CÓILÍN Inis scéal dúinn a Mhaitiais.

[*É do shuí ar chloch atá ar an ngiodán féir agus na malraigh do shuí ina thimpeall.*]

MAITIAS Cén scéal a inseos mé?

FÉICHÍN Eachtra an Ghearráin Ghlais!

MÁIRTÍN Preachán na gCearc is an Dreoilín!

BRIOCÁN Fathach an Dá Cheann!

CÓILÍN Imeachta an Phíobaire i gCaisleán an tSeilmide!

Na Malraigh *(d'aon ghuth)* Imeachta an Phíobaire i gCaisleán an tSeilmide!

MAITIAS Déanfaidh sin. Bhí Seilmide ann fadó agus fadó a bhí. Dá mbeadh sinne ann an uair sin ní bheadh sinn anois ann; bheadh scéal úr nó seanscéal again agus níor dhóichide sin ná bheith gan aon scéal. 'Sé an áit chónaithe a bhí ag an Seilmide seo an caisleán is breátha dá bhfaca súil riamh. Ba mhó i bhfad agus ba bhreátha míle uair é ná Caisleán Mhéibhe i Rath Cruachan nó ná Caisleán Ard-Rí Éireann féin i dTeamhair na Rí. Thug an Seilmide seo grá do Dhamhan Alla.

CÓILÍN Ní hea, a Mhaitiais, nach do Shnáthaid Mhór a thug sé grá?

MAITIAS M'anam go bhfuil an ceart agat. Céard atá ag teacht orm?

PÁDRAIC Lean leat a Mhaitiais.

MAITIAS Bhí an Spigneanta seo an-dathúil ar fad.

BRIOCÁN Cén Spigneanta, a Mhaitiais?

MAITIAS An Spigneanta a dtug sé grá di.

MÁIRTÍN Ach cheap mé gur do Shnáthaid Mhór a thug sé grá?

MAITIAS An ea? Tá an scéal ag imeacht uaim. Bhí an Píobaire seo i ngrá le hiníon Rí Chonnacht.

EOGHAN Ach níor labhair tú ar an bPíobaire fós, a Mhaitiais!

MAITIAS Nár labhras? An Píobaire – sea, ar m'anam, an Píobaire – tá mé ag cailleadh mo mheabhrach. Breathnaigí, a chomharsana, ní bhacfaimid leis an an scéal inniu. Bíodh amhrán againn.

CÓILÍN Haigh didil dum!

MAITIAS Bhfuil sibh sásta?

NA MALRAIGH Táimid.

MAITIAS Déanfaidh sin.

[*É do ghabháil na rann seo ina ndiaidh.*]

MAITIAS
Haigh didil dum, an cat is a mháthair
D'imigh go Gaillimh ag marcaíocht ar bhardal.

NA MALRAIGH Is haidh didil dum!

MAITIAS
Haigh didil dum, do tháinig an bháisteach
Gur fliuchadh go craiceann an cat is a mháthair.

NA MALRAIGH Is haidh didil dum!

MAITIAS
Haidh didil dum, ba dhóbair go mbáifí
An cat is is a mháthair, mo chreach is mo chrá iad!

NA MALRAIGH Is haidh didil dum!

MAITIAS Do rug leis go Gaillimh –

CÓILÍN –Ar éigin –

MAITIAS Maith thú, a Chóilín. Do rug leis go Gaillimh ar éigin sa tsnámh iad.

NA MALRAIGH Is haidh didil dom!

[*A cheann do chroitheadh go tuirseach do Shean-Mhaitias; é do labhairt de ghuth brónach.*]

MAITIAS Tá mo chuid amhrán ag imeacht uaim, a chomharsana. Is geall le seanveidhlín mé a mbeadh a chuid sreanga briste.

CUIMÍN Nach bhfuil an "Báidín" agat i gcónaí, a Mhaitiais?

MAITIAS Tá ar m'anam: beidh sé sin agam fad is beo mé. Ní chaillfidh mé an "Báidín" go gcuirtear san uaigh mé. An mbeidh sé againn?

NA MALRAIGH Beidh!

MAITIAS Bhfuil sibh réidh le dul ag iomramh?

NA MALRAIGH Táimid!

[*Iad do chur cuma orthu féin amhail is go mbeidís ag iomramh. Sean-Mhaitias do ghabháil na rann seo ina ndiaidh.*]

MAITIAS Crochfaidh mé seol is gabhfaidh mé siar,

NA MALRAIGH Oró, mo churraichín ó!

MAITIAS Is go hoíche 'le Eoin ní thiocfaidh mé aniar,

NA MALRAIGH Oró, mo churraichín ó!

MAITIAS Nach breá í mo bháidín ag snámh ar an gcuan,

MAITIAS Oró, mo churraichín ó.

MAITIAS Na maidí dá dtarraingt –

[*É do stad den cheol go tobann, agus a lámh do chur lena bhaithis.*]

PÁDRAIC Céard atá ort, a Mhaitiais?

MAITIAS Rud éicint a tháinig ar mo cheann. Ní tada é. Céard do bhí mé ag rá?

CÓILÍN Bhí tú ag rá an "Báidín" a Mhaitiais, ach ná bac leis mura n-áiríonn tú féin go maith. Bhfuil tú tinn?

MAITIAS Tinn? Ar ndóigh, níl mise tinn. Céard a dhéanfadh tinn me? Tosóimíd arís. Nach breá í mo bháidín ag snámh ar an gcuan.

NA MALRAIGH Oró mo churraichín ó!

MAITIAS Na maidí dá dtarraingt go láidir –

[*É do stad arís.*]

MAITIAS A chomharsana, tá an "Báidín" féin imithe uaim.

[*Iad do fhanúint ina dtost scaitheamh, an seanfhear ina shuí agus a cheann cromtha ar a ucht, agus na malraigh ag féachaint air go brónach. An seanfhear do labhairt de gheit:*]

MAITIAS An iad sin na daoine ag teacht abhaile ón Aifreann?

CUIMÍN Ní hiad. Ar ndóigh, ní bheidh siad ar fágáil go ceann leath uaire fós.

CÓILÍN Tuige nach dtéann tusa ag an Aifreann, a Mhaitiais?

[*An seanfhear d'éirí ina sheasamh agus a lámh do chur lena bhaithis arís. É do labhairt go borb i dtosach agus ina dhiaidh sin go mín:*]

MAITIAS Tuige a rachainn? … Níl mé sách maith. Ar ndóigh, ní éistfeadh Dia liom… Céard tá mé a rá?... *(É do gháirí)* Agus tá an "Báidín" caillte agam, deir sibh? Nach mé an díol trua agaibh gan mo "Báidín"!

[*É do thriall trasna an bhóthair go mall. Cóilín d'éirí agus a ghualainn do chur faoi láimh an tseanfhir le cuidiú leis ag dul trasna an bhóthair dó. Na malraigh do thosnú ag imirt cnaipí go ciúin. Sean-Mhaitias do shuí ar an gcathaoir arís agus Cóilín do theacht ar ais. Darach do labhairt de ghlór íseal.*]

DARACH Tá rud éigin ar Shean-Mhaitias inniu. Ní dhearna sé dearmad ar an "mBáidín" riamh roimhe.

CUIMÍN Chuala mé m'athair ag rá le mo mháthair an oíche cheana gur gearr eile a mhairfeadh sé.

CÓILÍN Meas tú an bhfuil sé an-aosta?

PÁDRAIC Tuige ar chuir tú an ceist sin air i dtaobh an Aifrinn? Nach bhfuil a fhios agat nach bhfacthas ar Aifreann é le cuimhne na ndaoine?

DARACH Chuala mé Sean-Chuimín Éanna ag rá lem' athair go bhfaca sé féin Sean-Mhaitias ar Aifreann nuair a bhí sé ina stócach.

CÓILÍN Meas tú cén fáth nach dtéann sé ar Aifreann anois?

PÁDRAIC (i gcogar) Ar ndóigh, deirtear nach gcreideann sé go bhfuil aon Dia ann.

CUIMÍN Chuala mise athair Sheáin Éamuinn a rá gurb é an chaoi rinne sé peaca uafásach éigin i dtús a shaoil agus nuair nach dtabharfadh an sagart apsalóid dó ar faoistin gur tháinig cuthach feirge air is gur mhionnaigh sé nach dtaobhódh sé sagart nó seipéal go deo arís.

DARACH Ní mar sin a chuala mise é. Aon oíche amháin nuair a bhí mé ar mo leaba bhí na seandaoine ag caint is ag cogar cois tine agus chuala mé Máire an Droichid ag rá leis na seanmhná eile gurb é an chaoi dhíol Maitias a anam le Fear Mór éicint a casadh dó uair ar mhullach Chnoc an Daimh, agus nach ligfeadh an fear seo dó an tAifreann a chleachtadh.

PÁDRAIC Meas tú an é an diabhal a chonaic sé?

DARACH Níl a fhios agam. "Fear Mór" a dúirt Máire an Droichid.

CUIMÍN Ní chreidfinn focal de. Ar ndóigh, má dhíol Maitias a anam leis an diabhal caithfidh sé gur drochdhuine atá ann.

PÁDRAIC Ní drochdhuine é, muis. Nach cuimhneach leat an lá a dúirt Íosagán gur dhúirt a athair go mbeadh Maitias i measc na naomh Lá an tSléibhe?

PÁDRAIC Is cuimhneach go maith.

CÓILÍN Cá bhfuil Íosagán uainn inniu?

DARACH Is iondúil nach dtagann sé nuair a bhíos duine fásta ag breathnú orainn.

CUIMÍN Nach raibh é anseo seachtain ó shin nuair a bhí Sean-Mhaitias ag breathnú orainn?

DARACH An raibh?

CUIMÍN Bhí.

PÁDRAIC Bhí, agus coicís 's an lá inniu freisin.

DARACH Tá seans go dtiocfaidh sé inniu mar sin.

[*Cuimín d'éirí agus do bhreathnú soir.*]

CUIMÍN Ó feách chughainn é!

[*Íosagán do theacht ar an láthair, i. gasúr beag donn, cóta bán air, agus é gan bróga gan caipín ar nós na malrach eile. Na malraigh do bheannú dó.*]

NA MALRAIGH 'Sé do bheatha, a Íosagáin.

ÍOSAGÁN Dia is Muire dhaoibh.

[*É do shuí ina measc, lámh leis faoi mhuineál Dharaigh; na malraigh do thosnú ag imirt arís go ciúin socair, gan gleo gan imreasán. Íosagán do thosnú ag imirt leo. Maitias d'éirí de gheit ar theacht ar an láthair d'Íosagán, agus do sheasamh ag féachaint air. Tar éis scathaimh dóibh ag imirt é do theacht chucu agus ansin do sheasamh arís agus do ghlaoch anonn chuige ar Chóilín.*]

MAITIAS A Chóilín!

CÓILÍN Abair!

MAITIAS Gabh i leith anseo chugham.

[*Cóilín d'éirí agus do dhul anonn chuige.*]

MAITIAS Cé hé an malrach údan fheicim in bhur measc le coicís, é sin a bhfuil an cloigeann donn air – ach fainic nach bánrua atá sé: níl a fhios agam an dubh nó fionn é a an chaoi a bhfuil an ghrian ag scalladh air. An bhfeiceann tú é – é siúd a bhfuil a lámh faoi chloigeann Dharaigh?

CÓILÍN Sin é Íosagán.

MAITIAS Íosagán?

CÓILÍN Sin é an t-ainm a thugas sé air féin.

MAITIAS Cé dár díobh é?

CÓILÍN Níl a fhios agm ach deir sé go bhfuil a athair ina rí.

MAITIAS Cá gcónaíonn sé?

CÓILÍN Níor inis sé é sin riamh dúinn, ach deir sé nach fada uainn a theach.

MAITIAS An mbíonn sé in éindí libh go minic?

CÓILÍN Bíonn nuair a bhíos muid ag caitheamh aimsire dúinn féin mar seo. Ach imíonn sé uainn nuair a thagas daoine fásta sa láthair. Imeoidh sé anois uainn chomh luath is a thosós na daoine ag teacht abhaile ón Aifreann.

[*Na malraigh d'éirí agus d'imeacht ina nduine agus ina nduine ag críochnú an chluiche dóibh.*]

CÓILÍN Ó! Tá said ag dul ag caitheamh léim!

[*É do rith amach i ndiaidh na coda eile. Íosagán agus Darach d'éirí agus do ghluaiseacht. Maitias do theacht ar aghaidh agus do ghlaoch ar Íosagán, roimh imeacht dó.*]

MAITIAS A Íosagáin!

[*An leanbh d'iontú ar ais agus do theacht chuige ar rith.*]

MAITIAS Tar i leith agus suigh ar mo ghlúin go fóillín, a Íosagáin.

[*An leanbh do thabhairt a láimhe i láimh an tseanfhir agus iad do thriall trasna an bhóthair cos ar chois. Maitias do shuí ar a chathaoir agus do tharraingt Íosagán chuige.*]

MAITIAS Cá gcónaíonn tú a Íosagáin?

ÍOSAGÁN Ní fada as seo mo theach. Cad chuige nach dtagann tú ar cuairt chugham?

MAITIAS Bheadh faitíos orm i dteach ríoga. Deirtear liom go bhful d'athair ina rí.

ÍOSAGÁN Is é Ard-Rí an domhain é. Ach níor ghá duit faitíos a bheith ort roimhe. Tá sé lán de thrócaire agus de ghrá.

MAITIAS Is baolach liom nár choinnigh mé a dhlí.

ÍOSAGÁN Iarr maithiúnas air. Déanfadsa is mo mháthair idirghuí ar do shon.

MAITIAS Is trua nach bhfaca mé roimhe seo thú, a Íosagáin. Cá raibh tú uaim?

ÍOSAGÁN Bhí mé anseo i gcónaí. Bím ag taisteal na mbóithre is ag siúl na gcnoc is ag treabhadh na dtonn. Bím i lár an phobail nuair a chruinníos said isteach i mo theach. Bím i measc na bpáistí a fhágas siad ina ndiaidh ag cleasaíocht ar an tsráid.

MAITIAS Bhí mise ró-fhaiteach, nó ró-uaibhreach, le dul isteach i do theach, a Íosagáin: i measc na bpáistí a fuair mé thú.

ÍOSAGÁN Níl aon áit ná am dá mbíonn páistí ag súgradh dóibh féin nach mbímse ina bhfochair. Amannta feiceann siad mé: amannta eile ní fheiceann.

MAITIAS Ní fhaca mise thú go dtí le gairid.

ÍOSAGÁN Bíonn na daoine fásta dall.

MAITIAS Agus ina dhiaidh sin gealladh dom thú fheiceáil, a Íosagáin.

ÍOSAGÁN Thug m'athair cead dom mé féin a fhoilsiú duit de bhrí gur thug tú grá dá pháistí beaga.

[*Glórtha na ndaoine do theacht ón Aifreann do theacht aniar.*]

ÍOSAGÁN Caithfidh mé imeacht anois uait.

MAITIAS Lig dom imeall do chóta a phógadh.

[*Imeall an chóta do phógadh dó.*]

MAITIAS An bhfeicfidh mé arís thú, a Íosagáin?

ÍOSAGÁN Feicfir.

MAITIAS Cén uair?

ÍOSAGÁN Anocht.

[*Íosagán d'imeacht. An seanfhear do sheasamh ar lic a dhorais ag féachaint ina dhiaidh.*]

MAITIAS Feicfidh mé anocht é.

[*Na daoine do ghabháil an bhóthair aniar ag teacht abhaile ón Aifreann.*]

CRÍOCH NA ROINNE SIN

An Dara Roinn

[*Seomra Shean-Mhaitiais. É an-dorcha. An seanfhear ina luí ar a leaba. Duine do bhualadh ar an doras taobh amuigh. Maitias do labhairt de ghlór lag:*]

MAITIAS Gabh isteach.

[*An Sagart do theacht isteach.*]

AN SAGART Go mbeannaí Dia anseo.

MAITIAS Dia is Muire dhuit. Cé hé seo chugham?

AN SAGART An sagart.

MAITIAS Tá fáilte romhat a Athair. Ba mhaith liom labhairt leat. Suigh anseo lem' ais.

[*An Sagart do shuí le hais na leaba agus faoistin an tseanfhir d'éisteacht. Maitias do labhairt arna bheith críochnaithe dóibh.*]

MAITIAS Cé dúirt leat go raibh tú ag teastáil uaim, a Athair? Bhí mé ag guí Dé go dtiocfá ach ní raibh aon teachtaire agam le cur faoi do dhéin.

AN SAGART Ach chuir tú teachtaire faoi mo dhéin, ar ndóigh?

MAITIAS Níor chuireas.

AN SAGART Níor chuiris? Ach tháinig garsúinín beag agus bhuail sé ar mo dhoras. Agus dúirt sé go raibh mo chúnamh ag teastáil uait.

[*An seanfhear do do dhíriú aniar sa leaba agus faobhar ina shúile.*]

MAITIAS Cé an sórt garsúinín a bhí ann, a Athair?

AN SAGART Garsúinín beag caoin a raibh cóta bán air.

MAITIAS Ar thug tú faoi deara mar bheadh scáile solais thart timpeall a chinn?

AN SAGART Thugas, agus chuir sé ionadh mór orm.

[*Osclaítear an doras. Íosagán do sheasamh ar an tairsigh agus a dhá láimh sínte amach aige chum Maitias; solas iontach timpeall a éadain agus a chinn.*]

MAITIAS A Íosagáin!

[*É do thitim siar ar an leaba agus é marbh; an sagart do dhruidim go socair leis an leaba agus do dhúnadh a shúl.*]

A CHRÍOCH-SAN

[Tús eile, Scríbhinní]

[*Níl na carachtair Briocán nó Máirtín sa leagan seo agus tugtar a gcuid línte do na buachaillí eile. Níl na "fir agus mná" luaite ach oiread. Tá miondifríochtaí eile ann ach is í an difríocht is mó ná go bhfuil tús agus deireadh éagsúil sa dara leagan seo.*]

ÍOSAGÁN

An fhoireann anseo síos:

Íosagán	**Malraigh:**
Sean-Mhaitias	Darach
An Sagart	Cóilín
	Pádraic
	Féichín
	Eoghan
	Cuimín

Tuigtear go bhfuil Darach agus Pádraic beagán níos sine ná na malraigh eile.

Áit don chluiche seo
Cladach ina aice le baile in Iar-Chonnacht
Aimsir dó
An aimsir atá i láthair

An Chéad Roinn

[*Cladach in aice le baile in Iar-Chonnacht. Teach ar thaobh na láimhe deise. Glór cloig do theacht aniar go glé glinn. Osclaítear doras an tí. Seanfhear, .i. Sean-Mhaitias, do theacht amach ar lic an dorais agus do sheasamh scaitheamh ag breathnú siar an bóthar. É do shuí ansin ar chathaoir atá taobh amuigh den doras, a dhá láimh i ngreim i maide, a cheann cromtha aige, agus é ag éisteacht go haireach le glór an chloig. An*

clog do stad dá bhualadh. Darach, Pádraic agus Cóilín do theacht aníos
ón bhfarraige agus iad ag cur orthu a gcuid éadaigh tar éis bheith ag
snámh dóibh.]

DARACH *(agus é ag síneadh a mhéir chun na farraige)* Tá na blátha
bána i ngarraí an iascaire.

PÁDRAIC Tá, muise.

CÓILÍN Cá bhfuil siad?

DARACH Féach uait ar an bhfarraige iad.

CÓILÍN Ní blátha bána iad sin. Sin iad na caiple bána.

DARACH Is cosúil le blátha bána iad.

CÓILÍN Ní hea, deir Sean-Mhaitias gurb iad sin na caiple bána
atá ag ag gluaiseacht ina gcos-in-airde trasna na farraige ón Tír
Eile.

PÁDRAIC Chuala mé Íosagán ag rá gur blátha iad.

CÓILÍN Cén chaoi a bhféadfadh blátha fárraige?

PÁDRAIC Agus cén chaoi a bhféadfadh caiple gluaiseacht ar
an bhfarraige?

CÓILÍN Go réidh, dá mba caiple sí a bheadh iontu.

PÁDRAIC Agus nach bhféadfadh blátha fás ar an bhfarraige
chomh furasta céanna dá mba blátha sí a bheadh iontu? Nach
minic a chonaic tú na bileoga báite ag Loch Eiliúrach? Agus nach
bhféadfadh siad fás ar an bhfarraige chomh maith le ar an loch?

CÓILÍN Níl a fhios agam an bhféadfadh.

PÁDRAIC D'fhéadfadh, muis.

DARACH Bhí an fharraige go breá inniu, a dhuine!

CÓILÍN Bhí, ach bhí sí diabhalta fuar.

PÁDRAIC Tuige nach mbeadh fuacht ortsa nuair nach ndeachaigh tú isteach ach go dtí do ghlúine?

CÓILÍN Ar ndóigh, bhí faitíos orm go leagfadh na tonntracha mé dá ngabhfainn isteach níos faide. Bhí siad uafásach mór.

DARACH Sin a thaitníos liom, a dhuine. An cuimhneach leat an tonn mhór mhillteach úd a tháinig os ár gcionn?

PÁDRAIC Sea, agus Cóilín ag screadaíl go raibh sé báite.

CÓILÍN Chuaigh sí síos mo scornach, chuaigh sin, agus is beag nár mhúch sí mé.

PÁDRAIC Ar ndóigh, bhí do bhéal oscailte agat, agus tú ag béicíl. Do b'aisteach an scéal é muna ngabhfadh sí síos do scornach.

CÓILÍN Thug an ceann údan mo dhóthain de dom. Choinnigh mé as a mbealach ina dhiaidh sin.

DARACH Bhfuil a gcuid éadaigh ortha ag na *lads* eile fós?

PÁDRAIC Tá, seo aníos iad.

CÓILÍN Féach an bhail atá ar ghruaig Fhéichín!

[*Féichín, Eoghan agus Cuimín do theacht aníos ón bhfarraige agus iad ag triomú a gcuid gruaige.*]

CUIMÍN Céard a imreos muid inniu?

[Críoch eile: Scríbhinní]

AN SAGART Thugas, agus chuir sé ionadh mór orm.

[*Osclaítear an doras. Íosagán do sheasamh ar an tairsigh agus a dhá láimh sínte amach aige chun Maitias; solas iontach timpeall a éadain agus a chinn.*]

MAITIAS Ba mhaith thú, a Íosagáin. Níor chinn tú orm, a ghrá. Bhí mé ró-uaibhreach le dul isteach i do theach, ach ina dhiaidh sin gealladh dom thú fheiceáil. "Bhí mé anseo i gcónaí" ar seisean. "Bím ag taisteal na mbóthar is ag siúl na gcnoc is ag treabhadh na dtonn. Bím i lár an phobail nuair a chruinníos siad isteach i mo theach. Bím i measc na bpáistí 'fhágas siad ina ndiaidh ag cleasaíocht ar an tsráid." I measc na bpáistí a fuair mé thú, a Íosagáin. "An bhfeicfidh mé arís thú". "Feicfir" a deir sé. "Feicfidh tú anocht mé". 'Sé do bheatha, a Íosagáin.

[*É do thitim siar ar an leaba agus é marbh; an sagart do dhruidim go socair leis an leaba agus do dhúnadh a shúl.*]

A CHRÍOCH-SAN

NOTES

1 Foinse: *An Macaomh*, Imleabhar 1, Uimhir 2, Nollaig 1909, lgh. 40-49.

2 Cuimín, leagan ceana de Cuimme nó Colm. Cóilín, Pádraic, Darach, Briocán, Máirtín, Eoghan: ainmneacha atá coitianta i gConamara. Tá ceangal ar leith ag Naomh Briocán le ceantar Ros Muc. Ó Chontae na hIarmhí Naomh Féichín, ón bhfocal "Fiach": deirtear gur bhunaigh sé mainistir i gConga. Tá an t-ainm in úsáid sa mhórcheantar sin fós. Féach Pádraic Ó Riain, *A Dictionary of Irish Saints* (Dublin: Four Courts Press, 2011), 309–11

3 Íosagán: Íosa beag. Scríobh an Piarsach gearrscéal leis an teideal céanna a foilsíodh ar dtús in *An Claidheamh Soluis* ar an 22 Nollaig 1906. Is cóiriú ar an ngearrscéal an dráma seo. I ndán a cumadh thart ar 900AD cuirtear cuntas ar theacht Ísúcán chuici i mbéal Naomh Íde. Is léir go raibh suim ag an bPiarsach i Naomh Íde ó d'ainmnigh sé a scoil do chailíní aisti. Is suimiúil chomh maith go raibh Íde mar aite ag Ísúcán/Íosagán – léirigh an Piarsach suim leanúnach i dtábhacht an 'aite' i gcultúr na nGael. Déantar lá fhéile Íde a cheiliúradh fós in Iarthar Luimnigh (15 Eanair). Féach Gerard Murphy *Early Irish Lyrics: eight to twelve century* (Dublin: Four Courts Press, 1998), pp.26–9; agus Pádraic Ó Riain, *A Dictionary of Irish Saints* (Dublin: Four Courts Press, 2011), pp.375–8.

4 'Hide and Seek' a thug an Piarsach ar an gcluiche seo sa leagan Béarla den dráma.

1.5 Beatrice Elvery's illustration for Pearse's short story 'Íosagán' from *Íosagán agus Scéalta Eile*, 1907. Léaráid de chuid Beatrice Elvery don ghearrscéal 'Íosagán' in *Íosagán agus Scéalta Eile*, 1907.

1.6 Programme for the production of *Íosagán* which was staged alongside *The Singer* in December 1917 in the National Foresters' Hall, Rutland Square (Parnell Square). Clár don léiriú ar *Íosagán* nuair a stáitsíodh an dráma sin i dteannta *The Singer* i mí na Nollag 1917 sa National Foresters' Hall, Cearnóg Rutland (Cearnóg Pharnell). (Image courtesy of Pearse Museum/le caoinchead ó Mhúsaem na bPiarsach)

110

ÍOSAGÁN[1]

First performed in original Irish version in Feb 1910 in Cullenswood House. Staged along with Padraic Colum's The Destruction of the Hostel.

CHARACTERS

Daragh and Pádraic are a little older than the other boys.

Íosagán[2]	**Boys**[4]:
Old Matthias[3]	Dara
The Priest	Pádraic
	Cóilín
	Cuimín
	Feichín
	Eoghan

PLACE

A sea-strand beside a village in Iar-Connacht[5]

TIME

The present

SCENE I

[*A sea-strand beside a village in Iar-Connacht. A house on the right-hand side. The sound of a bell comes east, very clearly. The door of the house is opened. An aged man, old Matthias, comes out on the door-flag and stands for a spell looking down the road. He sits then on a chair that is outside the door, his two hands gripping a stick, his head bent, and he listening attentively to the sound of the bell. The bell stops ringing. Daragh, Pádraic, and Cóilín come up from the sea and they putting on their share of clothes after bathing.*]

DARAGH (*stretching his finger towards the sea*) The flowers are white in the fisherman's garden.

PÁDRAIC They are, *muise*.[6]

CÓILÍN Where are they?

DARAGH See them out on the sea.

CÓILÍN Those are not white flowers. Those are white horses.

DARAGH They're like white flowers.

CÓILÍN No; Old Matthias says those are the white horses that go galloping across the sea from the Other Country.

PÁDRAIC I heard Íosagán saying they were flowers.

CÓILÍN And what way would flowers grow on the sea?

PÁDRAIC And what way would horses travel on the sea?

CÓILÍN Easy, if they were fairy horses would be in them.

PÁDRAIC And wouldn't flowers grow on the sea as easy, if they were fairy flowers would be in them? Isn't it often you saw the water-lilies on Loch Ellery? And couldn't they grow on the sea as well as on the lake?

CÓILÍN I don't know if they could.

PÁDRAIC They could, *muise*.

DARAGH The sea was fine today, lad.

CÓILÍN It was, but it was devilish cold.

PÁDRAIC Why wouldn't you be cold when you'd only go into your knees?

CÓILÍN By my word, I was afraid the waves would knock me down if I'd go in any further. They were terrible big.

DARAGH That's what I like, lad. Do you mind yon terrible big one that came over our heads?

PÁDRAIC Aye, and Cóilín screaming out he was drowned.

CÓILÍN It went down my throat; it did that, and it nearly smothered me.

PÁDRAIC Sure, you had your mouth open, and you shouting. It would be a queer story if it didn't go down your throat.

CÓILÍN Yon one gave me enough. I kept out of their way after that.

DARAGH Have the other lads on them yet?

PÁDRAIC Aye. Here they are.

[*Feichín, Eoghan and Cuimín come up from the sea and they drying their hair.*]

CUIMÍN What'll we play today?

CÓILÍN "Blind Man's Buff!"

PÁDRAIC Ara, shut up, yourself and your "Blind Man's Buff."

CÓILÍN "High Gates," then!

PÁDRAIC No. We're tired of those "High Gates."

DARAGH "Hide and Seek!"

FEICHÍN Away!

EOGHAN "Fox and Chickens!"[7]

CÓILÍN No. We'll play "*Lúrabóg Lárabóg.*"[8]

PÁDRAIC I'll make a *lúrabóg* of you!

CÓILÍN You do be always at me, Pádraic. *(Pádraic catches hold of him.)* Listen to me, will you?

CUIMÍN Ara, listen to him, Pádraic.

DARAGH Listen to him.

[*Pádraic lets him go.*]

CÓILÍN Speak yourself, Pádraic, if you won't give leave to anyone else.

PÁDRAIC Let's jump!

EOGHAN Let's jump! Let's jump!

DARAGH I'll bet I'll beat you, Pádraic.

PÁDRAIC At jumping, is it?

DARAGH Aye.

PÁDRAIC Didn't I beat you the day before yesterday at the School Rock?

DARAGH I'll bet you won't beat me today. Will you try?

PÁDRAIC I won't. My feet are sore. (The other boys begin laughing; Pádraic speaks with a shamed face.) I'd rather play ball.

EOGHAN Ball! Ball!

DARAGH Has anyone a ball?

CUIMÍN And if they had, itself, where would we play?

PÁDRAIC Against Old Matthias's gable-end. There's no nicer place to be found.

CÓILÍN Who has the ball?

CUIMÍN My soul, I haven't it.

DARAGH No, nor I.

PÁDRAIC You yourself, Cóilín, had it on Friday.

CÓILÍN By my word, didn't the master grab it where I was hopping it in the school at Catechism?[9]

FEICHÍN True for you, lad.

CUIMÍN My soul, but I thought he'd give you the rod that time.

CÓILÍN He would, too, only he was expecting the priest to come in.

DARAGH It's the ball he wanted. He'll have a game with the peelers today after Mass.

PÁDRAIC My soul, but he will, and it's he can beat the peelers, too.

DARAGH He can't beat the sergeant. The sergeant's the best man of them all. He beat Hoskin's and the red man together last Sunday.

FEICHÍN Ara, stop! Did he beat them?

DARAGH He did, *muise*. The red man was raging, and the master and the peelers all laughing at him.

PÁDRAIC I bet the master will beat the sergeant.

DARAGH I'll bet he won't.

PÁDRAIC Do ye hear him?

DARAGH I'll bet the sergeant can beat any man in this country.

PÁDRAIC Ara, how do you know whether he can or not?

DARAGH I know well he can. Don't I be always watching him?

PÁDRAIC You don't know!

DARAGH I do know! It's I that know it!

[*They threaten each other. A quarrel arises among the boys, a share of them saying, "The sergeant's the best!" and others, "The master's best!" Old Matthias gets up to listen to them. He comes forward, twisted and bent in his body, and barely able to drag his feet along. He speaks to them quietly, laying his hand on Daragh's head.*]

MATTHIAS O! O! O! My shame ye are!

PÁDRAIC This fellow says the master can't beat the sergeant playing ball.

DARAGH By my word, wouldn't the sergeant beat anybody at all in this country, Matthias?

MATTHIAS Never mind the sergeant. Look at that lonesome wild goose that's making on us over Loch Ellery! Look!

[*All the boys look up.*]

DARAGH Where's she coming from, Matthias?

MATTHIAS From the Eastern World. I would say she has travelled a thousand miles since she left her nest in the lands to the north.

CÓILÍN The poor thing. And where will she drop?

MATTHIAS To Aran she'll go, it's a chance. See her now out over the sea. My love you are, lonesome wild goose!

CÓILÍN Tell us a story, Matthias.

[*He sits on a stone by the strand-edge, and the boys gather round him.*]

MATTHIAS What story shall I tell?

FEICHÍN "The Adventures of the Grey Horse!"

CUIMÍN "The Hen-Harrier and the Wren!"

PÁDRAIC "The Two-Headed Giant!"

CÓILÍN "The Adventures of the Piper in the Snail's Castle!"

EOGHAN Aye, by my soul, "The Adventures of the Piper in the Snail's Castle!"

THE BOYS *(with one voice)* "The Adventures of the Piper in the Snail's Castle!"

MATTHIAS I'll do that. "There was a Snail in it long ago, and it's long since it was. If we'd been there that time, we wouldn't be here now; and if we were, itself, we'd have a new story or an old story, and that's better than to be without e'er a story at all. The Castle this Snail lived in was the finest that man's eye ever saw. It was greater entirely, and it was a thousand times richer than Meave's Castle in Rath Cruachan, or than the Castle of the High-King of Ireland itself in Tara of the Kings. This Snail made love to a Spider –"[10]

CÓILÍN No, Matthias, wasn't it to a Granny's Needle he made love?

MATTHIAS My soul, but you're right. What's coming on me?

PÁDRAIC Go on, Matthias.

MATTHIAS "This Nettle-Worm was very comely entirely –"

FEICHÍN What's the Nettle-Worm, Matthias?

MATTHIAS Why, the Nettle-Worm he made love to.

CUIMÍN But I thought it was to a Granny's Needle he made love.

MATTHIAS Was it? The story's going from me. "This Piper was in love with the daughter of the King of Connacht –"

EOGHAN But you didn't mention the Piper yet, Matthias!

MATTHIAS Didn't I! "The Piper ..." yes, by my soul, the Piper – I'm losing my memory. Look here, neighbours, we won't meddle with the story today. Let's have a song.

CÓILÍN "Hi diddle dum!"

MATTHIAS Are ye satisfied?

THE BOYS We are.

MATTHIAS I'll do that. *(He sings the following rhyme)* "Hi diddle dum, the cat and his mother, That went to Galway riding a drake"

THE BOYS "And hi diddle dum!"

MATTHIAS "Hi diddle dum, the rain came pelting,
And drenched to the skin the cat and his mother."

THE BOYS "And hi diddle dum!"

MATTHIAS "Hi diddle dum, 'twas in the deluge
The cat and his mother would both be drowned."

THE BOYS "And hi diddle dum!"

MATTHIAS "Hi diddle dum, my jewel the drake was,
That carried his burden –"

CÓILÍN Swimming –

MATTHIAS Good man, Cóilín. "That carried his burden swimming to Galway."

THE BOYS "And hi diddle dum!"

[*Old Matthias shakes his head wearily; he speaks in a sad voice.*]

MATTHIAS My songs are going from me, neighbours. I'm like an old fiddle that's lost all its strings.

CUIMÍN Haven't you the "*Báidín*" always, Matthias?[11]

MATTHIAS I have, my soul; I have it as long as I'm living. I won't lose the "*Báidín*" till I'm stretched in the clay. Shall we have it?

THE BOYS Aye.

MATTHIAS Are ye ready to go rowing?

THE BOYS We are!

[*They order themselves as they would be rowing. Old Matthias sings these verses.*]

MATTHIAS "I will hang a sail, and I will go west."

THE BOYS "*Oró, mo churaichín, O!*"

MATTHIAS "And till St. John's Day will not rest."[12]

THE BOYS "*Oró, mo churaichín, O!Oró, mo churaichín. O!'S óró, mo bháidín!*"[13]

MATTHIAS "Isn't it fine, my little boat, sailing on the bay."

THE BOYS "*Oró, mo churaichín, O!*"

MATTHIAS "The oars pulling –"

[*He stops suddenly, and puts his hand to his head.*]

PÁDRAIC What's on you, Matthias?

EOGHAN Are you sick, Matthias?

MATTHIAS Something that came on my head. It's nothing. What's this I was saying?

CÓILÍN You were saying the "*Báidín*", Matthias, but don't mind if you don't feel well. Are you sick?

MATTHIAS Sick? By my word, I'm not sick. What would make me sick? We'll start again:

"Isn't it fine, my little boat, sailing in the bay."

THE BOYS "*Oró, mo churaichín, O!*"

MATTHIAS "The oars pulling strongly –" *(He stops again.)* Neighbours, the "*Báidín*" itself is gone from me. *(They remain silent for a spell, the old man sitting and his head bent on his breast, and the boys looking on him sorrowfully. The old man speaks with a start.)* Are those people coming home from Mass?

CUIMÍN No. They won't be free for a half hour yet.

CÓILÍN Why don't you go to Mass, Matthias?

[*The old man rises up and puts his hand to his head again. He speaks angrily at first, and after that softly.*[14]]

MATTHIAS Why don't I go? … I'm not good enough. By my word, God wouldn't hear me. … What's this I'm saying? … (He laughs.) And I have lost the "*Báidín*", do ye say? Amn't I the pitiful object without my "*Báidín*!"

[*He hobbles slowly across the road. Cóilín rises and puts his shoulder under the old man's hand to support him. The boys begin playing "jackstones" quietly. Old Matthias sits on the chair again, and Cóilín returns. Daragh speaks in a low voice.*]

DARAGH There's something on Old Matthias today. He never forgot the "*Báidín*" before.

THE BOYS I heard my father saying to my mother, the other night, that it's not long he has to live.

CÓILÍN Do you think he is very old?

PÁDRAIC Why did you put that question on him about the Mass? Don't you know he hasn't been seen at Mass in the memory of the people?

DARAGH I heard Old Cuimín Enda saying to my father that he himself saw Old Matthias at Mass when he was a youth.

CÓILÍN Do you know why he doesn't go to Mass now?

PÁDRAIC *(in a whisper)* It's said he doesn't believe there's a God.

CUIMÍN I heard Father Sean Eamonn saying it's the way he did some terrible sin at the start of his life, and when the priest wouldn't give him absolution in confession there came a raging anger on him, and he swore an oath he wouldn't touch priest or chapel for ever again.

DARAGH That's not how I heard it. One night when I was in bed the old people were talking and whispering by the fireside, and I heard Máire of the Bridge saying to the other old women that it's the way Matthias sold his soul to some Great Man he met once on the top of Cnoc-a'-Daimh, and that this Man wouldn't allow him to go to Mass.

PÁDRAIC Do you think was it the devil he saw?

DARAGH I don't know. A "Great Man", said Máire of the Bridge.

CUIMÍN I wouldn't believe a word of it. Sure, if Matthias sold his soul to the devil it must be he's a wicked person.

PÁDRAIC He's not a wicked person, *muise*. Don't you mind the day Íosagán said that his father told him Matthias would be among the saints on the Day of the Mountain?[15]

CUIMÍN I mind it well.

CÓILÍN Where's Íosagán from us today?

DARAGH He never comes when there does be a grown person watching us.[16]

CUIMÍN Wasn't he here a week ago today when old Matthias was watching us?

DARAGH Was he?

CUIMÍN He was.

PÁDRAIC Aye, and a fortnight today, as well.

DARAGH There's a chance he'll come today, then.

[*Cuimín rises and looks east.*]

CUIMÍN O, see, he's coming.

[*Íosagán enters – a little, brown-haired boy, a white coat on him, and he without shoes or cap like the other boys. The boys welcome him.*]

THE BOYS God save you, Íosagán!

ÍOSAGÁN God and Mary save you!

[*He sits among them, a hand of his about Daragh's neck; The boys begin playing again, gently, without noise or quarrelling. Íosagán joins in the game. Matthias rises with a start on the coming of Íosagán, and stands gazing at him. After they have played for a spell he comes towards them, and then stands again and calls over to Cóilín.*]

MATTHIAS Cóilín!

CÓILÍN What do you want?

MATTHIAS Come here to me. (Cóilín rises and goes to him.) Who is that boy I see among you this fortnight back – he, yonder, with the brown head on him – but take care it's not red he is; I don't know is it black or is it fair he is, and the way the sun is burning on him? Do you see him – him that has his arm about Daragh's neck?

CÓILÍN That's Íosagán.

MATTHIAS Íosagán?

CÓILÍN That's the name he gives himself.

MATTHIAS Who are his people?

CÓILÍN I don't know, but he says his father's a king.

MATTHIAS Where does he live?

CÓILÍN He never told us that, but he says his house isn't far away.

MATTHIAS Does he be among you often?

CÓILÍN He does, when we do be amusing ourselves like this. But he goes from us when grown people come near. He will go from us now as soon as the people begin coming from Mass.[17]

[*The boys rise and go, in ones and twos, when they have finished the game.*]

CÓILÍN O! They are going jumping.

[*He runs after the others. Íosagán and Daragh rise and go. Matthias comes forward and calls Íosagán.*]

MATTHIAS Íosagán! (*The Child turns back and comes towards him at a run.*) Come here and sit on my knee for a little while, Íosagán. (*The Child links his hand in the old man's hand, and they sit cross the road together. Matthias sits on his chair and draws Íosagán to him.*) Where do you live, Íosagán?

ÍOSAGÁN Not far from this my house is. Why don't you come to see me?

MATTHIAS I would be afraid in a royal house. They tell me that your father's a king.

ÍOSAGÁN He is High-King of the World. But there's no call for you to be afraid of Him. He's full of pity and love.

MATTHIAS I fear I didn't keep His law.

ÍOSAGÁN Ask forgiveness of Him. I and my Mother will make intercession for you.[18]

MATTHIAS It's a pity I didn't see You before this, Íosagán. Where were You from me?

ÍOSAGÁN I was here always. I do be travelling the roads and walking the hills and ploughing the waves. I do be among the people when they gather into My house. I do be among the children they do leave behind them playing on the street.

MATTHIAS I was too shy, or too proud, to go into Your house, Íosagán: among the children, it was, I found You.

ÍOSAGÁN There isn't any place or time the children do be making fun to themselves that I'm not with them. Times they see Me; other times they don't see Me.

MATTHIAS I never saw You till lately.

ÍOSAGÁN All the grown people do be blind.

MATTHIAS And it has been granted me to see You, Íosagán.

ÍOSAGÁN My Father gave Me leave to show Myself to you because you loved His little children. *(The voices are heard of the people returning from Mass.)* I must go from you.

MATTHIAS Let me kiss the hem of Your coat.[19]

ÍOSAGÁN Kiss it.

[*He kisses the hem of His coat.*]

MATTHIAS Shall I see You again, Íosagán?

ÍOSAGÁN You will.

MATTHIAS When?

ÍOSAGÁN Tonight.

[*Íosagán goes. The old man stands on the door-flag looking after Him.*]

MATTHIAS I will see Him tonight.

[*The people pass along the road, returning from Mass.*]

CURTAIN

Scene II

[*Old Matthias's room. It is very dark. The old man lying on his bed. Someone knocks outside the door. Matthias speaks in a weak voice.*]

MATTHIAS Come in. *(The Priest enters. He sits down beside the bed and hears the old man's confession. When they have finished, Matthias speaks.)* Who told you I was wanting you, Father? I was praying God that you'd come, but I hadn't a messenger to send for you.

PRIEST But, sure, you did send a messenger for me?

MATTHIAS No.

PRIEST You didn't? But a little boy came and knocked at my door, and he said you were wanting my help.

[*The old man straightens himself back in the bed, and his eyes flash.*]

MATTHIAS What sort of a little boy was he, Father?

PRIEST A mannerly little boy, with a white coat on him.

MATTHIAS Did you take notice if there was a shadow of light about his head?

PRIEST I did, and it put great wonder on me.

[*The door opens. Íosagán stands on the threshold, and He with His two arms stretched out towards Matthias; a miraculous light about His face and head.*]

MATTHIAS Íosagán! You're good, Íosagán. You didn't fail me, love. I was too proud to go into Your house, but at the last it was granted me to see You.[20] "I was here always," says He. "I do be travelling the roads and walking the hills and ploughing the waves. I do be among the people when they gather into My house. I do be among the children they do leave behind playing on the street." Among the children, it was, I found You, Íosagán. "Shall I see You again?" "You will," says He. "You'll see Me tonight." Sé do bheatha, a Íosagán![21]

[*He falls back on the bed, and he dead. The Priest goes softly to him and closes his eyes.*]

CURTAIN

NOTES

1 From *Collected Works of Pádraic H. Pearse: Plays, Stories, Poems* (Dublin: Phoenix Publishing Co. Ltd., 1917).

2 Íosagán: little Jesus in Irish. Pearse wrote a short-story with the same title (published 22nd December, 1906, *An Claidheamh Soluis*) of which the play is a quite close staging. In a poem composed c.900AD the figure of St Íde/Ita describes how Christ came to her as the infant Ísúcán. Pearse's interest in St Ita is evident in his use of her name for the girl's school, and given Pearse's stated interest in the Gaelic idea of fosterage it is noteworthy that in the poem Ita fosters Jesus. [Her feast-day (15th Jan) is still celebrated in West Limerick. See Gerard Murphy *Early Irish Lyrics: eight to twelve century* (Dublin: Four Courts Press, 1998), pp.26–9; and Pádraic O Riain *A Dictionary of Irish Saints* (Dublin: Four Courts Press, 2011), pp.375–8].

3 Old Matthias: Matthias was chosen by lot to take the place of Judas Iscariot as one of the twelve apostles [Acts 1: 23-26]: So they proposed two, Joseph called Barabbas, who was also known as Justus, and Matthias. Then they prayed and said, 'Lord, you know everyone's heart. Show us which one of these two you have chosen to take the place in this ministry and apostleship from which Judas turned aside to go to his own place'. And they cast lots for them, and the lot fell to Matthias; and he was added to the eleven apostles.

4 Pearse chooses boys names common to the Connemara area in the west of Ireland.

5 Iar-Connacht: West Connacht.

6 Muise: emphatic interjection

7 Blind Man's Buff, High Gates, Hide and Seek, Fox and Chicken: a series of childhood games involving hiding, searching, catching.

8 A guessing game played by children.

9 Catechism: doctrinal questions and answers used to reinforce religious orthodoxies.

10 Made love: sweet words rather than the modern sexual connotation.

11 Báidín: referring to the song 'Oró, mo churaichín. O! / 'S óró, mo bháidín' that they sing a little later.

12 St John's Day: June 24th. St John's Eve, a mid-summer celebration, is still marked with bonfires along the West coast of Ireland.

13 Oró, mo churaichín, O! /Oró, mo churaichín. O! / 'S óró, mo bháidín!: A children's song about a traditional boat.

14 Matthias has possibly broken with the Catholic Church because of its denunciation of Fenianism.

15 Day of Last Judgment [Revelation 20: 11-12]: Then I saw a great

white throne and the one who sat on it; the earth and the heaven fled from his presence, and no place was found for them. And I saw the dead, great and small, standing before the throne, and books were opened. And the dead were judged according to their works, as recorded in the books.

16 It is important that the child-Jesus avoids the company of adults with the exception of Old Matthias; the detail reinforces Pearse's vision of children as the keepers of truth and hope.

17 The fact that the action happens outside the ritual space of Catholicism further reinforces the sense that Pearse is presenting the necessity of working outside the confines of orthodox powers.

18 Mother: Mary. Marian intercession is a longstanding and powerful tradition within Irish Catholicism.

19 Let me kiss the hem of Your coat: the imagery recalls Luke 8: 43–48: Now there was a woman who had been suffering from hemorrhages for twelve years; and though she had spent all she had on physicians, no one could cure her. She came up behind him and touched the fringe of his clothes, and immediately her hemorrhage stopped. Then Jesus asked, 'Who touched me?' When all denied it, Peter said, 'Master, the crowds surround you and press in on you'. But Jesus said, 'Someone touched me; for I noticed that power had gone out from me'. When the woman saw that she could not remain hidden, she came trembling; and falling down before him, she declared in the presence of all the people why she had touched him, and how she had been immediately healed. He said to her, 'Daughter, your faith has made you well; go in peace'.

20 The ending confers a sacred blessing on Irish republicanism and those who act in its name.

21 Sé do bheatha, a Íosagán!: A salutation to Íosagán.

1.7 Desmond Carney, a ghlac ról 'Giolla na Naomh' in *An Rí*, Scoil Éanna, The Hermitage, Rathfarnham sa bhliain 1912. Desmond Carney in the role of 'Giolla na Naomh' in *An Rí*, St. Endas, The Hermitage, 1912. (Le caoinchead ó Mhúsaem na bPiarsach/Image courtesy of Pearse Museum)

1.8 Sonra ón Burke Memorial le James Pearse/Detail from Burke Memorial by James Pearse. (Le caoinchead ó Mhúsaem na bPiarsach/Image courtesy of Pearse Museum)

AN RÍ[1]

.i. Fáithchluiche
Céadléirithe: Scoil Éanna, 15 Meitheamh 1912,
Scoil Éanna (Ráth Fearnáin)
Pádraic Mac Piarais do scríobh.

AN FHOIREANN ANSEO THÍOS

Macra	Rí
Giolla na Naomh *.i. mac beag*	Laochra
Manaigh	Giollanra
Ab	Bantracht
Míle	

ÁIT DON CHLUICHE SEO
Seanmhainistir

[*Faiche os comhair na mainistreach. Glórtha manach ag cantain. Buabhall do labhairt trén gcantain. An mac beag do rith ón mainistir amach agus do sheasamh ar an bhfaiche ag féachaint faoi dhéin na hairde inar labhair an buabhall.*]

AN MAC BEAG A Chonaill, a Dhiarmaid, a Ghiolla na Naomh!

[*Glórtha macra dá fhreagairt.*]

AN MAC BEAG Tá slua ag triall aduaidh!

[*An macra do theacht ar an bhfaiche.*]

MAC DÍOBH Cá bhfuil sé?

AN CHÉAD MHAC Féach uait sa ngleann é.

AN TREAS MAC Is é slua an Rí é.

AN CEATHRÚ MAC Tá an Rí ag triall chun catha.

[*An buabhall do labhairt arís, agus é níos gaire. An macra do dhul ar bharr múir na mainistreach. Cluintear siosmarnach an tslua agus é ag gluaiseacht.*]

AN CHÉAD MHAC Chím na heachraí agus na marcaigh.

AN DARA MAC Chím na claimhte agus na sleánna.

AN CEATHRÚ MAC Chím na suaitheantais agus na meirgí.

AN TREAS MAC Chím meirge an Rí.

AN CEATHRÚ MAC Chím an Rí!

AN CHÉAD MHAC Cé acu an Rí?

AN CEATHRÚ MAC An fear ard álainn atá ar an each dubh.

GIOLLA NA NAOMH Beannaímis don Rí.

AN MACRA *(d'aitheasc aon duine)* Beir bua chatha agus choscartha, a Rí!

[*Glórtha laochra agus macra ag moladh an Rí. Fuaim agus formán an tslua ag gluaiseacht chun an chatha. Ceol adharc agus píob. Ciúnas.*]

AN CHÉAD MHAC Ba mhian liom bheith im' Rí.

GIOLLA NA NAOMH Cad chuige?

AN CHÉAD MHAC Tá ór agus airgead ag an Rí.

AN DARA MAC Tá seoda uaisle aige ina sheodteach.

AN TREAS MAC Tá eich sheanga agus cúnna calma aige.

AN CEATHRÚ MAC Tá claíomh colg-ghéar cinn óir agus craoiseach chrannramhar cheannghorm agus sciath dhearg dhearscnaithe dhealrach. Do chonacas lá i dtigh m'athar é.

AN CHÉAD MHAC Cén dealbh agus cén déanamh do bhí air?

AN CEATHRÚ MAC Do bhí sé ard uasal. Do bhí sé láidir leathanguailneach. Folt fada fionn air. Éadan álainn uaibhreach air. Dhá shúil ghéara ghlasa aige. Ionar sróil lena chneas. Léine lánmhaiseach dhearg agus cochall geal air faoina cholainn. Brat ríoga corcuir uime. Seacht ndath air, idir ionar agus léine agus cochall agus brat. Dealg airgid ar a bhrollach. Mionn ríoga faoina cheann, agus dath an óir air. Dhá sciathán mhóra ag éirí os cionn a chinn agus iad chomh geal le sciatháin an fhaoileáin agus chomh mór le sciatháin an iolair. Do ba laochta an fear é.

AN DARA MAC Agus cad í an chuma nó an fheáchaint do bhí ar a éadan?

AN TREAS MAC An raibh cuma bhorb bhagarthach air?

AN CEATHRÚ MAC Do bhíodh ar uairibh.

AN CHÉAD MHAC An mbíodh sé gáireach?

AN CEATHRÚ MAC Do rinne sé aon gháire amháin.

AN DARA MAC Cad í an chuma is mó do bhíodh air? Borb nó gáireach?

AN CEATHRÚ MAC Cuma bhrónach. An uair do bhíodh sé ag agallamh na ríograí agus na laochra do bhíodh sé borb agus gáireach gach re seal, ach an uair do bhíodh sé ina thost do bhíodh sé brónach.

AN CHÉAD MHAC Cad é an brón atá air?

AN CEATHRÚ MAC Níl a fhios agam. Na mílte do mharaigh sé, b'fhéidir.

AN DARA MAC Na cealla do chreach sé, b'fhéidir.

131

AN TREAS MAC Na catha do briseadh air.

GIOLLA NA NAOMH Mo thrua an Rí bocht!

AN DARA MAC Níor mhaith leatsa a bheith i do Rí, a Ghiolla na Naomh?

GIOLLA NA NAOMH Níor mhaith. Do b'fhearr liom bheith im' mhanach go nguífinn ar an Rí.

AN CEATHRÚ MAC Do b'fhéidir domsa flaitheas na críche seo do ghabháil ar bheith foirfe dom, óir is den bhfuil ríoga m'athair.

AN DARA MAC Agus is den bhfuil ríoga m'athairse mar an gcéanna.

AN TREAS MAC Is ea, agus m'athairse.

AN CEATHRÚ MAC Ní ligfead an ríocht le haon agaibh. Is liomsa í!

AN DARA MAC Ní leat, ach liomsa.

AN TREAS MAC Is cuma cé leis í, is agamsa bheas sí.

AN DARA MAC Ní hagat, ná ag éinne ded' threibh.

AN CEATHRÚ MAC (ag breith ar shlat shailí agus á croitheadh) Imreod nimh mo chlaímh oraibh. Cosnód mo ríocht ar mo naimhde.[2] A Ghiolla na Naomh, guigh ar an Rí!

[Glór cloig do theacht ón mainistir.]

GIOLLA NA NAOMH Tá an clog ag labhairt.

[Muintir na mainistreach do theacht ar an bhfaiche ina nduine agus ina nduine nó ina mbeirteanna agus an tAb ina ndeireadh. An macra do dhul ar fhód ar leith. Gleo an chatha do theacht i gcéin.]

AN tAB A chlann, tá an Rí ag fearadh catha in aghaidh a bhíobha.

132

AN CHÉAD MHANACH Do briseadh ar an Rí seo gach cath ina ndeachaigh go nuige seo.

AN tAB Aisling do chonacas inniu agus mé i bhfianaise mo Dhé do foilsíodh dom go mbrisfear ar an Rí arís.

AN DARA MANACH Monuar!

AN TREAS MANACH Monuar!

AN CHÉAD MHANACH Inis dúinn, a Athair, fáth na mbriseadh do-áirithe seo.

AN tAB An dóigh libh go nglacfar iobairt ó lámha truaillithe. Dhoirt an Rí seo fuil na neamhchiontach. Do rinne tána agus creacha. Do ghéarlean na boicht. Do thréig muinteoras Dé agus do chuaigh i gcairdeas méirleach.

AN CHÉAD MHANACH Is fíor sin. Gidhe, is maith an comhrac a dhéanann an Rí anois, mar atá, comhlann[3] d'fhearadh ar son a mhuintire.

AN tAB Aingeal do mba chóir do chur ag doirteadh fíona agus briseadh arán na híobartha seo. Ní do Rí urchóideach is doirte an fíon uasal a bhíos i gcuislí dea-laoch. Ní ar fhoráil Rí chiontaigh is ciorruithe caomhcholainneacha. A deirim libh nach nglacfar an íobairt uaidh.

AN CHÉAD MHANACH Agus an ciontach cách i gcionta an Rí? Má bhuaitear ar an Rí beidh a dhólás ar chách. Céard faoi a n-imrítear díoltas ar chách mar gheall ar chionta an Rí? Ar an Rí féin an éiric.[4]

AN tAB Is ciontach gach cine i gcionta a ríograí.[5] A deirim libh nach saorfar an cine seo go ngabhfaidh chucu Rí ionraic.

AN DARA MANACH Cá bhfaightear Rí ionraic?

AN tAB Níl a fhios agam muna bhfaightear i measc na mac mbeag seo.

[*Bíodh an macra i dtimpeall an Aba anois.*]

AN CHÉAD MHANACH Agus an amhlaidh a bheas an cine faoi dhaorsmacht go bheith inchomhraic do na mic bheaga seo? Ní hé cás an Rí is trua liom ach cás an chine. Do chualas mná ag gol aréir. An mbeidh mná ag gol sa gcríoch seo go bráth?

AN TREAS MANACH Ar éirí ón mainistir amach dom inné, do bhí fear marbh ar imeall na coille. Is uafásach cathanna.

AN DARA MANACH Ní hea, is aoibhinn cathanna! An uair do bhíomar ag déanamh ar Nóna anois[6], a Athair, do chualas tré shalmaireacht na mbráthar glór buabhaill. Do ling mo chroí, agus do b'áil liom éirí ón áit a rabhas agus dul i ndiaidh an cheoil mheanmnaigh úd. Do ba chuma liom dá mba chun mo bháis do gheobhainn.

AN tAB Aitheasc óganaigh an t-aitheasc sin. Fanann gach seanóir leis an mbás agus téann gach óganach ina choinne. Dá dtiocfadh fear fuilteach ón ionad coimhghleice úd isteach san áit chiúin seo, mar a gcanann manaigh agus mar a n-imríonn leanaí, agus cách do ghríosadh chun a leanúna sa gcoimheascar, níl aon anseo nach n-éireodh agus a leanúint, ach mé féin agus an seanbhráthair a bhuaileas ár gclog. Níl aon agaibhse a bhráithre óga, níl aon de na mic bheaga seo, nach n-éireodh uaim agus dul sa gcath. Cuireann ceol úd na gcathmhílí croíthe na n-óg ar meisce.

AN DARA MANACH Oireann an mheisce don óige.

AN CHÉAD MHANACH A bhráthair, is olc do labhartha.

AN tAB Tá leann lánmheisciúil ann is ólta do gach óganach, óir an té nár ól de go bheith ar meisce dó ní bhfuair eolas ar an mbeatha. Is leis an leann úd a chuirfeas Dia croíthe na naomh ar meisce. Ní choscfainn oraibh bhur meisce, a fheara óga!

AN CHÉAD MHANACH Ní léir dom a bhrí seo, a Athair.

AN tAB An dóigh leat dá labhródh an glór álainn uafásach úd lena mbíonn na hóganaigh ag síorfhanúint agus cluas le

134

héisteacht orthu, é do labhairt anois san ionad úd mar a bhfuil an lucht cathaithe agus na heachraí agus an ceol, go gcoinneoinn sibh dá n-éireodh sibh chum a fhreagartha? An dóigh libh go mba mhór liom aon agaibh don bhás agus é ag labhairt den ghlór álainn uafásach úd, an dóigh leat go mba mhór liom dó an mac is dílse liom de na mic bheaga seo? Do ligfinn uaim sibh uile, cé gurbh uaigneach domsa agus don seanbhráthair anseo.

AN DARA MAC Ní rachadh Giolla na Naomh, a Athair.

AN tAB Céard faoi a ndeireann tú sin?

AN DARA MAC A dúirt sé go mb'fhearr leis bheith ina mhanach.

AN tAB Nach rachása sa gcath, a Ghiolla na Naomh?

GIOLLA NA NAOMH Do rachainn. Do rachainn im' ghiolla don Rí go bhfreastalóinn air an uair do thréigfeadh cách é.

AN tAB Ach is do na naoimh is giolla thú, a Ghiolla na Naomh, agus ní don Rí.

GIOLLA NA NAOMH Níor mhor don Rí bocht giolla beag nach dtréigfeadh é an uair do bhrisfí an cath air agus cách dá thréigean.

AN tAB Tá an ceart ag an leanbh seo. Clú atá uainne, ach dualgas giolla do dhéanamh atá uaidhsean.

[*Glórtha bróin agus buartha.*]

AN CHÉAD MHANACH Is eagal liom go bhfuil buaite ar an Rí!

AN tAB Téigh ar an múr agus inis dúinn a bhfeicfir.

AN CHÉAD MHANACH (*iar ndul ar an múr dó*) Tá fear chughainn agus é ag teitheadh.

AN DARA MANACH Cén chosúlacht atá air?

AN CHÉAD MHANACH Fear fuilteach fann, agus a chosa ar foluain agus ar fuaidreadh faoi.

AN DARA MANACH An fear de mhuintir an Rí é?

AN CHÉAD MHANACH Is ea.

[*An míle do theacht ar an láthair agus é tréithlag.*]

AN MÍLE Tá buaite ar an Rí!

NA MANAIGH Monuar, monuar!

AN MÍLE Tá buaite ar an Rí a deirim libh. Lucht na leabhar agus na gclog, ba bheag bhur gcabhair dúinn sa chomhrac crua![7] Tá buaite ar an Rí!

AN tAB Cá bhfuil an Rí?

AN MÍLE Tá sé ag teitheadh roimhe.

AN tAB Tabhair tuarascáil an chatha dúinn.

AN MÍLE Ní fhanann urlabhra agam. Tugtar deoch dom.

AN tAB Tugtar deoch don bhfear seo.

[*An mac beag dá ngairmtear Giolla na Naomh do thabhairt uisce dó.*]

AN tAB Labhair linn anois agus tabhair dúinn tuarascáil an chatha.

AN MÍLE Ba fhear comhlainn deichniúr gach fear dinn. Ba fear comhlainn céid an Rí. Ach cár bhfearrde sinn ar ngaisce? Do buadh orainn agus do theitheamar romhainn. Tá na céadta bonn le bonn ar an mbán.

NA MANAIGH Monuar, monuar!

[*Glórtha arda amuigh.*]

AN DARA MANACH Cé tá chughainn?

AN CHÉAD MHANACH An Rí!

[Eachra, marcaigh, laochra, giollanra, srl. do theacht ar an láthair agus an Rí ina bhfochair. An Rí do dhul ar a ghlúine i láthair an Aba, iar gcaitheamh a chlaímh ar lár dó.]

AN RÍ Tabhair do mhallacht dom, a fhir le Dia, agus lig dom dul d'éag. Tá buaite orm. Tá buaite ar mo mhuintir. Deich gcath do fhearas in aghaidh mo bhíobha agus do briseadh orm gach cath díobh. Mé do thug fearg Dé ar an gcríoch seo. Iarr ar do Dhia gan a fhearg d'imirt ar mo chine feasta ach a himirt ormsa. Déan trócaire ar mo mhuintir, a fhir le Dia!

AN tAB Déanfaidh Dia trócaire ortsa.

AN RÍ Do thréig Dia mise.

AN tAB Do thréigise Dia.

AN RÍ Do thréig Dia mo mhuintir.

AN tAB Níor thréig agus ní thréigfidh. Saorfaidh sé an cine seo má ghabhann siad chucu rí ionraic.

AN RÍ Tabhair dóibh mar sin rí ionraic. Tabhair dóibh duine de do mhanaigh nó duine de na macaibh beaga seo le bheith ina rí orthu. An cath ar do choimirce, a fhir le Dia!

AN tAB Ní hea, ach ar choimirce chlaíomh Rí ionraic. Labhraigí liom, a chlann, agus insígí dom cé is ionraice in bhur measc?

AN CHÉAD MHANACH Do pheacaíos-sa.

AN DARA MANACH Do pheacaíos-sa.

AN TREAS MANACH A Athair, do pheacaíomar uile.

AN tAB Do pheacaíos-sa mar an gcéanna. Níl aon dá bhfuil in aois fir nár pheacaigh. Nach luath a mhalartaítear gaois an linbh ar bhaois an fhir! Is eagnaí sibh, a leanaí, a bhfuil bhur suim in bhur mbréagáin agus ár suimne inar bpeacaí. Is léir dom an ní seo anois. Do gheobhad Rí ionraic i measc na mac beag seo. Labhraigí liom, a mhaca, agus insigí dom cé is ionraice in bhur measc.

AN MACRA *(d'aitheasc aon duine)* Giolla na Naomh.

AN tAB An mac beag a bhíos ag freastal ar chách. Tá an ceart agaibh. An té is isle is é is airde.[8] A Ghiolla na Naomh, an mbeir id' Rí ar an gcine seo?

GIOLLA NA NAOMH Táim ró-óg, a Athair. Táim rólag.

AN tAB Gabh i leith chugham a leanbh. *(An leanbh do dhul chuige.)* A dhalta d'oileas, má iarraim ort an ní seo, an ndéanfair é?

GIOLLA NA NAOMH Bead umhal duitse, a Athair.

AN tAB An dtabharfair aghaidh ar an gcath?

GIOLLA NA NAOMH Déanfad dualgas Rí.

AN tAB A mhic bheag, do b'fhéidir gurb é do bhás do gheofá.

GIOLLA NA NAOMH Mo chion an bás, más é a ordaítear dom.

AN tAB Nach ndúras go n-iarrann na hóga an bás? Scaipeann siadsan a gcuirimidne i dtaisce go cúramach; tóraíonn siadsan a séanaimidne. Tá an glór álainn uafásach tar éis labhartha leis an leanbh seo. Freagrófar tú, a eachlaigh, a bháis![9] Ní mór liom duit mo dhalta.

AN RÍ A Ab, orm féin mo chosaint féin. Ní mharófar leanbh ar mo shonsa.

AN tAB Thugais dom do chlaíomh, agus do bheirimse don leanbh seo é. A deirim leat go bhfuil Dia tar éis labhartha tré ghlór a sheaneachlaigh, tríd an nglór álainn uafásach a thigeas ó chroí na gcomhlann.

GIOLLA NA NAOMH Lig dom an ní beag seo do dhéanamh, a Rí. Cosnód do mheirge go maith. Do bhéarfad chughat an claíomh thar n-ais tar éis an chatha. Mise do ghiolla beag a dhéanfas faire an fhaid a chodlós an Rí, ar bheith tuirseach dó. Codlódsa anocht agus déanfairse faire.

AN RÍ Mo thrua, mo thrí thrua!

GIOLLA NA NAOMH Do bhíomarna inár gcodladh aréir agus tusa ag taisteal na gcríoch dorcha. An Rí bhoicht, is fada do do thriallta. Ní bheidh mo thriallsa ach gairid.

AN tAB Géill don chaoiniarracht seo, a Rí. A deirim leat go bhful Dia tar éis labhartha.

AN RÍ Ní thuigim do Dhia.

AN tAB Cé a thuigfeas é? Ní tuiscint is toil leis, ach umhla. Tá an leanbh seo umhal agus de bhrí go bhfuil sé umhal déanfaidh Dia mórbhearta tríd. Caithfir géilleadh sa ní seo, a Rí.

AN RÍ Géillim, géillim! Is mairg dom nár thit san ionsaí catha úd!

AN tAB Baintear a éadach den leanbh go gcuirtear uime éide Rí.

[A éadach do bhaint den leanbh.]

Cuirtear ionar ríoga le cneas an linbh.

[Ionar ríoga do chur air, agus cuaróga ar a chosa.]

Cuirtear léine ríoga uime.

[Léine ríoga do chur air.]

Cuirtear uime an brat ríoga.

[An brat ríoga do bhaint den Rí agus do chur ar an mac.]

Cuirtear mionn ríoga faoina cheann.

[An mionn ríoga do bhaint den Rí agus do chur faoi cheann an mhic.]

Tugtar dó sciath an Rí.

[*Sciath an Rí do thabhairt dó.*]

Beannacht ar an sciath seo! Go mba dhaingean í i gcoinne bíobha.

AN LAOCHRA Beannacht ar an sciath seo!

AN tAB Tugtar dó craoiseach an Rí.

[*An chraoiseach do thabhairt dó.*]

Beannacht ar an gcraoiseach seo! Go mba ghéar í i gcoinne bíobha!

AN LAOCHRA Beannacht ar an gcraoisigh seo!

AN tAB Tugtar dó claíomh an Rí.

[*An claíomh do thabhairt dó.*]

Beannacht ar an gclaíomh seo! Go mba chrua é in aghaidh bíobha!

AN LAOCHRA Beannacht ar an gclaíomh seo!

AN tAB Gairmim Rí den mhac beag seo, agus cuirim an cath ar a choimirce in ainm Dé.

AN RÍ (*ar ndul ar a ghlúine roimh an mac*) Umhlaím duit, a Rí, agus cuirimid an cath ar do choimirce.

AN LAOCHRA srl (*iar ndul ar a nglúine i bhfianaise an mhic*) Umhlaímid duit, a Rí agus cuirimid an cath ar do choimirce.

GIOLLA NA NAOMH Gabhaim lem' ais an cath do chosaint in ainm Dé.

AN tAB Tugtar each dó.

[*Each do thabhairt dó.*]

Scaoiltear meirge an Rí.

[An mheirge do scaoileadh.]

Tabhair d'aghaidh ar an gcath, a Rí.

GIOLLA NA NAOMH *(iar ndul ar a ghlúine i bhfianaise an Aba):* Beannaigh mé, a athair.

AN tAB Beannacht ort, a mhic bhig.

AN LAOCHRA Beir bua chatha agus choscartha, a Rí!

[An Rí beag, iar ndul ar muin eich dó, do ghluaiseacht chun an chatha, agus an laochra agus an giollanra uime. An tAb, an Rí, na manaigh agus an macra ag féachaint orthu.]

AN tAB A Rí, do bhronnas ort an tseod do b'uaisle dá raibh im' theach. Ba gheal liom an leanbh úd.

AN RÍ A shagairt, níor ghlacas riamh óm fhoríthe duais do ba ríogúla.

AN CHÉAD MHANACH Táid i láthair an chatha.

AN tAB A Dhia láidir, láidrigh lámh an linbh seo. Daingnigh a chos. Géaraigh a chlaíomh. Go mba mhéadú meanman agus ardú aigne dó glaine a chroí agus umhlaíocht a mheoin. A aingle do rinne na príomhchathanna, a sheanlaochra Dé, déanaidh cró catha ina thimpeall agus caithigí roimhe le lanna lasracha.

NA MANAIGH AGUS AN MACRA Ámén, Ámén,

AN tAB A Dhia, saor an cine seo trí chlaíomh an linbh ionraic.

AN RÍ Agus a Chríost do céasadh ar an gcnoc, tabhair an leanbh slán ón gcath contúirteach.

AN tAB A Rí, a Rí, ní cheannaítear an tsaoirse ach le mórluach.

[Buabhall do labhairt.]

Tugtar tuarascáil an chatha dúinn.

[*An Chéad Mhanach agus an Dara Manach do dhul ar an múr.*]

AN CHÉAD MHANACH Tá an dá shlua ar aghaidh a chéile.

[*Buabhall eile do labhairt.*]

AN DARA MANACH Binn sin! Sin é buabhall an Rí!

AN CHÉAD MHANACH Tá gártha os ard ag slua an Rí.

[*Gártha eile.*]

Tá an namhaid á bhfreagairt.

AN CHÉAD MHANACH Tá na sluaite ag dul i gcomhdháil a chéile.

AN DARA MANACH Tá ina throid eatarthu.

AN CHÉAD MHANACH Tá ár muintir ag géilleadh.

AN TREAS MANACH Ná habair sin.

AN DARA MANACH Mo bhrón, táid ag géilleadh.

[*Buabhall do labhairt.*]

AN TREAS MANACH Binn sin arís! Ba thráthúil do labhrais, a bhuabhall an Rí!

AN CHÉAD MHANACH Tá meirge an Rí ag dul sa gcath.

AN DARA MANACH Chím an Rí beag!

AN TREAS MANACH An bhfuil sé ag dul sa gcath?

AN CHÉAD MHANACH Tá.

NA MANAIGH AGUS AN MACRA *(d'aon ghuth)* Beir bua chatha agus choscartha, a Rí!

AN DARA MANACH Tá sé ina throid mhaith anois.

AN CHÉAD MHANACH Do tháinig dhá fharraige le chéile ar an maigh.

AN DARA MANACH Dhá fharraige fhraochta![10]

AN CHÉAD MHANACH Tá farraige díobh ag trá.

AN DARA MANACH An namhaid atá ag dul ar gcúl!

AN CHÉAD MHANACH Tá an Rí beag ag dul tríothu.

AN DARA MANACH Tá sé ag dul tríothu mar do ghabhadh seabhac trí mhionéin.

AN CHÉAD MHANACH Nó mar do gheobhadh faolchú trí thréad caorach ar mhachaire.

AN DARA MANACH Mar bhorbshruth tré bhearna sléibhe!

AN CHÉAD MHANACH Tá sé ina raon ruathair roimhe.

AN DARA MANACH Tá séisilbhe mór sa gcath. Tá sé ina chosán comhgháireach roimh mharc an Rí.

AN CHÉAD MHANACH A chinn órga os cionn an áir! A lann lonnrach lánábhal an Rí!

AN DARA MANACH Tá an namhaid ag teitheadh!

AN CHÉAD MHANACH Tá buaite orthu! Tá buaite orthu! Tá sé ina dheargraon ruathair! Déantar libh na gártha maíte!

AN DARA MANACH Mo bhrón!

AN CHÉAD MHANACH Mo bhrón, mo bhrón!

AN tAB Céard sin?

AN CHÉAD MHANACH Tá an Rí beag ar lár.

AN tAB An bhfuil an bua aige?

AN CHÉAD MHANACH Tá, ach tá sé féin ar lár. Ní fheicim a cheann órga. Ní fheicim a lann lonnrach. Táthar ag tógáil a choirp den bhán.

AN tAB An bhfuil an namhaid ag teitheadh?

AN DARA MANACH Táid. Táid ag teitheadh agus tá an tóir ina ndiaidh. Táid scaipthe. Táid scaipthe mar do scaipfí ceo. Nílid le feiscin ar an magh!

AN tAB A bhuí le Dia?

[*Cluintear caoineadh.*]

Do freagraíodh tú, a ghlóir uafásaigh, a sheaneachlaigh, d'fhreagair mo dhalta.

AN TREAS MANACH Táthar ag breith chughainn linbh mhairbh.

AN RÍ A dúirt sé gurb eisean do chodlódh anocht agus gur mise do dhéanfadh faire.

[*Laochra do theacht ar an bhfaiche agus corp an Rí bhig ar chróchar acu; bantracht dá chaoineadh. Leagtar an cróchar i lár na faiche.*]

Thug sé mo chlaíomh thar n-ais chugham. Do chosain sé mo mheirge go maith.

AN tAB (*ag tógáil an chlaímh den chróchar*) Beir leat an claíomh.

AN RÍ Ní bhéarfad, ach a fhágáil aigesean. Níor cheart do Rí a chodladh a dhéanamh gan claíomh aige. Ba Rí fíorchalma é seo.

[*An claíomh do thógáil as lámh an Aba don Rí agus a leagan ar an gcróchar arís. An Rí do dhul ar a ghlúine.*]

AN RÍ Umhlaím duit, a Rí mhairbh agus a leanbh bhuaigh;

pógaim thú a ghealcholainn, óir do ghlainese do shaor mo mhuintir.

[*Clár éadain Ghiolla na Naomh do phógadh dó. Tosnaítear ar an gcaoineadh arís.*]

AN tAB Ná caointear an leanbh seo, óir do cheannaigh sé saoirse dá chine. Déantar libh na gártha maíte agus cantar libh caintic ag moladh Dé.

[*"Te Deum" do ghabháil dóibh ag breith an choirp isteach sa mhainistir dóibh.*[11]]

A CHRÍOCHSAN

NOTES

1 Foinse: *An Macaomh*, edited by P. H. Pearse, Imleabhar II, Uimhir 2, Bealtaine , 1913, lgh. 18- 26, MS 15, 004.
2 Deotranaimí 32:41: 'Nuair a bheidh faobhar ar mo chlaíomh lonrach, agus go dtéim i mbun cúis na córa, déanfaidh mé díoltas a imirt ar mo naimhde, agus díolfaidh mé an comhar le lucht m'fhuatha', An Bíobla Naofa.
3 Cath/cogadh ('battle').
4 'Eric', fine, ransom, retribution, requital, restitution (Ua Duinnín)
5 Is léir ón aistriú Béarla a dhein an Piarsach féin ar an bhfrása 'cionta a ríograidh' ('the sins of its princes') agus ó na bunfhoinsí gur 'ríogradh' i bhfoirm an ghinidigh atá anseo – 'a dynasty, a line of kings' de réir an Duinnínigh. 'Ríogaí' atá ag Ó Buachalla.
6 'Nones': oifig de chuid na hEaglaise – a bhíodh ar siúl i dtosach ag an naoú huair.
7 Meabhraítear friotal na laoithe Fiannaíochta sa tagairt seo do 'lucht na leabhar agus na gclog', go háirithe na hagallaimh idir Oisín agus Naomh Pádraig mar a gcuirtear saoirse agus gliondar na Págántachta agus an dúlra i gcodarsnacht le saol rialta na mainistreach agus an chreidimh Chríostaí.
8 Matha 20:16: 'Sin mar a bheidh a bhfuil ar deireadh ar tosach agus a bhfuil ar tosach ar deireadh'. An Bíobla Naofa.
9 Meabhraítear an líne 'Fada liom do teacht/a sheaneachlaigh Dé' sa dán 'Fada liom do theacht' anseo. Féach Ciarán Ó Coigligh, Filíocht

Ghaeilge Phádraig Mhic Phiarais, (Baile Átha Cliath: An Clóchomhar) 1981, lch. 45.

10 Meabhraítear friotal na scéalta gaisce san íomháine agus san uaim atá anseo.

11 Te Deum, ó 'Te Deum Laudamus' ('Molaimid Thú a Dhia'), iomann molta de chuid na Luath-Chríostaíochta. Chantaí Te Deum ar chloisteáil tuairisce faoi bhua i gcath chomh maith.

1.9 Photograph of Desmond Carney who played 'Giolla na Naomh' in *An Rí*/*The King*. (Image courtesy of Pearse Museum/Le caoinchead ó Mhúsaem na bPiarsach)

1.10 Sculpture of two angels by James Pearse/Beirt aingeal le James Pearse.
(Image courtesy of Pearse Museum/Le caoinchead ó Mhúsaem na bPiarsach)

THE KING[1]

A Morality. Translated from the Irish of P.H. Pearse[2]
First performed in original Irish version 15th June 1912 in the grounds
of St Enda's (Rathfarnham).

CHARACTERS

Boys	A Soldier
Giolla na Naomh ('the Servant	A King
of the Saints'), a little boy	Heroes
Monks	Gillies[3]
An Abbot	Women

PLACE
An ancient monastery

A green before the monastery. The voices of monks are heard chanting.
Through the chanting breaks the sound of a trumpet.[4] A little boy runs
out from the monastery and stands on the green looking in the direction
whence the trumpet has spoken.

THE BOY Conall, Diarmaid, Giolla na Naomh!

[*The voices of other boys answer him.*]

FIRST BOY There is a host marching from the North.[5]

[*The boys come out upon the green.*]

SECOND BOY Where is it?

FIRST BOY See it beneath you in the glen.

THIRD BOY It is the King's host.

FOURTH BOY The King is going to battle.

[*The trumpet speaks again, nearer. The boys go upon the rampart of the monastery. The murmur of a marching host is heard.*]

FIRST BOY I see the horses and the riders.

SECOND BOY I see the swords and the spears.

FOURTH BOY I see the standards and the banners.

THIRD BOY I see the King's banner.

FOURTH BOY I see the King!

FIRST BOY Which of them is the King?

FOURTH BOY The tall comely man on the black horse.

GIOLLA NA NAOMH Let us salute the King.

THE BOYS *(with the voice of one)* Take victory in battle and slaying, O King!

[*The voices of warriors are heard acclaiming the King as the host marches past with din of weapons and music of trumpet and pipes. Silence succeeds.*]

FIRST BOY I would like to be King.

GIOLLA NA NAOMH Why?

FIRST BOY The King has gold and silver.

SECOND BOY He has noble jewels in his jewel-house.

THIRD BOY He has slender steeds and gallant hounds.

FOURTH BOY He has a keen-edged gold-hilted sword and a mighty-shafted blue-headed spear and a glorious red-emblazoned shield. I saw him once in my father's house.[6]

FIRST BOY What was he like?

FOURTH BOY He was tall and noble. He was strong and broad-shouldered. He had long fair hair. He had a comely proud face. He had two piercing grey eyes. A white vest of satin next his skin. A very beautiful red tunic, with a white hood, upon his body. A royal mantle of purple about him. Seven colours upon him, between vest and tunic and hood and mantle. A silver brooch upon his breast. A kingly diadem upon his head, and the colour of gold upon it. Two great wings rising above his head, as white as the two wings of a seagull and as broad as the two wings of an eagle. He was a gallant man.

SECOND BOY And what was the look of his face?

THIRD BOY Did he look angry, stern?

FOURTH BOY He did at times.

FIRST BOY Had he a laughing look?

FOURTH BOY He laughed only once.

SECOND BOY How did he look mostly? Stern or laughing?

FOURTH BOY He looked sorrowful. When he was talking to the kings and the heroes he had an angry and a laughing look every second while, but when he was silent he was sorrowful.

FIRST BOY What sorrow can he have?

FOURTH BOY I do not know. The thousands he has slain perhaps.

SECOND BOY The churches he has plundered.

THIRD BOY The battles he has lost.

GIOLLA NA NAOMH Alas, the poor King!

SECOND BOY You would not like to be a King, Giolla na Naomh?

GIOLLA NA NAOMH I would not. I would rather be a monk that I might pray for the King.

FOURTH BOY I may have the kingship of this country when I am a man, for my father is of the royal blood.

SECOND BOY And my father is of the royal blood too.

THIRD BOY Aye, and mine.

FOURTH BOY I will not let the kingdom go with either of you. It is mine!

SECOND BOY It is not, but mine!

THIRD BOY It matters not whose it is, for I will have it!

SECOND BOY No, nor anyone of your house!

FOURTH BOY *(seizing a switch of sally and brandishing it)* I will ply the venom of my sword upon you! I will defend my kingdom against my enemies! Giolla na Naomh, pray for the King![7]

[*A bell sounds from the monastery.*]

GIOLLA NA NAOMH The bell is ringing.

[*The people of the monastery come upon the green in ones and twos, the Abbot last. The boys gather a little apart. Distant sounds of battle are heard.*]

THE ABBOT My children, the King is giving battle to his foes.

FIRST MONK This King has lost every battle into which he has gone up to this.

THE ABBOT In a vision that I saw last night as I knelt before my God it was revealed to me that the battle will be broken on the King again.

SECOND MONK My grief!

THIRD MONK My grief!

FIRST MONK Tell us, Father, the cause of these unnumbered defeats.

THE ABBOT Do you think that an offering will be accepted from polluted hands? This King has shed the blood of the innocent. He has made spoils and forays. He has oppressed the poor. He has forsaken the friendship of God and made friends with evil-doers.

FIRST MONK That is true. Yet it is a good fight that the King fights now, for he gives battle for his people.

THE ABBOT It is an angel that should be sent to pour out the wine and to break the bread of this sacrifice. Not by an unholy King should the noble wine that is in the veins of good heroes be spilt; not at the behest of a guilty King should fair bodies be mangled. I say to you that the offering will not be accepted.

FIRST MONK And are all guilty of the sins of the King? If the King is defeated its grief will be for all. Why must all suffer for the sins of the King? On the King the eric.[8]

THE ABBOT The nation is guilty of the sins of its princes. I say to you that this nation shall not be freed until it chooses for itself a righteous King.

SECOND MONK Where shall a righteous King be found?

THE ABBOT I do not know, unless he be found among these little boys.

[*The boys have drawn near and are gathered about the Abbot.*]

FIRST MONK And shall the people be in bondage until these little lads are fit for battle? It is not the King's case I pity but the case of the people. I heard women mourning last night. Shall women be mourning in this land till doom?

THIRD MONK As I went out from the monastery yesterday there was a dead man on the verge of the wood. Battle is terrible.

SECOND MONK No, battle is glorious! While we were singing our None but now[9], Father, I heard, through the psalmody[10] of the brethren, the voice of a trumpet. My heart leaped, and I would fain have risen from the place where I was and gone after that gallant music. I should not have cared though it were to my death I went.

THE ABBOT That is the voice of a young man. The old wait for death, but the young go to meet it. If into this quiet place where monks chant and children play there were to come from yonder battlefield a blood-stained man, calling upon all to follow him into the battle-press, there is none that would not rise and follow him, but I myself and the old brother that rings our bell. There is none of you, young brothers, no, nor any of these little lads, that would not rise from me and go into the battle. That music of the fighters makes drunk the hearts of young men.

SECOND MONK It is good for young men to be made drunk.

FIRST MONK Brother, you speak wickedness.

THE ABBOT There is a heady ale which all young men should drink, for he who has not been made drunk with it has not lived. It is with that ale that God makes drunk the hearts of saints. I would not forbid you your intoxication, O young men!

FIRST MONK This is not plain, Father.

THE ABBOT Do you think if that terrible beautiful voice for which young men strain their ears were to speak from yon place where the fighters are, and the horses, and the music, that I would stay you did ye rise to obey it? Do you think I would grudge any of you, do you think I would grudge the dearest of these little boys, to death calling with that beautiful voice? I would let you all go, though I and the old brother should be very lonely here.

SECOND BOY Giolla na Naomh would not go, Father.

THE ABBOT Why do you say that?

SECOND BOY He said that he would rather be a monk.

THE ABBOT Would you not go into the battle, Giolla na Naomh?

GIOLLA NA NAOMH I would. I would go as gilly to the King that I might serve him when all would forsake him.

THE ABBOT But it is to the saints that you are gilly, Giolla na Naomh, and not to the King.

GIOLLA NA NAOMH It were not much for the poor King to have one little gilly that would not forsake him when the battle would be broken on him and all forsaking him.

THE ABBOT This child is right. While we think of glory he thinks of service.

[*An outcry as of grief and dismay is heard from the battlefield.*]

FIRST MONK I fear me that the King is beaten!

THE ABBOT Go upon the rampart and tell us what you see.

FIRST MONK (*having gone upon the rampart*) A man comes towards us in flight.

SECOND MONK What manner of man is he?

FIRST MONK A bloodstained man, all spent, his feet staggering and stumbling under him.[11]

SECOND MONK Is he a man of the King's people?

FIRST MONK He is.

[*A Soldier comes upon the green, all spent.*]

THE SOLDIER The King is beaten!

THE MONKS My sorrow, my sorrow!

THE SOLDIER The King is beaten I say to you! O ye of the books and the bells, small was your help to us in the hard battle![12] The King is beaten!

THE ABBOT Where is the King?

THE SOLDIER He is flying.

THE ABBOT Give us the description of the battle.

THE SOLDIER I cannot speak. Let a drink be given to me.

THE ABBOT Let a drink be given to this man.

[*The little boy who is called Giolla na Naomh gives him a drink of water.*]

THE ABBOT Speak to us now and give us the description of the battle.

THE SOLDIER Each man of us was a fighter of ten. The King was a fighter of a hundred. But what availed us our valour? We were beaten and we fled. Hundreds lie sole to sole on the lea.

THE MONKS My sorrow, my sorrow!

[*A din grows.*]

SECOND MONK Who comes?

FIRST MONK The King!

[*Riders and gillies come upon the green pell-mell, the King in their midst. The King goes upon his knees before the Abbot, and throws his sword upon the ground.*]

THE KING Give me your curse, O man of God, and let me go to my death! I am beaten. My people are beaten. Ten battles have I fought against my foes and every battle of them has been broken on me. It is I who have brought God's wrath upon this land. Ask your God not to wreak his anger on my people henceforth, but to wreak it upon me. Have pity on my people, O man of God!

THE ABBOT God will have pity on them.

THE KING God has forsaken me.

THE ABBOT You have forsaken God.

THE KING God has forsaken my people.

THE ABBOT He has not, neither will He. He will save this nation if it choose a righteous King.

THE KING Give it then a righteous King. Give it one of your monks or one of these little lads to be its King. The battle on your protection, O man of God!

THE ABBOT Not so, but on the protection of the sword of a righteous King. Speak to me, my children, and tell me who among you is the most righteous?

FIRST MONK I have sinned.

SECOND MONK And I.

THIRD MONK Father, we have all sinned.

THE ABBOT I too have sinned. All that are men have sinned. How soon we exchange the wisdom of children for the folly of men! O wise children, busy with your toys while we are busy with our sins! I see clearly now. I shall find a sinless King among these little boys. Speak to me, boys, and tell me who is most innocent among you?

THE BOYS *(with one voice)* Giolla na Naomh.[13]

157

THE ABBOT The little lad that waits upon all! Ye are right. The last shall be first.[14] Giolla na Naomh, will you be King over this nation?

GIOLLA NA NAOMH I am too young, Father. I am too weak.

THE ABBOT Come hither to me, child.

[*The child goes over to him.*]

O fosterling that I have nourished, if I ask this thing of you, will you not do it?

GIOLLA NA NAOMH I will be obedient to you, Father.

THE ABBOT Will you turn your face into the battle?

GIOLLA NA NAOMH I will do the duty of a King.

THE ABBOT Little one, it may be that your death will come of it.

GIOLLA NA NAOMH Welcome is death if it be appointed to me.

THE ABBOT Did I not say that the young seek death? They are spendthrift of all that we hoard jealously; they pursue all that we shun. The terrible, beautiful voice has spoken to this child. O herald death, you shall be answered! I will not grudge you my fosterling.

THE KING Abbot, I will fight my own battles: no child shall die for me!

THE ABBOT You have given me your sword, and I give it to this child. God has spoken through the voice of His ancient herald, the terrible, beautiful voice that comes out of the heart of battles.

GIOLLA NA NAOMH Let me do this little thing, King. I will guard your banner well. I will bring you back your sword after the battle. I am only your little gilly, who watches while the tired King sleeps. I will sleep tonight while you shall watch.[15]

THE KING My pity, my three pities!

GIOLLA NA NAOMH We slept last night while you were marching through the dark country. Poor King, your marchings have been long. My march will be very short.

THE ABBOT Let this gentle asking prevail with you, King. I say to you that God has spoken.

THE KING I do not understand your God.

THE ABBOT Who understands Him? He demands not understanding, but obedience. This child is obedient, and because he is obedient, God will do mighty things through him. King, you must yield to this.

THE KING I yield, I yield! Woe is me that I did not fall in yonder onset!

THE ABBOT Let this child be stripped that the raiment of a King may be out about him. *(The child is stripped of his clothing.)* Let a royal vest be out next the skin of the child. *(A royal vest is put upon him.)* Let a royal tunic be put about him. *(A royal tunic is put about him above the vest, and sandals upon his feet.)* Let the royal mantle be put about him. *(The King takes off the royal mantle and it is put upon the child.)* Let a royal diadem be put upon his head. *(The King takes off the royal diadem and it is put upon the child's head.[16])* Let him be given the shield of the King. *(The shieldbearer holds up the shield.)* A blessing upon this shield! May it be firm against foes!

THE HEROES A blessing on this shield!

[The shield is put on the child's left arm.]

THE ABBOT Let him be given the spear of the King. *(The spearbearer comes forward and holds up the spear.)* A blessing on this spear! May it be sharp against foes!

THE HEROES A blessing on this spear!

THE ABBOT Let him be given the sword of the King. *(The King lifts his sword and girds it around the child's waist. Giolla na Naomh draws the sword and holds it in his right hand.)* A blessing on this sword! May it be hard to smite foes!

THE HEROES A blessing on this sword!

THE ABBOT I call this little lad King and put the battle under his protection in the name of God.

THE KING *(kneeling before the boy)* I do homage to thee, O King, and I put the battle under thy protection.

THE HEROES, MONKS, BOYS, etc. *(kneeling)* We do homage to thee, O King, and we put the battle under thy protection.

GIOLLA NA NAOMH I undertake to sustain the battle in the name of God.

THE ABBOT Let a steed be brought him.

[*A steed is brought.*]

Let the banner of the King be unfurled.

[*The banner is unfurled.*]

Turn thy face to battle, O King!

GIOLLA NA NAOMH *(kneeling)* Bless me, Father.

THE ABBOT A blessing on thee, little one.

THE HEROES etc. *(with one voice)* Take victory in battle and slaying, O King!

[*The little King mounts and, with the heroes and soldiers and gillies, rides to the battle. The Abbot, the King, the Monks, and the Boys watch them.*]

THE ABBOT King, I have given you the noblest jewel that was in my house. I loved yonder child.

THE KING Priest, I have never received from my tributary kings a kinglier gift.

FIRST MONK They have reached the place of battle.

THE ABBOT O strong God, make strong the hand of this child. Make firm his foot. Make keen his sword. Let the purity of his heart and the humbleness of his spirit be unto him a magnifying of courage and an exaltation of mind. Ye angels that fought the ancient battles, ye veterans of God, make a battle-pen about him and fight before him with flaming swords.

THE MONKS AND BOYS Amen, Amen.

THE ABBOT O God, save this nation by the sword of the sinless boy.

THE KING And O Christ that was crucified on the hill, bring the child safe from the perilous battle.

THE ABBOT King, King, freedom is not purchased but with a great price.

[*A trumpet speaks.*]

Let the description of the battle be given us.

[*The First Monk and the Second Monk go upon the rampart.*]

FIRST MONK The two hosts are face to face.

[*Another trumpet speaks.*]

SECOND MONK That is sweet! It is the trumpet of the King!

[*Shouts.*]

FIRST MONK The King's host raises shouts.

[*Other shouts.*]

SECOND MONK The enemy answers them.

FIRST MONK The hosts advance against each other.

SECOND MONK They fight.

FIRST MONK Our people are yielding.

THIRD MONK Say not so.

SECOND MONK My grief, they are yielding.

[*A trumpet speaks.*]

THIRD MONK Sweet again! It is timely spoken, O trumpet of the King!

FIRST MONK The King's banner is going into battle.

SECOND MONK I see the little King!

THIRD MONK Is he going into the battle?

FIRST MONK Yes.

THE MONKS AND BOYS *(with one voice)* Take victory in battle and slaying, O King!

SECOND MONK It is a good fight now.

FIRST MONK Two seas have met on the plain.

SECOND MONK Two raging seas!

FIRST MONK One sea rolls back.

SECOND MONK It is the enemy that retreats!

FIRST MONK The little King goes through them.

SECOND MONK He goes through them like a hawk through small birds.

FIRST MONK Yea, like a wolf through a flock of sheep on a plain.

SECOND MONK Like a torrent through a mountain gap.

FIRST MONK It is a road of rout before him.

SECOND MONK There are great uproars in the battle. It is a roaring path down which the King rides.

FIRST MONK O golden head above the slaughter! O shining terrible sword of the King!

SECOND MONK The enemy flies!

FIRST MONK They are beaten! They are beaten! It is a red road of rout! Raise shouts of exaltation!

SECOND MONK My grief!

FIRST MONK My grief! My grief!

THE ABBOT What is that?

FIRST MONK The little King is down!

THE ABBOT Has he the victory?

FIRST MONK Yes, but he himself is down. I do not see his golden head. I do not see his shining sword. My grief! they raise his body from the plain.[17]

THE ABBOT It's thanks to God!

[*Keening is heard.*]

Thou hast been answered, O terrible voice! Old herald, my foster child has answered.

THIRD MONK They bear hither a dead child.

THE KING He said that he would sleep tonight and that I should watch.

[*Heroes come upon the green bearing the body of Giolla na Naomh on a bier; there are women keening it. The bier is laid in the centre of the green.*]

163

THE KING He has brought me back my sword. He has guarded my banner well.

THE ABBOT *(lifting the sword from the bier)* Take the sword.

THE KING No, I will let him keep it. A King should sleep with a sword. This was a very valiant King.

[*He takes the sword from the Abbot and lays it again upon the bier. He kneels.*]

I do homage to thee, O dead King, O victorious child! I kiss thee, O white body, since it is thy purity that hath redeemed my people.

[*He kisses the forehead of Giolla na Naomh. They commence to keen again.*]

THE ABBOT Do not keen this child, for he hath purchased freedom for his people. Let shouts of exultation be raised and let a canticle be sung in praise of God.[18]

[*The body is borne into the monastery with a Te Deum.[19]*]

[The Scene Closes]

NOTES

1 As published in *An Macaomh*, Vol. II No.2, May 1913.

2 This is Pearse's own translation of his work.

3 Gillies: servants or attendants.

4 Trumpet: In the New Testament the trumpet is often eschatological or apocalyptic.

5 Host: An armed company or multitude of men; an army (OED).

6 Reminiscent of the formulaic language and alliteration used to describe battles and journeys in Gaelic hero-tales and classical literature.

7 'the venom of my sword upon you': Old Testament imagery, recalls Deuteronomy 32: 41: 'When I whet my flashing sword, and my hand takes hold on judgment; I will take vengeance on my adversaries, and will repay those who hate me.'

8 Eric: a blood-fine, ransom, retribution, restitution: from the Irish éiric.

9 None: One of the daily offices in the Western Church, forming the fifth of the canonical hours of prayer and originally appointed for the ninth hour of the day (OED).

10 Psalmody: the singing of psalms.

11 The image is that prophesised by the Abbot minutes earlier.

12 The reference to 'books and bells' is reminiscent of the imagery used in some of the Fenian or Ossianic lays, where Oisín's celebration of nature and freedom in the pagan world is contrasted with the regulated life of the Christian monks.

13 In what follows the image of the child-king suffering for the sins of others establishes Giolla na Naomh as a Christ-like figure bringing redemption to a troubled land.

14 Matthew 20: 16: 'So the last shall be first, and the first will be last.'

15 Giolla na Naomh here foretells his own death and thus reinforces the ideals of redemptive sacrifice that are central to the play.

16 Diadem: A crown; an ornamental cincture or covering for the head, worn as a symbol of honour, esp. of royal dignity (OED).

17 In the same edition of *An Macaomh* that *The King* was published in Pearse recounted his famous dream: 'I dreamt that I saw a pupil of mine, one of our boys at St. Enda's, standing alone upon a platform above a mighty sea of people; and I understood that he was about to die there for some august cause, Ireland's or another. He looked extraordinary, proud and joyous, lifting his head with a smile almost of amusement; I remember noticing his bare, white throat and the hair on his forehead stirred by the wind, just as I had often noticed them on the hurling-field. I felt an inexplicable exhilaration as I looked down on him ...' (*An Macaomh*, May 1913, pp.6–7).

18 Canticle: A song, properly a little song; a hymn (OED).

19 *Te Deum*: An ancient Latin hymn of praise in the form of a psalm, sung as a thanksgiving on special occasions, as after a victory or deliverance (OED).

1.11 Image of a young boy with a rifle which was published alongside the script of *Owen* in *Fianna* magazine, December 1915. Grianghraf de bhuachaill óg agus raidhfil aige. In iris *Fianna*, mí na Nollag 1915 a foilsíodh, i dteannta script *Owen*. (Image courtesy of Trinity College/Le caoinchead ó Choláiste na Tríonóide).

1.12 Photograph of some of the volunteers associated with St. Enda's pictured on Easter Sunday 1916. Back row, left to right: Éamonn Bulfin, Conor McGinley, Desmond Ryan, Fintan Murphy, Peter Slattery. Front row, left to right: Brian Joyce, Frank Burke, Eunan McGinley, Joseph Sweeney. Bulfin, Murphy, and the two McGinleys would later take part in the 1917 production of *The Singer*. Iarscoláirí agus múinteoirí ó Scoil Éanna an lá roimh Éirí Amach na Cásca: Éamonn Bulfin, Conor McGinley, Desmond Ryan, Fintan Murphy, Peter Slattery ar cúl, clé go deas. Brian Joyce, Frank Burke, Eunan McGinley, Joseph Sweeney chun tosaigh. Ghlac Bulfin, Murphy agus an bheirt Mhac Fhionnlaoich páirt i léiriú *The Singer* sa bhliain 1917. Image courtesy of Pearse Museum/Le caoinchead ó Mhúsaem na bPiarsach.

OWEN[1]

NOTE FROM PEARSE

I have translated into English for 'Nodlaig na bhFiann' a little dramatic episode which I wrote in Irish for my pupils of St. Enda's College and which they performed at Ceilidhe[2] in the Dublin Mansion House in the winter of 1913, and at a Ceilidhe in the Hall of the Colmcille Branch of the Gaelic League. Companies of the Fianna[3] may find the English version suitable for performance at some of their Ceilidhthe. At the St. Enda's performance we gave the play a western setting, the bigger boys wearing bawneens[4] and the smaller boys the long frocks worn by children in the Connacht Gaedhealtacht.[5] 'The Hawk of the Hill' was the name given to James Stephens, the Chief Organiser of the Irish Republican Brotherhood. Stephens had left Ireland in 1866, but his name would still be used as a watchword by his followers.

CHARACTERS

A School Master	Owen
Shawn	Other Boys
Darach	A Ballad Singer[6]
Patrick	Policemen

TIME
March 4th, 1867[7]

[*A country schoolhouse. There is a door at the back, with a window beside it; another window to the right. The boys' caps and satchels hang on pegs on the wall. The Master is seated at his desk, reading. A class of older boys is working on slates in the benches; some smaller boys are writing on copybooks.*]

THE MASTER *(raising his eyes from his book)* Has anyone finished yet? Well, Shawn?

SHAWN No, sir; not yet.

THE MASTER Hurry up now like good lads. When you've that one done I'll let you home; it is on the stroke of three. (Reads to himself.) "Whether in the attack or in the defence cover is all-important. Cover is of two kinds: cover from fire and cover from view. An ordinary hedge, a comparatively small embankment, a loose stone wall, a mere depression in the ground, will afford cover from view. For effective fire cover —"[8]

[*The voice of Ballad Singer singing "The Wearin o' the Green" is heard. The Master and the boys listen. The singer seems to be at a little distance at first. When he starts the second stanza, "I met with Napper Tandy", he has apparently come up to the school door, and he sings clearly and loudly.[9] As soon as the second stanza is finished a knock is heard at the door.*]

THE MASTER Open the door, Shawn.

[*Shawn rises and opens the door. A Ballad Singer with ballads in his hand comes into the schoolroom. Shawn returns to his bench.*]

THE BALLAD SINGER God save all here.

THE MASTER God and Mary save you.

THE BALLAD SINGER Would you buy a ballad from me, Master?

THE MASTER What ballads have you got?

THE BALLAD SINGER I've got "The Wearin o' the Green", and "Bold Robert Emmet".[10]

THE MASTER Give me "Bold Robert Emmet".[11]

THE BALLAD SINGER Here you are, my jewel. A grand song *(he hands a ballad to the Master, who gives him a penny)*. God spare you your health. *(Coming closer to the Master, and speaking in a low voice)*. Are you Malachy Hession, schoolmaster of this place?

THE MASTER I am.

THE BALLAD SINGER I've got a message for you.

THE MASTER Who is the message from?

THE BALLAD SINGER From them that you know.

THE MASTER Give me a sign.

THE BALLAD SINGER Did you ever hear tell of the Hawk o' the Hill?[12]

THE MASTER I did.

THE BALLAD SINGER I am one of his friends.

THE MASTER Who do you come from?

THE BALLAD SINGER I was in a house in Dublin. There came into it a short dark man by the name of Devoy.[13] He was from Kill, in the County Kildare. He met you once at the fair of Oughterard.

THE MASTER You may give me your message.

THE BALLAD SINGER *(slowly and emphatically)* This is the night.

THE MASTER Tonight?

THE BALLAD SINGER Tonight.

THE MASTER This is great news, man.

THE BALLAD SINGER Aye is it. There'll be ballad singers crying ballads of tonight's story when you and I are dead.

THE MASTER I'll go down the boreen with you, and we can talk going down.[14] The lads maybe would hear us if we talked here. *(To the boys)* – Work on, boys, till I come back.

[*The Master and the Ballad Singer go out. As soon as the door is closed Shawn springs to his feet and runs to the window.*]

SHAWN They're going down the boreen!

DARACH Are they?

SHAWN They're at the gate!

PATRICK Dads!

SHAWN They're going out on the road!

OWEN Arrah, ye divils, let's have some fun!

DARACH All right. Leap-frog!

[*They spring to their feet and play leap-frog round the room. At the height of the uproar Owen seizes the Master's cane and mounts the rostrum.*]

OWEN I'm to be the Master, lads! *(Striking the desk with the cane lads and mimicking the Master's voice.)* Silence, silence! *(The boys sit down and pretend to work at the sum.)* Has anyone finished yet?

THE BOYS *(shouting discordantly)* No, sir! Yes, sir! I, sir! You, sir!

OWEN *(striking the desk)* Hold your tongues!

SHAWN Hold your tongue yourself.

OWEN Stand up, Shawn Johnny! (Shawn stands up) Hold out your hand!

[*Owen attempts to cane him but Shawn withdraws his hand at each stroke. Owen jumps from the rostrum and Shawn turns tail. Owen is chasing Shawn when the door opens and the Master enters. The Boys bolt back to their places, but Owen is caught in the middle of the floor.*]

THE MASTER What is all this about? What are you doing there?

OWEN Nothing, sir.

THE MASTER Give me that cane *(Owen gives it to him and the Master looks at him threateningly.)* You will go over there to the corner, and you will stay in after the other boys. *(Owen goes over to the corner and sits down on a bench, where he amuses himself by drawing caricatures of the Master on a slate.)* Well, boys, have you finished that sum?

SEVERAL OF THE BOYS Yes, sir!

THE MASTER What answer did you get, Patrick?

PATRICK Six pounds seventeen shillings and threepence.

SHAWN No, there's a halfpenny in it.

PATRICK Oh, aye! Six pounds seventeen shillings and threepence halfpenny.

THE MASTER The boys that got that answer will hold up their hands (several hold up their hands). Good! I'll let you off now.

[*The Boys, with the exception of Owen, take their books and caps, and go out, each saying "Good Evening, sir," as he leaves.*]

THE MASTER Good evening, boys. *(When the last has gone out the Master stands in the doorway looking after them.)* No, but goodbye! Who'll be your next master, I don't know. *(He seem to muse for a few seconds, then, springing into activity, he closes the door, tidies up some books etc., and finally takes the poker from the fireplace and, using it as a lever, raises a board in the floor; going down on one knee he takes a rifle from its hiding place under the boards.)* So here you are. Well, you'll do from some good man tonight, with the help of God *(he lays it down beside him).* The ammunition *(he takes out a bag of ammunition).* The sword *(he takes out a sword).* What's the best way to bring these with me now? Aye, I'll twist my coat around them. It's … *(his eyes travel to the place where his greatcoat hangs on the wall, and he sees Owen, who has been watching all his movements with wondering wide-open eyes).* Lord God, I forgot the boy! He has seen – Come here to me, Owen. *(Owen comes over to him.)* Owen, do you know what this is?

OWEN Isn't it a gun?

THE MASTER Yes.

OWEN Is it a soldier's gun?

THE MASTER It is; a rifle, they call it.

OWEN Did it ever kill anybody?

THE MASTER It didn't, – not yet.

OWEN Is it heavy?

THE MASTER Very heavy; you'd hardly be able to carry it.

OWEN Where do you put the bullet?

THE MASTER In there. Look (he shows how to insert the cartridge.) And then you press this little thing, like that.

OWEN Are you going to kill anyone with it?

THE MASTER *(laughing)* No. Or, I mean – *(he lays aside the rifle and, sitting down on a chair, draws Owen towards him).* Owen, I am your Master, and I must not tell you an untruth. Whisper. I am going to trust you. I am going to let you share a great secret. There are some of us here, there are men in every place in Ireland, that are going to fight tonight. To fight for Ireland. Poor Ireland, Owen that has been down for so long.

OWEN Is it the English ye are going out to fight?

THE MASTER Yes, the English.

OWEN Can I go with ye?

THE MASTER No. You are too young, Owen. You couldn't carry a gun.

OWEN I could carry bullets for ye. I could be your drummer to beat the charge and give ye heart, when ye'd be charging at them.

THE MASTER No, Owen, I can't take you with us. I ask you one thing. If the police hear that I have this gun or these bullets or this sword, they will take me tonight. If they knew that I've had them here for a year I'd have been taken long ago. Owen, I'm the captain of the boys that'll be rising in this countryside.

If the police catch me before the sun sets tonight there'll be no one to lead the lads when they come together. They'll be waiting for their captain to lead them. You must promise me now that you won't say a word about this gun or about the bullets or about the sword to anyone. Do you promise me that?

OWEN I do.

THE MASTER Not a word to anyone?

OWEN I promise.

THE MASTER Not to your own father and mother? Or to any of the lads?

OWEN I won't say a word to anyone.

THE MASTER That's a good boy. Give me your hand. *(They shake hands.)* Run off home now. Good-bye.

OWEN Good-bye, sir. *(He takes his books and cap and opens the door. As he goes out he starts and turns back.)* Sir, the police are coming up the boreen.

THE MASTER The police!

OWEN *(pointing)* Look!

THE MASTER *(looking)* God help me now! The Ballad Singer must have been seen coming to the school. Perhaps he's taken. What's the best thing to do? I must get out through this window. If I get to the crossroads before them I'm safe. This will be too heavy to bring with me *(he hastily conceals the rifle, ammunition, and sword, and replaces the board; he takes his hat and coat)*. Whip off home, Owen. *(He comes over to him and kisses on the forehead.)* May God protect you! *(He goes out through the window which is to the right.)*

OWEN I must keep them out until he's at the crossroad.

[*He dashes to the door, shuts it, and piles some of the benches against it. He barricades the two windows with blackboards. Then he listens.*]

173

A VOICE *(without)* Halt!

[*The clicks of heels and of rifles is heard.*]

OWEN *(dashing to the window through which the Master has escaped, and cautiously looking out, half-raising the blackboard)* He's not past the fence yet. If they catch him now, he's done.

[*A knocking at the door.*]

THE VOICE Open! Open! Open this door in the Queen's name!

OWEN If I fire a bullet at them they'll think the Master is here still, and they won't go after him.

[*He seizes the poker, prises up the board, takes out the rifle, and loads it, while the knocks and shouts redouble.*]

THE VOICE Open! Open! *(After a pause)* Break in the door, men.

[*The smashing of wood is heard. Owen raises the rifle, and takes aim. The door is broken in.*]

OWEN Now! *(He fires)*

THE VOICE A volley. Ready, aim, fire!

[*A volley is fired into the house and Owen falls forward on his face. When the smoke clears away a number of policemen, armed with rifles, push their way in. One kneels down beside Owen.*

THE POLICEMAN *(who is kneeling)* It's only a little lad.

ANOTHER Is he dead?

THE POLICEMAN He is.

[*They take off their helmets and the curtain descends.*]

NOTES

1 As found in *Fianna*, December 1915 (TCD, Early Printed Books, IN 20.90&91 no.22).

2 Ceilidhe: event usually involving song and dance.

3 Fianna Éireann: nationalist youth organisation.

4 Bawneens: waistcoat or jacket.

5 Gaedhealtacht: Irish-speaking district.

6 Pearse acknowledged the influence of popular political ballads on his own identity and Irish nationalism in general in his auto-biographical fragment. He recalled, for example, his Aunt Margaret's singing of political ballads and songs: she 'sang in her old crooning voice old ballads and snatches of songs in Irish and in English.' 'Aunt Margaret spoke of Wolfe Tone and of Robert Emmet as a woman might speak of the young men – the strong and splendid young men – she had known in her girlhood.' (*Autobiographical Fragment*, see Mary Brigid Pearse, *The Home-Life of Pádraig Pearse*, 1934). For a discussion of Pearse's interest in nationalist ballads see Róisín Ní Ghairbhí 'A People that did not Exist: Reflections on Some Sources and Contexts for Patrick Pearse's Militant Nationalism' in Ruán O Donnell, ed., *The Impact of the 1916 Rising: Among the Nations* (Irish Academic Press, 2008) pp.165–86, esp. 167–70.

7 1867: year of the Fenian Rising. Pearse heard a ballad singer sing songs of Emmet and Tone and speak of local Fenians while staying with his grandfather Patrick Brady (See 'From a Hermitage', pp.204–5).

8 In this short play Pearse explicitly links education with preparation for military action.

9 Napper Tandy: James Napper Tandy (1740–1803), a leader of the 1798 United Irishmen rebellion.

10 Popular ballads sung in support of Irish nationalist cause.

11 Robert Emmet: leader of a failed rebellion in 1803; one of the pantheon of nationalist leaders admired by Pearse.

12 As Pearse explains in his brief introduction this is a reference to James Stephens (1825–1901), a key leader of the Fenian movement. Pearse also wrote an adventure story for boys entitled 'The Wandering Hawk'.

13 Devoy: John Devoy (1842–1928), another significant Fenian leader.

14 Boreen: from the Irish *bóithrín*, meaning a small road or laneway.

THE IRISH THEATRE

HARDWICKE STREET

PLAY-BILL

THURSDAY, FRIDAY, AND SATURDAY, MAY
20TH, 21ST, AND 22ND, 1915. THREE NIGHTS AT
8.15 P.M., AND SATURDAY MATINEE AT 2.30 P.M.

THE STUDENTS OF ST. ENDA'S COLLEGE WILL PERFORM

IOSAGAN

A Miracle Play

BY P. H. PEARSE

Maitias, an Old Man	-	FRANK CONNOLLY
Darach		JOSEPH BUCKLEY
Padraic		BERNARD SWEENEY
Coilin		BRIAN MacGINLEY
Briccan	Boys	EDWARD FINUCANE
Eoghan		DONAL SWEENEY
Cuimin		OWEN CRONIN
Iosagan	-	DIARMAID MacGINLEY
A Priest	-	FRANK BURKE

Place, the seashore near a village in Iar-Connacht.

The lowering of the curtain for half-a-minute towards the end of the play represents the lapse of eight hours.

The name *Iosagan* is a loving diminutive of *Iosa* and may be translated *Jesukin*. "In bringing the Child Jesus into the midst of a group of boys disputing about their games, or to the knee of an old man who sings nursery rhymes to children, I am imagining nothing improbable, nothing outside the bounds of the everyday experience of innocent little children and reverent-minded old men and women. I know a priest who believes that he was summoned to the deathbed of a parishioner by our Lord in person."

The play was originally produced at St. Enda's College in February, 1910.

THE MASTER

A Miracle Play

BY P. H. PEARSE

(Translated by the Author from his Original Irish)

Art		EUNAN MacGINLEY
Breasal		JOSEPH SWEENEY
Maine	Pupils of Ciaran	DESMOND MURPHY
Ronan		AUGUSTINE GEARY
Ceallach		DAVID SEARS
Ciaran, a Teacher	-	WILLIAM PEARSE
Iollann Beag, a little Pupil of Ciaran's	-	OWEN CLARKE
A King's Messenger	-	DESMOND RYAN
Daire, a King	-	EAMONN BULFIN
Michael	-	JOHN KILGALLON

Place, a cloister in a wood.

The play is now produced for the first time.

The persons in both plays are named in the order of their entry.

The airs sung are by Thomas MacDonnell.

During the interval Mr. Pearse will deliver a short address on the Irish Style of Dramatic Speaking. The address will be illustrated by the performance of the only surviving fragment of an Irish drama prior to the language revival. The fragment was taken down in Co. Kerry in 1898, and is part of a play that was enacted among the people up to sixty or seventy years ago. The subject is the hero Dunlaing and his Fairy Lover, and the action takes place just before the Battle of Clontarf.

Dunlaing Og - - MICHAEL O'SULLIVAN
An Leannan Sidhe - MARY BULFIN

1.13 Programme for the production of *The Master* and *Íosagán* in the Irish Theatre, May 1915. Clár *The Master* agus *Íosagán* don léiriú san Irish Theatre, Bealtaine 1915. (Le caoinchead ó Mhúsaem na bPiarsach/Image courtesy of Pearse Museum).

THE MASTER[1]

*First performed 20th May 1915 at the Irish Theatre,
Hardwicke Street.*

CHARACTERS

Ciarán, *the Master*[2]   Ronán
Pupils[3]:   Ceallach
Iollann Beag[4]   Daire, *the King*
Art   Messenger
Breasal   The Archangel Michael[5]
Maine

[*A little cloister in a woodland. The subdued sunlight of a forest place comes through the arches. On the left, one arch gives a longer vista where the forest opens and the sun shines upon a fair hill. In the centre of the cloister two or three steps lead to an inner place, as it were a little chapel or cell.*

Art, Breasal, and Maine are busy with a game of jackstones about the steps. They play silently. Ronán enters from the left.]

RONÁN Where is the Master?

ART He has not left his cell yet.

RONÁN He is late. Who is with him, Art?

ART I was with him till a while ago. When he had finished his thanksgiving he told me he had one other little prayer to say which he could not leave over. He said it was for a soul that was in danger. I left him on his knees and came out into the sunshine.

177

MAINE Aye, you knew that Breasal and I were here with the jackstones.

BREASAL I served his Mass yesterday, and he stayed praying so long after it that I fell asleep.[6] I did not stir till he laid his hand upon my shoulder. Then I started up and said I, "Is that you, little mother?" He laughed and said he, "No, Breasal, it's no one so good as your mother."

RONÁN He is merry and gentle this while back, although he prays and fasts longer than he used to. Little Iollann says he tells him the merriest stories.

BREASAL He is fond of little Iollann.

MAINE Aye; when Iollann is late, or when he is inattentive, the Master pretends not to notice it.

BREASAL Well, Iollann is only a little lad.

MAINE He is more like a little maid, with his fair cheek that reddens when the Master speaks to him.

ART Faith, you wouldn't call him a little maid when you'd see him strip to swim a river.

RONÁN Or when you'd see him spring up to meet the ball in a hurley match.

MAINE He has, certainly, many accomplishments.

BREASAL He has a high, manly heart.

MAINE He has a beautiful white body, and, therefore, you all love him; aye, the Master and all. We have no woman here and so we make love to our little Iollann.[7]

RONÁN (laughing) Why, I thrashed him ere-yesterday for putting magories[8] down my neck!

MAINE Men sometimes thrash their women, Ronán. It is one of the ways of loving.

ART Maine, you have been listening to some satirist making satires. There was once a Maine that was called Maine Honey-mouth. You will be called Maine Bitter-Tongue.[9]

MAINE Well, I've won this game of jackstones. Will you play another?

CEALLACH *(enters hastily)* Lads, do you know what I have seen?

ART What is it, Ceallach?

CEALLACH A host of horsemen riding through the dark of the wood. A grim host, with spears.

MAINE The King goes hunting.

CEALLACH My grief for the noble deer that the King hunts!

BREASAL What deer is that?

CEALLACH Our Master, Ciarán.

RONÁN I heard one of the captains say that the cell was to be surrounded.

ART But why does the King come against Ciarán?

CEALLACH It is the Druids that have incited him. They say that Ciarán is over-turning the ancient law of the people.

MAINE The King has ordered him to leave the country.

BREASAL Aye, there was a King's Messenger here the other day who spoke long to the Master.

ART It is since then that the Master has been praying so long every day.

RONÁN Is he afraid that the King will kill him?

ART No, it is for a soul that is in danger that he prays. Is it the King's soul that is in danger?

MAINE Hush, the Master is coming.

CIARÁN *(comes out from the inner place; the pupils rise)* Are all here?

BREASAL Iollann Beag has not come yet.

CIARÁN Not yet?

CEALLACH Master, the King's horsemen are in the wood.

CIARÁN I hope no evil has chanced to little Iollann.

MAINE What evil could chance to him?

CEALLACH Master, the King is seeking you in the wood.

CIARÁN Does he not know where my cell is?

BREASAL The King has been stirred up against you, Master, rise and fly before the horsemen surround the cell.

CIARÁN No, if the King seeks me he will find me here … I wish little Iollann were come. *(The voice of Iollann Beag is heard singing. All listen.)* That is his voice.

ART He always comes singing.

MAINE Aye, he sings profane songs in the very church porch.

RONÁN Which is as bad as if one were to play with jackstones on the church stones.

CIARÁN I am glad little Iollann has come safe.

[*Iollann Beag comes into the cloister singing.*]

IOLLANN BEAG *(sings)*
We watch the wee ladybird fly far away,
With an óró and an iero and an úmbó éró.[10]

ART Hush, Iollann. You are in God's place.

IOLLANN BEAG Does God not like music? Why then did he make the finches and the chafers?

MAINE Your song is profane.

IOLLANN BEAG I didn't know.

CIARÁN Nay, Maine, no song is profane unless there be profanity in the heart. But why do you come so late, Iollann Beag?

IOLLANN BEAG There was a high oak tree that I had never climbed. I went up to its top, and swung myself to the top of the next tree. I saw the tops of all the trees like the green waves of the sea.

CIARÁN Little truant!

IOLLANN BEAG I am sorry, Master.

CIARÁN Nay, I am not vext with you.[11] But you must not climb tall trees again at lesson time. We have been waiting for you. Let us begin our lesson, lads. *(He sits down.)*

CEALLACH Dear Master, I ask you to fly from this place ere the King's horsemen close you in.

CIARÁN My boy, you must not tempt me. He is a sorry champion who forsakes his place of battle. This is my place of battle. You would not have me do a coward thing?

ART But the King has many horsemen. It is not cowardly for one to fly before a host.

CIARÁN Has not the high God captains and legions? What are the King's horsemen to the heavenly riders?

CEALLACH O my dear Master! –

RONÁN Let be, Ceallach. You cannot move him.

CIARÁN Of what were we to speak today? (*They have sat down around him.*)

ART You said you would speak of friendship and kindly fellowship.

CIARÁN Aye, I would speak of friendship and kindly fellowship. Is it not a sad thing that every good fellowship is broken up? No league that is made among men has more than its while, its little, little while. Even that little league of twelve in Galilee was broken full soon.[12] The shepherd was struck and the sheep of the flock scattered. The hardest thing our dear Lord had to bear was the scattering of His friends.

IOLLANN BEAG Were none faithful to Him?

CIARÁN One man only and a few women.

IOLLANN BEAG Who was the man?

CEALLACH I know! It was John, the disciple that He loved.

CIARÁN Aye, John of the Bosom they call him, for he was Iosa's[13] bosom friend. Can you tell me the names of any others of His friends?

ART There was James, his brother.

RONÁN There was Lazarus, for whom He wept.

BREASAL There was Mary, the poor woman that loved Him.

MAINE There was her sister Martha, who busied herself to make him comfortable and the other Mary.

182

CEALLACH Mary and Martha; but that other Mary is only a name.

CIARÁN Nay, she was the mother of the sons of Zebedee. She stands for all lowly, hidden women, all the nameless women of the world who are just the mothers of their children. And so we name her one of the three great Marys, with poor Mary that sinned, and with Mary of the Sorrows, the greatest of the Marys. What other friend can you tell me of?

IOLLANN BEAG There was John the Baptist, His little playmate.

CIARÁN That is well said. Those two Johns were good comrades to Iosa.

RONÁN There was Thomas.

CIARÁN Poor, doubting Thomas. I am glad you did not leave him out.

MAINE There was Judas who betrayed Him.

ART There was Peter who –

IOLLANN BEAG Aye, good Peter of the Sword!

CIARÁN Nay, Iollann, it is Paul that carries a sword.

IOLLANN BEAG Peter should have a sword, too. I will not have him cheated of his sword! It was a good blow he struck!

BREASAL Yet the Lord rebuked him for it.

IOLLANN BEAG The Lord did wrong to rebuke him. He was always down on Peter.

CIARÁN Peter was fiery, and the Lord was very gentle.

IOLLANN BEAG But when He wanted a rock to build His church on He had to go to Peter. No John of the Bosom then,

PATRICK PEARSE: COLLECTED PLAYS

but the old swordsman. Paul must yield his sword to Peter. I do not like that Paul.

CIARÁN Paul said many hard things and many dark things. When you understand him, Iollann, you will like him.

MAINE Let him not arrogate a sword merely because his head was cut off, and Iollann will tolerate him.

CIARÁN Who has brought me a poem today? You were to bring me poems of Christ's friends.

BREASAL I have made a Song for Mary Magdalene. Shall I say it to you?

CIARÁN Do, Breasal.

BREASAL *(chants)*:
O woman of the gleaming hair
(Wild hair that won men's gaze to thee),
Weary thou turnest from the common stare,
For the *shuiler*[14] Christ is calling thee.

O woman, of the snowy side,
Many a lover hath lain with thee,
Yet left thee sad at the morning tide;
But thy lover Christ shall comfort thee.

O woman with the wild thing's heart,
Old sin hath set a snare for thee;
In the forest ways forspent thou art,
But the hunter Christ shall pity thee.

O woman spendthrift of thyself,
Spendthrift of all the love in thee,
Sold unto sin for little pelf[15],
The captain Christ shall ransom thee.

O woman that no lover's kiss
(Tho' many a kiss was given thee)
Could slake thy love, is it not for this
The hero Christ shall die for thee?

CIARÁN That is a good song, Breasal. What you have said is true, that love is a very great thing. I do not think faith will be denied to him that loves. ... Iollann was to make me a song today, too.

IOLLANN BEAG I have made only a little rann.[16] I couldn't think of rhymes for a big song.

CIARÁN What do you call your rann?

IOLLANN BEAG It is the Rann of the Little Playmate. It is a rann that John the Baptist made when he was on the way to Iosa's house one day.

CIARÁN Sing it to us, Iollann.

IOLLANN BEAG *(sings)*
Young Iosa plays with me every day
(With an óró and an iero)
Tig and Pookeen and Hide-in-the-Hay[17]
(With an óró and an iero)

We race in the river with otters gray,
We climb the tall trees where red squirrels play,
We watch the wee lady-bird far away,
(With an óró and an iero and an imbó éro).

[*A knocking is heard.*]

CIARÁN Run and open the postern[18], Iollann.

CEALLACH Master, this may be the King's people.

CIARÁN If it be, Iollann will let them in. *(Iollann Beag goes to the door.)*

CEALLACH Why have good men such pride?

[*A King's Messenger appears upon the threshold. Iollann Beag holds the curtain of the door while the Messenger speaks.*]

MESSENGER Who in this house is Ciarán?

CIARÁN I am Ciarán.

MESSENGER I bring you greeting from the King.

CIARÁN Take back to him my greeting.

MESSENGER The King has come to make the hunting of this wood.

CIARÁN It is the King's privilege to hunt the woods of the cantred.[19]

MESSENGER Not far from here is a green glade of the forest in which the King with his nobles and good men, his gillies[20] and his runners, has sat down to meat.

CIARÁN May it be a merry sitting for them.

MESSENGER It has seemed to the King an unroyal thing to taste of the cheer of this greenwood while he is at enmity with you; for he has remembered the old saying that friendship is more welcome at meat than ale or music. Therefore, he has sent me to say to you that he has put all enmity out of his heart, and that in token thereof he invites you to share his forest feast, such as it is, you and your pupils.

CIARÁN The King is kind. I would like well to come to him, but my rule forbids me to leave this house.

MESSENGER The King will take badly any refusal. It is not usual to refuse a King's invitation.

CIARÁN When I came to this place, after journeying many long roads of land and sea, I said to myself: "I will abide here henceforth, this shall be the sod of my death". And I made a vow to live in this little cloister alone, or with a few pupils, I who had been restless and a wanderer, and a seeker after difficult things; the King will not grudge me the loneliness of my cloister?

MESSENGER I will say all this to the King. These lads will come with me?

CIARÁN Will ye go to the King's feast, lads?

BREASAL May we go, Master?

CIARÁN I will not gainsay you.

MAINE It will be a great thing to sit at the King's table.

CEALLACH Master, it may turn aside the King's displeasure for your not going if we go in your name. We may, perchance, bring the King here, and peace will be bound between you.

CIARÁN May God be near you in the places to which you go.

CEALLACH I am loath to leave you alone, Master.

CIARÁN Little Iollann will stay with me. Will you not, little Iollann?

[*Iollann Beag looks yearningly towards the Messenger and the others as if he would fain go; then he turns to Ciarán.*]

IOLLANN BEAG I will.

CIARÁN *(caressing him)* That is my good little lad.

ART We will bring you back some of the King's mead[21], Iollann.

IOLLANN BEAG Bring me some of his apples and his hazel-nuts.

RONÁN We will, and, maybe, a roast capon, or a piece of venison.

[*They go out laughing. Ceallach turns back in the door.*]

CEALLACH Good-bye, Master.

CIARÁN May you go safe, lad. *(To Iollann)* You are my whole school now, Iollann.

IOLLANN BEAG *(sitting down at his knee)* Do you think the King will come here?

CIARÁN Yes, I think he will come.

IOLLANN BEAG I would like to see him. Is he a great, tall man?

CIARÁN I have not seen him for a long time; not since he and I were lads.

IOLLANN BEAG Were you friends?

CIARÁN We were fostered together.

IOLLANN BEAG Is he a wicked King?

CIARÁN No; he has ruled this country well. His people love him. They have gone into many perilous places with him, and he has never failed them.

IOLLANN BEAG Why then does he hate you? Why do Ceallach and the others fear that he may do you harm?

CIARÁN For twenty years Daire and I have stood over against each other. When we were at school we were rivals for the first place. I was first in all manly games; Daire was first in learning. Everyone said "Ciarán will be a great warrior and Daire will be a great poet or great teacher." And yet it has not been so. I was nearly as good as he in learning, and he was nearly as good as me in manly feats. I said that I would be his master in all things and he said he would be my master. And we strove one against the other.

IOLLANN BEAG Why did you want to be his master?

CIARÁN I do not know. I thought that I should be happy if I were first and Daire only second. But Daire was always first. I sought out difficult things to do that I might become a better man than he: I went into far countries and won renown among strange peoples, but very little wealth and no happiness; I sailed into seas that no man before me had sailed into, and saw islands that only God and the angels had seen before me; I learned outland[22] tongues and read the books of many peoples and their old lore; and when I came back to my own country I found that Daire was its king, and that all men loved him. Me they had forgotten.

IOLLANN BEAG Were you sad when you came home and found that you were forgotten?

CIARÁN No, I was glad. I said, "This is a hard thing that I have found to do, to live lonely and unbeloved among my own kin. Daire has not done anything as hard as this." In one of the cities that I had sailed to I had heard of the true, illustrious God, and of men who had gone out from warm and pleasant houses, and from the kindly faces of neighbours to live in desert places, where God walked alone and terrible; and I said that I would do that hard thing, though I would fain have stayed in my father's house. And so I came into this wilderness, where I have lived for seven years. For a few years I was alone; then pupils began to come to me. By-and-bye the druids gave out word that I was teaching new things and breaking established custom; and the King has forbade my teaching, and I have not desisted, and so he and I stand opposed as of old.

IOLLANN BEAG You will win this time, little Master.

CIARÁN I think so; I hope so, dear. (Aside.) I would I could say "I know so." This seems to me the hardest thing I have tried to do. Can a soldier fight for a cause of which he is not sure? Can a teacher die for a thing he does not believe? … Forgive me, Lord! It is my weakness that cries out. I believe, I believe; help my unbelief. (To Iollann Beag.) Why do you think I shall win this time, Iollann – I who have always lost?

IOLLANN BEAG Because God's great angels will fight for you. Will they not?

CIARÁN Yes, I think they will. All that old chivalry stands harnessed in Heaven.

IOLLANN BEAG Will they not come if you call them?

CIARÁN Yes, they will come. *(Aside.)* Is it a true thing I tell this child or do I lie to him? Will they come at my call? Will they come at my call? My spirit reaches out and finds Heaven empty. The great halls stand horseless and riderless. I have called to you, O riders, and I have not heard the thunder of your coming. The multitudinous, many-voiced sea and the green, quiet earth have each its children, but where are the sons of Heaven? Where in all this temple of the world, this dim and wondrous temple, does its God lurk?

IOLLANN BEAG And would they come if I were to call them – old Peter, and the Baptist John, and Michael and his riders?

CIARÁN We are taught that if one calls them with faith they will come.

IOLLANN BEAG Could I see them and speak to them?

CIARÁN If it were necessary for any dear purpose of God's, as to save a soul that were in peril, we are taught that they would come in bodily presence, and that one could see them and speak to them.

IOLLANN BEAG If the soul of any dear friend of mine be ever in peril I will call upon them. I will say, "Baptist John, Baptist John, attend him. Good Peter of the Sword, strike valiantly. Young Michael, stand near with all the heroes of Heaven!"

CIARÁN *(aside)* If the soul of any dear friend of his were in peril! The peril is near! The peril is near!

[*A knock at the postern; Iollann Beag looks towards Ciarán.*]

CIARÁN Run, Iollann, and see who knocks. *(Iollann Beag goes out.)* I have looked back over the journey of my life as a man at evening might look back from a hill on the roads he had travelled since morning. I have seen with a great clearness as if I had left this green, dim wood and climbed to the top of that far hill I have seen for seven years now, yet never climbed. And I see that all my wayfaring has been in vain. A man may not escape from that which is in himself. A man shall not find his quest unless he kill the dearest thing he has. I thought that I was sacrificing everything, but I have not sacrificed the old pride of my heart. I chose self-abnegation, not out of humility, but out of pride: and God, that terrible hidden God, has punished me by withholding from me His most precious gift of faith. Faith comes to the humble only ... Nay, Lord, I believe: this is but a temptation. Thou, too, wast tempted. Thou, too, wast forsaken. O valiant Christ, give me Thy strength! My need is great. *(Iollann Beag returns.)*

IOLLANN BEAG There is a warrior at the door, Master, that asks a shelter. He says he has lost his way in the wood.

CIARÁN Bid him to come in Iollann. *(Iollann Beag goes to the door again.)* I, too, have lost my way. I am like one that has trodden intricate forest paths that have crossed and recrossed and never led him to any homestead; or like a mariner that has voyaged on a shoreless sea yearning for a glimpse of green earth, yet never descrying it. If I could find some little place to rest, if I could but lie still at last after so much wayfaring, after such clamour of loud-voiced winds, methinks that would be to find God; for is not God quiet, is not God peace? But always I go on with a cry as of baying winds or of vociferous hounds about me. ... They say the King hunts me today: but the King is not so terrible a hunter as the desires and doubts of a man's heart. The King I can meet unafraid, but who is not afraid of himself? *(Daire enters, wrapped in a long mantle, and stands a little within the threshold: Iollann Beag behind him. Ciarán looks fixedly at him; then speaks.)* You have hunted well today, O Daire!

DAIRE I am famed as a hunter.

CIARÁN When I was a young man I said, "I will strive with the great untamed elements, with the ancient, illimitable sea and the anarchic winds;" you, in the manner of Kings, have warred with timid, furtive creatures, and it has taught you only cruelty and craft.

DAIRE What has your warfare taught you? I do not find you changed, Ciarán. Your old pride but speaks a new language. ... I am, as you remind me, only a King; but I have been a good King. Have you been a good teacher?

CIARÁN My pupils must answer.

DAIRE Where are your pupils?

CIARÁN True; they are not here.

DAIRE They are at an ale-feast in my tent. ... *(Coming nearer to Ciarán.)* I have not come to taunt you, Ciarán. Nor should you taunt me. You seem to have spent your life pursuing shadows that fled before you; yea, pursuing ghosts over wide spaces and through the devious places of the world: and I pity you for the noble manhood you have wasted. I seem to you to have spent my life busy with the little, vulgar tasks and the little, vulgar pleasures of a King: and you pity me because I have not adventured, because I have not been tried, because I have not suffered as you have. It should be sufficient triumph for each of us that each pities the other.

CIARÁN You speak gently, Daire; and you speak wisely. You were always wise. And yet, methinks, you are wrong. There is a deeper antagonism between you and me than you are aware of. It is not merely that the little things about you, the little, foolish, mean, discordant things of a man's life, have satisfied you, and that I have been discontent, seeking things remote and holy and perilous –

DAIRE Ghosts, ghosts!

CIARÁN Nay, they alone are real; or, rather, it alone is real. For though its name be many, its substance is one. One man may call it happiness, another will call it beauty, a third will call it holiness, a fourth will call it rest. I have sought it under all its names.

DAIRE What is it that thou have sought?

CIARÁN I have sought truth.

DAIRE And have you found truth? *(Ciarán bows his head in dejection.)* Ciarán, was it worth your while to give up all goodly life to follow that mocking phantom? I do not say that a man should not renounce ease. I have loved ease. But I have loved power, and victory, and life, and men, and women, and the gracious sun. He who renounces these things to follow a phantom across a world has given his all for nothing.

CIARÁN Is not the mere quest often worthwhile, even if the thing quested be never found?

DAIRE And so you have not found your quest?

CIARÁN You lay subtle traps for me in your speeches, Daire. It was your way at school when we disputed.

DAIRE Kings must be subtle. It is by craft we rule. ... Ciarán, for the shadow you have pursued I offer you a substance; in place of vain journeying I invite you to rest ... If you make your peace with me you shall be the second man in my kingdom.

CIARÁN *(in scorn and wrath)* The second man!

DAIRE There speaks your old self, Ciarán. I did not mean to wound you. I am the King, chosen by the people to rule and lead. I could not, even if I would, place you above me; but I will place you at my right hand.

CIARÁN You would bribe me with this petty honour?

DAIRE No. I would gain you for the service of your people. What other service should a man take upon him?

CIARÁN I told you that you did not understand the difference between you and me. May one not serve the people by bearing testimony in their midst to a true thing even as by feeding them with bread?

DAIRE Again you prate of truth.[23] Are you fond enough to think that what has not imposed even upon your pupils will impose upon me?

CIARÁN My pupils believe. You must not wrong them, Daire.

DAIRE Are you sure of them?

CIARÁN Yes, I am sure. *(Aside.)* Yet sometimes I thought that that gibing Maine did not believe. It may be –

DAIRE Where are your pupils? Why are they not here to stand by you in your bitter need?

CIARÁN You enticed them from me by guile.

DAIRE I invited them; they came. You could not keep them, Ciarán. Think you my young men would have left me, in similar case? Their bodies would have been my bulwark against a host.

CIARÁN You hint unspeakable things.

DAIRE I do but remind you that you have today no disciples; *(smiling)* except, perhaps, this little lad. Come, I will win him from you with an apple.

CIARÁN You shall not tempt him!

DAIRE *(laughing)* Ciarán, you stand confessed: you have no faith in your disciples; methinks you have no faith in your religion.

CIARÁN You are cruel, Daire. You were not so cruel when we were lads.

DAIRE You have come into my country preaching to my people new things, incredible things, things you dare not believe yourself. I will not have this lie preached to men. If your religion be true, you must give me a sign of its truth.

CIARÁN It is true, it is true!

DAIRE Give me a sign. Nay, show me that you yourself believe. Call upon your God to reveal Himself. I do not trust these skulking gods.

CIARÁN Who am I to ask that great Mystery to unveil Its face? Who are you that a miracle should be wrought for you?

DAIRE This is not an answer. So priests ever defend their mysteries. I will not be put off as one would put off a child that asks questions. Lo, here I bare my sword against God; lo, here I lift up my shield. Let one of his great captains come down to answer the challenge!

CIARÁN This the bragging of a fool.

DAIRE Nor does that answer me. Ciarán, you are in my power. My young men surround this house. Yours are at an ale-feast.

CIARÁN O wise and far-seeing King! You have planned all well.

DAIRE There is a watcher at every door of your house. There is a tracker on every path of the forest. The wild boar crouches in his lair for fear of the men that fill this wood. Three rings of champions ring round the tent in which your pupils feast. Your God had need to show Himself a God!

CIARÁN Nay, slay me, Daire. I will bear testimony with my life.

DAIRE What will that prove? Men die for false things, for ridiculous things, for evil things. What vile cause has not its heroes? Though you were to die here with joy and laughter you would not prove your cause a true one. Ciarán, let God send down an angel to stand between you and me.

CIARÁN Do you think that to save my poor life Omnipotence will display Itself?

DAIRE Who talks of your life? It is your soul that is at stake, and mine, and this little boy's, and the souls of all this nation, born and unborn.

CIARÁN (aside) He speaks true.

DAIRE Nay, I will put you to the proof. (To Iollann.) Come hither, child. (Iollann Beag approaches.) He is daintily fashioned, Ciarán, this last little pupil of yours. I swear to you that he shall die unless your God sends down an angel to rescue him. Kneel boy. (Iollann Beag kneels.) Speak now, if God has ears to hear.

[He raises his sword.]

CIARÁN (aside) I dare not speak. My God, my God, why hast Thou forsaken me?[24]

IOLLANN BEAG Fear not, little Master, I remember the word you taught me. … Young Michael, stand near me!

[The figure of a mighty Warrior, winged, and clothed in light, seems to stand beside the boy. Ciarán bends on one knee.]

DAIRE Who art thou, O Soldier?

MICHAEL I am he that waiteth at the portal. I am he that hasteneth. I am he that rideth before the squadron. I am he that holdeth a shield over the retreat of man's host when Satan cometh in war. I am he that turneth and smiteth. I am he that is Captain of the Host of God.

[*Daire bends slowly on one knee.*]

CIARÁN The Seraphim and the Cherubim[25] stand horsed. I hear the thunder of their coming ... O Splendour!

[*He falls forward, dead.*]

CURTAIN

NOTES

1 From *Collected Works of Pádraic H. Pearse: Plays, Stories, Poems* (Dublin: Phoenix Publishing Co. Ltd., 1917).

2 CIARÁN: the name recalls Ciarán of Clonmacnoise, the sixth-century saint who founded the monastery at Clonmacnoise in Co. Offaly. Pearse's ideas on education were heavily influenced by the philosophy of knowledge and reflection at Clonmacnoise.

3 Pupils: in this play Pearse gives the pupils names largely derived from the Ulster Cycle in Irish mythology. For more on Pearse's familiarity with this tradition see Philip O'Leary, *The Prose Literature of the Gaelic Revival: 1881–1921*, esp. pp.223–79.

4 IOLLANN BEAG: little Iollann. There are various Iollanns in Gaelic literature. The name recalls, for example, the warrior from the Ulster Cycle 'Fair-Haired Iollann' whose bravery provides a model for Iollann Beag's brave stand in *The Master*. Another Iollann, known as Iollann Iolchruthaith (Iollann the rejuvenator), and another possible point of reference for the action in *The Master*, is evoked in a fourteenth-century poem by Gofraidh Fionn Ó Dálaigh where Gofraidh compares his own young son to Iollann as he seeks to placate the Earl of Desmond. In verses 7-28 (Poem IX) a reference is made to Fionntán whose youthful form was restored to him by the

kiss of Iollann Iolchruthaith (see 'The Historical Poems of Gofraidh Fionn Ó Dálaigh', *The Irish Monthly*, January 1919, pp. 509–62). A character named Iollann also features in the romance *Iollan Láimhdhearg mac Righ Gréag* whose death is evoked in Yeats's dramatic poem 'The Shadowy Waters' (1900).

5 Book of Revelation [12:7-9]: And war broke out in heaven; Michael and his angels fought against the dragon. The dragon and his angels fought back, but they were defeated, and there was no longer any room for them in heaven. The great dragon was thrown down, the ancient serpent, who is called the Devil and Satan, the deceiver of the whole world – he was thrown down to the earth, and his angels were thrown down with him.

6 The story recalls that of Christ praying in the garden of Gethsemane whilst His disciples fall asleep (Matthew 26: 36-41): Then Jesus went with them to a place called Gethsemane: and he said to his disciples, 'Sit here while I go over there and pray'. He took with him Peter and the two sons of Zebedee, and began to be grieved and agitated. Then he said to them, 'I am deeply grieved, even to death; remain here, and stay awake with me'. And going a little further, he threw himself on the ground and prayed, 'My father, if it is possible, let this cup pass from me; yet not what I want but what you want'. Then he came to the disciples and found them sleeping; and he said to Peter, 'So, you could not stay awake with me one hour? Stay awake and pray that you may not come into the time of trial; the spirit is indeed willing, but the flesh is weak'.

7 Make love: sweet words rather than the modern sexual connotation.

8 Name given to the fruit from the hawthorn bush.

9 References two characters from the Ulster Cycle: Maine Honeymouth and Bricriu of the Bitter Tongue – each of whom is adept at using language to provoke a response from their listeners.

10 Children's nonsense rhyme.

11 Vext: angry / annoyed.

12 Little league of twelve in Galilee: Christ's twelve disciples.

13 Iosa: the Irish name for Jesus, often used by Pearse in his writings.

14 Shuiler: a wayfaring man, a traveller.

15 Pelf: goods that have been stolen or ill-gotten.

16 Rann: a verse.

17 Childhood games.

18 Postern: an outer door or gate.

19 Cantred: a district.

20 Gillies: attendants or servants.

21 Mead: a form of ale made from fermented honey and water.

22 Outland: foreign.

23 Prate of truth: Daire dismisses Ciarán's talk of truth as useless chatter.

24 Ciarán here echoes the words Christ spoke on the cross [Matthew 27: 45-46]: From noon on, darkness came over the whole land until three in the afternoon. And about three o'clock Jesus cried in a loud voice, 'Eli, Eli, lama sabachthani?' that is, 'My God, my God, why have you forsaken me?'

25 Seraphim, cherubim: heavenly beings who reside at different levels in the hierarchy of angels.

1.14 Photograph of Gypsy Walker who played 'Sighle' in the first production of *The Singer* in 1917 and for whom the part was written. Grianghraf de Gypsy Walker i gcéad léiriú *The Singer* sa bhliain 1917. Is di a scríobh Mac Piarais páirt Shighle. (Image courtesy of Mr. Dave Kenny/Le caoinchead ó Mr. Dave Kenny)

1.15 Programme for the first production of *The Singer* and restaging of *Íosagán* in December 1917. Clár do chéad léiriú *The Singer*. (Image courtesy of Pearse Museum/Le caoinchead ó Mhúsaem na bPiarsach)

THE SINGER[1]

First performance December 1917, Foresters' Hall, Parnell Square.[2]
First public performance, Liverpool, 1918.[3]

CHARACTERS

MacDara, *the Singer*[4]
Colm, *his brother*
Máire Ní Fhiannachta, *Mother*
of MacDara and Colm
Sighle, *a foster-daughter of the*
family

Maoilsheachlainn, *local*
Schoolmaster
Cuimín Éanna[5]
Diarmaid of the Bridge.

[*The wide clean kitchen of a country house. To the left a door which, when open, shows a wild country with a background of lonely hills; to the right a fireplace, beside which another door leads to a room. Candle burns on the table.*

Máire Ní Fhiannachta, a sad grey-haired woman, is spinning wool near the fire.[6] Sighle, a young girl, crouches in the ingle nook, carding. She is barefooted.]

MÁIRE Mend the fire, Sighle jewel.

SIGHLE Are you cold?

MÁIRE The feet of me are cold.

[*Sighle rises and mends the fire, putting on more turf; then she sits down again and resumes the carding.*]

201

SIGHLE You had a right to go to bed.

MÁIRE I couldn't have slept child. I had a feeling that something was drawing near to us. That something or somebody was coming here. All day yesterday I heard footsteps abroad on the street.[7]

SIGHLE 'Twas the dry leaves. The quicken trees in the gap were losing their leaves in the high wind.[8]

MÁIRE Maybe so. Did you think that Colm looked anxious in himself last night when he was going out?

SIGHLE I may as well quench the candle. The dawn has whitened.

[*She rises and quenches the candle; then resumes her place.*]

MÁIRE Did you think, daughter, that Colm looked anxious and sorrowful in himself when he was going out?

SIGHLE I did.

MÁIRE Was he saying anything to you?

SIGHLE He was.

[*They work silently for a few minutes; then Sighle stops and speaks.*]

SIGHLE Máire Ní Fhiannachta, I think I ought to tell you what your son said to me. I have been going over and over it in my mind all the long hours of the night. It is not right for the two of us to be sitting at this fire with a secret like that coming between us. Will I tell you what Colm said to me?

MÁIRE You may tell me if you like, Sighle girl.

SIGHLE He said to me that he was very fond of me.

MÁIRE *(who has stopped spinning)* Yes, daughter?

202

SIGHLE and … he asked me, if he came safe out of the trouble, would I marry him.

MÁIRE What did you say to him?

SIGHLE I told him that I could not give him any answer.

MÁIRE Did he ask you why you could not give him an answer?

SIGHLE He did; and I didn't know what to tell him.

MÁIRE Can you tell me?

SIGHLE Do you remember the day I first came to your house, Máire?

MÁIRE I do well.

SIGHLE Do you remember how lonely I was?

MÁIRE I do, you creature. Didn't I cry myself when the priest brought you in to me? And you caught hold my skirt and wouldn't let it go but cried till I thought your heart would break. 'They've put my mammie in the ground', you kept saying. 'She was asleep, and they put her in the ground'.

SIGHLE And you went down on your knees beside me and put your two arms around me and put your cheek against my cheek and said nothing but 'God comfort you, God comfort you'. And when I stopped crying a little you brought me over to the fire. Your two sons were at the fire, Máire. Colm was in the ingle where I am now; MacDara was sitting where you are. MacDara stooped down and lifted me on to his knee – I was only a weeshy child.[9] He stroked my hair. Then he began singing a little song to me, a little song that had sad words in it, but that had joy in the heart of it, and in the beat of it; and the words and the music grew very caressing and soothing like … like my mother's hand when it was on my cheek, or my mother's kiss on my mouth when I'd be half asleep –

MÁIRE Yes, daughter?

SIGHLE And it soothed me and soothed me; and I began to think that I was at home again, and I fell asleep in MacDara's arms – oh, the strong strong arms with his soft voice soothing me. When I woke up long after that I was still in his arms with my head on his shoulder. I opened my eyes and looked up at him. He smiled at me and said 'That was a good long sleep',[10] I … I put up my face to be kissed, and he bent down his head and kissed me.[11] He was so gentle, so gentle. *(Máire cries silently.)* I had no right to tell you all this. God forgive me for bringing those tears to you, Máire Ní Fhiannachta.

MÁIRE Whisht, girl. You had a right to tell me. Go on, jewel. My boy, my poor boy!

SIGHLE I was only a weeshy child –

MÁIRE Eight years you were, no more, the day the priest brought you into the house.[12]

SIGHLE How old was MacDara?

MÁIRE He was turned fifteen – fifteen[13] he was on St. MacDara's day[14], the year your mother died.

SIGHLE This house was as dear nearly to me as my mother's house from that day. You were good to me, Máire Ní Fhiannachta, and your two boys were good to me, but –

MÁIRE Yes, daughter?

SIGHLE MacDara was like sun and moon to me, like dew and rain to me, like strength and sweetness to me. I don't know did he know I was so fond of him. I think he did, because –

MÁIRE He did know, child.

SIGHLE How do you know that he knew? Did he tell you? Did you know?

MÁIRE I am his mother. Don't I know every fibre of his body? Don't I know every thought of his mind? He never told me; but well I knew.[15]

SIGHLE He put me into his songs. That is what made me think he knew. My name was in many a song that he made. Often when I was at the *fosaíocht*[16] he would come up into the green *mám*[17] to me, with a little song that he had made. It was happy for us in the green mám that time!

MÁIRE It was happy for us all when MacDara was here.

SIGHLE The heart in the breast of me nearly broke when they banished him from us.

MÁIRE I knew it well.

SIGHLE I used to lie awake in the night with his songs going through my brain, and the music of his voice. I used to call his name up in the green *mám*. At Mass his face used to come between me and the white Host.[18]

MÁIRE We have both been lonely for him. The house has been lonely for him.

SIGHLE Colm never knew I was so fond of MacDara. When MacDara went away Colm was kinder to me than ever – but indeed he was always kind.

MÁIRE Colm is a kind boy.

SIGHLE It was not till yesterday he told me he was fond of me; I never thought it. I liked him, but I never thought there would be word of marriage between us. I don't think he would have spoken of it was it not for the trouble coming. He says it will be soon now.

MÁIRE It will be very soon.

Blurring of eroticised and religious images of boy/manhood [handwritten annotation in top margin]

SIGHLE I shiver when I think of them all going out to fight. They will go out laughing: I see them with their cheeks flushed and their red lips apart. And then they will lie very still on the hillside – so still and white, with no red in their cheeks, but maybe a red wound in their white breasts or their white foreheads. Colm's hair will be dabbled with blood.[19]

MÁIRE Whisht, daughter.[20] That is no talk for one that was reared in this house. I am his mother, and I do not grudge him.

SIGHLE Forgive me. You have known more sorrow than I, and I think only of my own sorrow. *(She rises and kisses her.)* I am proud other times to think of so many young men, young men with straight strong limbs and white smooth flesh, going out into great peril because a voice has called to them to right the wrong of the people. Oh, I would like to see the man that has set their hearts on fire with the breath of his voice! They say that he is very young. They say that he is one of ourselves, a mountainy man that speaks our speech, and has known hunger and sorrow.

MÁIRE The strength and the sweetness he has comes maybe out of his sorrow.[21] *Two of MacDara qualities* [handwritten annotation]

SIGHLE I heard Diarmaid of the Bridge say that he was at the Fair of Uachtar Ard yesterday. There were hundreds in the streets striving to see him.

MÁIRE I wonder would he be coming here into Cois Fharraige or is it into the Joyce Country[22] he would go? I don't know but it's his coming I felt all day yesterday and all night. I thought maybe it might be –

SIGHLE Who did you think it might be?

MÁIRE I thought it might be my son that was coming to me.

SIGHLE Is it MacDara?

206

MÁIRE Yes, MacDara.

SIGHLE Do you think would he come back to be with the boys in the trouble?

MÁIRE He would.

SIGHLE Would he be left back now?

MÁIRE Who would let or stay him and he homing like a homing bird? Death only; God between us and harm!

SIGHLE Amen.

MÁIRE Here is Colm in to us.

SIGHLE *(looking out of the windows)* Aye, he's on the street.

MÁIRE Poor Colm!

[*The door opens and Colm comes in. He is a lad of twenty.*]

COLM Did you not go to bed, mother?

MÁIRE I did not, Colm. I was too uneasy to sleep. Sighle kept me company all night.

COLM It's a pity of the two of you to be up like this.

MÁIRE We would be more lonesome in bed than here chatting. Had you many boys at the drill tonight?

COLM We had them. There were ten and three score.[23]

MÁIRE When will the trouble be, Colm?

COLM It will be tomorrow or after tomorrow; or maybe sooner. There's a man expected from Galway with the word.

MÁIRE Is it the mountains you'll take to, or to march to Uachtar Ard or to Galway?

COLM It's to march we'll do, I'm thinking. Diarmaid of the Bridge and Cuimín Éanna and the master will be in to us shortly. We have some plans to make, and the master wants to write some orders.

MÁIRE Is it you will be their captain?

COLM It is, unless a better man comes in my place.

MÁIRE What better man would come?

COLM There is talk of the Singer coming. He was at the Fair of Uachtar Ard yesterday.

MÁIRE Let you put on the kettle, Sighle, and ready the room. The master will be asking a cup of tea. Will you lie down for an hour, Colm?

COLM I will not. They will be in on us now.

MÁIRE Let you make haste, Sighle. Ready the room. Here, give me the kettle.

[*Sighle, who has brought a kettle full of water, gives it to Máire Ní Fhiannachta, who hangs it over the fire; Sighle goes into the room.*]

COLM (*after a pause*) Was Sighle talking to you, mother?

MÁIRE She was, son.

COLM What did she say?

MÁIRE She told me what you said to her last night. You must be patient, Colm. Don't press her to give you an answer too soon. She has strange thoughts in her heart, and strange memories.

COLM What memories has she?[24]

MÁIRE Many a woman has memories.

COLM Sighle has no memories but of this house and of her mother. What is she but a child?

MÁIRE And what are you but a child? Can't you have patience? Children have memories, but the memories sometimes die. Sighle's memories have not died yet.

COLM This is queer talk. What does she remember?

MÁIRE Whisht, there's someone on the street.

COLM *(looking out of the window)* 'Tis Cuimín and the master.

MÁIRE Be patient, son. Don't vex your poor head. What are you both but children yet?

[*The door opens and Cuimín Éanna and Maoilsheachlainn come in. Cuimín is middle-aged; Maoilsheachlainn past middle age, turning grey, and a little stooped.*]

CUIMÍN and MAOILSHEACHLAINN *(entering)* God save all here.

MÁIRE God save you, men. Will you sit? The kettle is on the boil. Give the master the big chair, Colm.

MAOILSHEACHLAINN *(sitting down near the fire on the chair which Colm places for him)* You're early stirring, Máire.

MÁIRE I didn't lie down at all, master.

MAOILSHEACHLAINN Is it to sit up all night you did?

MÁIRE It is then. Sighle kept me company.

MAOILSHEACHLAINN 'Tis a pity of the women of the world. Too good they are for us, and too full of care. I'm afraid that there was many a woman on this mountain that sat up last night. Aye, and many a woman in Ireland. 'Tis women that keep all the great vigils.[25]

MÁIRE *(wetting the tea)* Why wouldn't we sit up to have a cup of tea ready for you? Won't you go west into the room?

MAOILSHEACHLAINN We'd as lief drink it here beside the fire.[26]

MÁIRE Sighle is readying the room. You'll want the table to write on, maybe.

MAOILSHEACHLAINN We'll go west so.

MÁIRE Wait till Sighle has the table laid. The tea will be drawn in a minute.

COLM *(to Maoilsheachlainn)* Was there any word of the messenger at the forge, master?

MAOILSHEACHLAINN There was not.

CUIMÍN When we were coming up the boreen I saw a man breasting Cnoc an Teachta that I thought might be him.

MAOILSHEACHLAINN I don't think it was him. He was walking slowly, and sure the messenger that brings that great story will come on the wings of the wind.

COLM Perhaps it was one of the boys you saw going home from the drill.

CUIMÍN No, it was a stranger. He looked like a mountainy man that would be coming from a distance. He might be someone that was at the Fair of Uachtar Ard yesterday, and that stayed the evening after selling.

MAOILSHEACHLAINN Aye, there did a lot stay, I'm told, talking about the word that's expected.

CUIMÍN The Singer was there, I believe. Diarmaid of the Bridge said that he spoke to them all at the fair, and that there did a lot stay in the town after the fair thinking he'd speak to them again. They say he has the talk of an angel.

MAOILSHEACHLAINN What sort is he to look at?

CUIMÍN A poor man of the mountains. Young they say he is, and pale like a man that lived in cities, but with the dress and the speech of a mountainy man; shy in himself and very silent, till he stands up to talk to the people. And then he has the voice of a silver trumpet, and words so beautiful that they make the people cry. And there is terrible anger in him, for all that he is shrinking and gentle. Diarmaid said that in the Joyce Country they think it is some great hero that has come back again to lead the people against the Gall[27] or maybe an angel or the Son of Mary Himself that has come down on the earth.

MAOILSHEACHLAINN *(looking towards the door)* There's a footstep abroad.

MÁIRE *(who has been sitting very straight in her chair listening intently)* That is my son's step.

COLM Sure, amn't I here, mother?

MÁIRE That is MacDara's step.

[*All start and look first towards Máire, and then towards the door, the latch of which has been touched.*]

MAOILSHEACHLAINN I wish it was MacDara, Máire, 'tis maybe Diarmaid or the mountainy man we saw on the road.

MÁIRE It is not Diarmaid. It is MacDara.

[*The door opens slowly, and MacDara, a young man of perhaps twenty-five, dressed like a man of the mountain stands on the threshold.*]

MACDARA God save all here.

ALL And you likewise.

MÁIRE *(who has risen and is stretching out her hands)* I felt you coming to me, little son!

MACDARA *(springing to her and folding her in his arms)* Little mother, little mother!

[*While they still embrace Sighle re-enters from the room and stands still on the threshold looking at MacDara.*]

MÁIRE *(raising her head)* Along all the quiet roads and across all the rough mountains and through all the crowded towns I felt you drawing near to me.

MACDARA Oh, the long years, the long years!

MÁIRE I am crying for pride at the sight of you. Neighbours, neighbours, this is MacDara, the first child that I bore to my husband.

MACDARA *(kissing Colm)* My little brother! *(To Cuimín)* Cuimín Éanna! *(To Maoilsheachlainn)* Master! *(They shake hands.)*

MAOILSHEACHLAINN Welcome home.

CUIMÍN Welcome home.

MACDARA *(looking round)* Where is – *(He sees Sighle in the doorway)* Sighle! *(He approaches her, and takes her hand)* Little, little Sighle! … I … Mother, sometimes when I was in the middle of great crowds I have seen this fireplace, and you standing with your hands stretched out to me as you stood a minute ago, and Sighle in the doorway of the room; and my heart has cried out to you.

MÁIRE I used to hear the crying of your heart. Often and often here by the fireplace or abroad on the street I would stand and say, 'MacDara is crying out to me now. The heart in him is yearning'. And this while back I felt you very near to me. Do you remember me saying, Sighle, that I felt someone coming, and that I thought maybe it might be MacDara?

SIGHLE You did.

MÁIRE I knew that something glorious was coming to the mountain with today's dawn. Red dawns and white dawns I have seen on the hills, but none like this dawn. Come in, jewel, and sit down a while in the room. Sighle has the table laid. The tea is drawn. Bring in the griddle-cakes, Sighle. Come in, master. Come in, Cuimín.

MAOILSHEACHLAINN No, Máire, we'll sit here a while. You and the children will like to be by yourselves. Go in west, children. Cuimín and I have plans to make. We're expecting Diarmaid of the Bridge in.

MÁIRE We don't grudge you a share of our joy, master. Nor you, Cuimín.

CUIMÍN No, go on in, Máire. We'll go west after you. We want to talk here.

MÁIRE Well, come in when you have your talk out. There's enough tea on the pot for everybody. In with you, children.

[*MacDara, Colm, Sighle, and Máire Ní Fhiannachta go into the room, Sighle carrying the griddle-cakes and Máire the tea.*]

MAOILSHEACHLAINN This is great news, MacDara to be back.

CUIMÍN Do you think will he be with us?

MAOILSHEACHLAINN Is it a boy with that gesture of the head, that proud laughing gesture, to be a coward or a stag? You don't know the heart of this boy, Cuimín; the love that's in it, and the strength. You don't know the mind he has, so gracious, so full of wisdom. I taught him when he was only a little ladeen.[28] 'Tis a pity that he had ever to go away from us. And yet, I think, his exile had made him a better man. His soul must be full of great remembrances.[29]

CUIMÍN I never knew rightly why he was banished.

MAOILSHEACHLAINN Songs he was making that were setting the people's hearts on fire.

CUIMÍN Aye, I often heard his songs.

MAOILSHEACHLAINN They were full of terrible love for the people and of great anger against the Gall. Some said there was irreligion in them and maybe blasphemy against God. But I never saw it, and I don't believe it. There are some would have us believe that God is on the side of the Gall, and well, word came down from Galway or from Dublin that he would be put in prison and maybe excommunicated if he did not go away. He was only a gossoon of eighteen or maybe twenty. The priest counselled him to go, and not to bring sorrow on his mother's house. He went away one evening without taking leave or farewell of anyone.

CUIMÍN Where has he been since, I don't know?

MAOILSHEACHLAINN In great cities, I'd say, and in lonely places. He has the face of a scholar or of a priest or of a clerk on him. He must have read a lot, and thought a lot, and made a lot of songs.

CUIMÍN I don't know is he as strong a boy as Colm?

MAOILSHEACHLAINN He's not as robust in himself as Colm is, but there was great strength in the grip of his hand. I'd say that he'd wield a camán or a pike with any boy on the mountain.[30]

CUIMÍN He'll be a great backing to us if he's with us. The people love him on account of the songs he used to make. There's not a man that won't do his bidding.

MAOILSHEACHLAINN That's so. And his counsel will be useful to us. He'll make better plans than you or I, Cuimín.

CUIMÍN I wonder what's keeping Diarmaid.

MAOILSHEACHLAINN Some news that was at the forge or at the priest's house, maybe. He went east the road to see if there was sign of a word from Galway.

CUIMÍN I'll be uneasy till he comes.

[*He gets up and walks to the window and looks out; Maoilsheachlainn remains deep in thought by the fire. Cuimín returns from the window and continues:*]

Is it to march we'll do, or to fight here in the hills?

MAOILSHEACHLAINN Out Maam Gap we'll go and meet the boys from the Joyce Country. We'll leave some to guard the Gap and some at Leenane. We'll march the road between the lakes through Maam and Cornamona and Clonbur to Cong. Then we'll have friends on our left at Ballinrobe and on our right at Tuam. What is there to stop us but the few men the Gall have in Clifden?

CUIMÍN And if they march against us we can destroy them from the mountains.

MAOILSHEACHLAINN We can. It's into a trap they'll walk.

[*MacDara appears in the doorway of the room with a cup of tea and some griddle-cake in his hand.*]

MACDARA I've brought you out a cup of tea, master. I thought it long you were sitting here.

MAOILSHEACHLAINN (*taking it*) God bless you, MacDara.

MACDARA Go west, Cuimín. There's a place at the table for you now.

CUIMÍN (*rising and going in*) I may as well. Give me a call, boys, when Diarmaid comes.

MAOILSHEACHLAINN This is a great day, MacDara.

MACDARA It is a great day and a glad day, and yet it is a sorrowful day.

MAOILSHEACHLAINN How can the day of your home-coming be sorrowful?

MACDARA Has not every great joy a great sorrow at its core? Does not the joy of homecoming enclose the pain of departing? I have a strange feeling, master. I have only finished a long journey, and I feel as if I were about to take another long journey. I meant this to be a homecoming, but it seems only like a meeting on the way … When my mother stood up to meet me with her arms stretched out to me I thought of Mary meeting her Son on the Dolorous Way.

MAOILSHEACHLAINN That was a queer thought. What was it that drew you home?

MACDARA Some secret thing that I have no name for. Some feeling that I must see my mother and Colm and Sighle again. A feeling that I must face some great adventure with their kisses on my lips. I seemed to see myself brought to die before a great crowd that stood cold and silent; and there were some that cursed me in their hearts for having brought death into their houses. Sad dead faces seemed to reproach me – oh, the wise sad faces of the dead – and the keening of women rang in my years. But I felt that the kisses of those three warm on my mouth would be as wine in my blood, strengthening me to bear what men said and to die with only love and pity in my heart, and no bitterness.

MAOILSHEACHLAINN It was strange that you should see yourself like that.

MACDARA It was foolish. One has strange lonesome thoughts when one is in the middle of crowds. But I am glad of that thought, for it drove me home. I felt so lonely away from here … My mother's hair is greyer than it was.

MAOILSHEACHLAINN Aye, she has been aging. She has had great sorrows: your father dead and you banished. Colm is grown a fine strapping boy?

MACDARA He is. There is some shyness between Colm and me. We have not spoken yet as we used to.

MAOILSHEACHLAINN When boys are brought up together and then parted for a long time there is often shyness between them when they meet again. Do you find Sighle changed?

MACDARA No; and yet – yes. Master, she is very beautiful. I did not know a woman could be so beautiful. I thought that all beauty was in the heart, that beauty was a secret thing that could be seen only with the eyes of reverie or in a dream of some unborn splendour. I had schooled myself to think physical beauty an unholy thing. I tried to keep my heart virginal; and sometimes in the street of a city when I have stopped to look at the white limbs of some beautiful child, and have felt the pain that the sight of great beauty brings, I have wished that I could blind my eyes so that I might shut out the sight of everything that tempted me. At times I have rebelled against that, and have cried aloud that God would not have filled the world with beauty, even to the making drunk of the sight, if beauty were not of heaven. But then again I have said, 'This is the subtlest form of temptation, this is to give to one's own desire the sanction of God's will'. And I have hardened my heart, and kept myself cold and chaste as the top of a high mountain. But now I think I was wrong, for beauty like Sighle's must be holy.

MAOILSHEACHLAINN Surely a good and comely girl is holy. You question yourself too much, MacDara. You brood too much. Do you remember when you were a gossoon[31] how you cried over the wild duck whose wing you broke by accident with a stone, and made a song about the crane whose nest you found ravished, and about the red robin you found perished on the doorstep? And how the priest laughed because you told him in confession that you had stolen drowned lilies from the river?

MACDARA *(laughing)* Aye, it was at a station in Diarmaid of the Bridge's, and when the priest laughed, my face got red, and everyone looked at us, and I got up and ran out of the house.

MAOILSHEACHLAINN *(laughing)* I remember it well. We thought it was what you told him you were in love with his housekeeper.

MACDARA It's little but I was, too. She used to give me apples out of the priest's apple-garden. Little brown russet apples, the sweetest I ever tasted. I used to think that the apples of the Hesperides[32] that the Children of Tuireann[33] went to quest must have been like them.

MAOILSHEACHLAINN It's a wonder but you made a poem about them.

MACDARA I did. I made a poem in Deibhidhe of twenty quatrains.

MAOILSHEACHLAINN Did you make many songs while you were away?

MACDARA When I went away first my heart was as if dead and dumb and I could not make any songs. After a little while, when I was going through the sweet green country and I used to come to little towns where I'd see children playing, my heart seemed to open again like hard ground that would be watered with rain. The first song I made was about the children that I saw playing in the street of Kilconnell. The next song I made was about an old dark man that I met on the causeway of Aughrim. I made a glad proud song when I saw the broad Shannon flow under the bridge of Athlone. I made many a song after that before I reached Dublin.

MAOILSHEACHLAINN How did it fare with you in Dublin?

MACDARA I went to a bookseller and gave him the book of my songs to print. He said that he dared not print them, that the Gall would put him in prison and break up his printing press. I was hungry and I wandered through the streets. Then a man who saw me read an Irish poster on the wall spoke to me and asked me where I came from. I told him my story. In a few days he came to me and said that he had found work for me, to teach Irish and Latin and Greek in a school. I went to the school and taught in it for a year. I wrote a few poems and they were printed in a paper. One day the brother who was over the school came to me and asked me was it I that had written those poems. I said it was. He told me then that I could not teach in the school any longer. So I went away.

MAOILSHEACHLAINN What happened to you after that?

MACDARA I wandered in the streets until I saw a notice that a teacher was wanted to teach a boy. I went to the house and a lady engaged me to teach her little son for ten shillings a week. Two years I spent at that. The boy was a winsome child, and he grew into my heart. I thought it a wonderful thing to have the moulding of a mind, of a life, in my hands. Do you think that, you who are a schoolmaster?

MAOILSHEACHLAINN It's not much time I get for thinking.

MACDARA I have done nothing all my life but think: think and make poems.

MAOILSHEACHLAINN If the thoughts and the poems are good, that is a good life's work.

MACDARA Aye, they say that to be busy with the things of the spirit is better than to be busy with the things of the body. But I am not sure, master. Can the Vision Beautiful alone content a man? I think a true man is divine in this, like God, he must needs create, he must needs do.

MAOILSHEACHLAINN Is not a poet a maker?[34]

MACDARA No, he is only a voice that cries out, a sigh that trembles into rest. The true teacher must suffer and do. He must break bread to the people; he must go into Gethsemane[35] and toil up the steep of Golgotha[36] … Sometimes I think that to be a woman and to serve and suffer as women do is to be the highest thing. Perhaps that is why I felt it proud and wondrous to be a teacher, for a teacher does that. I gave to the little lad I taught the very flesh and blood and breath that were my life. I fed him on the milk of my kindness; I breathed into him my spirit.

MAOILSHEACHLAINN Did he repay you for that great service?

MACDARA Can any child repay its mother? Master, your trade is the most sorrowful of all trades. You are like a poor mother who spends herself in nursing children who go away and never come back to her.

MAOILSHEACHLAINN Was your little pupil untrue to you?

MACDARA Nay, he was so true to me that his mother grew jealous of me. A good mother and a good teacher are always jealous of each other. That is why a teacher's trade is the most sorrowful of all trades. If he is a bad teacher his pupil *wanders* away from him. If he is a good teacher his pupil's folk grow jealous of him. My little pupil's mother bade him choose between her and me.

MAOILSHEACHLAINN Which did he choose?

MACDARA He chose his mother. How could I blame him?

MAOILSHEACHLAINN What did you do?

MACDARA I shouldered my bundle and took to the roads.

MAOILSHEACHLAINN How did it fare with you?

MACDARA It fares ill with one who is so poor that he has no longer even his dreams. I was the poorest *shuiler*[37] on the roads of Ireland, for I had no single illusion left to me. I could neither pray when I came to a holy well nor drink in a public-house when I had got a little money. One seemed to me as foolish as the other.

MAOILSHEACHLAINN Did you make no songs in those days?

MACDARA I made one so bitter that when I recited it at a wake they thought I was some wandering wicked spirit, and they put me out of the house.

MAOILSHEACHLAINN Did you not pray at all?

MACDARA Once as I knelt by the cross of Kilgobbin, it became clear to me, with an awful clearness, that there was no God.[38] Why pray after that? I burst into a fit of laughter at the folly of men in thinking that there was a God. I felt inclined to run through the villages and cry aloud, 'People, it is all a mistake; there is no God'.

MAOILSHEACHLAINN MacDara, this grieves me.

MACDARA Then I said, 'Why take away their illusion? If they find out that there is no God their hearts will be as lonely as mine'. So I walked the roads with my secret.

MAOILSHEACHLAINN MacDara, I am sorry for this. You must pray, you must pray. You will find God again. He has only hidden His face from you.

MACDARA No, He has revealed His face to me. His face is terrible and sweet, Maoilsheachlainn. I know it well now.

MAOILSHEACHLAINN Then you found him again?

MACDARA His name is suffering. His name is loneliness. His name is abjection.

MAOILSHEACHLAINN I do not rightly understand you, and yet I think you are saying something that is true.

MACDARA I have lived with the homeless and with the breadless. Oh, Maoilsheachlainn, the poor, the poor![39] I have seen such sad childings[40], such bare marriage feasts, such candleless wakes! In the pleasant country places I have seen them, but oftener in the dark, unquiet streets of the city. My heart has been heavy with the sorrow of mothers, my eyes have been wet with the tears of children. The people, Maoilsheachlainn, the dumb, suffering people[41]: reviled and outcast, yet pure and splendid and faithful. In them I saw, or seemed to see again, the face of God. Ah, it is a tear-stained face, defiled with ordure, but it is the Holy Face![42]

[*A page of the manuscript is either missing or skipped over by Pearse at this point: the character Diarmaid now appears in the scene.*]

MAOILSHEACHLAINN What news have you with you?

DIARMAID The Gall have marched from Clifden.

MAOILSHEACHLAINN Is it into the hills?

DIARMAID By Letterfrack they have come, and the Pass of Kylemore, and through Glen Inagh.

COLM And no word from Galway yet?

DIARMAID No word, nor sign of a word.

COLM They told us to wait for the word. We've waited too long.

MAOILSHEACHLAINN The messenger may have been caught. Perhaps the Gall are marching from Galway too.

COLM We'd best strike ourselves, so.

CUIMÍN Is it to strike before the word is given?

COLM Is it to die like rats you'd have us because the word is not given?

CUIMÍN Our plans are not finished. Our orders are not here.

COLM Our plans will never be finished. Our orders may never be here.

CUIMÍN We've no one to lead us.

COLM Didn't you elect me your captain?

CUIMÍN We did: but not to bid us rise out when the whole country is quiet. We were to get the word from the men that are over the people. They'll speak when the time comes.

COLM They should have spoken before the Gall marched.

CUIMÍN What call have you to say what they should or what they should not have done? Am I speaking lie or truth, men? Are we to rise out before the word comes? I say we must wait for the word.[43] What do you say, Diarmaid, you that was our messenger to Galway?

DIARMAID I like the way Colm has spoken, and we may live to say that he spoke wisely as well as bravely; but I'm slow to give my voice to send out the boys of this mountain – our poor little handful – to stand with their poor pikes against the big guns of the Gall. If we had news that they were rising in the other countrysides; but we've got no news.

CUIMÍN What do you say, master? You're wiser than any of us.

MAOILSHEACHLAINN I say to Colm that a greater one than he or I may give us the word before the day is old. Let you have patience, Colm.

COLM My mother told me to have patience this morning, when MacDara's step was on the street. Patience, and I after waiting seven years before I spoke, and then to speak too late!

223

MAOILSHEACHLAINN What are you saying at all?

COLM I am saying this, master: that I'm going out the road to meet the Gall, if only five men of the mountain follow me.

[*Sighle has appeared in the doorway and stands terror-stricken.*]

CUIMÍN You will not, Colm.

COLM I will.

DIARMAID This is throwing away men's lives.

COLM Men's lives get very precious to them when they have bought out their land.

MAOILSHEACHLAINN Listen to me, Colm –

[*Colm goes out angrily, and the others follow him, trying to restrain him. Sighle comes to the fire, where she kneels.*]

SIGHLE *(as in a reverie)* 'They will go out laughing', I said, but Colm has gone out with anger in his heart. And he was so kind. Love is a terrible thing. There is no pain so great as the pain of love … I wish MacDara and I were children in the green mám and that we did not know that we loved each other … Colm will lie dead on the road to Glen Inagh, and MacDara will go out to die… There is nothing in the world but love and death.

[*MacDara comes out of the room.*]

MACDARA *(in a low voice)* She has dropped asleep, Sighle.

SIGHLE She watched long, MacDara. We all watched long.

MACDARA Every long watch ends. Every traveller comes home.

SIGHLE Sometimes when people watch it is death that comes.

MACDARA Could there be a royaller coming, Sighle? … Once I wanted life. You and I to be together in one place always: that is what I wanted. But now I see that we shall be together for a little time only; that I have to do a hard, sweet thing, and that I must do it alone. And because I love you I would not have it different. … I wanted to have your kiss on my lips, Sighle, as well as my mother's and Colm's. But I will deny myself that. *(Sighle is crying)* Don't cry, child. Stay near my mother while she lives – it may be for a little while of years. You poor women suffer so much pain, so much sorrow, and yet you do not die until long after your strong young sons and lovers have died.

[*Máire's voice is heard from the room, crying:* MacDara!]

MACDARA She is calling me.

[*He goes into the room; Sighle cries on her knees by the fire. After a little while voices are heard outside, the latch is lifted, and Maoilsheachlainn comes in.*]

SIGHLE Is he gone, master?

MAOILSHEACHLAINN Gone out the road with ten or fifteen of the young lads. Is MacDara within still?

SIGHLE He was here in the kitchen a while. His mother called him and he went back to her.

[*Maoilsheachlainn goes over and sits down near the fire.*]

MAOILSHEACHLAINN I think that maybe Colm did what was right. We are too old to be at the head of work like this. Was MacDara talking to you about the trouble?

SIGHLE He said that he would have to do a hard, sweet thing, and that he would have to do it alone.

[*A murmur is heard as of a crowd of men talking as they come up the hill.*]

SIGHLE What is that noise like voices?

MAOILSHEACHLAINN It is the boys coming up the hillside. There was a great crowd gathering below at the cross.[44]

[*The voices swell loud outside the door. Cuimín, Éanna, Diarmaid, and some others come in.*]

DIARMAID The men say we did wrong to let Colm go out with that little handful. They say we should all have marched.

CUIMÍN And I say Colm was wrong to go before he got his orders. Are we all to go out and get shot down because one man is hotheaded? Where is the plan that was to come from Galway?

MAOILSHEACHLAINN Men, I'm blaming myself for not saying the thing I'm going to say before we let Colm go. We talk about getting word from Galway. What would you say, neighbours, if the man that will give the word is under the roof of this house?

CUIMÍN Who is it you mean?

MAOILSHEACHLAINN (*going to the door of the room and throwing it open*) Let you rise out, MacDara, and reveal yourself to the men that are waiting for your word!

ONE OF THE NEWCOMERS Has MacDara come home?

[*MacDara comes out of the room. Máire Ní Fhiannachta stands behind him in the doorway.*]

DIARMAID (*starting up from where he has been sitting*) That is the man that stood among the people in the fair of Uachtar Ard! (*He goes up to MacDara and kisses his hand*) I could not get near you yesterday, MacDara, with the crowds that were round you. What was on me that didn't know you? Sure I had a right to know that sad, proud head. Máire Ní Fhiannachta, men and women yet unborn will bless the pains of your first childing.

226

[*Máire Ní Fhiannachta comes forward slowly and takes her son's hand and kisses it.*]

MÁIRE NÍ FHIANNACHTA *(in a low voice)* Soft hand that played at my breast, strong hand that will fall heavy on the Gall, brave hand that will break the yoke! Men of this mountain, my son MacDara is the Singer that has quickened the dead years and all the quiet dust! Let the horsemen that sleep in Aileach rise up and follow him into the war! Weave your winding-sheets, women, for there will be many a noble corpse to be waked before the new moon!

[*Each comes forward and kisses his hand.*]

MAOILSHEACHLAINN Let you speak, MacDara, and tell us it is time.

MACDARA Where is Colm?

DIARMAID Gone out the road to fight the Gall, himself and fifteen.

MACDARA Had not Colm spoken by his deed already?

CUIMÍN You are our leader.

MACDARA Your leader is the man that spoke first. Give me a pike and I will follow Colm. Why did you let him go out with fifteen men only? You are fourscore on the mountain.

DIARMAID We thought it a foolish thing for fourscore to go into battle against four thousand, or maybe forty thousand.

MACDARA And so it is a foolish thing. Do you want us to be wise?

CUIMÍN This is strange talk.

MACDARA I will talk to you more strangely yet. It is for your own souls' sakes I would have had the fourscore go, and not for Colm's sake, or for the battle's sake, for the battle is won whether you go or not.

[*A cry is heard outside; one rushes in terror-stricken.*]

THE NEWCOMER Young Colm has fallen at the Glen foot!

MACDARA The fifteen were too many. Old men, you did not do your work well enough. You should have kept all back but one. One man can free a people as one Man redeemed the world. I will take no pike. I will go into the battle with bare hands. I will stand up before the Gall as Christ hung naked before men on the tree!

[*He moves through them, pulling off his clothes as he goes. As he reaches the threshold a great shout goes up from the people. He passes out and the shout dies slowly away. The other men follow him slowly. Máire Ní Fhiannachta sits down at the fire, where Sighle still crouches.*]

CURTAIN

Appendix to *The Singer*

[*The following version of dialogue from the play is contained in some extra pages (MS 8232) found with Pearse's manuscript.*]

CUIMÍN Our plans are not finished. Our orders are not here.

COLM Our plans will never be finished. Our orders may never be here.

CUIMÍN We've no one to lead us.

COLM Didn't you elect me your Captain?

CUIMÍN We did, but not to bid us rise out when the whole country is quiet. We were to get the word from the men that are over the people. They'll speak when the time comes. *(The door opens again, and Féichín comes in with two or three others.)* Am I speaking lie or truth, men? Colm here wants us to rise out before the word comes. I say we must wait for the word. What do you say, Féichín, you that's got a wiser head than these young fellows?

FÉICHÍN God forgive me if I'm wrong, but I say we should wait for our orders.

CUIMÍN What do you say, Diarmaid?

DIARMAID I like you, Colm, for the way you spoke well and bravely; but I'm slow to give my voice to send out the boys of this mountain – our poor little handful – to stand with their poor pikes against the big guns of the Gall. If we had news that they were rising in the other countrysides; but we've got no news.

COLM Master, you haven't spoken yet. I'm afraid to ask you to speak.

MAOILSHEACHLAINN Cuimín is right when he says that we must not rise until we get the word; but what do you say, neighbours, if the man that'll give the word is under the roof of this house?

DIARMAID What do you mean?

MAOILSHEACHLAINN *(going to the door of the room and throwing it open)* Let you rise out, MacDara, and reveal yourself to the men that are waiting for your word!

FÉICHÍN Has MacDara come home?

[*MacDara comes out of the room; Máire and Sighle stand behind him in the doorway.*]

DIARMAID *(starting up from where he has been sitting)* That is the man that stood among the people in the fair of Uachtar Ard! *(He goes up to MacDara and kisses his hand)* I could not get near you yesterday, MacDara, the crowds were so great. What was on me that I didn't know you? Sure I ought to have known that sad, proud head. Máire Ní Fhiannachta, men and women yet unborn will bless the pains of your first childing.

MÁIRE *(comes forward and takes her son's hand and kisses it)* Soft hand that played at my breast, strong hand that will fall heavy on the Gall, brave hand that will break the yoke! Men of this mountain, my son MacDara is the Singer that has quickened the dead years and the young blood. Let the horsemen that sleep in Aileach rise up today and follow him into the war!

[*They come forward one by one and kiss his hand; Colm and Sighle last.*]

COLM The Gall have marched from Clifden, MacDara. I wanted to rise out today, but these old men think it is not yet time.

CUIMÍN We were waiting for the word.

MACDARA And must I speak the word? Old men, you have left me no choice. I had hoped that more would not be asked of me than to sow the secret word of hope, and that the toil of the reaping would be for others. But I see that one does not serve.

NOTES

1 Patrick Pearse, *The Singer* (National Library of Ireland, MS 7389)
2 See *Irish Press*, 27th April 1966, p.12.
3 See *Irish Independent*, 19th August 1938, p.6.
4 Macdara: much venerated saint associated with Saint MacDara's island off the coast of Connemara, where his feast day is still celebrated on July 16th.
5 Cuimín Éanna: (Cuimín) pet-name for Cuimme or Colum; (Éanna) saint associated with the Aran Islands and whom Pearse named his school in honour of; his feast day is March 21st.
6 The opening scene featuring an isolated cottage with an old woman waiting pensively for news of loved ones has clear echoes of J.M. Synge's *Riders to the Sea*.

7 The play is dominated by this sense of foreboding, of major action on the cusp of happening.

8 Quicken trees: rowan or mountain ash.

9 Weeshy: small.

10 Manuscript (Ms 7389) reads: 'He smiled at me and said "That was a good long sleep" and then he bent down his head and kissed me on the lips' – Pearse redacts image of MacDara bending down to kiss her.

11 Manuscript (Ms 7389) reads: 'he bent down his head and kissed me on the lips' – Pearse has scribbled out final three words. Pearse clearly struggled with this image of the kiss between the older boy and young girl. He steers away from idea of MacDara taking the lead, preferring instead the image of the girl putting up her face to be kissed; he also steers away from the more clearly sexual image of a kiss on the lips.

12 Manuscript originally read: 'Eight years you were, no more, the day the priest brought you into the house after your mother's funeral'.

13 The age difference clearly gave Pearse some pause for thought – manuscript originally gives MacDara's age as sixteen – Pearse swaps between these two options a number of times before settling on fifteen.

14 MacDara's Day: July 16th.

15 See Pearse's poem 'The Mother': 'I do not grudge them: Lord I do not grudge / My two strong sons that I have seen go out / To break their strength and die.'

16 fosaíocht: herding cattle while they are grazing (Ua Duinnín).

17 mám: a mountain pass or summit (Ua Duinnín).

18 Gaelic folksongs about unrequited love such as Donal Óg sometimes alluded to how the deserting lover had taken God from the speaker. Pearse's translation of Donal Óg appeared in his *Specimens for an Irish Anthology*.

19 Pearse was aware that citation of blood imagery in his writings might be controversial and he explicitly noted its recurrence as a theme in Gaelic literature. ('I do not defend this bloodthirstiness any more than I apologise for it. I simply point it out as the note of a literature.') Ghosts, 1915. For a discussion of Pearse's use of blood imagery see Róisín Ní Ghairbhí, 'A People that did not Exist: Reflections on Some Sources and Contexts for Patrick Pearse's Militant Nationalism' in Ruan O' Donnell, ed., *The Impact of the 1916 Rising: Among the Nations*, Irish Academic Press, 2008, esp. p.165 and p.179–83. The imagery deployed in parts of this dialogue also finds a clear echo in much of

the poetry associated with the First World War.

20 Whisht: quiet / hush.

21 The description – 'strength and sweetness' – echoes that used by Sighle when talking about MacDara earlier.

22 Joyce Country: an area of County Galway.

23 Ten and three score: 70.

24 Manuscript (Ms 7389) originally read: 'What memories has she? Sure she never had another boy?'

25 See Pearse's poem 'The Mother': We suffer in their coming and their going / And tho' I grudge them not, I weary, weary / Of the long sorrow – And yet I have my joy? My sons were faithful, and they fought.

26 as lief: be as happy to / prefer to.

27 The Gall: the English.

28 Ladeen: young boy.

29 The idea of memory – personal and communal – is a recurring concern for Pearse in this play.

30 Camán: hurley stick.

31 Gossoon: child.

32 Hesperides: in Greek mythology the Hesperides were nymphs who lived in a beautiful garden near Mt. Atlas. In this garden grew the tree with the golden apples which Gaia had given as a present to Hera on her wedding to Zeus.

33 Children of Tuireann: figures from Irish mythology who were sent on a series of near-impossible quests resulting in their deaths.

34 There is an echo here of the Romantic conception of poets as the 'unacknowledged legislators of the world' (P.B. Shelley, 'A Defence of Poetry').

35 Gethsemane: the garden where Jesus prays and asks 'My father, if it is possible, let this cup pass from me; yet not what I want but what you want' (Matthew 26: 36-41).

36 Golgotha: the place where Jesus' crucifixion took place.

37 shuiler: a wayfarer or travelling man.

38 cross of Kilgobbin: a famous High Cross in County Dublin.

39 Pearse's sympathy with socialism is often under-examined. See especially his series 'From A Hermitage', in which he wrote: 'My instinct is with the landless man against the Lord of lands, and with the breadless man against the master of millions. I may be wrong, but I do hold it a most terrible sin that there should be landless men in this island of waste yet fertile valleys and that there should be

breadless men in this city where great fortunes are made and enjoyed' ['From a Hermitage', Irish Freedom Press, 1915, p.177].

40 childings: births.

41 The imagery here provides a sacred validation to the Republican principle that the people are sovereign (for similar imagery see Pearse's poem 'The Rebel').

42 In the manuscript (NL MS 7389) MacDara goes on to say: 'This is rhetoric. I mean that I found such purity, such faithfulness, such patience, in the houses of the poor that I believed again in God'.

43 There is a curious prescience in this debate over the timing of a rising and the wait for orders to come.

44 The cross: there is a double allusion at work here – the cross as in the crossroads but also as in the cross of the crucifixion.

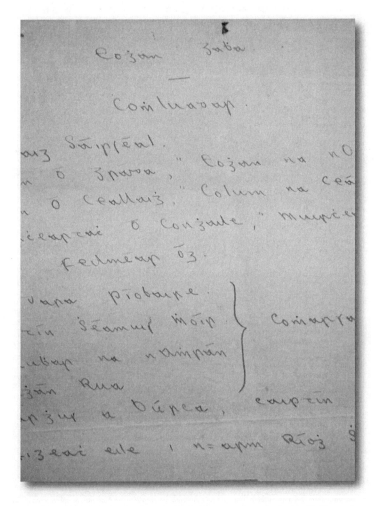

1.16 Lámhscríbhinn *Eoghan Gabha*, dráma nár críochnaíodh/Pearse's handwritten script for the unfinished *Eoghan Gabha*. (Image courtesy of the National Library of Ireland/Le caoinchead ó Leabharlann Náisiúnta na hÉireann)

EOGHAN GABHA[1]

Léirithe den chéad uair ag Comhaltas Drámaíochta na Tulaigh Móire ar an 27ú Deireadh Fómhair, 1953, in Amharclann an R.I.A.M. (Royal Irish Academy of Music) mar chuid d'Fhéile an Oireachtais.[2]

COMHLUADAR

Pádraig Sáirséal[3]

Eoghan Ó Gráda, "Eoghan na nOrd", Gabha.

Colm Ó Ceallaigh, "Colm na Ceártan", *príntíseach Eoghain.*

Muircheartach Ó Conghaile, "Muircheartach na mBan", *Feilméar Óg.*

Comharsana:

Mac Dara Píobaire

Máirtín Shéamuis Mhóir

Conchubhar na nAmhrán

Seán Rua

Fearghus A' Búrca, *Caiptín in airm Rí Shéamuis*[4]

Máire, *iníon Eoghain*

Brid an Phíobaire, *iníon le Mac Dara*

Comharsana idir fhir, mhná, bhuachaillí, chailíní, pháistí

AN CHÉAD GHNÍOMH

ÁIT
Ceárta Eoghain

UAIN
Lá Márta sa mbliain 1689

EOGHAN *(ag gábháil fhoinn)* Síos, suas, srl. Bhfuil an crú capaill sin críochnaithe agat, a Choilm?

COLM Ara, níl ná baol air.

EOGHAN Maise, dá mba capall féin bheifeá a dhéanamh ní fhéadfá tuilleadh moille a bhaint aisti! Tá an deamhan ort le fallsacht, a Choilm.

[*Tosaíonn sé ag gabháil fhoinn arís.*
   Síos, suas, srl.]

COLM Seo duit. An ndéanfaidh sé sin cúis?

EOGHAN *(ag breathnú ar an gcrú)* Há! Há! Há! An dtugann tú crú capaill air sin?

COLM Céard eile?

EOGHAN Cá bhfios domsa céard eile? Ní thabharfainnse crú capaill air ar aon nós.

COLM Tabhair pé ainm is maith leat air.

EOGHAN Ara, a bhuachaill mo chroí, ní thabharfainn é sin do King Billy féin.

COLM Cén locht atá air?

EOGHAN Cén locht atá air? É bheith gan chuma, gan chruth, gan dealbh, gan déanamh, gan maise, gan maitheas. M'anam maise go scanródh an púca féin dá bhfeicfeadh sé é! 'n Domhnach, dá gcuirfeá an rud sin faoi chapall dhéanfá bacach í faoi cheann ceathrú uaire!

COLM Níl aon rath orm. Ní thig liomsa leasú.

EOGHAN Níl aon rath ort: an anois fuair tú fios air sin? Nach mbím dá fhuagairt duit oíche is de ló nach bhfuil aon mhaith leat? Ag brionglóideach 'sea bhíonns tú i leaba cion fir a dhéanamh sa gceártain. Agus nuair nach mbíonn tú ag brionglóideach, bíonn tú ag sodar i ndiaidh na mban agus ag déanamh filíochta – slán an chomhartha – agus ag damhsa. Is breá an rud an damhsa, ach ní chruinníonn sé na pingineacha.

COLM Bhí teanga líofa agat i gcónaí, a Eoghain.

EOGHAN Maise, scéal beag ort: tá tú chomh sleamchúiseach le mac bean treafa na buaile a sháigh a mhéar isteach sa tine i leaba an phrócaire! Tá tú chomh tuathalach le Donncha Daoi a thacht é féin agus é ag cur a charbhat air féin! Tá tú chomh fallsa le Micheál fada a fuair bás den ocras mar gheall ar bheith ró-fhallsa lena chuid bídh 'ithe!

COLM Dia leat a Eoghain: níor chlis an dea-chaint riamh ort.

EOGHAN Theastódh dea-chaint ó dhuine uaireanta.

COLM Níl aon mhaith bheith liom. Ní dhéanfaidh mé gabha choíche.

EOGHAN Agus ó tharla go bhfuil a fhios sin agat, 'tuige in ainm na seacht ndiabhal ar thaobhaigh tú mo cheárta? Deirtear go bhfuil ardléann agat agus go bhfuil tú in ann Laidin agus Fraincis a thuiscint. Más amhlaidh atá, cad é an chiall nach ndearnadh sagart díot, nó bráthair, nó máistir scoile, nó file, nó rud ar bith ar thalamh an domhain thar a bheith ag cur daoine macánta as a meabhair le do chuid leibideachta?

COLM Mé féin a thogh an cheard seo, a Eoghain, agus bí cinnte go raibh ciall agam leis.

EOGHAN Deirtear go mbíonn a chiall féin ag an amadán.

COLM Fíor duit, a Eoghain. M'anam gur fíor do phort, mar a dúirt Tadhg.

EOGHAN Beidh port eile dá sheinm agatsa, a bhuachaill, mura gcuire tú caoi is fearr ar an gcrú capaill sin. Tá mise ag dul soir go teach an tsiúinéara le cos nua a fháil don ráca seo. Bíodh an crú capaill sin ar bhealach níos fearr agat faoi cheann ceathrú uaire nó bíodh ort féin.

[*Amach leis.*]

COLM Mais go n-imí an diabhal 's an deamhan leat! Agus go poll Tighe Liabáin led' chrú capaill![5]

[*Caitheann sé uaidh é.*]

Deamhan dreas eile a bhuailfeas mé. Sleamchúiseach, mar dhea! 'Sea agus fallsa! Tuathalach ina theannta sin! Is tuathalach leis chuile dhuine nach bhfuil ina ghabhainn chomh maith leis féin! Má ta, bíodh, mar a dúirt an Barrach.

[*Suíonn sé faoi os comhair na tine agus a smig ar a dhá láimh.
    Tagann Máire isteach.*]

MÁIRE Cá bhfuil m'athair a Choilm?

COLM (*gan cor as*) D'imigh sé soir go teach an tsiúinéara le cos nua d'fháil do ráca Mháirtín Shéamuis.

MÁIRE Tuige nach bhfuil tú ag obair?

COLM Tuige mbeinn?

MÁIRE Tuige mbeifeá?

COLM Sea, tuige mbeinn? Tá mé réidh leis an obair. Níl aon mhaith liom.

MÁIRE (*ag cur a láimhe ar a ghualainn*) Ceard tá ort a Choilm? Tá rud éicint ag cur as duit.

COLM Is iomaí rud atá ag cur as dom a Mháire.

MÁIRE Inis dom iad. B'fhéidir go bhféadfainn na bearta crua a réiteach.

COLM B'fhéidir leis an Athair Síoraí go bhféadfá. Ach an ndéanfá?

MÁIRE Nach bhfuil fhios agat go ndéanfainn rud ar bith a chuirfeadh áilleacht ort.

COLM Grá mo chroí thú! Ta's agam go ndéanfá. Tá t-athair tar éis íde na muc agus na madraí a thabhairt dom mar gheall ar bheith leisciúil agus tuathalach agus chuile short. Tá fhios agam i mo chroí istigh go bhfuil lom na fírinne aige. Ní dhéanfaidh mé gabha choíche, a Mháire. Gabha! Há ! Há! Há! Dia dá réiteach! B'fhearr liom bheith im' thincéar, mar ansin bheadh cead mo chos agus mo chinn agam.

MÁIRE A Choilm, tá mí-ádh éicint inniu ort. Féach, tá an tine ag dul as, beidh m'athair ag tíocht ar ais ar an bpointe. Seo, seo oibrigh leat. Séidfidh mise an bolg duit.

COLM Ná déan, a Mháire, ar do bhás ná déan! Ní bhuailfidh mé dreas eile ar an inneoin seo má mhairim an céad. Tá mé ag imeacht anocht, a Mháire.

MÁIRE Ag imeacht! Nár lige Dia!

COLM Agus an ndeireann tú liom nár mhaith leat mé 'imeacht?

MÁIRE Ar ndóigh, níor mhaith. Níl de chompánach agam ach tú agus m'athair. A Choilm, nárbh aoibhinn dúinn le bliain anois ag scéalaíocht cois tine, ag damhsa chuile thráthnóna nuair a bhailíomar na comharsana sa gceártain ag éisteacht le ceol na n-éanlaithe agus le glór na gaoithe amuigh sa gcoill?

COLM B'aoibhinn, a Mháire. A Dhia, nárbh aoibhinn! – A Mháire tá tú tar éis focla a ligint as do bhéal amach a chuir áilleacht ar mo chroí. Éist liom go ceann nóiméidín. Tá rún agam le scaoileadh – rún atá ag baint codlata díom le bliain. Nach suífidh tú, a Mháire?

[*Suíonn sí, brúnn seisean anall ina haice.*]

Níl ionamsa anois ach printíseach gabhann. Is mé an cheád duine de ghinealach mo shinsear a raibh ceard aige, thar cleachtadh a n-arm. Cailleadh m'athair agus mé im' mhalrach.

MÁIRE Agus cén t-ainm agus cén sloinne a bhí ar d'athair, a Choilm?

COLM An t-ainm agus an sloinne céanna tá ormsa.

MÁIRE Ach níl againne ort ach Colm na Ceártan.

COLM Colm Ó Ceallaigh a bhí ar m'athair agus Colm Ó Ceallaigh atá ormsa.

MÁIRE Colm Ó Ceallaigh! Is minic a chuala mé an t-ainm sin. Nárbh é Colm Ó Ceallaigh a chosain Gaillimh ar na Sasanaigh in aimsir Chromuell – é féin agus Preston?[6] Arbh é an Ceallach sin d'athairse?

COLM B'shin é m'athairse, a Mháire. In aimsir na ruaige, baineadh a chuid talún de, agus b'éigean dó dul ar teitheadh faoi na coillte agus na sléibhte. Fuair bodach éigin de Chlann Londain a raibh de thalamh aige agus níor bheag é. Rugadh mise i gcoill Mhílic Thiar ar bhruach an locha san am a bhí m'athair ar cheilt ann.[7] Fuaireas léann ó m'athair ar dtús agus ina dhiaidh sin ó shagart a bhí ar cheilt sa choill chéanna. Básaíodh m'athair agus mé deich mbliana d'aois – Fuair mo mháthair bás dhá bhliain roimhe sin.

MÁIRE Agus, a Choilm bhoicht, céard a rinne tú tar éis bhás d'athar?

COLM Ní raibh baol orm, a Mháire. D'fhan mé i measc na Rapairí agus ba Rapaire mé féin ón gcéad lá bhíos in ann claíomh a tharraingt as truaill.

MÁIRE Mo mhíle grá iad na Rapairí! Nuair nach raibh de dhídean againn ach iad sheas said go cróga i mbearna an bhaoil. Agus raibh tusa id' Rapaire a Choilm?

COLM Bhíos, a Mháire. Lá amháin – bhfuil tú ag éisteacht liom?

MÁIRE Táim.

COLM Lá amháin – tá sé anois trí bliana ó shin – tháinig mé féin agus beirt eile dár mbuachaillí go dtí an teach seo. Bhí macra Sasanach ar ár lorg. Bhí dhá scór acu ann. Chuardaigh said an choill ó mhaidin agus nuair nár éirigh leo breith orainn scaoil said a gcuid con 'nár ndiaidh.

MÁIRE Beannacht Dé linn!

COLM Thug d'athairse fosca oíche dúinn agus d'fhanamar i bhfolach sa scioból amuigh go maidin. B'in í an chéad uair a chonaic mé thú a Mháire. Ní raibh tú ach id' pháiste an t-am sin.

MÁIRE Is cuimhin lim go maith é, a Choilm. Is cuimhin liom an triúr Rapaire a tháinig go dtí an doras agus iad fuar fliuch báite; agus nuair a chualas go rabhthas ar bhur dtóir bhí an trua agam daoibh.

COLM Bhí a Mháire – bhí tú ag caoineachán go truamhéalach nuair a chuala tú an crua-chás a bhí orainn.

MÁIRE Agus ar tusa ceann don triúr sin, a Choilm?

COLM Ba mé, a Mháire. Ní raibh tú thar aois páiste mar a deirim leat, ach a Mháire, thug mé searc mo chroí duit an oíche sin. Bhí tú chomh geanúil, chomh binnbhriathrach, chomh caoinghlórach; bhí do chuid gruaige go clipeach ag titim ina dualaibh ar do sheál-bhráid. Bhí luisne i do chaoinleacainn le náire roimh na stráinséirí. A Mháire, od' ghealchois go dtí clár mín d'éadain ní raibh ball díot nach dtug mé mo mhíle grá dó. An gcloiseann tú mé a Mháire? D'imigh mé ar maidin lá arna mhárach agus go ceann bliana eile ní fhaca mé thú. Ach pé bith áit a ghabhainn ó shin amach bhí tú mar réalt eolais nó mar lóchrainn ó Dhia, ag dul romham sa lá agus san oíche fuair fuar gáifeach d'fheicinn an réalt eolais sin ag scaipeadh dorchadas na dubhchoille.

[*Cuireann sé a lámh faoina bráid.*]

MÁIRE Agus a Choilm, tuige a d'fhág tú an choill agus thréig na Rapairí?

COLM Níor thréigeas iad, a Mháire. Tháinig scaipeadh orainn. Básaíodh cuid againn agus chuaigh cuid eile thar sáile go dtí an Fhrainc nó an Spáinn.

MÁIRE Tuige nár imigh tusa, a Choilm, nuair a d'imigh an chuid eile?

COLM A Mháire, nach bhfuil fhios agat? Tá go raibh tusa anseo. Thairg mé mo sheirbhís dod' athair agus ghlac sé liom. Níor inis mé dó cé a bhí ionam, mar bhí fhios agam nár chara dom' athair é. Bhí imreas agus easaontas idir na Ceallaigh agus na Grádaigh le cuimhne na ndaoine. Uair amháin d'éirigh rí-rá éigin eatarthu ag aonach. Bhí m'athair agus d'athairse ann. Ins an gcoimheascair mharaigh muintir m'athar dearthái d'atharsa. Ón lá sin amach níor labhair Ceallach le Grádach. Dá mbeadh fhios ag d'athair gurb é Mac Choilm Uí Cheallaigh atá faoi dhíon a thí níorbh aoibhinn dom.

MÁIRE Cuireann do scéala iontas orm, a Choilm.

COLM Ag éirí ina sheasamh. Is iomaí cor sa saol seo a Mháire. Is beag a shíl m'athair uair go mbeadh a mhacsan Colm an Rapaire ina phríntíseach ag Eoghan na nOrd feadh dhá bhliain. Sea, agus is lag a shíl an líne a bhí in Éirinn leathchéad bliain ó shin go mbeadh a ginealach ag iarraidh déirce inniu.

MÁIRE Tóg suas go chroí, a Choilm, b'fhéidir le Rí na Glóire go bhfuil an lá sin thart anois.

COLM A Mháire, táim ag imeacht uait anocht. Deirtear go bhfuil Rí Séamus lena chuid féin a fháil arís. Beidh claimhte á nochtadh in Éirinn sula bhfad. Táim ag imeacht go Baile Átha Cliath mar a bhfuil Risteárd Talbóid ag cruinniú slua.[8] Sul má imeos mé tá ceist agam ort, a Mháire. Ón oíche sin tháinig mé anseo im'dhíbeartach ag teitheadh roimh mo naimhde thug mé grá mo chléibhe dhuit. A rúin ghil, an bpósfaidh tú mé?

MÁIRE Pósfaidh a Choilm. Nár thug mé féin grá duit le dhá bhliain?

COLM Tóg suas d'éadan geanúil, a Mháire agus lig dom do bhéal a phógadh. *(Pógann sé í)* A Mháire is milse ná sméartha do phóg. Ceann eile, a ghrá. *(Pógann sé arís í, tagann Eoghan isteach agus é dá pógadh).*

EOGHAN A chladhaire, scaoil uait í! Dár Críost! Ní bhrisfidh tú a clú!

COLM Ná labhair a thuilleadh a Eoghan na nOrd. Ní scriosadóir ban mise. Tá sí geallta dom i gcleamhnas.

EOGHAN Tá craiceann na bréige ar do chaint, a mhéirdrigh.

COLM Fiafraigh di féin an fíor a n-abraim leat?

EOGHAN A Mháire, an fíor a chaint?

MÁIRE Is fíor, a athair.

EOGHAN Céard deir tú? Ní chloisim i gceart tú.

MÁIRE Is fíor gach a n-abrann sé, a athair. Táimid geallta dá chéile.

EOGHAN Glan leat as mo radharc ar an bpointe, a Mháire, 'gcluin tú? Fág sin, a deirim leat. *(Tugann sí iarracht faoi labhairt:)* A Mháire, ó bogadh sa chliabhán tú níor leag mé mo lámh ort, ach, dar Críost, muna ngéilleann tú dom ní chosnóidh do leannán orm tú.

MÁIRE A athair, a chuid.

EOGHAN Ná labhair, a deirim leat. Imigh ort ar do bhás. *(Imíonn sí agus dúnann Eoghan an doras.)* ...Anois a scriosadóir! Tá an teach fúinn féin. Céard tá le rá agat liom?

COLM A Eoghain na nOrd. Thug tú cladhaire anocht orm. Sin ainm nár tugadh riamh roimhe orm ná ar dhuine dem' threibh...

EOGHAN Do threabhsa! Dár ndóighnín. Táimid ag dul 'un cinn. Nach mór an mórtas atá ag mo chathsa agus gan é ach óg!

COLM Thug tú cladhaire anocht orm, agus thug tú ainm eile orm níos measa ná sin. Bíodh fhios agat nach ceachtar acu mé. Is dána an fear tú a Eoghain ach dá dhánacht thú, tá sé mór agat drochainm a thabhairt ar mhac m'atharsa.

EOGHAN Agus cérbh é d'athairse?

COLM Colm Ó Ceallaigh. Tá barúil agam gur chuala tú caint air.

EOGHAN Colm Ó Ceallaigh! Agus an tusa a mhacsan?

COLM Is mé.

EOGHAN Dia dár gcumhdach! Mac le Colm Ó Ceallaigh – mac le Colm an áir- mac leis an bhfear dá dtug mé fuath mo chroí!...Éist liom, a Choilm Uí Cheallaigh, ós é sin d'ainm agus do shloinne, éist liom, a deirim leat. Dá mba printíseach bocht tú mar shíl mé bheith ionat ní sheánfainn m'iníon ort mar gheall ar tú bheith bocht. Ach ó tá 's agam anois cé tá ionat, bíodh 's agat nach bpósfaidh sí choíche tú. Níl agam ar an saol ach í. 'Sí an t-uan is measa liom dem' threibh. 'Sí an seod is uaisle atá agam. Ba mhó liom a bás ná mo bhás féin. Ach dár Rí na nGrás! B'fhearr liom dá sínfí fuar marbh os mo chomhair í ná dá bpósfadh sí tusa.

COLM Más amhlaidh atá, bíodh, a Eoghain. An leaba a thoghfas duine dó féin, luífeadh sé uirthi. Shíl mé go mbeadh d'iníon agam dod' dheoin ach ó tharla nach mbeidh beidh sí agam dod ainneoin. (Gluaiseann sé go dtí an doras.)

EOGHAN Fan id' sheasamh, a deirim leat. Ar do bhás, ná corraigh. Is mairg a théanns roimh Eoghan na nOrd.

COLM Ná ceap go bhfuil faitíos orm romhat, a Eoghain. Tá's agam an cháil atá amuigh ort. Deirtear nach bhfuil fear in Éirinn a d'fhéadfadh an t-Ord sin a thógáil ach tú féin. Deirtear go bhfuil tú in ann thú iarainn a lúbadh i do dhá láimh agus é a dhíriú amach arís. B'fhéidir go bhféadfainnse na cleasa céanna a dhéanamh. Dúirt tú liom lá mar mhagadh go raibh mo lámh chomh mín le lámh sagairt. B'fhéidir go raibh an ceart agat.

Ach féach an lámh sin a Eoghain! *(Nochtann sé a lámh.)* Bíodh go bhfuil a cneas mín agus geal, tá a fhéitheanna chomh teann led' chuid féin. Ná coisc orm imeacht. Táim réidh leatsa agus led' cheártain. Tá obair éifeachtach thar crú capaill a dhéanamh. Tá deaslámhacht ann thar crú a chasadh. B'fhéidir le Dia na bhFeart go gcloisfeá scéala sul i bhfad.

[*Caitheann sé a aprún uaidh agus amach leis.*]

EOGHAN Maise, grá mo chroí é! Shilfeá gur mac rí a bhí ann! Cá bhfaighinn fear ab uaisle ardmheannaighe dom' uan geal? Glaofaidh mé air. *(Téann sé go dtí an doras.)* A Choilm! Ach fan! Céard é seo tá mé rá? Nach mac le Colm Ó Ceallaigh é? Nach mac leis an bhfear a mharbhaigh Féidhlim Bán é? A Dhia Mhóir, cuidigh liom! Ná lig dom bás mo dhearthár a dhearmad. Tá Colm ardaigeantach uasal, ach tá buachaillí chomh maith leis, ar an mbaile. Ní ghéillfidh mé dó. Is mise a thoghfas fear dom' iníon. Thogh mé Muircheartach Ó Conghaile di agus dar Príosta pósfaidh sí faoi cheann ráithe é! Beidh sé anseo anocht. Labhróidh mé leis. Pósfar i ndiaidh Cásca iad. *(Cloistear fear.)* Éist! Éist! Cé hé seo chughainn? M'anam gurb é Muircheartach féin atá ann! Maith an áit a raibh sé! *(Tosaíonn sé ag obair ar chnámh a dhíchill.)*

MUIRCHEARTACH *(agus é amuigh, ag gábháil fhoinn)*
"Dá mbeinn 'mo bhadóir is deas a shnámhfainn an fharraige anonn,
Agus scríobhfainn cúpla líne ag mo ghrá faoi fhonn;
Bheinn ag éalú le mo chéad searc is ag fáisceadh a coim,
Is an lá nach bhféadaim bean a bhréagadh níl an báire liom."
Go mbeannaí Dia dá bhfuil anseo ach amháin an cat 's an mada.

EOGHAN Go mbeannaí an fear céanna duitse.

MUIRCHEARTACH Cén scéal é?

EOGHAN Scéal fada ar an anró.

MUIRCHEARTACH 'n Domhnach, bíonn an t-anró ar bharr do theanga i gcónaí.

EOGHAN Bíonn amannta, agus amannta eile nach mbíonn. Bhfuil aon bharr nuacht agat féin?

MUIRCHEARTACH Deirtear go bhfuil Rí Séamus ar an sáile.

EOGHAN Míle moladh le mac Dé!

MUIRCHEARTACH Tá barúil agam go mbeifear ag seasamh in aghaidh Bil Bradaigh go gairid.[9]

EOGHAN Níl aon amhras agam ort nach mbeifear.

MUIRCHEARTACH *(ag gábháil fhoinn)*
"Tá ribín le mo chéad searc i mo phóca thíos,
Agus feara Éireann ní fheádfaidís an chumha a bhaint díom
Tá mé réidh leat go ndéantar dom cónra chaol
Is go bhfásfaidh an féar ina dhiaidh trí mo lár aníos."
"Dona go leor a tháilliúir", mar a deir Tadhg:
"Bhéarfainn comhairle do na mná óga dá nglacfaidís uaim é,
Gan a bheith ag comhrá leis na hógfhir ná ag creidiúint a scéal,
Níl na gcomhrá ach mar dhoirtfeá braon uisce ar ghé,
Is a Dhia na Glóire go gcuirtear comhairle mo leasa orm féin!
Tabhair mo mhallacht do t'athair agus do do mhaithrín féin,
Nár thug scoil duit ar tús t'óige le mo láimh a léamh,
Is moch ar maidin a chuirfinn chughat brí mo scéil,
Is bíodh mo bheannacht leat go gcastar ort in uaigneas mé."

EOGHAN Táimid an-ceolmhar inniu, a Mhuircheartaigh.

MUIRCHEARTACH Bhfuil aon dochar ann?

EOGHAN Níl mé a rá go bhfuil.

MUIRCHEARTACH *(ag gábháil fhoinn)* "Tá cúl gruaige ar mo bhuachaill —"

EOGHAN Ara, caith uait. Tá rud éicint agam le rá leat.

MUIRCHEARTACH Abair leat. Tá mo phort seinnte, mar a dúirt an gandal nuair a bhí bean an tí ag casadh a mhuiníl.

EOGHAN Ar chuala tú go bhfuil Máire ag dul a'pósadh?

MUIRCHEARTACH Dar brí na ngabhar, níor chualas. I ndáiríre?

EOGHAN Tá sí dul a'pósadh tar éis Cásca.

MUIRCHEARTACH Agus an dochar fiafraí cé phósfas í?

EOGHAN Ara, bíodh ciall agat a bhuachaill! Cé phósfadh sí ach tú féin?

MUIRCHEARTACH Mise?

EOGHAN Cé eile?

MUIRCHEARTACH Dheamhan a bhfuil 'fhios agam cé eile.

[*Tosaíonn sé ag feadaíl.*]

EOGHAN Caith uait do chuid leibideachta. Nach bhfuil tú i ngrá léi?

MUIRCHEARTACH Tá mé i ndianghrá léi le blianta.

EOGHAN Maith go leor. Tabharfaidh mé leathchéad punt mar spré daoibh agus buaile na creige san aguisín.

MUIRCHEARTACH Ach fuirigh ort, a Eoghain. Bhfuil fhios ag Máire féin go bhfuil sí le pósadh?

EOGHAN Beidh fhios aici ar ball.

MUIRCHEARTACH Agus rud eile. Shíl mé go raibh sí féin agus Colm na Ceártan an-mhór le chéile?

EOGHAN Stop do bhéal, a deirim leat! Dá mbeadh a hanam ag seasamh air ní phósfaidh sí Colm na Ceártan. 'Sé an fear a thoghfas mise a phósfas sí agus is tusa mo rogha.

MUIRCHEARTACH Ach cogar i leith a Eoghain. Níor mhaith liom dul romhat, ach nach bhfuil a fhios agat go bhfuil mé féin agus Bríd an Phíobaire ag labhairt le chéile?

EOGHAN Do chroíse ón seabhac, a dhuine, an ag dul as do mheabhair atá tú? Bríd an Phíobaire! Nár bhreá an cleamhnas é! B'fhéidir go ndéanfaidh sí píobaire díot féin! A Mhuircheartaigh, tá mise tar éis m'iníon féin a thairiscint duit. Cé acu is fearr leat?

MUIRCHEARTACH Dheamhan a bhfuil fhios agam.

EOGHAN Dheamhan a bhfuil fhios agat! A Mhuircheartaigh, tá dhá cheist agam ort.

MUIRCHEARTACH Abair leat.

EOGHAN Bhfuil tú i ngrá le Máire s'agamsa?

MUIRCHEARTACH Nár dhúirt mé leat go bhfuilim.

EOGHAN Maith go leor. Bhfuil tú i ngrá le Bríd an Phíobaire?

MUIRCHEARTACH Nár dhúirt mé leat go bhfuilim.

EOGHAN Muise, lagar an bháis ort, a bhromaire.

MUIRCHEARTACH Fan ort, a Eoghan. Níl an cheist chomh furasta le réiteach is cheapanns tú. Breathnaigh anseo. Ba mhaith leatsa dá bpósfainn Máire. Maith go leor. D'fheilfeadh sí go maith dom. Ach tá Colm na Ceártan ar buile agus i ngrá léise.

EOGHAN Go hIfreann le Colm na Ceártan!

MUIRCHEARTACH Tá Colm ar buile agus i ngrá le Máire, agus tá faitíos m'anama orm go bhfuil sise i ngrá leis. Tá Bríd an Phíobaire i ngrá liomsa. Tá mise i ngrá leis an mbeirt acu.

EOGHAN Muise, lagar an bháis ort, a bhromaire.

[*Tagann Máirtín Shéamuis Mhóir isteach.*]

MÁIRTÍN Go mbeannaí an Rí anseo.

EOGHAN, MUIRCHEARTACH Go mba hé duit.

[*Tosaíonn Eoghan ag obair arís ar a mhine géire.*]

EOGHAN Suigh fút, a Mháirtín, agus téigh tú féin.

MÁIRTÍN Tá mé tuirseach im' shuí. Im' shuí ata mé i gcónaí *(buaileann sé faoi).*

MUIRCHEARTACH Bhfuil scéal ar bith agat?

MÁIRTÍN Dheamhan scéal muna bhfaighim uaitse é. Cá bhfuil Colm a Eoghain?

EOGHAN Is cuma liom sa tubaiste cá bhfuil sé.

MÁIRTÍN Níl aon chall duit smailc a bhaint asam a Eoghain. Ní raibh aon dochar sa cheist.

EOGHAN Ná tóg orm é, a Mháirtín. Tá mí-ádh éicint inniu orm.

MUIRCHEARTACH Seo chughainn fear na n-amhrán. 'Sé do bheatha, a Chonchubhair.

[*Tagann Conchubhar isteach.*]

CONCHUBHAR Go mba hé daoibh a chomhluadair. Feicim an Píobaire ag dul amach an bóthar.

[*Tagann scata de chomharsana isteach. Fir agus mná agus cailíní agus buachaillí agus páistí: beannaíonn gach duine acu go cneasta le comhluadar an tí.*]

MÁIRTÍN Seo chughainn an Píobaire.

[*Tagann MacDara agus Bríd isteach.*]

MACDARA Bail ó Dhia anseo!

CONCHUBHAR Dia leat, a Phíobaire. Maith an t-am tháinig tú.

MUIRCHEARTACH Séid suas, a Phíobaire. Tá cosa na gcailíní ag damhsa cheana.

IAD UILIG Glanaigí an t-úrlár. Amach libh a bhuachaillí agus a chailíní!

[*Séideann an píobaire; damhsann siad pas. Cruinníonn na seandaoine thar an tine ag cur agus ag cúiteamh. Glaotar "Go neartaí Dia sibh!" "Dia leat, a Phíobaire!" "Thug sé amach í" agus araile agus iad ag damhsa. Tá Eoghan ag obair i gcónaí.*]

MÁIRTÍN Ara, caith uait an t-ord sin, a Eoghain. Tá cion fir déanta agat inniu.

EOGHAN A chomharsana, tá an damhsa seo ag goilleadh orm. Chítear dom go bhfuil cogadh agus bás ar na gaotha anocht. *(Stadtar den damhsa.)* A bhuachaillí, tá loingeas ar an sáile ag déanamh ar Éirinn. B'fhéidir go bhfuil sé i gcuan cheana féin. Is fear go mbeidh an rosc catha dá sheinm thart faoin tír. A Chonchubhair, buail suas amhrán, amhrán a chuirfeas misneach 'nár gcroíthe.

MÁIRTÍN Déan, a Chonchubhair!

CONCHUBHAIR Maith go leor, a chomharsana. Tabharfaidh mé "Gráinne Mhaol" daoibh.[10]

IAD UILIG "Nár laga Dia thú"; "Go maire tú do ghuth".

CONCHUBHAIR *(ag gábháil fhoinn)* Bí meanmach srl.

[*Buailtear ar an doras. Seo isteach Seán Rua.*]

SEÁN Shroich loingeas na bhFrancach Ceann tSáile trí lá ó shin. Tá Rí Séamus anois i gCorcaigh.[11]

IAD UILIG Forrú-ú-ú!

EOGHAN I ndáiríre, a bhuachaillí? Cé tá ina fhochair?

SEÁN Tá ceithre chéad oifigeach idir Fhrancaigh agus Ghaeil. Cloisim go bhfuil De Rosen ann agus Berwick agus a'gcluin sibh, a chairde? – Sáirséal an chroí mhóir agus na láimhe láidre![12]

[*Preabann Eoghan ar stól.*]

EOGHAN Seo beatha gan bás do Rí Séamus! Seo beatha gan bás do Phádraig Sáirséal! Seo beatha gan bás do Ghráinne Mhaol!

AN COMHLUADAR Forú-ú-ú!

[*Tá Eoghan in airde ar stól i lár an ardáin: tá na daoine eile cruinnithe ina thimpeall ag glaoch ar Rí Séamus, Pádraig Sáirséal agus Gráinne Mhaol. Druidtear an brat anuas agus iad ag gábháil "Gráinne Mhaol".*]

AN COMHLUADAR Ó, srl.

An Dara Gníomh

Áit
Sráid os comhair ceártan
Uain
Tráthnóna Iúil sa mbliain 1690

[*Tagann Colm isteach agus é gléasta mar oifigeach le Rí Séamus.*]

COLM (*ag féachaint siar*) Bhfuil tú ag tíocht a Fhearghuis?

FEARGHUS (*amuigh*) Táim. Go poll Tigh Liabáin leis na clocha seo! Tá mo chosa briste acu.

COLM Tabhair aire duit féin. Is clochach an spota é. Bhfuil an Sáirséalach ag tíocht?

FEARGHUS Tá sé lem' shála. Ó bú! Bú! Dia le m'anam!

COLM Céard tá anois ort?

FEARGHUS Och! Sciorr mo chos agus is iontach nár leagadh mé.

COLM 'n Domhnach, ní shílfeá gur Gaillimheach tú má bhaineann an cnoicín sin tuisle asat.

[*Tagann Fearghus isteach.*]

FEARGHUS Caith uait, a deirim leat. 'Dhóbair go ndearnadh cruas de chnámha in aghaidh na creige.

[*Tagann Sáirséal isteach.*]

Maise, beannacht Dé duit, a Choilm, nach greannmhar an áit seo le ceárta a dhéanamh. Níl an chreag sin in airíocht le capall a shiúl chor le duine.

COLM Ar ndóigh, tá bealach eile ar an taobh thiar den chreig. Thángamar an cóngar.

SÁIRSÉAL An cóngar! Maise, beannacht Dé duit. "Más cam díreach an bóthar, 'sí an tslí mhór an aicearra." Nach uaigneach an ball é! Bhfuil sé i bhfad go Cill Dalua?

COLM An bhfeiceann tú an spota geal sin fad do sheanradhairc uait?

SÁIRSÉAL Feicim.

COLM Sin cuan de Loch Deirg. An bhfeiceann tú an cnoc maol sin ar an taobh thall don loch?

COLM Tá an cnoc sin i gContae an Chláir. Níl Cill Dalua deich mile ar an taoibh ó dheas den chnoc sin.

SÁIRSÉAL Agus níl Luimneach os cionn deich mile siar ó dheas ó Chill Dalua.

FEARGHUS Tá sé deich míle go leith.

SÁIRSÉAL Maith go leor. Sroichfimid Cill Dalua anocht agus beimid i Luimneach le maidin an lae amárach. Arb é seo an ceárta, a Choilm?

COLM 'Sí. Buailigí isteach.

SÁIRSÉAL Nach dtiocfaidh tú in éindí linn?

COLM Ní thiocfad. B'fhearr liom fuireacht anseo.

SÁIRSÉAL Tuige?

COLM Tá gá leis. Fuireod anseo libh anseo.

SÁIRSÉAL Aoibhneas duine a thoil. Ní bhacfaidh mé leat.

[*Buaileann sé an doras.*]

EOGHAN *(agus é istigh)* Cé hé sin amuigh?[13]

SÁIRSÉAL Tá mise agus duine eile.

EOGHAN I ndáiríre? Bhfuil tú cinnte gur thú féin atá ann?

SÁIRSÉAL D'fhéadfainn an leabhar a thabhairt ann.

EOGHAN Agus an dochar fiafraí cé tú féin?

SÁIRSÉAL Saighdiúir bocht atá ag déanamh ar Luimneach.

EOGHAN *(ag an doras)* Cé acu Gaeil nó Gaill sibh?

SÁIRSÉAL Nach léir duit gur Gaeil sinn de réir teanga?

EOGHAN Cé acu le Rí Séamus nó le Rí Liam sibh?

SÁIRSÉAL Ní le ceachtar acu. Ní ghéillimid do Rí ar thalamh an domhain.[14]

EOGHAN Cé leis sibh, mar sin, in ainm na tubaiste?

SÁIRSÉAL Ní le Rí sinn, ach le banríon.

EOGHAN Ní thuigim brí do chainte, a dhuine uasail. Cé hí an bhanríon ar léi sibh?

SÁIRSÉAL Is iomaí ainm agus sloinne atá uirthi. 'Sé an t-ainm is mó a thugann na Connachtaigh uirthi Gráinne Mhaol.

EOGHAN *(ag breith ar láimh air)* Maise, mo ghrá sibh, na páistí bheas agaibh. Saighdiúirí sibh le Gráinne boicht. Buíochas leis an Athair síoraí go bhfuil seadairí fearúla ag seasamh le ceart Ghráinne i ndeireadh na dála. Raibh sibh ag an mBóinn?

SÁIRSÉAL Bhíomar.

EOGHAN Nach bocht mar briseadh orainn ann! Ghol mé mo dhóthain nuair a chualas na scéala.

SÁIRSÉAL Níor briseadh orainn, a ghabha. Ní orainne a briseadh ach ar Rí Séamus! Dar prícín, nár chumasach an Taoiseach é, lena leathbhróg Gaelach agus a leathbhróg Gallda! Dá raibh Liam bradach féin mar cheannfort orainn agus Séamuisín mar cheannfhort ar na Gallaibh, ní bhrisfí orainn![15]

EOGHAN Ach cogar mé seo, a dhuine uasail. Cloisim go bhfuil Sáirséal na Féile tar éis na Gaill a ruagairt ó Bhaile Átha Luain?

SÁIRSÉAL Cloisim féin go bhfuil.

EOGHAN Grá mo chroí é, Pádraig! Murach é ba chráite cás Ghráinne Mhaol inniu. Níl saighdiúir aici ach é. Le Séamus nó le Liam an chuid eile, ach fearacht sibh féin, a uaisle, níor thug Pádraig a chroí ach do Ghráinne Mhaol. Cá bhfuil sé anocht, meas sibh, ós rud é go bhfuil ruaigthe aige ar Douglas agus a raibh os comhair Átha Luain.

SÁIRSÉAL Is dóigh go bhfuil sé ag déanamh ar Luimneach chomh maith le cách.

EOGHAN Tá mé ceapadh go ngabhfaidh sé an bealach seo mar sin. Nach raibh sé in aice le Beannachair seachtain ó shin?

SÁIRSÉAL Sin é a chloisim.

EOGHAN Thabharfainn a bhfuil agam ar an saol lena lámh a chreathadh.

FEARGHUS B'fhéidir nach bhfuil sé rófhada uait.

EOGHAN An ag magadh fúm atá tú?

FEARGHUS Dheamhan magadh. Cén t-ainm atá ar an áit seo?

EOGHAN Ceárta na Creige thugtar air.

FEARGHUS 'n Domhnach maise níl Pádraig Sáirséal i bhfad ó Cheárta na Creige anocht.

[NEAMHCHRÍOCHNAITHE]

NOTES

1 Foinse: MS 15, 004. Ní fios cén uair go cruinn a cumadh an script neamhchríochnaithe seo: athaimsíodh é sa bhliain 1953 i dtigh Éamonn Bulfin in aice le Biorra. Féach 'A Forgotten Play by Patrick Pearse' *The Irish Press*, June 8, 1953. Níor foilsíodh an dráma riamh roimhe seo.

2 'Oireachtas Lá na nÓg, Priest Says Ireland Needs Her Youth', *Irish Independent*, 28 October 1953.

3 Pádraig Sáirséal (Patrick Sarsfield) c.1660–1693, ceannaire ar fhás a cháil mar gheall ar a chuid gaiscí ar thaobh na gCaitliceach sa tréimhse tar éis Chath na Bóinne sa bhliain 1690. Tháinig sé chun cinn mar cheannaire de réir mar a bhí ag teip ar mhisneach na gcinnirí eile, go háirithe Iarla Thír Chonaill agus de Lauzun. Is léir go bhfuil an mhír den dráma lena mbaineann Sáirséal suite an tráth go raibh lucht leanúna an tSáirséalaigh ag teacht chucu féin agus ag déanamh ar Luimneach tar éis scaipeadh Chath na Bóinne agus tar éis dó féin seal a chaitheamh ag mBeannachair. Tá cáil ar leith ar an ionsaí a dhein Sáirséal ar chuid d'fhórsaí Rí Liam ag Baile an Fhaoitigh tar éis dó éalú amach as Cathair Luimnigh i ndoircheacht na hoíche agus suas le sé chead marcach eile leis. Ach is léir go bhfuil an t-aicsean sa chuid seo de dhráma Mhic Phiarais suite sular tharla léigear Luimnigh nó ionsaí cáiliúil sin an tSáirséalaigh ar fhórsaí Liam – cé go luaitear cuid de na logainmneacha a bhain cáil amach mar chuid de scéal Sarsfield anseo, Cill Dalua, mar shampla.

4 Séamus II, an ceannaire Seacaibíteach/Caitliceach. Sa bhliain 1690 thug an Rí Séamus agus Liam Oráiste aghaidh ar a chéile ag Cath na Bóinne. Bhain cúlra polaitíochta comhaimseartha na hEorpa leis an gcath ach samhlaítear sa ghnáthchultúr é mar chath idir na Gaeil Chaitliceacha agus na Protastúnaigh. Tá cuntas cuimsitheach ar

pholaitíocht na ré in Eamonn Ó Ciardha, *Ireland and the Jacobite Cause 1685–1766, a fatal attachment,* (Dubin: Four Courts), 2002.

5 Go Poll Tighe Liabáin. 'Go háit iargúlta' an chiall atá anseo, is dócha. Bhí Poll Tighe Liabháin i ndeisceart na Gaillimhe (i measc áiteanna eile) agus luaitear an nath in *Foras Feasa ar Éirinn.* Féach William Mahon, aist., Seán Ó Neachtain, *The History of Éamon O'Clery,* (Conamara: Cló Iarchonnachta), 2000, p. 180

6 Ba é an Gionarál Preston, gobharnóir an bhaile, a bhí i gceannas ar chosaint na Gaillimhe agus an baile faoi léigear ag Sir Charles Coote. Tá cuntas ar an léigear le fáil in Eamon P. Duffy, 'The Siege and Surrender of Galway 1651–1652', *Journal of the Galway Archaeological and Historical Society,* Vol. 39, 1983/1984, pp. 115-142.

7 Meabhraíonn an tagairt do Choill Mhílic eachtraí ar leith de chuid chogaí na 1640aidí. Bhí seasamh déanta ag fórsaí Connachtacha faoi cheannas Iarla Clanricarde. Bhí éirithe le Clanricarde fórsaí a bhí faoi cheannas Colonel Daniel Axtell a ruaigeadh tamall ó dheas de Bhaile Átha Luain agus bhí fórsa an Ghionaráil Preston tar éis teacht i gcabhair ar Clanricarde. Ach bhí méadaithe ar fhórsaí Axtell chomh maith agus chuir siad an ruaig ar na Connachtaigh i gcath a thit amach ag Mílic (ar an tSionainn) i mí Dheireadh Fómhair na bliana 1650.

8 Richard Talbot, 1630–1691 ('Lying Dick Talbot'), Iarla Thír Chonaill, Saighdiúir agus ceannaire Seacaibíteach a dhein airm a shlógadh do na Seacaibítigh. D'imigh chun na Fraince chun cúnamh a lorg tar éis Chath na Bóinne, d'fhill ar Éirinn sa bhliain 1691 ach fuair bás go gairid ina dhiaidh sin. Bhí teannas idir é agus Sarsfield sa deireadh agus amhras ar dhaoine áirithe faoi.

9 Liam Oráiste.

10 Foilsíodh an dán 'A Shaoi Ghlain don Phríomhscoth' le Seán Clárach Mac Domhnaill, a bhfuil Gráinne Mhaol mar shiombal d'Éirinn ann, in *Amhráin Sheaghain Chláraigh Mhic Dhomhnaill,* eag. An tAthair Pádraig Ua Duinnín, An dara heagar, (BÁC: Conradh na Gaeilge), 1902, lgh. 40-41 agus luaitear 'fonn Ghráinne Mhaol' leis an dán. Tá fáistine sa dán sin 'go sínfidh an Rí ceart le Gráinne Mhaol'. Is eol dúinn go raibh *Bards of the Gael and Gall* le George Sigerson, a raibh leagan Béarla de dhán Mhic Dhomhnaill ann, léite ag an bPiarsach. Féach George Sigerson, *Bards of the Gael and Gall,* Fisher Unwin, London, 1897, p.271. Nuair a dhein an Piarsach a leagan féin den amhrán traidisiúnta 'Séarlas Óg' ('An Dord Féinne') (arbh ionann é agus an t-amhán a dtugtar 'Óró sé do bheatha abhaile' go coitianta air anois) chuir sé línte breise faoi Ghráinne Mhaol ann. Ghlac an Piarsach le moladh Ruairí Mac Easmuinn go mbainfí leas as an

seanamhrán sin 'Searlas Óg' mar amhrán mairseála do na hÓglaigh tar éis cruinnithe sa Ghaillimh sa bhliain 1914 agus foilsíodh leagan cóirithe Mhic Phiarais leis an tagairt do Ghráinne Mhaol san *Irish Volunteer* ar an 27.2.1915. Féach Ciarán Ó Coigligh, eag., *Filíocht Ghaeilge Phádraig Mhic Phiarais*, An Clóchomhar, 1981, lgh.41-42; 91-92. Le haghaidh eolais ghinearálta faoi Ghráinne Mhaol agus faoi thagairtí di sa litríocht agus sa bhéaloideas féach Anne Chambers, *Granuaile, The Life and Times of Grace O'Malley, c.1530–1603*, Wolfhound Press, 1998.

11 Ar an 12ú nó an 17ú Márta a tháinig Rí Séamus i dtír i gCionn tSáile. Féach John Todhunter, *Life of Patrick Sarsfield*, Fisher Unwin, 1895, p.28.

12 Gionarál Francach ab ea De Rosen. Bhí sé i láthair agus Doire faoi léigear. Glaodh ar ais as Éirinn é mar gheall ar an teannas a chruthaigh a chuid iompair. Ba mhac mídhlisteanach le Séamus II é an chéad Diúc Berwick, James Fitzjames, 1670-1734. Bhí cáil air as a chrógacht agus ghlac sé páirt ghníomhach i gCath na Bóinne. Tar éis bhás an tSáirséalaigh, phós sé a bhaintreach.

13 Tá an líne chéanna san amhrán cáiliúil 'Éamonn an Chnoic'. Rapaire cáiliúil i dTiobraid Árann ab ea Éamonn an Chnoic/Éamonn Ó Riain.

14 Deirtear go raibh an-díoma ar Shairséal agus ar go leor eile maidir le hiompar Rí Séamus ag Cath na Bóinne.

15 Cuirtear ráiteas mar seo i mbéal an tSairséalaigh sa bhéaloideas.

1.17 Portrait of Patrick Sarsfield, Earl of Lucan (d.1693), English, 17th century (artist unknown). Pádraig Sáirséal. (Courtesy of the National Gallery of Ireland/Le caoinchead ón Dánlann Náisiúnta.)

EOGHAN THE SMITH[1]

First performance (in Irish): Comhaltas Drámaíochta na Tulaigh Móire, 27 October 1953, in the R.I.A.M (Royal Irish Academy of Music) theatre, as part of the Oireachtas Festival.[2]

CAST

Patrick Sarsfield[3]

Eoghan O'Grady, "Eoghan of the Hammers", *Blacksmith*

Colm O'Kelly, "Colm of the Forge", *Eoghan's apprentice*

Muircheartach Ó Conghaile, "Muircheartach na mBan", (Muircheartach of the Women), *a young farmer*

Macdara the Piper

Máirtín Shéamuis Mhóir

Conchubhar na nAmhrán (Conchubhar of the Songs) Neighbours

Seán Rua

Fergus Burke, *a captain in King James' army*[4]

Máire, *Eoghan's daughter*

Bríd an Phíobaire/Bríd of the Piper, *a daughter of Mac Dara*

Neighbours, including men, women, boys, girls and children.

THE FIRST ACT

PLACE
Eoghan's Forge
TIME
The first of March in the year 1689

EOGHAN *(singing)* Síos, suas, etc.
Have you finished that horseshoe Colm?

COLM Ara, I have not and no fear I have.

EOGHAN Muise, if it were a horse itself you were making you couldn't delay more with it! You are the devil with laziness, Colm. *(He starts singing again)* Síos, suas, etc.

COLM Here you are. Will that do?

EOGHAN *(looking at the shoe)* Ha! Ha! Ha! Do you call that a horseshoe?

COLM What else?

EOGHAN How do I know what else? I wouldn't call it a horseshoe anyway.

COLM Give it whatever name you like.

EOGHAN Ara my boy, I wouldn't give that to King Billy himself.

COLM What's wrong with it?

EOGHAN What's wrong with it? It has neither shape nor make nor look appearance nor ornament nor any use. Upon my soul, muise, a ghost itself would get a fright if he saw it! By Sunday, if you put that thing under a horse you would make it lame in a quarter of an hour!

COLM I am no good. I can't improve.

EOGHAN You are no good: is it now you found that out? Don't I be announcing it to you night and day that you are no good. Dreaming you do be instead of doing a man's share in the forge. And when you are not dreaming, you are chasing after women and composing poetry – signs beyond – and dancing. Dancing is a fine thing but it doesn't gather the pennies.

COLM You always had a way with words, Eoghan.

EOGHAN Muise, a quick summary of you: you are as sloppy as the son of the ploughwoman who stuck his finger in the fire instead of the poker! You are as clumsy as Donnacha Daoi who choked himself and he putting his tie on him! You are as lazy as Micheál Fada who died of hunger from being too lazy to eat his food!

COLM God be with you Eoghan, you were never short of clever words.

EOGHAN A person would want clever words sometimes.

COLM There's no use in me. I will never make a smith.

EOGHAN And since you know that, why in the name of the seven devils did you come to my forge? It's said you have great learning and that you can understand French and Latin. If that is so, why did you not become a priest or a brother or a schoolmaster or a poet or anything at all on the face on the earth instead of sending honest people out of their minds with your carelessness?

COLM It was myself chose this trade Eoghan, and you can be sure I had a reason for it.

EOGHAN It's said a fool himself has his reasons.

COLM True for you, Eoghan. Upon my soul but "is fíor do phort", like Tadhg said.

EOGHAN You'll be playing a different tune, boy, unless you put proper shape on that horseshoe. I am going over to the carpenter's house to get a new handle for this rake. Let that horseshoe be in a better way by you in a quarter of an hour or it's your own lookout.

(He goes out.)

COLM Musha, may the devil and the demon go with you! And to hell with your horseshoe! *(He throws it away from him)*. I won't hit it another go. Sloppy, mar dhea! Yes, and lazy! Clumsy as well as that! Everyone is clumsy to him who isn't as good a smith as himself! If that is the case, then let it be, like Barry said.

[*He sits down before the fire with his chin on his two hands.*
    Máire enters.]

MÁIRE Where is my father Colm?

COLM *(without moving)* He went over to the carpenter's house to get a new handle for Máirtín Shéamuis' rake.

MÁIRE Why aren't you working?

COLM Why would I?

MÁIRE Why would you?

COLM Yes, why would I? I'm finished with work. I'm no good.

MÁIRE *(putting her hand on his shoulder)* What's wrong with you Colm? Something is upsetting you.

COLM There's many a thing upsetting me Máire.

MÁIRE Tell me about them. Maybe I could solve your difficulties.[5]

COLM Maybe with the everlasting Father you could. But would you?

MÁIRE Don't you know that I would do anything at all that would make you happy.

COLM *Grá mo chroí thú!*[6] I know you would. Your father is after laying into me for being lazy and clumsy and everything else. I know in my heart he is telling the truth. I will never make a smith, Máire. A smith! Ha! Ha! Ha! God save us! I'd rather be a tinker because then I could go freely where my head and my feet wanted.

MÁIRE Colm, there is some mí-ádh on you today. Look, the fire is going out, my father will be coming back any minute. Here, here, be working away. I will blow the bellows for you.

COLM Do not, Máire, on your death, do not! I will never use this anvil again if I live to be a hundred. I am leaving tonight Máire.

MÁIRE Leaving! God forbid!

COLM And are you saying to me that you don't want me to leave?

MÁIRE Of course I don't want you to. I have no companion but you and my father. Colm, wasn't it lovely for us for the last year to be telling stories by the fire, dancing every evening when we gathered the neighbours in the forge listening to the music of the birds and to the sound of the wind outside in the wood?

COLM It was lovely, Máire. God, wasn't it lovely! Máire, you are after letting words out of your mouth that gladdened my heart. Listen to me for a little minute. I have a secret to tell – a secret that is stopping me sleeping with a year. Won't you sit, Máire? *(She sits, he moves over beside her.)* I am only a smith's apprentice now. I am the first person of my people who had a trade, other than using their arms. My father died and I a young boy.

MÁIRE And what name and surname had your father, Colm?

COLM The same name and surname is on me.

MÁIRE But we call you nothing except Colm of the Forge.

COLM Colm O'Kelly was my father's name and Colm O'Kelly is my name.

MÁIRE Colm O'Kelly! It's often I heard that name. Wasn't it Colm O'Kelly who defended Galway from the English in the time of Cromwell – himself and Preston?[7] Was that O'Kelly your father?

263

COLM That was my father, Máire. In the time of the driving out, his land was taken from him, and he had to go on the run among the woods and the mountains. Some bodach of London's seed got all his land – and it was no little land. I was born in Mílic Thiar wood on the shore of the lake at the time my father was in hiding there. I got learning from my father first of all and then from a priest who was hiding in the same wood. My father was killed and I ten years old – my mother died two years before that.[8]

MÁIRE And poor Colm, what did you do after the death of your father?

COLM There was no fear of me, Máire. I stayed among the Raparees and I was a Raparee myself from the first time I could draw a sword from a sheath.

MÁIRE My thousand praises to the Raparees! When we had no protection but them they stood boldly in the gap of danger. And were you a Raparee, Colm?

COLM I was, Máire. One day – are you listening to me?

MÁIRE I am.

COLM One day – it's three years ago now – myself and two more of our boys came to this house. A troop of Englishmen were after us. There were two score of them. They searched the wood from morning and when they didn't succeed in catching us they set their hounds after us.

MÁIRE God bless us!

COLM Your father gave a night's shelter to us and we stayed hiding in the barn outside until morning. That was the first time I saw you, Máire. You were only a child that time.

MÁIRE I remember it well, Colm. I remember the three Raparees who came to the door and they drowned cold wet;[9] and when I heard that ye were being chased I had a lot of pity for ye.

COLM You did, Máire – you were crying pitifully when you heard the hard situation we were in.

MÁIRE And were you one of those three, Colm?

COLM I was, Máire. You weren't above the age of a child, like I say, but Máire, I gave you the love of my heart that night.[10] You were so lovely, so sweet-spoken, so gentle-voiced; your hair falling freely in tresses on the edge of your shawl. There was a flush in your lovely cheek with shyness before the strangers. Máire, from your bright leg to your gentle forehead there wasn't a part of you that I didn't give my thousand loves to. Do you hear me Máire? I left the next morning and for another year I didn't see you. But wherever I went since then you were like a star of knowledge or a lantern from God, going before me in the day and in the cold terrible night I used to see that star of knowledge scattering the darkness of the black wood.

[*He puts his arm around her.*]

MÁIRE And Colm, why did you leave the wood and leave the Raparees behind?

COLM I didn't leave them behind, Máire. We were separated. Some of us died and others went abroad to France or Spain.

MÁIRE Why didn't you go Colm when the rest went?

COLM Máire, do you not know? It is that you were here. I came as a servant to your father and he accepted me. I didn't tell him who I was, because I knew he was not a friend of my father. As far back as people can remember there was contention and disunity between the Kellys and the Gradys. One time there was some kind of a rí-rá between them at a fair. My father and your father were there. In the skirmish the people of my father killed your father's brother. From that day onward no Kelly spoke to a Grady. If your father knew it was the son of Colm O'Kelly under his roof it would not bode well for me.

MÁIRE Your story surprises me, Colm.

COLM *(getting up)* There's many a twist in this life, Máire… it's little my father once thought that his son Colm the Raparee would be Eoghan of the Hammers apprentice for two years. Yes, and it's little the line that was in Ireland half a century ago thought that their descendants would be begging today.

MÁIRE Raise up your heart, Colm, maybe by the King of Glory that that day is over now.

COLM Máire, I'm leaving you tonight. It is said that King James is to get what is his again. Swords will be bared in Ireland before long. I am going to Dublin where Richard Talbot is gathering a crowd.[11] Before I go I have a question for you Máire. Since that night when I came here as an outcast fleeing from my enemies I gave you the love of my heart. My bright darling, will you marry me?

MÁIRE I will marry you Colm. Didn't I love you myself with two years?

COLM Lift up your lovely face, Máire and let me kiss your mouth. *(He kisses her.)* Máire, your kiss is sweeter than berries. Another one, my love. *(He kisses her again, Eoghan comes in while he is kissing her.)*

EOGHAN You rogue, let her go! By Christ! You will not take her honour!

COLM Don't say any more Eoghan of the Hammers. I am not a destroyer of women. She is engaged to me.

EOGHAN There is a cover of a lie on your talk, you slut.

COLM Ask herself is what I am saying to you true?

EOGHAN Máire, is his talk true?

MÁIRE It is true, father.

EOGHAN What are you saying? I can't hear you right.

MÁIRE Everything he says is true, father. We are engaged to each other.

EOGHAN Clear out of my sight right now, Máire, do you hear? Leave, I say. *(She attempts to speak)* Máire, since you were rocked in the cradle I didn't lay my hand on you, but by Christ, if you don't yield to me your lover will not protect you.

MÁIRE Father, dear.

EOGHAN Don't speak, I tell you. Leave on your death. *(She leaves and Eoghan closes the door)* …Now you destroyer! We have the house to ourselves. What have you to say to me?

COLM Eoghan of the Hammers. You called me a rogue tonight. That's a name that was never given to me ever before or to anyone of my people.

EOGHAN Your people! Of course. We are making progress. Isn't it plenty of pride my man has and he only young!

COLM You called me a rogue tonight, and you called me another name worse than that. Let you know that I am neither. You are a bold man Eoghan but bold as you are, you have some nerve to vilify the son of my father.

EOGHAN And who was your father?

COLM Colm O'Kelly. I have an idea you heard talk of him.

EOGHAN Colm O'Kelly! And are you his son?

COLM I am.

EOGHAN God protect us! A son of Colm O'Kelly, a son of Colm of the slaughter – a son of the man I gave my heart's hatred! … Listen to me, Colm O'Kelly, since that is your name and your surname, listen to me, I tell you. If I thought you were a poor apprentice as I thought I wouldn't deny my daughter to

267

you for being poor. But since I know now who you are, let you know she will never marry you. I have nothing in this life but her. She is the best loved lamb of my people. She is my most noble jewel. Her death would be more to me than my own death. But God of Grace! I would prefer her to be stretched cold dead in front of me than for her to marry you.

COLM If that is the way, then that is the way, Eoghan. The bed a man makes, let him lie in it. I thought I would have your daughter with your will but since I won't, I will have her despite you. *(He moves to the door.)*

EOGHAN Stay standing, I tell you. On your death, don't move. Pity him who goes before Eoghan of the Hammers.

COLM Don't think I am afraid of you Eoghan. I know your reputation. It's said there isn't a man in Ireland could take that hammer but yourself. It's said you can bend an iron tongs in your two hands and straighten it out again. Maybe I could do the same tricks. You said to me one day as a joke that my hand was as smooth as a priest's hand. Maybe you were right. But look at that hand, Eoghan! (He shows his hand). Even though its skin is smooth and white its veins are as strong as your own. Don't stop me leaving. I am finished with you and your forge. There is worthwhile work besides making a horseshoe. There is skill besides turning a shoe. Maybe with the help of God Almighty that you will hear news before long.

[He casts aside his apron and goes out.]

EOGHAN *Muise, grá mo chroí é*! You would think him a king's son! Where would I find a more noble ardmheannaighe for my bright lamb? I will call him. *(He goes to the door.)* Colm! But wait! What is this I am saying? Isn't he a son of Colm O'Kelly? Isn't he a son of the man who killed Féidhlim Bán? God, help me! Don't let me forget the death of my brother. Colm is highminded and noble, but there are boys as good as him around here. I won't yield to him. It is I will choose a man for my daughter. I chose Muircheartach Ó Conghaile for her and by Christ[12] she will marry him in three months! He will be here tonight. I will speak to him. They will be married after Easter. *(A man is heard.)* Listen! Listen! Who is this coming? Upon my soul but it is Muircheartach himself! Isn't it well he is here! *(He starts working as hard as he can).*

MUIRCHEARTACH *(outside, singing)*
"If I were a boatman I would swim the sea over,
And I'd write some true lines to my lover;
I'd be escaping with my first love and embracing her waist,
And the day I can't entice a woman is the luckless day".
God bless all here except for the cat and the dog.

EOGHAN May the same man bless you.

MUIRCHEARTACH What news?

EOGHAN A long story of misery.

MUIRCHEARTACH By Sunday, misery is always on the tip of your tongue by you.

EOGHAN There are times it is and times it isn't. Have you any strange news yourself?

MUIRCHEARTACH It is said King James is on the sea.

EOGHAN The son of God be praised a thousand times!

MUIRCHEARTACH I have an idea there will be a stand against Bill Bradach soon[13].

EOGHAN I have no doubt but that there will be.

MUIRCHEARTACH *(singing)*
A ribbon of my first love is in my pocket below,
And the men of Ireland couldn't take away my sorrow
I am finished with you til my narrow coffin is made
And til up through me grow the green grass blades.
"Bad enough, tailor", like Tadhg says:

"I would advise the young women if they'd listen to me
Not to talk with the young men or their story believe
Their talk is like water being poured onto geese,
And God of Glory, that to good advice I pay heed!
Curse your father and your mothereen,
Who gave no schooling in your youth to you so my hand you
could read.
Tis early in the morning I would tell you what I mean
And have my blessing til the lonely place where next we'll meet."

EOGHAN We are very musical today, Muircheartach.

MUIRCHEARTACH Is there any harm in it?

EOGHAN I'm not saying there is.

MUIRCHEARTACH *(singing)* My boy's hair is curly-

EOGHAN Ara, give over. I have something to say to you.

MUIRCHEARTACH Say away. "My tune is up", like the gander
said when the woman of the house was twisting his neck.

EOGHAN Did you hear Máire is going to get married?

MUIRCHEARTACH By dad, I did not. Truthfully?

EOGHAN She is going to get married after Easter.

MUIRCHEARTACH And is there any harm asking who will
marry her?

EOGHAN Ara, have sense boy! Who will she marry but
yourself?

MUIRCHEARTACH Me?

EOGHAN Who else?

MUIRCHEARTACH Devil I know who else.

(He starts whistling.)

270

EOGHAN Give over your clowning. Aren't you in love with her?

MUIRCHEARTACH I am deeply in love with her with years.

EOGHAN Fair enough. I will give fifty pounds as a dowry to ye and the craggy enclosure in addition.

MUIRCHEARTACH But hold on, Eoghan. Does Máire herself know she is to get married?

EOGHAN She will know soon.

MUIRCHEARTACH And another thing. I thought she and Colm of the Forge were great with each other?

EOGHAN Hold your mouth, I tell you! If her soul depended on it she won't marry Colm of the Forge. It's the man I choose she will marry and you are my choice.

MUIRCHEARTACH But listen to me Eoghan. I don't want to anticipate you but don't you know myself and Bríd an Phíobaire are talking together?

EOGHAN Your heart from the hawk, man, is it going out of your mind you are? Bríd an Phíobaire! Wouldn't it be a fine match! Maybe she will make a piper of yourself! Muircheartach, I'm after offering my own daughter to you. Which do you prefer?

MUIRCHEARTACH Devil if I know.

EOGHAN Devil if you know! Muircheartach, I have two questions for you.

MUIRCHEARTACH Be telling.

EOGHAN Are you in love with my Máire?

MUIRCHEARTACH Didn't I tell you I am.

EOGHAN Fair enough. Are you in love with Bríd an Phíobaire?

MUIRCHEARTACH Didn't I tell you I am.

EOGHAN *Muise*, the weakness of death on you, you boaster.

MUIRCHEARTACH Hold on, Eoghan. The question isn't as easy to settle as you think. Look here. You would like if I married Máire. Fair enough. She would suit me well. But Colm of the Forge is raging and in love with her.

EOGHAN To hell with Colm of the Forge!

MUIRCHEARTACH Colm is raging and in love with Máire, and I fear in my soul that she is in love with him. Bríd an Phíobaire is in love with me. I am in love with the two of them.

EOGHAN *Muise*, the weakness of death on you, you boaster.

[*Máirtín Shéamuis Mhóir enters.*]

MÁIRTÍN The King bless all here.

EOGHAN, MUIRCHEARTACH And yourself.

[*Eoghan starts working intensely.*]

EOGHAN Sit down, Máirtín, and warm yourself.

MÁIRTÍN I am tired sitting. I am always sitting. *(He sits down)*.

MUIRCHEARTACH Have you any news?

MÁIRTÍN Devil a story unless I get it from you. Where is Colm, Eoghan?

EOGHAN I don't care in the slightest where he is.

MÁIRTÍN There's no need for you to take it out on me Eoghan. There was no harm in the question.

EOGHAN Don't hold it against me, Máirtín. Nothing is going right for me today.

MUIRCHEARTACH Here is the man with the songs. God save you, Conchubhar.

[*Conchubhar enters.*]

CONCHUBHAR The same to all here. I see the piper going out the road.

[*Several neighbours enter. Men and women and girls and boys and children: each of them salute the company kindly.*]

MÁIRTÍN Here comes the Piper.

[*Mac Dara and Bríd enter.*]

MACDARA God save all here!

CONCHUBHAR God be with you, Piper. You came at a good time.

MUIRCHEARTACH Play up, Piper. The girls' legs are dancing already.

ALL Clear the floor. Out with ye boys and girls!

[*The piper plays; they dance a little. The old people gather around the fire discussing. People call "God strengthen ye!" "God be with you, Piper!" "He took her out" etc. while they are dancing. Eoghan is still working.*]

MÁIRTÍN Ara, lay that hammer aside, Eoghan You have a man's worth done today.

EOGHAN Neighbours, the dance is upsetting me. It seems to me there is war and death on the winds tonight. *(The dancing stops.)* Boys, there is a fleet on the sea making for Ireland. Maybe it has already reached harbour. 'Tis better that the battle cry be playing around the country. Conchubhar, play a song – a song that will put courage in our hearts.

MÁIRTÍN Do, Conchubhar!

CONCHUBHAR Fair enough, neighbours. I will give ye "Gráinne Mhaol".[14]

ALL "God strengthen you"; "Mind that voice".

CONCHUBHAR *(singing)* Be lively etc.

[*There is a knock on the door. Seán Rua enters.*]

SEÁN The French fleet reached Kinsale three days ago. King James is in Cork.[15]

ALL For- oo – oo!

EOGHAN Truthfully, boy? Who is with him?

SEÁN There are four hundred officers between Gaels and French. I hear De Rosen is there and Berwick and do ye hear, my friend? – Sarsfield of the big heart and strong hand![16]

[*Eoghan jumps on a stool.*]

EOGHAN Life without death to King James! Life without death to Patrick Sarsfield! Life without death for Gráinne Mhaol!

THE COMPANY For- oo- oo!

[*Eoghan is on top of a stool in the middle of the stage: the people are gathered around him calling on King Séamus, Patrick Sarsfield and Gráinne Mhaol. The curtain is lowered while they are singing "Gráinne Mhaol".*]

THE COMPANY O, etc

THE SECOND ACT

PLACE
The road in front of a forge
TIME
A July evening in the year 1690

[*Colm enters dressed as an officer of King James.*]

COLM *(looking behind)* Are you coming Fearghus?

FEARGHUS *(outside)* I am. To hell with these rocks! My legs are broken by them.

COLM Mind yourself. It's a stony spot. Is Sarsfield coming?

FEARGHUS He is right behind me. Ó bu! Bu! My God!

COLM What is wrong with you now?

FEARGHUS Och! My foot slipped and it's surprising I wasn't knocked.

COLM By Sunday, you wouldn't think you were a Galwayman if that little hill tripped you.

[*Fearghus enters.*]

FEARGHUS Give over, I tell you. Bones were nearly broken against the cliff. *(Sarsfield enters.)*

SARSFIELD *Muise*, God bless you, Colm, isn't it a strange place to put a forge. That cliff isn't suitable for a horse to walk not to mind a person.

COLM Of course, there is another way on the other side of the cliff. We came the shortcut.

SARSFIELD The shortcut! Muise, God bless you. "If the road is straight and twisty the main road is the shortcut." Isn't it a lonesome spot! Is it far to Killaloe?

COLM Do you see that bright spot as far away as you can see?

SARSFIELD I do.

COLM That is a harbour in Loch Derg. Do you see that bare hill on the far side of the lake?

COLM That hill is in County Clare. Killaloe is not ten miles to the south of that hill.

SARSFIELD And Limerick is not above ten miles south west from Killaloe.

FEARGHUS It's ten and a half miles.

SARSFIELD Fair enough. We will reach Killaloe tonight and we will be in Limerick by tomorrow morning. Is this the forge Colm?

COLM It is. Go on in.

SARSFIELD Won't you come with us?

COLM I won't. I'd rather wait here.

SARSFIELD Why?

COLM There's need for it. I will wait for ye here.

SARSFIELD Each to his own. I won't bother with you.

[*He knocks on the door.*]

EOGHAN *(inside)* Who is that outside?[17]

SARSFIELD It is me and another.

EOGHAN In truth? Are you sure it is yourself is there?

SARSFIELD I could swear on the book.

EOGHAN And is there any harm in asking who you are yourself?

SARSFIELD A poor soldier making for Limerick.

EOGHAN *(at the doors)* Are ye Gaels or foreigners?

SARSFIELD Isn't it clear to you that we are Gaels according to language?

EOGHAN Which do ye belong to, King James or King William?

SARSFIELD To neither. We yield to no king on earth.[18]

EOGHAN Who do ye belong to then, in the name of the disaster?

SARSFIELD We belong to no king, but a queen.

EOGHAN I don't understand the meaning of your talk, gentleman. Who is the queen ye belong to?

SARSFIELD She has many names and surnames. The name the Connacht people call her most is Gráinne Mhaol.

EOGHAN *(taking his hand)* Mush, my love to ye, and to the children ye will have. Ye are soldiers with poor Gráinne. Thanks to the everlasting Father that here are finally manly warriors standing with the rights of Gráinne. Were ye at the Boyne?

SARSFIELD We were.

EOGHAN Wasn't it a poor defeat we had there! I cried my fill when I heard the news.

SARSFIELD We were not beaten, smith. It wasn't us that was beaten but King James! By God, wasn't he a capable leader with one Gaelic shoe and one foreign shoe![19] If the rogue William himself was our commandant and Jamsie as commandant on the foreigners, we would not be defeated!

EOGHAN But listen to me, nobleman. I hear generous Sarsfield has driven the foreigners from Athlone?

SARSFIELD I hear myself he has.

EOGHAN My heart's love to him, Pádraig! Only for him Gráinne Mhaol would be a sorry case today. She has no soldier but him. The rest belong to James or William, but like yereselves, noble men, Patrick gave his heart to none but

Gráinne Mhaol. Where is he tonight, do ye think, since he has routed Douglas and all who were before Athlone.

SARSFIELD I think he is making for Limerick like everyone else.

EOGHAN I am thinking he will come this way then. Wasn't he beside Banagher a week ago?

SARSFIELD That's what I hear.

EOGHAN I would give all I own in the world to shake his hand.

FEARGHUS Maybe he is not too far from you.

EOGHAN Is it mocking me you are?

FEARGHUS No mocking. What is this place called?

EOGHAN It is called the Forge of the Crag.

FEARGHUS By Sunday, muise, Patrick Sarsfield is not far from the Forge of the Crag tonight.

NOTES

1 No date of composition available, previously unpublished. Source MS 15, 004, discovered in Éamonn Bulfin's home near Birr in 1953. See 'A Forgotten Play by Patrick Pearse' *The Irish Press,* June 8, 1953. Translation Róisín Ní Ghairbhí.
2 'Oireachtas Lá na nÓg, Priest Says Ireland Needs Her Youth', *Irish Independent,* 28 October 1953.
3 Patrick Sarsfield, c.1660–1693, a leader famed among the people for his leadership and exploits on the 'Catholic' side in the period following the Battle of the Boyne. He became more important as the resolve of other leaders, such as the Earl of Tyrconell and de Lauzun, was wavering. The scene in *Eoghan Gabha* which features Sarsfield takes place as Jacobites regroup and head towards Limerick in the aftermath of the Jacobite retreat after the Battle of the Boyne. Sarsfield is famed in folklore for his attack on a battle train (a party carrying weapons and other requisitions) at Ballyneety near Limerick.

Sarsfield had crept out of Limerick under cover of darkness with up to six hundred riders before staging his daring ambush. However the scene in the unfinished *Eoghan Gabha* takes place before that ambush and before the siege, although the mention of placenames like Killaloe evoke the famous 'ride of Sarsfield' which took place shortly after the period depicted here.

4 In 1690 the armies of the Catholic King James and the Protestant King William faced each other at the Battle of the Boyne. While there was a complex European backdrop to the battle it is commonly perceived in Ireland as a battle between Gaelic Catholics and Protestant settlers. For an overview of the Jacobite era in Ireland see Eamonn Ó Ciardha, *Ireland and the Jacobite Cause 1685–1766, a fatal attachment*, (Dubin: Four Courts, 2002).

5 The phrase used in the original Irish version for 'solve difficulties' is 'na bearta crua a réiteach' which echoes a line in a political song known in many versions as 'Na Bearta Crua'.

6 Literally 'love of my heart to you' but the phrase is used as a general emphatic phrase of encouragement or praise.

7 General Preston, as governor, was in charge of defending Galway when the town was under siege from the forces of Sir Charles Coote. For an account of the siege see Eamon P. Duffy, 'The Siege and Surrender of Galway 1651–1652', *Journal of the Galway Archaeological and Historical Society*, Vol. 39, 1983/1984, pp. 115–42.

8 The allusion to Mílic Wood refers to specific events which took place during the Confederate Wars in the years following the 1641 Rebellion. In this case Connacht forces under the command of the Earl of Clanricarde enjoyed initial success in holding out. Having repelled forces commanded by Colonel Daniel Axtell south of Athlone, Clanricarde's army was joined by General Preston's reinforcements. However Axtell's forces, also reinforced, routed the Connachtmen at a battle which took place at Mílic (on the Shannon) in October 1650.

9 The image and language in the original Irish are reminiscent of the well-known song 'Eamonn an Chnoic', where a Tipperary raparee, Éamonn Ó Riain, seeks shelter at a homestead.

10 The Irish word 'searc', used for 'love' in the original Irish version, refers specifically to romantic love.

11 Richard Talbot, ('Lying Dick Talbot'), 1630–1691, Earl of Tyrconnell, Jacobite soldier and leader who raised an army for the Royalists. Having gone to France to seek aid after the Battle of the Boyne, he returned to Ireland in 1691 but died shortly afterwards. There were tensions between him and Sarsfield.

12 The Irish version has 'Dar Príosta' instead of 'Dar Críost' in order to avoid swearing.

13 Bill Bradach, a disparaging nickname for William of Orange.

14 The poem 'A Shaoi Ghlain don Phríomhscoth' by Seán Clárach Mac Domhnaill, which features Gráinne Mhaol as a symbol of Ireland was published in *Amhráin Sheaghain Chláraigh Mhic Dhomhnaill*, eag. An tAthair Pádraig Ua Duinnín, An dara heagar, Conradh na Gaeilge, 1902, p. 40–1. Pearse owned a copy of this book. The tune for the song is described as 'Gráinne Mhaol'. The poem prophecises that 'the true king will lie with Gráinne Mhaol'. Pearse was also familiar with George Sigerson's *Bards of the Gael and Gall*, which featured Sigerson's English translation of Mac Domhnaill's poem about Ireland as Gráinne Mhaol. See George Sigerson, *Bards of the Gael and Gall*, Fisher Unwin, London, 1897, p.271. An image of Gráinne Mhaol as Ireland features in Pearse's adaptation of the traditional song 'Séarlas Óg' which he published as 'An Dord Féinne' (though the song is more commonly known as 'Óró sé do bheatha abhaile' today. Roger Casement had made the initial suggestion that 'Searlas Óg' should be adapted as a marching song for the Volunteers after a meeting held in Galway in 1914. Pearse's adaptation was published as 'Amhrán na nÓglach' ('The Volunteers' Song') in *The Irish Volunteer* on the 27.2.1915. See Ciarán Ó Coigligh, eag., *Filíocht Ghaeilge Phádraig Mhic Phiarais*, An Clóchomhar, 1981, p.41–2; 91–2. For an account of Gráinne Mhaol as a historical figure and as a figure in literature and folklore see Anne Chambers, *Granuaile, The Life and Times of Grace O'Malley, c.1530–1603*, Wolfhound Press, 1998.

15 King James is said to have landed in Kinsale on either the 12th or 17th March. See John Todhunter, *Life of Patrick Sarsfield*, Fisher Unwin, 1895, p.28.

16 De Rosen was a general on King James' side when they besieged Derry in 1689. He was recalled from Ireland because of his conduct and other tensions. The 1st Duke of Berwick, James Fitzjames, 1670–1734 was an illegitimate son of James II who was famed for his courage. He took an active part in the Battle of the Boyne. After the death of Sarsfield, Berwick married his widow.

17 The phrase 'Who is that outside?' ('Cé hé sin amuigh?') again echoes the song 'Éamonn an Chnoic'.

18 Sarsfield was said to be disgusted with James after the Battle of the Boyne.

19 The phrase was commonly used to refer to James.

TREATMENTS
of 'SCRIPTLESS'
PLAYS

1.18 Mary Bulfin a ghlac ról na Maighdine Muire in *An Pháis*/ Mary Bulfin as the Virgin in the Passion Play. (Image courtesy of Pearse Museum/Le caoinchead ó Mhúsaem na bPiarsach.)

1.19 Liam Mac Piarais mar Phíoláit/Willie Pearse as Pilate. (Image courtesy of Pearse Museum/Le caoinchead ó Mhúsaem na bPiarsach.)

Cluiche Trírannach dar teideal
AN PHÁIS
A Passion Play in Three Acts[1]
[ORIGINAL PROGRAMME/CLÁR]

Amharclann na Mainistreach / Abbey Theatre
7, 8 Aibreán / 7, 8 April 1911

LUCHT AN CHLUICHE
(de réir mar thiocfas siad i láthair) anseo síos:
Persons in the order of their entry:

Seisear Macaomh	Six Boys
An tAon Duine Dhéag, agus Peadar, agus Séamus agus Eoin orthu	The Eleven, including Peter and James and John
Íosa	Jesus
Iúdás, *i. duine den dáréag*	Judas, *one of the Twelve*
Óglach an Ardshagairt	The Servant of the High Priest
Ceann Feidhme an Fhorfhaire	The Captain of the Guard
Seisear den bhForfhaire	Six of the Guard
Iúdaigh	Jews
Beirt Iníon	Two maids
Scríobhaithe agus Sinsir	Scribes and Ancients
An tArdshagart	The High Priest
Beirt Shagart Eile	Two other priests
Beirt Bhuabhailldhe	Two trumpeters
Beirt Lictor	Two Lictors
Point Píoláit	Pontius Pilate
Beirt Ghiolla	Two Attendants
Barabbas	Barabbas
Mná Caointe	Keening Women

Muire, *i. Máthair Íosa*	Mary, *the Mother of Jesus*
Muire Magdailéan	Mary Magdalen
An Mhuire eile	The other Mary
Bheronice	Veronica
Siomóin Ceiréineach	Simon of Cyrene
Beirt Mhéirleach	Two Thieves

ÁIT DON CHLUICHE SEO
Place
An Chéad Roinn i nGairdín Gethsemane
(*Act One, The Garden of Gethsemane*)
An Dara Roinn, i gCúirt Phíoláit
(*Act Two, the Court of Pilate*)
Treas Roinn, ar chnoc Calbhari
(*Act Three, the Side of Calvery*)

AN SCÉAL

I: It is evening in Gethsemane. Certain boys of Jerusalem are singing old Jewish songs beneath the olive trees. As darkness gathers they leave the garden, into which presently come Jesus and the Eleven. Taking with him Peter and James and John, Jesus begins to grow sorrowful and to be sad; and bidding them watch with Him, He goes forward and prays. Thrice He prays that the chalice may pass away from Him if it be his Father's will; the disciples meanwhile sleep. At the third prayer an angel appears from Heaven, comforting Him. Rousing the disciples, He tells them that he is at hand who will betray Him. Then Judas, with a band of soldiers and servants from the chief priests and Pharisees, bearing torches and swords and clubs, enters the garden and betrays his Master with a kiss. Rebuking Peter, who strikes the servant of the high priest with a sword, Jesus delivers himself up and is led away. Then the disciples all leaving Him flee, except John who follows close to Jesus; but Peter follows afar off. Judas, now full of horror of his sin, is left in the garden alone.

II: In the courtyard of Pilate a crowd of Jews, including many of the scribes and ancients, are awaiting the arrival of the Governor and of the prisoner whose life is sought. They bow low as the priests enter. The latter tell the people what has happened in the high priest's court; that Jesus has blasphemed, declaring Himself to be the Son of God. The people cry out that He has deserved death. Trumpets sound, and preceded by lictors and soldiers Pilate enters. Jesus is called in to the inner court. Questioning Him apart, Pilate finds no cause in Him. Going out to the priests, the governor pleads for the silent prisoner, but they will have His blood: if Pilate let him go free he is no friend to Caesar. Give them rather Barrabas. Fearing a tumult, Pilate sends Jesus to be scourged. Then he shows Him to the people and asks them to choose between Him and Barrabas. They choose Barrabas. "What then shall I do with Jesus who is called Christ?" "Crucify Him!" "Shall I crucify your king?" "We have no king but Caesar!" Calling for water and washing his hands Pilate declares himself innocent of the blood of that just man, and the people cry out "His blood be upon us and upon our children!"

III: On the side of Calvary Peter and others await the coming of a sad procession which is winding out of Jerusalem. Up the hillside comes the sound of keening, and presently the women of Jerusalem, among them the three Marys, accompanied by the disciple that Jesus loved, emerge on the slope. Mary, the mother of Jesus, asks Peter for news of her Son: Peter can tell her only that he has seen Him in the midst of his foemen. Then Mary catches sight of a form bent beneath a cross: it is her Son. Staggering up the hillside Jesus meets His mother and comforts her; and turning to the keeners bids them weep not for Him but for themselves and for their children. Then, blessing them, he passes on to His death. Presently a shadow is flung across the hill as the cross is raised. The voices of the chief priests and ancients are heard mocking; and the gentle replies of Jesus; the voices of the thieves, one mocking, the other beseeching, and Jesus' reply; and the other word spoken from the cross. Finally crying out with a loud voice He gives up the ghost; and darkness spreads over the hill.

All the words put into the mouths of the characters are taken from the Gospels, with the exception of certain speeches in the last Act attributed to Jesus, Mary and Peter by a very old Irish tradition. The only other departure from the letter of the Gospels is in making the denials of Peter take place in the courtyard of Pilate instead of that of the high priest.

The song of the boys in Act One, the words of which are from the Psalms of David ("Laudate pueri Dominum," "Quare Fremuerunt" and "Domine ne in furore") and the keen of the women in Act Three have been composed by Mr. Thomas MacDonnell.

Miss Sage, Mus.B. will play passages from Rossini's "Stabat Mater" on the organ before the play. There will be no music during the intervals.

The audience is requested to abstain from applause during the performance and after it.

P.H.P.

DESMOND RYAN'S MEMORY OF THE PASSION PLAY[2]

The Passion Play in Irish, produced at the Abbey Theatre, Passion Week 1911, is worthy of more lengthy mention than Mr. Pearse has made in a short note in *An Macaomh*. Of it Mr. Padraic Colum wrote: 'It was made convincing by the simple sincerity of the composition and the reverence of the performance. No one who witnessed it had any doubt as to the fitness of the production. This Passion Play takes us back naturally to the origin of modern European drama. In a sense, it is the first serious theatre piece in Irish. It has root power. Naturally Irish drama begins with the Passion Play, the Miracle Play or the Morality Play. This Passion Play gives the emotion out of which a Gaelic drama may arise. If its production be ever made an annual event it might create a tradition of acting and dramatic writing in Irish'. It had been decided to make the play not an annual but a triennial event. Postponed at Easter 1914, the Easter of 1916 indefinitely postponed it.

The students of Sgoil Eanna and Sgoil Ide roused Dublin by their earnest, simple and unelaborated enacting of the Passion Play. Simplicity, dignity, reverence in the general staging and management, all these helped to make the play the magnificent success it was, but to P.H. Pearse the main credit must be given, because in the first place he arranged the play itself, and also because of the endless and untiring foresight and patience with which he carried through the work against many serious obstacles and difficulties.

To come to the play itself. The story, the scenes, the words were those of the Gospel. A few unavoidable deviations were made from the narrative for dramatic purposes. The denials of Peter were made to take place in the courtyard of Pilate instead of in that of the High Priest. In the last act certain speeches taken from an old Irish hymn *Caoineadh Mhuire*, were spoken by Jesus, Mary and Peter.

As the curtain rises on the first scene, the Garden of Gethsemane, certain boys of Jerusalem are playing and singing old Jewish songs beneath the olive trees. As darkness gathers, they leave the garden into which presently come Jesus and the Eleven. He warns them of his approaching betrayal and death. Peter, with vehemence, John and the other disciples gravely deny that they will desert Him. Taking with Him Peter and James and John, and bidding them watch with Him, He goes forward and prays. Thrice He prays that the chalice may pass away from Him, if it be His Father's will; the disciples meanwhile sleep. At the third prayer, an angel appears from Heaven comforting Him. Rousing the disciples, He tells them that He is at hand who will betray Him. A murmur, low and indistinct at first, soon loud and threatening, is heard outside; then Judas with a band of soldiers and servants from the chief priests and Pharisees enters the garden and betrays his Master with a kiss.

'Judas, dost thou betray the Son of Man with a kiss?' Then to the crowd: 'Whom seek ye?' 'Jesus of Nazareth.' 'I am He.' Peter strikes the High Priest's servant with his sword. Jesus rebukes him and touches the servant, who falls at His feet and kisses the hem of His garment. Turning to the guard and the crowd Jesus delivers Himself up and is led away. The disciples all leaving Him flee, except John, who follows close to Jesus, but Peter follows afar off. Judas, now full of the horror of his sin, is left in the garden alone.

The second scene shows the courtyard of Pilate. On low stone steps leading upwards to the inner court Peter sits alone. At the rear are a large open window and a balcony; on the right Pilate's judgment seat. To the left a crowd of Jews including many of the Scribes and Ancients are awaiting the arrival of the Governor and of the Prisoner, whose life is sought. A serving maid comes from the crowd and accosts Peter. 'Thou also wert with Jesus of Nazareth.' Peter is fierce in his denial. A second serving maid steps forward to repeat the accusation. Peter swears still more fiercely that he knows not the Man. A cry: 'The Priests!' from without. The latter enter, the crowd bowing low. They harangue the crowd, telling what has just happened in the High Priest's Court, that Jesus has blasphemed, declaring himself to be the Son of God. The multitude cry out that He is deserving of death. Trumpets sound and, preceded by lictors and the guards, Pilate enters. Christ is called into the inner court. The crowd passes round with hostile cries and menaces. Pilate questions at first half mockingly; then, wondering at Christ's calm demeanour and replies, he goes out to the priests, pleading that he finds no cause in the Man. But they will have blood, calling out that if Pilate let Him go, he is no friend to Caesar. Give them rather Barabbas. Fearing a tumult Pilate sends Jesus to be scourged. As he ponders over a warning letter from his wife, the guards lead back Christ crowned with thorns, reed in hand, and clothed in purple. Pilate leads Him to the balcony. 'Behold the Man.'

A terrible sound of a crowd passionate and vengeful comes from without. Only on Pilate raising his hand for the third time does it cease. Then Barabbas is led to the window. 'Release unto us Barabbas! Barabbas! Barabbas!' 'What then shall I do with Jesus who is called Christ?' Shouts: 'Crucify Him!' 'Crucify Him!' 'Shall I crucify your King?' 'We have no King but Caesar!' 'Crucify Him!' 'Crucify Him!' 'What evil hath He done?' 'Crucify Him!' 'Crucify Him!' Pilate calls for water and washes his hands. 'I am innocent of the blood of this Just Man. Look ye to it.' A shout, louder and more terrible than before, answers him: 'Let His blood be upon us and upon our children.'

The third scene shows the side of Calvary. Peter and others await the coming of the sad procession which is winding out of Jerusalem. Up the hill-side comes the sound of keening, and presently the women of Jerusalem, among them the three Marys, accompanied by the disciple whom Jesus loved, emerge on the slope. The Virgin turns to Peter. 'Oh, Peter! O, Apostle! Hast thou seen my Bright Love?' Peter answers: 'I saw Him even now in the midst of His foremen.' She turns to the women: 'Come hither, two Marys, till ye see my Bright Love.' Then Mary catches sight of a form bent under a cross, staggering up the hill-side. She asks Peter: 'Who is that noble Man beneath the Tree of Passion?' 'Dost thou not know thy Son, O Mother?' Jesus meets her and comforts her: 'Hush, O Mother, and be not sorrowful.'

Turning to the keeners He bids them weep not for Him, but for themselves and their children. Blessing them He passes on to His death. Presently a shadow is flung across the hill as the cross is raised. The voices of the Chief Priests and Ancients are heard mocking, and the gentle replies of Jesus, the voices of the thieves, one mocking, the other beseeching, and Jesus' reply. After a space Jesus again speaks. This time with the Blessed Virgin and St. John: 'Woman, behold thy Son. Son, behold Thy Mother.' A pause. 'I thirst.' Another pause: 'My God, my God, why hast Thou forsaken me?' A longer pause: 'It is consummated.' Then with a sigh: 'Father, into Thy Hands I commend My Spirit.'

Lightening flashes and peals of thunder roll. Darkness spreads across the hill, and the loud, poignant, agonized keening of the women rises.

The audience which, slowly and without applauding, passed out of the Abbey on the two nights of the performance had much to think of, the Irish medium, strange to most of it, had not veiled but intensified the meaning and pathos of the story. Some of us, too, thought, though to many it may seem an irreverence, that our national and individual struggle was in ways a faint reflection of the Great One just enacted. Is it not so? The Man is crucified as the Nation, and the Soul moves slowly, falteringly, towards the Redemption.

Sgoil Éanna did much towards creating the tradition of acting and dramatic writing of which Mr. Colum speaks. In June 1912 we produced *An Rí*, in the open air upon the banks of the river that runs through the Hermitage grounds. In Whitsuntide 1915 we produced *The Master* at the Irish Theatre, Hardwicke Street.

William Pearse took the part of Ciaran in *The Master*, and the Abbot in *An Rí*. Mr. Pearse wrote his 'masterpieces to order,' to quote his own jesting phrase, and with an eye upon special individuals for particular parts.

Mary Bulfin's memory of the Passion Play[3]

In the Holy Week of 1911 Mr Pearse produced a Passion Play in the Abbey Theatre. This play represented the chief incidents in the Passion of Christ as related in the Gospel.

Thomas McDonnell, a master of St. Enda's impersonated Christ. He also composed the music sung by the boys in the opening scene – that of the Garden of Gethsemane. Mr Mac Donnell also composed a very beautiful *caoine* for the women on Calvary.

Mr. Willie Pearse's impersonation of Pilate was considered wonderful, I remember, and was much discussed at the time. Personally the thing that most impressed me about Pilate was the astonishing variety of his frowns. Mr Willie could frown a thousand ways at once; and during the Passion Play we used to watch in awed fascination the perfectly marvellous things he did with his forehead. The Head himself was the impenitent thief – one of the thiefs anyway and Mr Thomas McDonagh the other.

I have a very distinct memory of Mr. McDonagh, on the night of the dress rehearsal, diving through a crowd of boys to get to the right side of the stage at the critical moment – and beginning to chant forth his speech while picking up a small boy whom he had knocked over!

The Head was also the voice in the crowd that called out to Pilate: *Má scaoilfidh tú an fear seo, ní cara Chaesar tú.* That sentence is the only bit of the whole play that has stayed in my mind.

Oddly enough, the thing I remember most vividly is Micheál Mac Ruaidhrí as Barrabas. I never in my life saw anyone so villainous as the smile of the mild and genial Micheál, when, clad in a leopard skin, he made his bow before Jesus. He looked a most devilish, horrible ruffian- however he managed it.

Mr Pearse didn't seem to worry too much about rehearsals. He told us simply and clearly what he wanted done; and once he was sure that each one really knew what he or she had to do, he was satisfied. He seemed to have a divine belief that everyone would rise to the occasion and perform their individual parts adequately at the actual performance, no matter how woodenly they behaved at the rehearsals. It was part of his general belief in human nature, I think.

NOTES

1 Treatment taken from Programme for original performance.
2 Desmond Ryan, 'A Retrospect', in *Padraic Pearse, The Story of a Success* (Dublin: Maunsel & Co., 1920), pp.101–9.
3 As found in Mary Brigid Pearse (ed.), *The Home-Life of Pádraig Pearse* (Dublin: Mercier Press, 1979), pp.120–1.

1.20 Image from original programme for St. Enda's Fête June 1913: 'The Week's Programme'. (Courtesy of Allen Library/Le caoinchead ó Mhúsaem na bPiarsach).

1.21 Image from original programme for St. Enda's Fête June 1913. (Image courtesy of Allen Library/Le caoinchead ó Leabharlann Uí Ailín).

THE DEFENCE
OF THE FORD

PEARSE'S ADVERTISEMENT FOR THE UPCOMING
PERFORMANCES OF THE DEFENCE OF THE FORD

An Claidheamh Soluis, May 31ˢᵗ 1913, p.9

In these days when "Ulster" talks of war it is appropriate to
remember that there was once real chivalry in Ulster, and that
it is Ulster that has given Ireland her greatest epic. The central
incidents of that epic will be represented in one of the pageants
which will be enacted at the St. Enda's Fête at Jones's Road
during the week June 9ᵗʰ to June 14ᵗʰ. The theme of the pageant
is the defence of the Ford by Cuchulainn and by the Boy-Corps
of Eamhain Macha against the provinces pending the rising of
the Ulster Chiefs. In Part I the Boy-Corps are seen at a hurling
match on the green of Eamhain. A messenger arrives with
tidings that the four provinces under Meadhbh have broken the
Ulster border, and that Cuchulainn who has been defending the
frontier alone lies wounded and spent. The Boy-Corps
volunteer to take the post of danger, and to hold it until Ulster
rises. They arm themselves and set out singing a marching song.
Part II shows the camp of the men of Ireland on the Ulster
border. They are singing by their watchfires. Suddenly they are
charged by the Boy-Corps who make three outsets upon them.
The boys fall after a gallant fight. Now Cuchulainn rouses

himself from his torpor and passes out to avenge the Boy-Corps. Part III shows the camp fires of Feardiach and Cuchulainn by the Ford. Meadbh has sent Feardiach, his bosom friend, against Cuchulainn and this is the third morning of their fight. After exchanging high courtesies they fall to battle, and Feardiach is slain. The Ulster hosts have now gathered and arrive at the frontier, which has been held until their coming by Cuchulainn and the boys. Over a hundred and fifty performers will take part in the spectacle, which is being arranged by Messrs. P.H. Pearse and Wm. Pearse.

A minor Pageant entitled "The Fianna of Fionn" will also be enacted during the week. Other attractions will be displayed by the "Fianna Eireann", a series of Aeridheachta, dancing on the green, and a whole round of sideshows. Prices of admission range from three-pence up.

SEAN O'CASEY LETTER TO *IRISH WORKER*, 7th JUNE 1913[1]

[O'Casey's Letter urging people to support Pearse's efforts, especially the upcoming The Defence of the Ford.*]*

The Irish Fête in Jones's Road

"Neart i n-ar lámhaibh, Fírinne i n-ar mbéalaibh, agus glaine i n-ar gcroidhthibh" – The Fenian character[2]

"They shall yet old men and old women dwell in the streets of Jerusalem, every man with his staff in his hand for very age. And the streets of the city shall be full of boys and girls playing in the streets thereof." – Zechariah 8: 4-5

St. Enda's College – Is it a great thing to be asked to help in the strengthening of the one natural Gaelic School in Ireland? Workers for Ireland, let us help now to fertilize the seed sown by Pádraig Mac Piarais by instant help and vigorous sympathy, that it may grow and bring forth fruit a hundred-fold to the glory of God and the honour of Ireland. Slave, and worse than slaves, are we if it should be that this man's hope and this man's efforts are as water spilled upon the ground. St. Enda's is the beginning, a glorious beginning – the acorn that may contain a forest of oak trees – ours now to do and say, "Live and flourish!" "We refuse," says P. Mac Piarais, "to worship the gods of Hume Street." Isn't it time for Irish Irelanders, not only to refuse to worship these gods, but to take them out, smash them to pieces, and grind the pieces in the Temple of Irish Ireland? How better to weaken what is strong than to strengthen what is weak? Every penny given to Scoil Enna is a link in the defensive armour of Ireland. Any Gael who refuses to help, or neglects to help, the efforts being made to strengthen and extend the influence of St. Enda's College, let him be anathema!

The Fête will commence on Monday, June the 9th, and go on every evening till Saturday, June the 14th. All kinds of amusements will make the Fête attractive to everybody, such as Shooting Galleries, Hobbie Horses, Aunt Sally Shows, Swing boats etc. As well, there will be exhibitions of drill, tent-pitching, and skirmishing by the Dublin National Boy Scouts. Pipers' Bands, and Brass and Reed Bands will enliven the hours with gay and stirring tunes. Open-air concerts will be held every night, at which every time will be as the handbills declare – "New, fresh, and good."

Irish dancing on the sward may be indulged in by all who love the merry gig and reel for a very nominal fee. The principal attraction will be the elaborate pageant, "The Defense of the Ford", depicting one of the 4 grandest episodes in Ireland's Heroic Past.

Two hundred performers will take part in this pageant. Here will be shown the Boy Corps of Ulster hurling on the field. The news of Cuchulainn's wounding; the march of the boys to defend the frontiers till the Hero recovers; the scene of the men of Ireland around their Camp Fires; the attack by the Boy

Corps of Ulster; and, finally, in the last act, the "Battle of the Ford" between the two Heroes, Cuchulainn and Feardiadh. Admission to the Grounds is only 3d., so that it certainly is possible for almost everyone to come upon one of the nights to witness a unique and instructive Festival. Three-day tickets may be had for one shilling; season tickets, admitting to all functions throughout the week, two and sixpence.

In one of his latter paragraphs in "An Macaomh," St. Enda's Manual, enumerating the teachers, Pádraig Mac Piarais says, "Bow to us, and pass on." We bow to you, A Phádraig, but we will not pass on. Our hopes are your hopes; your work shall be our work; we stand or fall together. Scoil Enna for Ireland, Ireland for Scoil Enna, amen, a Thighbhearna![3]

Craobh na nDealg[4]

EXTRACTS FROM SEAN O'CASEY, *DRUMS UNDER THE WINDOW*[5]

[*In his imaginative autobiography, O'Casey recounts in the third person the experience of attending the performances of* The Defence of the Ford.]

The pageant was held in Jones's Road Park, and the opening night was one of torrential rain, so that all who came crowded into the large hall of the grand-stand, to crouch there, saturated, gloomy, and low in heart as man could be. Pearse sat, the nadir of dejection, his grieving figure telling us that once more the damned weather had betrayed the Gael; with Douglas Hyde, who came to open it, roared out eulogy and boomed out windy joy, all the time the wind shook the sodden walls, and the rain slashed down on the roof above them.

Wind and water, thought Sean; we want only the fire now.

That came on the last day of the great event. The Boy Scouts had been careless with the oil, and had let a lot of it swim about the floor; then some hasty hand had flung a glow-match into a pool of oil, and in a moment the grand-stand and the dressing-rooms were crackling. Such a scene! All the performers dressed for the pageant thought of their every day clothes, and the money and watches hidden in the pockets, and ran from their places to save their goods. Pearse, still brooding on Cuchullain, was knocked over, and a great cry went up from the crowd to put the fire out, someone! […]

But the fire was quelled, the firemen went away, the pageant went on, and Sean saw again the Boy Corps of Emain Macha playing hurley, to be stopped by a messenger telling them that Connacht was marching on Ulster, and that Ulster's chumpians were in the punishment of a trance-stupor for great unkindness to a pregnant woman, that Cuchullain having fought Maeve's army for many days, was now in a deep sleep, and that they would have to take his place, which they did, all dying in defence of the black north. […]

And there it was on the green sward before him – *The Cattle Raid of Cooley*, with its mimic figures, coloured gaily in the floodlight, growing mighty through the mind's misty thought of what happened far away and long ago. The Boy Corps of Armagh playing hurley, veiled in blues, greens, reds, browns, and purple; the stopping of the game by the Messenger, Pearse himself, to tell them that Cuchullain, weary with the battle of many days, was asleep, and the boys Boy Corps would have to defend Ulster from the Men of Eireann till Cuchullain could stand to fight again, for the rest of the Ulster champions were in a trance-stupor …

And here was the bould Cuchullain challenging Maeve to send her champions out, with a Come on the whole of you, one by one, to meet your doom, and when I'm done with you, a lot of you'll be like little green leaves in a bible; and won't your Maeve be glad when she's at home with her feet on the fender, while the old kitchen kettle keeps singing a song, and Oillol, if he can get away, to smoke another pipeful in the shade of the old apple-tree.

The last came Ferdiah to fight with the hero, and Cuchullain's heart near failed him, for Ferdiah wore the same old school gorget[6] that he wore himself; but there was no way out, so they fought by day, and rested by night for a lunar month, till Cuchullain, full of wounds and mad with anger, could stick it no longer and killed Ferdiah without any hindrance; then came the caoining skirl of the pipes, and the sad rolling of the drum, mingling with the hues of red, brown, green, and purple kilts and shawls, ending a scene of a song that in colour, form, dignity of movement, and vigour of speech made the loveliest thing that had ever patterned the green sward of the playing-field of Jones's Road, or any other field, the world over; faired than anything the bowler-hatted Gael could think of now, much more do.

THE DEFENCE OF THE FORD

[*Summary of* The Defence of the Ford *from original fête programme.*][7]

ACT I- THE GREEN OF EAMHAIN MACHA

The Boy-Corps of Eamhain Macha hurl upon the green. They are startled by the voice of a Herald calling upon the Ulster Chiefs to rise, for the four provinces under Meadhbh of Connacht have broken the Ulster border. But the Ulstermen lie under the curse of Macha (laid upon their fathers for terrible sin) which deprives them of their manhood in their hour of need; so only the echo of Eamhain Macha's streets answers the Herald's voice. To the wondering boys the Herald relates that Meadhbh of Connacht comes to make the Táin Bó Cuailgne[8] and that with her march the provinces under their respective kings and the Ulster exiles under Feargus son of Róigh, bent on avenging upon King Conchubhar the slaying of the sons of

298

Uisneach.[9] 'Who guards the frontier?' 'The little Hound, the valiant Hound, The Hound of my heart – Cuchulainn – has held the provinces at bay for many days, giving single battle to their chiefs.' 'How fares it with Cuchulainn?' 'Alas he lies wounded.' 'Were it not a fitting thing for us, O boys', said Follamhain, Captain of the Boy Corps, 'to take our fathers' weapons and march to the frontier to hold the fords and passes til Ulster rises?' Thou has spoken well O Follamhain, Son of Conchubhar, and running they gird themselves with their fathers' swords and set out for the frontier singing a marching song.

ACT II – THE FRONTIER

Cuchulainn sleeps by a lonely camp-fire, watched by Laegh, his charioteer. He men of Ireland gather round their own campfires, singing and feasting. The music of boyish voices is borne to them on the wind. 'Who comes?' 'The Boy-Corps of Eamhain.' With ringing cheers, the Boy-Corps charge, making three onsets upon the men of Ireland, and at the end of the third onset all the Boy-Corps lie dead. The men draw off, sick with that slaughter. The Herald returns form Eamhain Macha, and rouses Cuchulainn. 'How long have I thus slept?' 'Three days and three nights.' 'Woe is me for the hosts have been unmolested for that space.' 'Not so.' 'Who has come against them?' 'The Boy-Corps of Eamhain.' 'How fares it with the Boy-Corps?' 'Alas, they lie dead in the fords and shallows.' 'Had I been there they would not have fallen. Yoke my chariot and bring me my arms of valour.' While Laegh yokes the chariot, Cuchulainn mourns the Boy-Corps, 'fallen, but not defeated'. Then, arming himself, he passes forth to avenge them.

ACT III – THE FORD

Meadhbh has persuaded Feardiadh, Cuchulainn's fellow-pupil and bosom friend, the only man of the men of Ireland who is his match in battle, to give him single combat. They have fought for three days, sharing at evening the same meal and the same couch, but on the third night they sleep apart. It is the morning of the fourth day. Feardiadh rises and goes to the ford. The men of Ireland come upon the plain to view the battle. They acclaim the arrival of Meadhbh and Aileall. 'Rise, Cuchulainn', says Laegh: 'Feardiadh is at the ford.' 'Alas, Feardiadh will fall by me today. Bring me my weapons.' Cuchulainn arms and goes to the ford. 'Welcome to me thy coming, Cuchulainn.' 'Not welcome to me thy coming Feardiadh, for it is to thy death thou comest.' 'Everyman must come to the sod of his death.' Having embraced like brothers, they fight. Cuchulainn is yielding. The men of Ireland laud Feardiadh. Laegh incites Cuchulainn: 'Remember the fame of thy people. Remember the need of Ulster.' Cuchulainn's battle-fury comes upon him and he slays Feardiadh. Then, catching him in his arms, he mourns him dead. Laegh leads him from the field, for he is wounded; the men of Ireland bear off the body of Feardiadh, the pipers playing his keen. But now the power of Macha's curse is spent and all Ulster has risen. The Ulster host arrives on the plain, under its chiefs; and as Conchubhar and the heroes of the Red Branch come up they are acclaimed by the warriors. Last, Cuchulainn, recovered from his fight with Feardiadh, come to join his over-king and Ulster hails him with a long shout of 'Hail Cuchulainn!'.

NOTES

1 David Krause (ed.), *The Letters of Sean O'Casey Vol. I* (London: Cassell, 1975), pp.27–8.
2 'Strength in our hands, truth in our mouths, and purity in our hearts.' 'Fenian' here refers to Fenian or Fiannaíocht literature.
3 A Thighbhearna!: Oh Lord!
4 Craobh na nDealg: The Thorny Branch, one of O'Casey's pseudonyms and a sideways poke at Douglas Hyde's pseudonym An Craoibhín Aoibhinn (The Pleasant Little Branch).

5 Sean O'Casey, *Drums Under the Window* (London: Macmillan & Co. Ltd., 1945), pp.278–84.

6 Gorget: a piece of armour to protect the throat area; an ornamental collar.

7 Information from orignal programme, courtesy of Allen Library.

8 The Cattle Raid of Cooley: *The Táin* is one of the great texts in Gaelic epic literature .

9 *Oidheadh Chloinne hUisneach* is another important story from the Rúraíocht or Ulster Cycle. It relates the story of Deirdre and the sons of Uisneach and the tragic end that befell them following events triggered by the jealousy of King Conchubhar. Deirdre had been destined for Conchubhar before she eloped with Naoise. AE (George Russell), Yeats and Synge all wrote plays based on the story.

1.22 Photograph of group of actors for *Fionn* in gardens of St. Enda's, The Hermitage, 1914. Buíon aisteoirí as *Fionn*, 1914. (Image courtesy of Pearse Museum/Le caoinchead ó Mhúsaem na bPiarsach.)

FIONN

A Dramatic Spectacle[1]

First performed June 13th 1914, St Enda's (Rathfarnham)

CHARACTERS

(in order of appearance)

Cup-Bearers	Conn of the Hundred Battles
Heroes	Pages
Chief Musician	Fionn
Druid	Lugh Lamhfhada
Art the Lonely	The Son of Miodhna
Coll Mac Morna	

Conn of the Hundred Battles sits at feast in Tara, with Goll Mac Morna, Chief of the Fianna, at his right hand. There is neither music nor mirth at the feast, for a great calamity is impending over Tara: the Son of Miodhna is come to burn down the royal city, and no valour avails against him, for he is a mighty enchanter. A young stranger enters the assembly. "One disinherited seeks hospitality," he cries. He is courteously bidden to the feast, and placed between the King and his son, Art the Lonely. Presently he asks the cause of the sorrow which is in the faces of all, and Conn relates to him the plight of Tara. "What shall be my reward if I save Tara?" "Thy inheritance," says the King, "be it great or small, and I give Goll Mac Morna and my son, Art the Lonely, as my guarantees in this." The assembly is lulled into sleep by the mysterious music of the Son of Miodhna; but the young stranger summons the god Lugh Lamhfhada, who gives him a wonderous spear, and with this

303

he slays the Son of Miodhna. Rousing the King and his heroes, the lad claims his promised reward. "Who, then, art thou?" "I am Fionn, the son of Cumhall, and the inheritance I claim is the Fiann leadership of Ireland." Goll puts his hand into Fionn's and becomes his man, and the young hero is acclaimed Chief of the Fianna.

IRISH TIMES, JUNE 15ᵗʰ 1914

The interesting experiment that has been going on for some years past at St. Enda's College of demonstrating the practicability of combining the somewhat elusive element of "nationality" with modern educational methods has met with a measure of success. St. Enda's College was established about six years ago as a secondary boarding school for boys. A fine old mansion, situated in that charming district of country lying a few miles south of the village of Rathfarnham, was secured for the college, and here the principal and his staff have been patiently working out their ideal of what an Irish school should be. A large number of boys are now in attendance at the college. Saturday was the annual *fete* day, and many past pupils and friends of the present pupils attended to take part in the social pleasures of the occasion. The weather during the afternoon was delightful, and the charming gardens and extensive grounds which adjoin the main building were greatly admired. The earlier part of the programme was devoted to athletic sports, in which both present and past pupils took part. Later on there was an adjournment to the lawn, where afternoon tea was served. While this was going on the school pipers played a programme of Irish airs, varying from the pathetic to the tragic. After tea, the guests were much interested in a dramatic spectacle which was performed in the grounds by the pupils. It was entitled "Fionn", and was founded on a legend of the Fianna, in which Fionn, the son of Cumhall, with a wonderous spear slays the Son of Miodhna, who had come to burn down the royal city of Tara. Those who took part in the spectacle were dressed in the picturesque costumes usually associated with the Fianna. The principal part, that of Conn of the Hundred Battles, was admirably played by Mr. William Pearse, while Mr. David Sears as Fionn was also excellent. The boys who took part were Alfred Gaynor, Joseph McGilligan, T. Carleton, E. MacGinley, T. Butler, B. Cooney, W. Kenny, F. Holden, C. MacGinley, Joseph Sweeney, John Hunt, Desmond Murphy, Owen Clarke, John Joyce, and F. O'Docherty. The prizes won at the sports were then distributed by Miss Pearse, and the school prizes by Dr. Douglas Hyde.

NOTES

1 Treatment taken from Programme for original performance.

APPENDICES

SELECTED EXTRACTS FROM
AN CLAIDHEAMH SOLUIS

Editors' Note: The following selection from Pearse's editorials in *An Claidheamh Soluis* from 1906 to 1908 provide a snapshot of his increasing interest in drama in the years between his joining of the Theatre of Ireland and the founding of St. Enda's. The writings also provide a fascinating insight into Pearse's views on the development of Irish language drama, on the *Playboy* controversy, and on folklore, culture, literature and politics in general.

May 19th 1906
Folklore and the Zeitgeist

We remember as a child sitting by a turf fire and listening to a grey-haired woman telling Irish folk-tales.[1] From that gentle seanchaidhe we first learned how gracious and noble is Mother Eire, how sweet a thing it is to love her, how proud a service to toil and to suffer for her.[2] In converse with her, too, we first realized that Eire has a voice and a speech of her own; from her we first learned to pronounce Irish words; from her we first heard the names of Cuchulainn and Fergus and Fionn, of Gráinne of the Fleets and the two mighty Aodhs; from her lips we first listened to the tale of

'... ...   Brian's wisdom,
Eoghan's genius, Sarsfield's daring,
Emmet's early grave, and Grattan's
Life-long epic of devotion.'

She loved all who had striven for Ireland from the shadowy heroes of old to those of her own blood and ours who died in '98 or been imprisoned in '67. Her heart had a corner for the Fianna of Fionn and another for the Fenians of John O'Mahony.[3]

She died when we were an Intermediate schoolboy. A year later we were promoted to the Irish class and for the first time saw Irish words in print. Our texts – it was Junior Grade, 1894 – were 'Laoi Oísín' and 'Diarmaid agus Gráinne'. We remember the thrill of pleasure with which we heard the familiar names, the eagerness with which we read the familiar tales. The turf fire was back and the dead voice was speaking to us again. Not content to limit our reading to the two texts prescribed by the programme, we wondered further afield, – finding our way, greatly daring, into the National Library and making the acquaintance of An Craoibhín's 'Leabhar Sgéalaidheachta' and 'Cois na Teineadh' and – later – of his 'Sgéalaidhe Gaedhealach'.[4] Here we were in the very heart of the land of mystery and romance on which so many years before that kindly hand had raised the curtain, bidding us look with the eyes of childish wonder. And in that land we strayed long and far; learning to know its broad highways and its quiet bóithríns, its shining spreading plains and its tangled enchanted woods.[5] At recurring examinations we gained only respectable and never brilliant marks; but all the time we were learning to realize ourselves as a child of our Mother and the heir of a tradition.

These recollections have come to us on sitting down to write an article on the Oireachtas folklore competitions.[6] We hope they are not wholly irrelevant. In our mind at least they have a subtle connection with the theme. We never listen to a seanchaidhe by a fireside or at a Feis but all this comes back to us; we never open a book of folklore or read a manuscript folktale submitted to us for publication but years slip away and we are again seated on an earthen floor beside a fire where a kettle sings. And is not this part of the charm of the folklore for us all? It stirs a long-silent chord in our hearts; it awakens dead voices; it recalls mornings long ago on sunny heights and evenings in fireside ingles; it appeals to all that is most inborn, hereditary, primal in our being; it is the voice of our own folk speaking to what is of the folk in us – and there is a good deal of the folk in us all, 'civilised', 'educated', labeled and ticketed off by the universities and examination-boards though we be. The folktale speaks the same language as the bird which sings in the blue, as the kine[7] which low in the buaile,[8] as the streamlet which babbles by the roadside, as the sparks which fly upward from a fire. The man from whom an old tale has no appeal is to be feared and pitied even as the man who is irritated by the prattle of children or repelled by the caress of a dumb animal. He is one apart; he is landless and kindless.

We have been re-reading An Craoibhín's 'Cois na Teineadh'. The Dedication and Preface, which were written in 1890, make strange reading today, – as indeed does nearly everything written about the

Irish language and Irish literature before the era of the Gaelic League. Wrote An Craoibhín sixteen years ago: 'To the memory of those truly cultured and unselfish men, the poet-scribes and hedge-schoolmasters of the last century and the beginning of this – men who may well be called the last of the Milesians – I dedicate this effort to preserve even a scrap of that native lore which in their day they loved so passionately, and for the preservation of which they worked so nobly, but in vain.' Would An Craoibhín write so today? Or would he commence a preface with these mournful words? – 'Irish and Scotch Gaelic folk-stories are, as a living form of literature, by this time pretty nearly a thing of the past. They have been trampled in the common ruin under the feet of the Zeitgeist, happily not before a large harvest has been reaped in Scotland, but, unfortunately, before anything worth mentioning has been done in Ireland to gather in the crop which grew luxuriantly a few years ago.'

Since that was written, the strong arms of An Craoibhín and others have grappled with the Zeitgeist, and lo! he has yielded up his spoil. Reverent hands have gathered up the fragments which he had trampled into the dust, piecing them together so cunningly and lovingly. Sixteen years ago An Craoibhín could write with absolute truth that nothing worth mentioning had been garnered in of the once luxuriant crop of Irish folklore; today we can write with equally absolute truth that the mass of Irish folklore which has been recovered and is now preserved for all time either in print or in the MS collection of the Oireachtas Committee already ranks with the largest collections of national folklore in the world, and will probably be quite the largest ere the last scrap has been harvested. A bhuidheachas soin le Dia![9]

An Craoibhín has published half-a-dozen volumes of folklore. Pádraig Ó Laoghaire has given us of the best of Béarra. Seosamh Laoide has rescued a fragment at least of the lore of Farney.[10] Others, publishing the result of their gleaning either in smaller books and booklets or in the columns of the *Irisleabhar, An Claidheamh*, and local newspapers, have probably doubled or trebled the harvest of the three main workers. But the amount of published Irish folklore forms only a fraction of the great body which has been saved from the Zeitgeist and of which the largest past is to be found in the piles of MS accumulated by the Oireachtas Committee during the past nine years. All this will someday be sorted, catalogued, examined, and published. But that is a matter which can wait, and in fact must wait: the things which cannot wait, which must not be allowed to wait, is the rescue of the large mass of folklore still unrecorded. And here is a task in the accomplishment of which the Oireachtas Committee demands and is entitled to the help of everyone who is qualified to render help.

The work is pressing. 'For the folklorist the Gospel saying is … more pregnant with meaning than for any other student of man's history – "the night cometh when no man can work."' For the seanchaidhes are passing from us, and with each one that goes down to his grave there disappears a fragment of as fair and noble an inheritance as ever was bequeathed to a race by its past. How many precious scraps of lore have been lost because someone omitted or was unable to commit them to paper on first hearing them, and on returning to look for them found that the seanchaidhe was dead! Think of Farney where An Laoideach[11] gleaned to such purpose ten years ago: had he delayed his visit until today we should never have had 'Sgéalaidhe Fearnmhaighe' or 'Sgéalaidhe Oirghiall',[12] for today all the seanchaidhes are gone, and those who are in their places, even the Irish speakers, are dumb. Think of Roscommon, whose whole lore, with the exception saved by An Craoibhín, has been lost within living memory. Think of Tirconnell, not a tithe of whose lore has been collected – some doubt whether it has any lore. Think of the Déise, where an Irish-speaking generation is dying out, and leaving behind it – nothing.[13]

A Gael who lives in a district where Irish is vernacular or who during the summer will have an opportunity of spending a few weeks in such a district, could undertake no more thoroughly useful and meritorious piece of work than the collection of songs and stories of the district and their forwarding to the Oireachtas. He may happen to win a prize, but the winning of prizes is not the objective: the objective is the saving of the national lore, down even to the last shred, from that Zeitgeist to whom the Gaelic League has flung down a challenge.

MAY 26th 1906
ABOUT LITERATURE

Perhaps the distinguishing characteristic of the intellect of ancient Ireland was its spirit of daring. Both in the world of action and in the world of thought the old Gael was a brave adventurer. His mind was abnormally inquisitive, restless, venturous, original. He mingled the spirit of the Vikings or of the Elizabethans with that of the olden Greeks and of the first Christian missionaries. It was his delight to make voyages of discovery on unknown seas, to penetrate virgin fastnesses, to climb untrodden heights, to venture down into unexplored depths; in general, to essay feats never before attempted or dreamt of. He took a keen intellectual and imaginative pleasure in efforts to overcome matter; a still keener and subtler pleasure in his adventures in the realm of the mind. In the domain of action he civilized Europe and discovered America. In the world of thought he speculated daringly in theology, sociology, and pure science – being the first, for one thing, to teach formally the sphericity of the earth and to expound the law of gravitation. In literature he invented the novel and (by contriving the rhymed stanza) laid the foundations of modern poetry. He gave Europe its first hymn, its first love-song, and its first mock-heroic. Among his minor achievements are the inventions of blank-verse, chain-rhyme, entrance-rhyme, burthens, broken staves, dis-syllabic and tri-syllabic rhymes, bilingual or macaronic verse. The *technique* of the poetry of modern civilized nations is purely Irish, or at least Celtic; the inspiration largely so. Take away what the Greek and the Celt have gifted to European literature and what remains?

Eclipse came for the Irish Gael just at the moment when he stood on the threshold of modern philosophy. As he had anticipated Columbus, Galileo, and Newton, so he was about to anticipate Bacon, Pascal, and the great moderns. Tolstoy he partially anticipated, Ibsen wholly. We have said that he invented the novel. The statement, amazing as it may seem to some, does not represent the summit of his achievement in this particular direction. He invented the novel of psychology. In *Diarmaid agus Gráinne* we have the first patient and detailed analysis of the *mind* of a human being that was attempted in Europe since the days of Greek drama. Has it ever occurred to anyone that Gráinne is a prototype of Hedda Gabler?

To what purpose this disquisition? To this purpose. Is it possible that the Gael has lost all that gallant adventuresomeness of spirit, all that soaring originality of intellect which characterized him in his great ages? Have the Breandans and the Fearghals and the Aonghuses and the unknown shapers of the first European novels left no intellectual descendants? Do Kerry mountainsides and Iar-Connacht heights and Tirconnell glens nurture today a race in which there lingers no breath of the old daring spirit, no spark of the old consuming fire, no trace of the old high resolve? Our sires sang poetry which set Europe aglow and which still rings down the evening gale in remote country places at home: we, apart from a few pure and strenuous notes that have recently been heard, can produce nothing better than half-English jingles and frigid imitations of eighteenth-century decadents. Our sires invented the novel: amongst us (apart from the creator of 'Séadna') only two have attempted anything longer than a storyette, both of these have dealt with incident rather than with character, and only one is readable. Our sires expounded the motions of the spheres and explained the daily ebb and flow of the tide: we have produced a table-book, an elementary arithmetic, and a geography primer, - all three admirable as far as they go, but covering how small an expense of the mighty ocean of science!

Of course, it were absurd at this stage of the movement to expect philosophical poetry, psychological novels, and deep treatises on metaphysics. But we *do* think that a little more originality, a little more boldness, a little more ambition on the part of Irish writers were both necessary and desirable. Last week we wrote a glorification of the folktale. But it must be distinctly understood that we hold the folktale to be a beautiful and graceful thing only in its own time and place, – and its time and place are the winter fireside, or the spring sowing-time, or the summer hay-making, or the autumn harvesting, or the country road at any season. This week we lay down the proposition that a living modern literature *cannot* (and if it could, should not) be built up on the folktale. The folktale is an echo of old mythologies, an unconscious stringing together of old memories and fancies: literature is a deliberate criticism of actual life. In point of form, the folktale is bound by a convention, which (by the way) is not a distinctly Irish, but rather a distinctly folk convention, – that is to say, a convention which, in essentials, obtains amongst the folk universally, whether in Ireland, in Bohemia, or in Afghanistan. Why impose the folk attitude of mind, the folk convention of form on makers of a literature? Why set up as a standard for the Irish writers of today a standard at which Aonghus O Dálaigh[14] and Seathrún Céitinn[15] would have laughed?

'Because we have no other standard', says someone who reads. But we have. We have the standards of the ancients. Irish literature gave models to Europe. Is it not high time that it should give models to Ireland? Let us, in attempting to re-make a literature here, follow not the folk, but the makers of literature who have preceded us.

Will the ancients suffice as exemplars? Frankly, we are afraid not. We must get into touch also with our contemporaries, – in France, in Russia, in Norway, in Finland, in Bohemia, in Hungary, wherever, in short, vital literature is being produced on the face of the globe. Two influences go to the making of every artist, apart from his own personality, – if, indeed, personality is not, in the main, only the sum of these influences: the influence of his ancestors and that of his contemporaries. Irish literature, if to live and grow, must get into contact on the one hand with its own past and on the other with the mind of contemporary Europe. It must draw the sap of its life from the soil of Ireland; but it must be open on every side to the free air of heaven.

We should have our literature modern not only in the sense of freely borrowing every modern form which it does not possess and which it is capable of assimilating, but also in texture, tone, and outlook. This is the twentieth century: and no literature can take root in the twentieth century which is not of the twentieth century. We want no Gothic revival. We would have the problems of today fearlessly dealt with in Irish: the loves and hates and desires and doubts of modern men and women. The drama of the land war; the tragedy of the emigration-mania; the stress and poetry and comedy of the language movement; the pathos and vulgarity of Anglo-Ireland; the abounding interest of Irish politics; the relations of priest and people; the perplexing education riddle; the drink evil; the increase of lunacy; such social problems as (say) the loveless marriage; – these are matters which loom large in our daily lives, which bulk considerably in our daily conversation: but we find not the faintest echoes of them in the Irish books that are being written. There would seem to be an amazing conspiracy amongst our writers to refrain absolutely from dealing with *life*, – the one thing with which, properly considered, literature has any concern!

We would have every young writer remember that his first duty is to be unafraid. If he has a message to deliver to the world, let him speak out: and the fact that his message is one that has not hitherto been delivered in Irish should not deter him; but rather urge him on. All honour to the ancients: but they have not said everything that is to be said on any subject, and there are some millions of subjects on which they have said nothing at all.

We commenced this article with the intention of redeeming a solemn promise to Séamus O Cathasaigh to write something about the Oireachtas literary competitions; but we have reached the limit of the space at our disposal without coming to the Oireachtas at all. Let the foregoing, therefore, serve as a réamh-rádh[16] to what we shall say next week: meantime we hope that intending Oireachtas competitors will chew upon our advice which is, in brief, –

'... Be bold
And resolute ...
Be lion-mettled, proud and take no
Care
Who chafes, who fretes ...' –

even though the chafers and the fretters include Oireachtas
adjudicators and newspaper reviewers!

JUNE 2nd 1906
LITERATURE, LIFE AND THE OIREACHTAS
COMPETITIONS

Commenting on our Irish leader of the week before last – of which
our English leader of last week was an expansion – the *Irish Peasant*
falls into pretty much the train of thought in which we were in when
we penned last week's homily on the function of literature. 'Ireland',
writes our contemporary, 'for a long time has been afraid of life.
When people are afraid of life there can be no literature or art worth
a moment's consideration. In Irish Ireland, however, we are not afraid
of life. But we have only discovered a little of its romance and wonder
yet. We have not got to the great stage of vision and enthusiasm in
which literature – which is something produced by people whose
souls are really alive – is possible. But we are rapidly approaching it'.

We hope so. And it was to erect a beacon-light for the guidance
of the marching host of young poets and storytellers that we wrote
our article. For it seemed to us that there was a danger to be feared
from the setting up of false standards, – a standard in poetry which
regards the observance of certain recently-devised canons of prosody
as the one thing essential to the making of an Irish poem, and a
standard in prose which takes the gossip by a country fireside or in a
village taproom as the high-water level both of its thought and of its
style. For form we would go to the ancients: and for subject-matter
we would have our young writers take (as the ancients did) Life; the
Life within them and the Life around them.

Our view of literature as a criticism of life has been objected to
as partial, – as covering only one aspect of the function of literature.
This, however, is to restrict unduly the connotations both of
'criticism' and 'life'. We do not mean that every piece of literature
must be didactic in aim – the world's greatest literature is for the most
part singularly un-didactic; neither do we suggest that every writer
ought to take up the discussion of knotty problems, psychological,
social, political, and so forth. We simply put in compendious form
the undoubted fact that every piece of literature, as indeed every piece
of art, expresses the *views* of its creator on whatsoever may happen
for the moment to be his theme. Even though it be the mere
recording of an impression – a water-colour sketch of a sea-beach, a
couplet describing an autumn sunset, a word-picture of a child met

in a country laneway – it is, as far as it goes, the author's *view* of something, and is in this sense a piece of criticism. It is a revelation of the artist's soul: a giving back again to others of something as *he* saw it and felt it; *his* interpretation of a fragment of life.

Now we hold that it is time for our Irish writers to make a brave effort to express *themselves*, – to tell us what they think, or at any rate (if they do not yet think) what they *feel*. So far for the most part they have not been doing so. They have simply been giving us photographic reproductions of everyday conversations in Irish-speaking districts. Their work in this direction has been useful from certain points of view. It has been invaluable in introducing students to the idioms of the living Irish language. But it is no more literature than would be a verbatim report of the daily conversation which goes on, say in the case-room of our printing-office. And it is as impossible as the foundation of a national literature as a series of photographs of Irish physiognomies and scenery taken by Messrs. Lawrence would be as the foundation of a national art.[17]

Confirmative of the contention that our writers have not commenced to put *themselves* into their books is the fact that so few distinctive 'styles' have been developed in Irish. Style is personality; and as we have only two or three unmistakable 'styles', it follows that only two or three personalities are being given expression to in modern Irish, – a thousand pities when one remembers that individualities are so varied and so rich amongst the writers and potential writers of the language. An tAthair Peadar has a style which is intensely personal, although he genially pretends that he writes only as ordinary folk talk in West Cork; and Conán Maol has a style which is perhaps the most strenuously individual note in all recent Irish literature; and two or three others have styles; but the vast majority of those who write Irish in books and in papers are mere photographers or imitators, without any characteristic outlook or bias or mode of expressing themselves. Almost any passage of Munster Irish that one comes across might have been written by almost any Munsterman; almost any passage of Connacht Irish by any Connachtman; there is no individual stamp on it: the personality, the man, the living soul of the writer speaking to you is to seek.

With this advice, then, that they should aim at making whatever they write in Irish a *personal* expression – their own view of something put in their own way – we commend the literary competitions at the forthcoming Oireachtas to Irish writers and would-be writers, native-speaking and otherwise. The competition to which we invite special attention is No.5: 'For the best Short Story dealing with Modern Irish Life. Length from 4,000 to 7,000 words.' We have theories of our own on the subject of the Short Story, as perhaps our readers are aware; and we foresee for this type of composition a mighty future in Irish and indeed European literature. In the past great thinkers and reformers have thrown much of their criticism of life into the novelistic and dramatic forms. The drama will always be a power, but we believe that the era of the ponderous novel beloved of nineteenth-century Europe is past. The evangels of the future will go forth in the form of light, crisp, vivid, arresting short stories. Gorki rather than Dickens suggests the style.

Literary criticism in Irish has been attempted with some little success. But we want deeper searchings, wider stretches of view, more unconventional and individual expressions of opinion than we have yet got. Competition No. 2 ('A Critical Essay on "the Place of the Lyric in Irish Poetry"') should draw forth good work, if students really competent come forward and if, coming forward, they let themselves 'go'. Writers whose bent is towards affairs rather than towards artistic and imaginative themes can discuss 'The Influence of Irish Local Elective Bodies on the Development of the Nation' (No.1) or 'What the Irish Press can do for the Language' – proposed (suggestively) by the *Freeman's Journal Co., Ltd.* (No.7). There are two competitions for Historical Essays, – No.8 ('Fiacha Mac Aodha' or 'Domhnall Cam' – we hope, by the way, that the mystery surrounding the identity hidden under this sinister-looking *soubriquet* has been satisfactorily cleared up), and No.9 ('Best Account of the Land Tenure in Ancient Ireland'). The substantial prize of £10 is offered for a Three-Act Historical Drama, and there is a further prize of £5 for a short Two-Act Play suitable for performance by children. We trust that there will be good and sincere work in both of these competitions, though we confess we do not expect the appearance of a master-piece: a great drama cannot grow up in a few years and without traditions.

We have now fulfilled our *geasa* to Séamus Ó Cathasaigh and tonight we shall lay us down to rest with the calm happiness of one who knows himself at peace with the world and with the Oireachtas Committee.[18]

JUNE 9ᵗʰ 1906, PP.6-7
TRADITIONALISM

A correspondent writes us: 'Now that you have come out of your shell and have been holding forth (very interestingly, if somewhat dogmatically) on such high themes as art, literature, and folklore, perhaps you will go on to give us the benefit of your views on one or two other vexed problems, – say, dancing and traditional music. Some of my friends are haunted by the suspicion that *An Claidheamh* is not quite orthodox on the dancing question, – a suspicion given rise to less by anything you have said on the topic than by your stony silence whenever it agitates the minds of Gaels. As for the subject of traditionalism, I feel that the pen which wrote the article on "Folklore and the Zeitgeist" could deal with it very sympathetically and illuminatingly'.

We are grateful to our friend; but wild horses would not draw from us an editorial expression of opinion on the dancing question. Not that we are without views – we hold views which we might mildly describe as startling; and if ever we conceive a desire to wreck the movement we may possibly give those views to the world in a special number of *An Claidheamh*, taking a railway-ticket to some remote wilderness on the eve of publication. Then from afar we shall, Bricriu-like, watch with glee the wranglings of the men of Erin. But for the present we keep our own counsel.[19]

It occurs to us, however, that we might rejoice the soul of Séamus Ó Cathasaigh by writing a little on the subject of traditionalism with (more or less) reference to the Oireachtas Syllabus. We believe we approach the theme with 'sympathy'; we hope we shall prove 'illuminating'; and we will do our best not to put our opinions too 'dogmatically'. Readers whom we chance to offend will, we trust, transfer their animosity to the correspondent who has drawn us.

The first point that it seems necessary to make is that 'traditionalism' is not essentially Irish. One finds a 'traditional' mode of singing and a 'traditional' mode of reciting in every land in which there is an unspoiled peasantry. We ourselves have heard French, Breton, Flemish, and German traditional singing; and we have heard French and Breton traditional recitation. The traditional style is not the *Irish* way of singing or of declaiming, but the *peasant* way; it is not, and never has been, the possession of the nation at large, but only of a class in the nation. There was traditional singing in Ireland in the days of Cormac Mac Airt[20]: but the traditional singing in Ireland was no more in favour in Cormac's court than it is in the court of Edward VII. Then, as now, the folk sang in their way, and the 'trained' musicians in theirs; just as the folk spoke, ate, dressed, and lived in one fashion, and the gentles and their hangers-on in another.

This is not written by way of decrying traditionalism. Quite the contrary. Its object is simply to put those capable of dealing with the subject from the technical standpoint on the right track, which they have not been on up to the present. They have seen in the traditional style the debris of an antique native culture. We see in it simply a peasant convention, which, in its essentials, is accepted by the folk everywhere.

Of course this peasant convention is not absolutely identical in any two countries. Irish traditional singing, though similar to, is not the same thing as Breton or Flemish traditional singing: it has its *Irish* as well as its *folk* characteristics. It is for experts to analyse it with a view to determining which of its peculiarities are distinctly Irish and which are simply due to the fact that it is the art of a peasantry.

We have suggested that there was in ancient Ireland a mode of singing which was not of the people, but was governed by rules deliberately framed by musicians and taught in schools. What the style was we have no means of knowing. It perished when the native culture perished. Only the steadfast folk, with their lowly but beautiful art, have remained to bear witness to the Ireland that was. The professional musician and the professional seanchaidhe passed away in the wake of the Earls.[21] Thus it comes that the only arts which have survived to us from Ireland's past are peasant arts; just as the only Irish speech which is living today is a peasant speech. And those who would build up a great national art – an art capable of expressing the soul of the whole nation, peasant and non-peasant – must do even as we propose to do with regard to the language: they must take what the peasants have to give them and develop it. And this, indeed, is simply doing over again what was done thousands of years ago by the earliest of the professional musicians and seanchaidhes.

We hope that traditional singing and traditional recitation, exactly as we know them, will always be heard in Ireland – by cottage fires in the winter evenings. We would not have them on the stages of great theatres; we would not bring them into the brawl of cities. Not that they are not worthy to be heard in the high places of art: but that they demand for their fitting rendering and their fitting appreciation an attitude of mind on the part of artist and of audience which is possible only in the light of a turf fire blazing on an earthen floor. They are of the countrysides and for the countrysides: let us keep them *in* the soul of Ireland, they need not be afraid of modern culture. They need not hesitate to learn voice-production; they need not boycott Mendelssohn or Chopin. Their art will be Irish because they themselves will be Irish; it will be Irish even though it may be free from some of the eccentricities which (being ignorant) we today look upon as most characteristic of the Irish style.

There are three or four singers (all more or less products of the Oireachtas) who have been working on the lines we suggest. Amongst

them are Mairghréad Ní Annagáin, Séamus Clanndiolúin, Pádraig O
Séaghdha, and Sighle Ní Ailgheasa. All these are palpably Irish: not
one of them is out-and-out 'traditional'. They form, in our opinion,
the nucleus of a native school of vocal art: and their method has been
to *develop* that which they have either inherited or assimilated from
the folk amongst whom they were born or have lived. Perhaps the
forthcoming Oireachtas will discover a new Mairghréad Ní Annagáin
or another Pádraig Ó Séaghdha.

JUNE 16ᵗʰ 1906
'THE IRISH STAGE'

The language movement has not yet produced a drama. When (and if)
the reader recovers from the fit of irritation into which this piece of
editorial dogmatism will probably throw him, he will, we trust, go on to
hear our explanation. Our explanation is simply this, that we differentiate
between the terms 'play' and 'drama'. 'Play' covers anything and
everything from 'Droghedy's March' up to a tragedy of Sophocles.
Obviously some plays are dramas, quite as obviously most are not. A
drama is a picture of human life intended and suitable for representation
by means of action. 'A picture of human life': a study of men and
women; an effort on the part of the dramatist to induce you to see the
march of lives and fates as he sees it. 'Intended and suitable for
representation by means of action': not a mere piece of philosophising
(though it may enshrine a world of philosophy); and yet not the mere
telling of a tale (though a tale of some sort it must almost of necessity
tell); but a picture so treated that, however well it may read as a piece of
prose or verse, it imperiously demands *viva voce* representation in order
that it may yield up its full message. This is drama.

Now, our point is that whilst we have many passable and a few
miserable plays in Irish, we have none that we can confidently rank
with the small class to which we reserve the name 'drama'. We have
none, that is, which give us the authors' views on life; nay, we have
hardly any which place before us men and women at all. Abstractions
we get which talk at us like phrase-books; these are labeled, and set
down on programmes and on the front pages of books under the
heading 'dramatis personae'. But they are not living, sentimental
human beings who think and talk and act in a certain way made
inevitable by their personalities. In a word, there is little or no
characterisation in our Irish plays. We have the same 'Bean Tighe', the

same 'Sean-Fhear', the same 'Fear Óg', the same 'Buachaill Aimsire', the same 'Cailín Comhursan' in a dozen plays: and these worthy folk foregather in the same kitchen, and dance the same dances, and chat in the same way about the same topics, no matter what part of Ireland they hail from, what period they are supposed to be living in, what events – grave or gay – they are taking part in. There is in our playwrightship something of the naiveté of the Moralities and Mysteries, in which, too, the characters were all types or abstractions rather than individuals.

One Irish writer only – An Craoibhín – has attempted a character-study in dramatic form. Unfortunately the attempt (*Teach na mBocht*) is the one piece from his pen which has no 'go' from the stage point of view: two old men hurling recriminations at one another from two beds do not make a drama. But the effort is noteworthy, as unique of its kind. An Craoibhín's *Pósadh*, too, whilst we hesitate to call it a drama, is an exceedingly beautiful piece of work – one of the most strangely moving things to have been written in Irish. Other playwrights, notably of course An tAthair Peadar, have evinced a remarkable gift for dramatic dialogue, and it is probably only their want of acquaintance with stage-craft that prevents them from giving us artistic dramas. Tomás Ó hAodha's achievement in producing two rattling melodramas – we use the word in no uncomplimentary sense – is probably the greatest that can so far be placed to the credit of the young Irish stage. It has taken other national theatres something like a hundred years to reach the point marked by *Seabhac na Ceathramhan Caoile*. So that there is no need to be pessimistic. If no dramatist of the Gael has yet sounded the depths or scaled the heights, we have got at least an attempt at psychology; three or four beautiful idylls in dramatic form; a great deal of vigorous dialogue; and (from Tomás Ó hAodha) two all-round good acting plays; - and this, in all the circumstances, is not a little.

July 7ᵗʰ 1906
'Irish Acting'

Three weeks ago we wrote an article on the Irish Stage, apparently apropos of nothing. It was in reality, whilst a continuation of our series of homilies on literature, intended as a Dion-Bhrollach to certain remarks we desire to make in view of the forthcoming performance of Irish plays at the Oireachtas.[22] Last year we rejoiced a great many people and offended a few by writing exactly what we taught (*sic.*) of the Oireachtas plays. This year we intend, más slán dúinn, once more to write exactly what we think.[23] Sincerity, without bitterness, is the first essential of criticism.

The plays which are to be produced at the Oireachtas are three in number. Tomás Ó hAodha's[24] *Seabhac na Ceathramhan Caoile* we have already described as a rattling melodrama. Given a reasonably good interpretation, it is bound to go on the stage with a swing that has been wanting in nearly every attempt at an Irish acting-play that has hitherto been made, Tomás' own *Seaghán na Sguab* being the most notable exception. Acts I and III, in particular, have been written with a fine eye for stage effect. And one will be glad to exchange the stereotyped cottage interior for An Cuimíneach's[25] library and the battlefield of Fontenoy. *The Land*, unlike almost every other Irish play we can think of, is a genuine criticism of life, is irreproachable in form, and has dramatic purpose and coherency: it is therefore that comparatively rare thing, a drama. (In parenthesis, it is a drama which we admire intensely without liking one bit, a personal attitude in which few, perhaps, will be found to join us.) How Pádraic Colum's beautiful and characteristic English will translate into Munster Irish we do not know. We suspect that there will be more of 'Tórna' than of Pádraic in the *mélange*, – '*mélange*' because we are not convinced that there exists between the minds of Tadhg Ó Donnchadha and Pádraic Colum that secret and indefinable sympathy which would enable the one to give a perfect and satisfying translation of the other; a fear of which the performance at the Oireachtas may happily disabuse us. Of *An tAtharrughadh Mór* we know nothing save that its broad comedy and good-humoured sarcasm have set all County Mayo a-laughing. If it adds to the geniality and zest of the Oireachtas it will be welcome.

The dramatic bill of this year's festival is thus decidedly interesting. It remains for us to hope that the actors will do justice to themselves and to the authors. Bluntly, we have hitherto got very little acting in Irish that has risen above the painfully mediocre. Two or three things we have heard on the Irish stage which will always haunt us, as the elocution of Bernhardt in *Frou-Frou*, or of Coquelin in *Cyrano de Bergerac*, or of Mrs. Patrick Campbell in *Magda* haunts one. Let us not be smiled at for our comparisons, or rather we do not care whether we are smiled at or not, for in matters artistic one ought never to be ashamed to write down a deliberately-formed judgment, however bizarre it may appear to all but oneself. Seriously, then, we place the acting of An Craoibhín in *An Pósadh* and of Sighle Ní Ailgheasa in *Seaghán na Sguab* and *Creideamh agus Gorta* on a level with the greatest acting we have ever seen; and very near to this we place the acting of

Maighréad Ní Ailgheasa in *Seaghán na Sguab* and certain of the speeches of Tomás Ó hAodha in the same play. Beautiful in its naiveté and reserve is some of the elocution of the Galway players who interpreted *An Deoraidhe* at the last Oireachtas, and whose work has for some years past been so interesting a feature of Feis Chonnacht. With these exceptions, however, we have seen little acting in Irish which could be called creditable even for amateurs. What is wrong?

Two things are wrong. The first thing is that most of those who have essayed the actor's art in Irish do not know how to speak. They can only talk. The second is that they – or perhaps those responsible for their training – are enslaved by English conventions and mannerisms. They are, in particular, obsessed by the Anglo-Saxon demon of restlessness – an awkward and unbecoming fidgetiness which is as remote from the vivacity of the South as it is from the reposefulness of the East. Two things we would recommend to Irish actors and stage-managers: first, to study the art of the Irish traditional reciter; and secondly, to pay an occasional visit to the Abbey Theatre. Not that the traditional reciter is a model to be religiously copied (for – other considerations apart – acting is essentially different from recitation), or that the Abbey Theatre has said the last word on the drama; but that the one puts the student in touch with Ireland, whilst the other puts him in touch with the best contemporary ideals. We hope we have shocked no one by mentioning the Abbey. At present the standard of the average Irish stage-manager seems to be – the Queen's.

AUGUST 4th 1906: OIREACHTAS SPECIAL ISSUE
IN MY GARDEN

I was 'lazing' the other evening in my garden – even Gaelic Leaguers 'laze' sometimes; and I am fortunate – or unfortunate – in possessing a garden full of quaint crannies and ingles which perpetually invite me to dalliance. My favourite nook is one overlooking the smooth lawn which stretches at one side of the house. From it I have a noble view of my elms, – I am rather proud of my elms, which are among the oldest and the loftiest near Dublin. Also, this particular alcove is fragrant in the evening with the scent of Cape Jessamine – and it is only in the evenings that I have time to 'laze'. So here you will often find me watching the sunset; and here I was on the particular evening already referred to.

Not watching the sunset, however, – it was only six-thirty in mid-July. I was reading the *Freeman's Journal* on the British Education Bill, and – I fell asleep. I did not seem to have slept very long when I was aroused by a step on the gravel walk. It was the postman, who seeing me in my wonted place, came up the walk to me with a bundle of letters and papers. As he laid them on the rustic table before me, he saluted me in Irish. I started for I had not known that the local post-office staff included an Irish speaker.

'You have Irish?' I said to him, speaking also in the vernacular.

'To be sure I have, Sir,' replied he with what sounded like a note of surprise in his voice. 'If I hadn't it's small chance I'd have in my present job.'

'Good!' I said, laughing at what I took to be a piece of sarcasm on the well-known attitude of the Post Office towards the things of the Gael.

As the postman turned to leave, I noticed he wore a uniform which I did not remember to have seen before. It was a very neat dark green, and on the collar, in small letters of white metal, was the cryptic inscription, 'P. na hE.'

'What does "P. na hE" stand for?' I asked.

'"Post na hEireann", of course, Sir.' The note of surprise in his voice seemed somewhat accentuated.

'Why, this is capital!' I exclaimed. 'Have we brought the Post Office round so far? Who would have dreamt of this two years – six months – ago? And I have seen nothing about it in the papers!'

The postman was now regarding me in downright astonishment, as though my enthusiasm were something incomprehensible to him. He saluted me and walked off, looking back uneasily once more.

I turned to the bundle of letters he had left on the table. They were all addressed in Irish, and, to my surprise, the familiar penciled translation was absent. On looking closer I discovered the stupendous fact that the very post-marks were in Irish!

'The Post Office *is* marching,' I said. 'Have they made An Craoibhín P.M.G or what does it all mean? Hallo, there's my copy of *An Claidheamh*! It will have something to say about this new development.'

The packet which I drew towards me seemed rather bulkier than *An Claidheamh* generally is.

'Have they enlarged the paper?' I asked myself. 'Strange that they did not give notice of it beforehand. Or stay, – this is probably the special Oireachtas number.'

I tore off the wrapper and spread the paper out. A large broadsheet, – and every word of it in Irish. Advertisements and all!

The front page consisted of a couple of signed editorials followed by crisp news notes. At the foot of the page was a literary feuilleton.

I ran my eyes down the columns of news. The first item that struck me was this (I roughly paraphrase the Irish in which it was written):

'The forthcoming Oireachtas promises to be one of the most remarkable in the long history of what has now grown to be our most venerable national institution. We say venerable because, though the Oireachtas is not so much more than a hundred years old – the first festival was held in 1897 – yet it is a link with a past which is remote from us less by reason of the span of years which has elapsed than in virtue of the enormous changes – intellectual, political, social – which have passed over our country since the days when Hyde, O'Leary, MacNeill, and their compeers first challenged the intellectual supremacy of a foreigner in Ireland.'

This paragraph was so stupifyingly unintelligible that I glanced at the top of the paper to see was it really *An Claidheamh*, and what was the date of it. Then for the first time I read the title: '*The Daily Claidheamh*;' and the date: Lughnasa 4, 2,006![26]

Had I, like Rip Van Winkle, slept a hundred years? Impossible! Was I being made the recipient of some strange revelations of futurity? Most improbable! Was this, then, merely a common or (both literally and figuratively) garden dream? With admirable presence of mind I determined to waste no time in debating these questions with myself lest (supposing I was asleep) I might awake before I had extracted all the information possible from my twenty-first century *Claidheamh*. So I turned eagerly back to the news column and read on: –

'The Oireachtas will as usual be formally opened by the Ard-Rí. A unique feature of this year's festival will be the presence, on the invitation of the State, of various distinguished foreign visitors and delegations. Among the more important potentates who will assist at the opening ceremonies are the Emperor of the French, the President of the Russian Republic, and the Protector of the Indian Commonwealth. Much interest is manifested in the visit of the French Emperor, as it is the first time that a Bonaparte Sovereign has set foot in Ireland. His Imperial Majesty, with the Russian and Indian Presidents, will be the guests of the Ard-Rí at the Palace of the Nation. Among the learned bodies which will be represented are the French Academy, the Hungarian Academy, the Norsk-Norsk Theatre, and the Japanese Society of Arts. The Oireachtas Oration will be delivered by the Cardinal-Archbishop of Dublin, and the writing of the Oireachtas Ode has been entrusted to Padraic Ó Domhnalláin, the brilliant young Connacht poet whose recent volume of verse we review elsewhere, – and who is, by the way, the direct descendent of Padraic Ó Domhnalláin, of Uachtar Ard, one of the pioneer Gaelic Leaguers of the early part of the last century.[27] The evening gatherings of the Oireachtas will be held in the Theatre of Ireland, whose auditorium, since the recent extensions, seats 15,000 people.'

In another part of the paper I found the following interesting details as to the ceremonies with which the approaching Oireachtas – the one-hundred-and-tenth – was to be opened: –

'The opening of the Oireachtas being timed to take place at 10 am, the royal procession will start from the Palace of the Nation at 9.30. The order will be as follows: - The Herald of Ireland, with his attendants; a detachment of the National Guard, headed by the Band of Pipers of the First Regiment of Light Infantry; a troop of Cuirassiers[28]; the Ministers; the Ard-Rí, attended by his staff, and escorted by mounted Chasseurs[29]; the Boy-Corps of the Palace; Cuirassiers.' (N.B. I use 'National Guard', 'Light Infantry', 'Cuirassiers', and 'Boy-Corps' to translate 'Fianna Éireann', 'Ceithearnaigh', 'Laochraidhe Luireach', 'Rapairí', and 'Macraidhe', respectively.)

'The following will be the route of the procession: – Plás na nArd-Riogh; Slighe na hÉireann; Sráid Dhomhnaill Uí Chonaill; Slighe Eoghan Uí Ghramhna; Slighe an Chraoibhín; Plás an Chraoibhín to Amharclann na hÉireann.[30]

The Ministries and other public buildings along the line of march will be decorated. The troops will salute at the Monument to Ireland Free in Plás na nÉireann and at the O'Growney Monument at the head of Slighe Eoghan Uí Ghramhna.

The Presidents and officers of the Gaelic League; the adjudicators and officials of the Oireachtas; the members of the Irish academy; the Bards (robed), with the distinguished personages specially invited, will be assembled on the platform around the base of the Hyde Monument in Plás an Chraoibhín. The general public will be accommodated in the temporary stands which line the four sides of the Plás.

On the arrival of the Ard-Rí, the cannon in Dún Bhaile Átha Cliath will fire a salute. The Oireachtas will then be formally opened in accordance with the ancient procedure revived – as our antiquarian readers will recollect – in 1913. The Herald of Ireland will proclaim the Peace of the Gael; the Bard of Ireland will invoke the spirit of Gaelic Thought and Imagination; and the Ard-Rí will declare the one-hundred-and-tenth Oireachtas in session. The trumpets and cannon will then salute the Oireachtas, and the National Hymn will be intoned'.

In a column of occasional jottings entitled 'Brúsgar,' I read the following interesting note[31]: -

'Some of our readers may not be aware of the fact that the Oireachtas was, some years after its institution or revival in 1897, mainly an indoor festival. We are so used to the open-air musters in Plás an Chraoibhín and in Páirc an Fhionn-Uisge that we find it difficult to realise that the Oireachtas Ode and Oration were once delivered in a stuffy hall to a sweltering audience. Our correspondent, Mac Uí Mhaol-Thuile of Inis-Chórthaidh, reminds us of the fact that the first al-fresco performance of plays in Páirc an Fhionn-Uisge occurred in 1921; and that the Ode and Oration were for the first time delivered in the open air in 1950. It must be remembered that – as a result of the draining of the bogs and the reforestation of the country – the temperature of Ireland has risen several degrees within the last century: which explains why it is now possible for us to hold nearly all our gatherings, whether for business or pleasure, in the open air. We who are used to a Baile Átha Cliath of shady boulevards and open-air cafes can hardly realise that our city had neither boulevards nor cafes in 1906. People then paraded sun-baked streets in summer and ploughed their way through sludge in winter; whilst they resorted for "refreshment" to evil-smelling dens known as "public-houses," which no decent women would enter.'

I next turned to the leading articles. The first discussed an educational measure recently introduced in the Dáil, or Lower Chamber of the Irish Parliament. The second dealt with Irish Drama, with special reference to the forthcoming performance of a new play by the great psychological dramatist, Aodh Ó hAodhagáin, at the

Oireachtas, mentioning incidentally that Ó hAodhagáin had in the previous year been the recipient of the Nobel Prize, and that a French translation of his *Parnell* had been *couronné* by the French Academy.[32] The third leader congratulated the nation on the amicable adjustment of a diplomatic dispute which had arisen between Ireland and the South African Republic.

Interested by the first editorial, I turned to the parliamentary column to read the report of the debate referred to. Only the gist of the speeches was given – a fact for which, mindful of the deadly verbatim of reports of the *Freeman*, I was grateful: –

'The senior member for Port Láirge introduced a Bill for the compulsory teaching of Japanese as a second language in seaport towns and cities. In recommending the measure to the Dáil, he dwelt on the immense and growing importance of Japanese as a commercial language. In fact, it bade fair to become a world-tongue. He conceived that Irish boys and girls, equipped with a sound commercial knowledge of Irish and Japanese – the two dominant tongues, the one of the West, the other of the East – would have an enormous advantage over the children of less progressive nations, such as Germany and France – not to mention England (laughter) – in which Japanese was not taught and Irish as yet only partially.

The Minister of Education (Reachtaire an Oideachais) regretted that the Government was unable to accept the measure. He quite agreed with the member for Port Láirge as to the commercial value of Japanese, though he was not impressed by his assurance that it was likely to become the universal language. Prophecies on that subject were generally unfortunate. A hundred years ago English writers and statesmen were optimistic enough – he might say foolish enough – to prophesy that English was about to become the universal language, and today they were face to face with the fact that English was spoken only by a few peasants in Somersetshire. Coming to principle, the policy of the Irish Education Department and of the Irish Government on the linguistic question was the policy which had been followed by them ever since their country had achieved independence, and which, if he was not mistaken, was first formulated by *An Claidheamh Soluis* (applause) upwards of a century ago. He might state that policy in two sentences: every child has the right to be taught its mother-tongue; every child ought to be taught, in addition, at least one other language. If they would bear with him, he would remind them of a few facts, now belonging to ancient history, but important to be borne in mind in any discussion on this subject. Almost the first act of the Revolutionary Government of 19- (the figure was unfortunately blotted) had been to establish a national education system embodying the two principles he had referred to. Under that system Irish was regarded as the vernacular or "first language" over one-third of the total area of the country, English being regarded as the vernacular over the remaining two-thirds. In the first-named area English, French, or German was taught as a "second language"; in the other, Irish was the "second language" almost universally adopted, though a few schools, chiefly in the North-East, adhered to French or German for a few years. Irish, as they were aware, rapidly extended its vernacular area, with the result that, in a generation and a half, it completely ousted English as the "first language". The conquest of England by the Russian Republic, and the splitting up of the British Empire into independent kingdoms and republics, soon destroyed the commercial value of English, which henceforth had only a literary and historical interest – its linguistic interest has always been small. Thus, English commenced to drop out of Irish schools even as a "second language", some tongue more valuable either from the intellectual or from the commercial standpoint, being adopted in its stead. At present the situation was this: every Irish child was taught Irish as a matter of course; every Irish child was taught, in addition, at least one other language. The Government laid down so much as de rigueur: it refused to go further and specify what languages should be taught in a given district in addition to the national language. That was a matter for the local management acting under the control of the district authority. He found that the languages most favoured were such classical literary languages (he did not refer to what were once known as Ancient Classics) as French, German, Italian, with the (in a sense) younger and more vigorous tongues of what he might call New Europe – Russian, Norwegian, Danish, Flemish, and Hungarian. In theory, any language might be taught – even English.

A member (interrupting) asked whether English was taught in *any* Irish school.

The Minister of Education – Yes, in three, - two in Béal Feirste and one in Rath Ó Máine (laughter).[33] Continuing, the Minister said that there was nothing to prevent the teaching of Japanese where desired, and in fact it had already been placed on the syllabus in Corcaigh, Port Láirge, Loch gCarmain, Báile Átha Cliath, and some other ports who had extensive trade with the East: but he was entirely opposed to setting the precedent of making any particular language, other than the national language, a compulsory subject of study anywhere. Apart from the general aspect of the question, there was the further important point that the Bill proposed by the member for Port Láirge would interfere with the right hitherto enjoyed by local school authorities of arranging the details of their own programmes. He hoped the Dáil would reject the Bill.

Other members having spoken, the Bill on a division was thrown out by 291 votes to 19.'

I found that the result of the debate was favourably commented upon in the editorial columns of *An Claidheamh*, where it was remarked: –

'On the linguistic question Ireland stands in 2006 exactly where the Gaelic League and *An Claidheamh Soluis* stood in 1906. She will stand there till the end. The mother tongue *de rigueur*, for the rest – liberty.'

On another page of the paper I found a column of literary reviews. One noticed a history of the National University (founded by public subscription in 1911, – *before* the War of Revolution, in which, by the way, its students played a prominent part); another reviewed a new novel by An tAthair Pádraic Ó Laoghaire, whom it hailed as the literary descendent of An tAthair Peadar, described as 'perhaps the foremost of literary figure of the revival of a century ago;' a third welcomed Pádraic Ó Domhnalláin's new book of verse; and a fourth discussed issues raised in a recently-published work entitled *A Hundred Years of Irish Literature*.[34] In the course of the last-mentioned review I read:

'We agree with the author that Irish poetry was saved from death from inanition by the movement which took its rise in

Connacht about the year 1910. Previously, Irish poets had wavered between two standards of form: the eighteenth century standard, which imposed metrical bonds so strict that they crushed out all thought; and the foreign or English standard, which though apparently affecting only externals, in reality affected the spirit of poetry itself, depriving it of the life-giving sap of native inspiration. The pioneers of what has come to be known as the Connacht movement, like Ronsard and his fellows in sixteenth-century France, set up again the standard of the Antique. As the poets of the *Pleiades* revived the *ballade*, the *rondeau*, and so on, so these Western poets revived the Ossianic Laoi, the Rosg, and some of the simpler forms of Dán Díreach. They raised, too, the banner of Liberty, and sand boldly and fearlessly of the lives, the loves, the hates, the joys, the sins, the sorrows of men, – even as the ancients did in Ireland, even as the poets of all time have done, – mocking at conventions, keeping in mind only the one sacred duty of the poet, – to utter the soul's thoughts, be those thoughts what they may.

With regard to the tons of eighteenth-century poetry disinterred from MSS about the beginning of the 20th century –'

At this moment, a voice broke in on my reading, I started, and dropped the paper, – which, to my surprise, turned into a copy of the *Freeman's Journal* (containing an article on the British Education Bill), as it fluttered to the ground from my hand. The bundle of letters and papers which the postman had brought had disappeared – if they had ever been there.

' ….' I said to myself as I stood up and followed the voice which had called me in to tea.

DEC 15th 1906
THE ENGLISH-SPEAKING TRADITION

Our leading articles for the past three months have been devoted to an examination of the actual situation in the Irish-speaking districts, and to the suggestion of remedies for the deplorable state of affairs revealed by that examination. We have seen that, speaking generally, vernacular Irish continues to die in its home; that it continues to die in spite of the fact (we again speak generally) that the public opinion of the Gaedhealtacht, so far as such a thing exists, has been converted to the view that it ought not to be allowed to die; that it continues to die, in other words, primarily and chiefly because THE HABIT of speaking English has become ingrained in Irish speakers and that the eradication of that habit has so far proved a task beyond the strength of the language movement.[35] We have seen the habit in full force in the home, in the school, in the church, on the political platform, in the public boardroom. We have seen that it imposes its tyranny on teachers who spend themselves in the effort to impart a reading and writing knowledge of the language to their pupils; on priests who are thoroughly convinced that the maintenance of the language is essential to the spiritual, intellectual, and material welfare of their flocks; on politicians who subscribe to the full programme of the Gaelic League; on League workers known throughout the length and breadth of the land as eager and effective writers, students, teachers, or propagandists. In theory, we all admit that Irish should be spoken; in practice we all – or nearly all – go on speaking English. In the Galldacht this is only ridiculous: in the Gaedhealtacht it is not ridiculous but tragical.[36]

THE UNCHECKED CONTINUANCE OF THE ENGLISH-SPEAKING TRADITION FOR ANOTHER TEN YEARS WILL MEAN THE DEATH OF THE IRISH LANGUAGE.

Let the tradition, then, be attacked on every League platform, in every League classroom, in every newspaper and periodical which the Gaelic League can influence. Let it be attacked from the pulpit, from the political platform, in the boardroom, in the schoolroom. Let it be attacked directly and indirectly, in season and out of season, night, noon, and morning.

This is a programme in which every Gaelic Leaguer can take part – it is a programme in which every Gaelic Leaguer *must* take part. It was by adopting a strenuous and utterly uncompromising attitude in a similar crisis that the Czechs succeeded in saving the spoken language in Bohemia. At the present day a Czech will reply to a foreigner who addresses him in German, but he will not reply to a Czech who does so. In Poland a hundred thousand children strike from school because they are required to repeat the Catechism in German. In Wales the audience at a political meeting storms the platform because it is addressed in English by the member for the constituency. We want a little of the Czech's, or the Pole's, or the Welshman's thoroughness, stiffneckedness, and contempt for 'respectability'.

9th February 1907
The Passing of Anglo-Irish Drama.[37]

If it is unlikely to have any other happy outcome – as we fear it is – the tragic-comedy which ran its absurd course at the Abbey Theatre last week will at least concentrate the attention of Gaels on the absolute necessity for the foundation of an Irish Theatre in the capital of Ireland. Anglo-Ireland has been shown at its worst, and a very unlovely worst it is. We cannot congratulate either the Theatre or its critics on the way in which they have acted in face of a crisis. On both sides there have been mock-heroics and hysterics; on both a shameful lack of tolerance and broadmindedness; on both an even more painful want of that saving sense of humour which in his most tense and electric moments never deserts the genuine Gael. If 'Art' has contrived to make itself look ridiculous so have the raucous cryers-down of 'Art'. And both are of Anglo-Ireland; wherein the true Gael who 'sees life steadily and sees it whole' may find a certain grim satisfaction.

Mr. Synge's play was indefensible. But it was defensible – and was ably defended – on almost every ground on which it was attacked. The objections to certain plain-spoken expressions which occurred in the dialogue as it was originally spoken were simply puerile. The serious resentment of the play as a libel on Irish character was almost as inept. Irish character does not need to be vindicated against Mr. J.M. Synge; and if it did, the audience went a passing strange way about vindicating it. But we do not believe that Mr. Synge intended his play either as a picture or as a caricature of Irish life. The charge which we bring against him is graver. Whether deliberately or un-deliberately, he is using the stage for the propagation of a monstrous gospel of animalism, of revolt against sweet and sane ideals, of bitter contempt for all that is fine and worthy, not merely in Christian morality, but in human nature itself. He lays the scenes of his plays in Ireland merely because Ireland is the country with whose scenery and life he is best acquainted: but it is not Ireland he libels so much as mankind in general, it is not against a nation he blasphemes so much as against the moral order of the universe.

In 'The Shadow of the Glen' we find Mr. Synge preaching contempt of what he would doubtless call the 'moral convention'; in 'The Well of the Saints' he railed against light, and sweetness, and knowledge, and charity; in 'The Playboy of the Western World' – not so much perhaps in the mere story or plot as in the amazingly powerful dialogue – he has produced a brutal glorification of violence, and grossness, and the flesh. In these three plays humanity is in savage revolt. In the beautiful and wonderfully impressive 'Riders to the Sea' humanity is represented as passive and despairing in the hands of some strange and unpitying God. A sinister and unholy gospel, truly.

The Anglo-Irish dramatic movement has now been in existence for ten years. Its net result has been the spoiling of a noble poet in Mr. W.B. Yeats, and the generation of a sort of Evil Spirit in the shape of Mr. J.M. Synge. 'By their fruits ye shall know them.'

'The Playboy of the Western World' was not a play to be howled down by a little mob. It was a play to be left severely alone by all who did not care to listen to it. The course taken by the objectors was not only undignified, but, as events proved, ineffective. It was, therefore, bad tactics, as well as an infringement of the liberty both of the author and players and of the public. On the other hand, the action of the Theatre authorities in introducing the police, in personally denouncing members of the audience, and in pressing their vindictiveness so far as to go down to the police courts in order to secure convictions, can only be described as lamentable. The author of 'Cathleen Ni Houlihan' at the head of a column of D.M.P. men was a sight which will long haunt the memory with that mixture of the odious and the ludicrous which clings to the recollection of the mean deeds of men made for finer things.[38]

Mr. Yeats triumphs for the moment; but he has lost far more than he has gained. As for Anglo-Irish drama – it is the beginning of the end.

AUGUST 15th 1908
THE PLAYS[39]

On Thursday evening, before a large audience, two of the prize Dramas were produced; the first being 'Bairbre Ruadh' by a young Connacht writer, Padraic Ó Conaire, now resident in London. The piece, which was produced by members of the London Gaelic League, is quite a simple little drama, dealing with the daughter of a Galway farmer, who is in love with a servant boy, while her brother makes a match for her with a publican in Galway. The servant boy wins, while the publican had to content himself with the heroine's sister, Cáit. It was regrettable that those any distance from the stage could not hear the play, and this gave a bad impression of what was a fairly good little drama.

Father O'Kelly's play, 'Ar Thaobh an Locha', was more elaborate, and much better presented. There are seven characters in this piece.

It depicts the trials of an evicted farmer, Maitiú Ó Ruairc, who is subsequently relieved of his difficulties by the timely arrival of his son, Michael, from America, who not only gets his father out of his troubles, but saves his sister, Una, from being compelled to wed the bailiff, Báille, instead of her lover, Feidhlim O'Griobhtha. Those who presented this Play did their work well, particularly Michael O Briain, who as the farmer Maitiú, spoke clearly and distinctly, and did his part in a very realistic manner.

On Friday night, two other Plays of quite a different character were presented. The first, 'Mac Carrthaigh Mór', by Padraig Ó Seadha ('Padraig na Léime') of Cahirdaniel, carried us back to stormy and stirring times in Irish history, and relates the efforts of the Mac Carrthaigh Dubh to oust Mac Carrthaigh Mór from the Chieftaincy of the Clan. The drama is an ambitious piece of work, evenly balanced; with the various incidents and dialogues very well sustained. On the whole those who presented the play did their parts very well, and spoke with ease and clearness, while the acting was generally natural and easy.

The Play which followed, 'An Duthchas', was by Máire Ní Chinnéide, B.A. (Mrs. Fitzgerald) a lady prominently connected with the Keating Branch for some years, who and has (*sic*) already gained a reputation as a Gaelic writer. This little drama is a very simple one, and gives a vivid picture of a young man who becomes a drunkard by commencing merely with a glass of wine, to drink his sweetheart's health; and by becoming addicted to drink he loses his inheritance. The play forcibly illustrates the remark once made by the late John Bright, that the sin of drunkenness began with the first glass. The little drama was excellently presented by the dramatic corps of the Keating Branch.

SEPTEMBER 26th 1908
MÓR SHIUBHAL NA NGAEDHEAL[40]

Sunday's Language Procession was a signal triumph, no other demonstration we believe in the history of the League, displayed so spontaneous an outburst of popular enthusiasm as that which manifested itself in Dublin on Sunday in spite of unfavourable weather conditions that prevailed.

We wrote last week that there were many reasons why the Gaelic League should show its strength and influence on Sunday – and it did so, there is no gainsaying the fact, it was the finest Gaelic League demonstration we have witnessed.

No one who saw the great, orderly, and dignified Procession, but felt how deserved were the compliments paid by An Craoibhín, and the Lord Mayor, to the band of zealous, earnest, and painstaking workers who brought it to so successful an issue. It was a huge undertaking for voluntary workers, yet the whole thing was planned and organised by Padraic Mac Giolla Íosa aided by willing hands from various Craobhacha in the city and suburbs.[41]

None but those having such work in hand can have even the remotest conception of the numberless details involved, the neglect of any of which might have disarranged the whole proceedings, yet in the vast throng forming a procession practically two miles in length, not a hitch occurred, section after section took up the places that were planned for them before hand; there was no rush, no uncertainty, no delay, every section went straight to its own position, and thus the most admirable order and decorum were preserved throughout from start to finish.

A striking feature of the procession was the Tableaux, illustrating in a vivid and realistic manner various periods of our country's story. These were also designed and executed by voluntary workers, who deserve every praise. Each tableau was a thing of beauty in itself, the whole series not only produced a fine artistic effect, but lent grace and dignity to the Procession. They helped to recall stirring and eventful incidents in our history, they recalled the glories of the past, and conveyed a message of hope for the future. Sunday's demonstration, with its historical tableaux, its industrial exhibits, its educational, temperance, trade and numberous (*sic*) other sections marching in serried ranks, proclaimed the voice of a resurgent Nation, it proclaimed that the Gael had truly risen, and was marching onwards, and rapidly approaching the day when he should once more occupy the premier position in his own country. It seemed like the culmination of a great struggle, it was a march of triumph. Who is it that could witness the vast concourse of people assembled and see the Procession on Sunday, or saw numbers the taking part in it (*sic*), that could doubt for a moment that Dublin was enthusiastically with the Gael. In that Procession, were grave and learned men, clergymen, and men learned in science, art and music, pioneers in industrial effort, and skilful tradesmen. Teachers and professors were there, and students in vast numbers – Ireland's hope – all proclaiming their adherence to the principles of the Gaelic League. They were there in order to support the Gaelic League's demands that our language should occupy its rightful position in the intellectual and social life of the Nation, that they were with us because they recognise that the Gaelic League has developed the moral character of such of our people as have been brought under its influence, stimulated them to intellectual improvement, and industrial efforts, which have already borne fruit. These various societies and organisations were with us in recognition of the work of the League in the cause of temperance, education, manliness, self-respect and Nationality in its highest sense.

As we wended our way in Sunday's great Procession, looking at the serried ranks marching before us, the solid mass of humanity which filled either side of the long route through which we passed, the immense number of youth that made us so hopeful of Ireland's future, while looking at all these yet, we, as Gaelic Leaguers, thought how empty would that pageant be, how shorn it would be of its interest, how lacking it would be in its effect, but for the presence of 'An Craoibhín Aoibhinn', whose winning personality, intense patriotism, wide and varied scholastic attainments, have largely been instrumental in placing the League in the prominent position it occupies today in Irish public life. The enthusiasm displayed by the vast multitude which Dr. Hyde addressed in the Phoenix Park on Sunday clearly showed the affection which the Gaels of Dublin entertain for 'An Craoibhín'.

Sunday's Demonstration was, owing to weather conditions, purely a local affair, practically it only represented the voice of Ireland's capital. Headed by its Chief Magistrate, Dublin spoke on Sunday with no uncertain voice, it proclaiming its adhesion to the principles of the Gaelic League, and endorsed its demand for the proper recognition of our National language in the curriculum of the new University.

This is the most vital issue that confronts us at the moment, and the speakers at the great meeting in the Park on Sunday realised the fact, Dr. Hyde himself dwelling upon the question with his usual vigour.

Altogether, the day's proceedings were such as to inspire even the most pessimistic with bright hopes for the future of the Language Movement.

NOVEMBER 14th 1908
OUR HERITAGE OF CHIVALRY

At the Commemoration Dinner at University College on Thursday week last a remarkable thing happened. Speaker after speaker had addressed the guests from the President's table. They were all good speakers. Some of them, indeed, are famous as orators, and on this occasion they did not belie their fame. The President of University

College, the Archbishop of Tuam, and the Chancellor of the Royal University dealt with grave themes in grave and dignified language, and each received and merited the applause of the distinguished audience. It was towards the end that the remarkable thing happened. The President in proposing the toast of the Professors of the College coupled it with the name of Dr. Sigerson.[42] Then there arose, not on the dais where the other speakers sat at the President's table, but in a place far down in the body of the hall, a man with a leonine head poised grandly on broad shoulders. Immediately there was an outburst not of mere hand-clapping but of cheering, loud and long and vehement. It was perfectly spontaneous in its coming. It was electric in its effect. The dignitaries on the President's dais looked startled, yet joined in vociferously. For many seconds – nay, actually for minutes – it continued. Then, amid a hush, Dr. Sigerson spoke, in massive and noble sentences, each one unfolding its length like a Miltonic verse, each one closing with a grand Miltonic music. He said not one word about the petty politics of the moment. His thoughts were with Ireland's past and with Ireland's gift to the nations – Ireland's two-fold gift of learning and chivalry. Listening to his words every young man there realised his noblest and finest self; realised, too, that he was the heir of a great tradition; and wondered vaguely why it was that that consciousness should awake in him so rarely. When the speaker sat down the cheering broke out and again lasted many seconds.

The present writer happened to be sitting beside Dr. Sigerson. On his other side sat the President of the Gaelic League. 'You had your audience with you', whispered An Craoibhín. 'Oh! the young men are always with me', replied Dr. Sigerson. And he had expressed a strange psychological truth. What is the secret bond of sympathy between this veteran of the days of Kickham and O'Leary and the young men of today? What but a common faith, a common hope, and a common love, all centring in the same dear Cause?

On Monday evening last Dr. Sigerson again addressed a Dublin audience. An Craoibhín was in the chair. The subject was 'The Celtic Origin of Chivalry'. In the course of a paper every sentence of which was luminous, Dr. Sigerson established conclusively Ireland's claim to priority in the manifestation of the spirit and customs of chivalry. There was no chivalry, properly so called, amongst Greeks and Romans. There is nothing essential the in (*sic.*) medieval chivalry that is not traceable to or at any rate anticipated by Irish chivalry in the first century. Waiving the question of the historic basis of the Cuchulainn saga, we have at all events a tradition at least as old as the seventh or eighth century of a heroic companionship existing in Ireland a few centuries earlier and acknowledging a code of chivalry loftier and more beautiful than any that ever obtained in Europe in the days of the Crusaders and the Troubadours. Grant that the Red Branch is a myth, and we are face to face with the stupendous fact that in the eighth century Irishmen were able to imagine heroic characters and heroic laws than which literature, tradition, and history have nothing greater to show. Whichever way you take it, Ireland's glory remains unique.

Standish O'Grady would like to set the boys and girls of Ireland reading the story of the young Napoleon. We too have glowed over that great tale of youthful endeavour, and sometimes with reverence we show our boys certain relics of Napoleon which we treasure at Sgoil Éanna. But the hero we would soonest place before Young Ireland as a shining ideal of youthful achievement is our own Cuchulainn.

When we were thinking out a scheme of decoration for Sgoil Éanna it seemed to us that it would be a noble thing to set somewhere where every boy that entered the School might see it a picture in which the boy Cuchulainn should be the central figure. Accordingly an Irish artist – Edwin Morrow – painted for us a semicircular panel for our entrance hall. It shows Cuchulainn taking arms. He had overheard Cathbhadh the Druid prophesy that the lad who took arms that day should do deeds that should always be remembered in Ireland but that his span of life should be short. Straightaway the little lad sought the presence of Conchobar. 'All victory and blessing be thine, O King: I come to demand arms this day'. And, after he had rejected all other arms as unworthy of him, he was armed with the famous weapons of Conchobar himself. Then came Cathbhadh, aghast to find that his favourite pupil had done this heroic but terrible thing. 'Thou, little child, shalt win great fame and glory, but thy life shall quickly pass'. Cuchulainn made the undaunted reply: 'I care not though I remain in being but one day and one night so that my deeds and my fame live after me'. These words, in the original Irish of the Book of Leinster Táin, are on a scroll around our panel at Sgoil Éanna.

It seems to us that with such an heroic inspiration in our own literature, we, men and boys of Ireland, have little need to go to foreign literatures or foreign legends to learn chivalry. Not only was Ireland the first nursing ground of chivalry, but chivalry in Ireland reached a finer flower than ever-afterwards in Europe. 'I give comfort to him who is wretched, I deal out mischief to him who is strong', said Cuchulainn. 'I do not slay women or children or folk unarmed'.

Compare the Flight at the Ford with similar episodes in other ancient literature. And Dr. Sigerson finds in the Cuchulainn saga an incident still more knightly, an incident than which, he says, if there be any higher achievement, accomplished or imagined, in historic romance, it is unknown to him. We refer to the march of the Macradh of Eamhain Macha to the relief of Cuchulainn and their fall on the Ulster frontier. The Táin tells the story very simply. Miss Milligan has woven it into ringing English verse.[43]

Down they came with shouts of contest and the sheen of falchions glancing,
And they rushed across the torrent on the vast invading horde;
There they fought and fell and perished, but they stayed the foe's advancing.
Till Cuchulainn rose from slumber with his matchless strength restored –
Till Cuchulainn stood, and, gazing from the woodland o'er the water,
Saw the white limbs tossed and mangled in the torrent on the rocks,
Saw the broken weapons shining in the shallow pools of slaughter,
And the ruddy stains of wounding on the brightness of their locks.

Then his heart was sore with sorrow and his eyes bedimmed with weeping
For the youths who had been keeping through long space of perilous hours,
In the beauty of their boyhood, whilst the Red Branch Knights were sleeping,
Watch and ward beside the ford against the Olnemactian powers.
Forth Cuchulainn went to glory, o'er the stream and plain-land glory,
But pausing in his passing ere his chariot westward rolled,
Their laud be thus repeated: O ye fallen, but not defeated,
Ye shall share the conqueror's fame, who kept the land for him to hold.[44]

NOTES

1 The figure recalled here is Pearse's grandaunt Margaret Brady.

2 Seanchaidhe: storyteller.

3 John O'Mahony: founding member of the Fenian Brotherhood in the United States.

4 An Craoibhín: Douglas Hyde, founding member of Gaelic League, dramatist and later first President of Ireland.

5 Bóithríns: laneways.

6 Oireachtas: annual competition festival instigated by the Gaelic League in 1897.

7 Kine: cattle.

8 Buaile: pasture.

9 A bhuidheachas soin le Dia!: Thank God for that.

10 Farney: an area of Co. Monaghan which was to some extent still Gaelic speaking at the turn of the twentieth century.

11 Seosamh Laoide, 1865–1939, scholar, folklorist, editor of Gaelic literature and language activist.

12 Fearnaigh/Farney and Oirialla/Oriel. Farney still had native speakers attending Oireachtas competitions in the early twentieth century. Oriel comprises a historical area around Louth, Monaghan, North Meath and South Armagh and is also known for its rich Gaelic heritage. The contention here that the seanchais were gone was premature.

13 The Déise: Gaelic-speaking area in Co. Waterford. The diagnosis that no-one would replace the then current Irish-speaking generation was overly pessimistic.

14 Aonghus O Dálaigh: sixteenth-century Irish poet.

15 Seathrún Céitinn: Geoffrey Keating, seventeenth-century poet and historian. Pearse translated his 'Óm sceol ar Ardmhaigh Fáil' in his 'Songs of the Irish Rebels'.

16 réamh-rádh: preface.

17 Messrs. Lawrence: William and John Lawrence – photographic entrepreneurs who built up an extraordinarily extensive collection of photographic images of the Irish landscape.

18 Geasa: literally a spell, here meaning promise or commitment.

19 Bricriu: a poet and troublemaker from the Ulster Cycle who took joy in observing the tensions and arguments that he had orchestrated.

20 Legendary High King of Ireland.

21 Reference to Turas na dTaoiseach/ Flight of the Earls, (Aodh Ó Néill and Ruaidhrí Ó Domhnaill/Hugh O'Neill and Rory O'Donnell) 1607. Here again Pearse's reading of the demise of elite Gaelic culture

is overly negative and the dichotomy he draws between high and 'peasant' culture is a little generalised.

22 Dion-Bhrollach: Preface.

23 más slán dúinn: if we're still here.

24 Tomás Ó hAodha, 1866–1935, a teacher and language activisit, was one of the first dramatists of the Gaelic Revival. The two plays mentioned were produced at the 1904 and 1906 Oireachtas Festivals.

25 Daithí Coimín, 1854–1907, Gaelic language activist, editor of Irisleabhar na Gaeilge, edited 'Laoi Oisín ar Thír na nÓg' (1880), 'Mac-Ghníomhartha Fhinn' (1902) Foras Feasa ar Éirinn Iml. a hAon (1902).

26 August 4th 2006.

27 A prose writer championed by Pearse.

28 Mounted Soldiers.

29 Light Infantry soldiers.

30 Plás na nArd-Riogh: Place of the High Kings; Slighe na hÉireann: Way of Ireland; Sráid Dhomhnaill Uí Chomaill: Daniel O'Connell Street; Slighe Eoghan Uí Ghramhna; Eugene O'growney Street; Slighe an Chraoibhín: Douglas Hyde Way; Plás an Chraoibhín: Douglas Hyde Place; Amharclann na hÉireann: The Theatre of Ireland.

31 Brúsgar: bits and pieces.

32 *couronné*: awarded a prize.

33 Belfast and Rathmines.

34 An tAthair Peadar: Father Peter O'Leary.

35 Gaedhealtacht: today, Irish-speaking districts. In 1906 the meaning still encompassed Gaelic culture in general.

36 Galldacht: those parts of Ireland where English is the dominant language.

37 J.M. Synge's *Playboy of the Western World* was premiered at the Abbey on January 26th 1907, the infamous 'riots' it provoked are the starting point for Pearse's article.

38 D.M.P: Dublin Metropolitan Police.

39 The Plays: as presented as part of the preceding Oireachtas competition.

40 Mór Shiubhal na nGaedheal: The Gaels' Parade

41 Craobhacha: Branches (of the Gaelic League).

42 Dr Sigerson: George Sigerson (1836–1925) – medical doctor and scholar, whose translations and writings on Gaelic literature had a seminal influence on Pearse.

43 Miss Milligan: Alice Milligan (1866–1953), Belfast-based poet, playwright and Gaelic League activist.

44 Alice Milligan, 'The Defenders of the Ford'.

SELECTED EXTRACTS FROM *AN MACAOMH*

Editors' Note: Pearse wrote extensively about his own plays and dramatic productions in *An Macaomh*, the journal of St. Enda's. The 'By Way of Comment' editorials showcase Pearse's skill at publicising his school's achievements and at transmitting his own thinking to an influential readership. The photographs of actors in costume which were published alongside the original scripts were professionally taken. As well as being a rich source for information on the dramatic productions themselves, the excerpts below allow us to observe the continuing developments in Pearse's understanding of Fiannaíocht and Rúraíocht literature from 1909 onwards, and to trace developments in his political and cultural thinking. The writings from which the excerpts are taken were prepared for publication in book form by Pearse before the Rising and were edited by Desmond Ryan as *The Story of A Success*. We have also included a piece by Stephen McKenna which descibes the impact of Pearse's return to the Pageant as a form of public theatre.

AN MACAOMH JUNE 1909

We must be worthy of the tradition we seek to recreate and perpetuate in Éire, the knightly tradition of the macradh of Eamhain Macha, dead at the Ford "in the beauty of their boyhood," the high tradition of Cúchulainn, better is short life with honour than long life with dishonour," "I care not though I were to live but one day and one night, if only my fame and my deeds live after me;" the noble tradition of the Fianna, " we, the Fianna, never told a lie, falsehood was never imputed to us," "strength in our hands, truth on our lips, and cleanness in our hearts ;" the Christ-like tradition of Colm Cille, "if I die, it shall be from the excess of the love I bear the Gael." It seems to me that with this appeal it will be an easy thing to teach Irish boys to be brave and unselfish, truthful, and pure; I am certain that no other appeal will so stir their hearts or kindle their imaginations to heroic things.

344

The value of the national factor in education would appear to rest chiefly in this, that it addresses itself to the most generous side of the child's nature, urging him to live up to is finest self. (...)

Our first attempt at the presentation of plays was at our St. Enda's Day celebration on March 20th, 21st, and 22nd last, when in the School Gymnasium, converted for the occasion into a beautiful little theatre, our boys performed An Craoibhín's *An Naomh ar Iarraidh* and Mr. Standish O'Grady's *The Coming of Fionn*.[1] We had an audience of over a hundred each evening, our guests on the third evening including Sir John Rhys, Mr. Eoin MacNeill, Mr. W. B. Yeats, Mr. Stephen Gwynn, and Mr. Padraic Colum. All these, especially Mr. Yeats, were very generous in their praise of our lads, who, I hope, will not be spoiled by the tributes they received from such distinguished men. The Press notices, too, were very kindly. The *Irish Independent* and the London *Sphere* published photographs. The *Freeman's Journal* dwelt on the beautiful speaking of the actors, which, it said, had none of the stiffness and crudeness usually characteristic of schoolboy elocution. Mr. D. P. Moran wrote in the *Leader*: "There was a prologue to each piece, and both were excellently spoken. Dr. Hyde's little play, *An Naomh ar Iarraidh*, was well done, and particularly well staged. *The Coming of Fionn* was likewise a striking performance. We are not enamoured much of the cult of words on the stage that has to fight for existence in the world, but words and their delivery are all-important in school-plays. The players in *The Coming of Fionn* spoke their words excellently, and half the pleasure of a pleasant performance was the distinct and measured declamation. Indeed, we can write with enthusiasm though some cynical people don't think we have any of the plays at Sgoil Éanna. The stage and costumes emanated from the school, and the costumes were striking. . . ." In the *Nation* Mr. W. P. Ryan wrote: "The whole environment and atmosphere were delightful, but the human interest aroused by the boys is what remains kindliest in the memory. Boys as players are often awkward, ill at ease, and unnatural, as if they could not take kindly to the make-believe. The boys in the Sgoil Éanna plays for the most part were serenely and royally at home. An Craoibhín's delicate and tender little drama was delicately and tenderly interpreted; it had a religious sense and atmosphere about it, and the miracle seemed fitting and natural. In *The Coming of Fionn* one could easily lose sight of the fact that it was dramatic representation; the boys for a time were a part of the heroic antiquity; dressed in the way they were, and intense and interested as they were, one could picture them in Tara or Eamhain without much straining of the imagination. The heroic spirit had entered into their hearts and their minds, and one realized very early indeed that the evening's life and spirit were not something isolated, a phase and charm to be dropped when they reappeared in ordinary garb. The evening's sense was a natural continuation of that and many other evenings and days when the spirit of Fionn and his heroic comrades had been instilled into their minds by those for whom the noble old-time love had a vivid and ever-active and effective meaning. Fionn and Cúchulainn and their high-heroic kin had become part of the mental life of the teachers and the taught. With much modern culture they had imbibed things of dateless age, things that time had tested and found periennially human and alive." (…)

And Mr. Padraic Colum wrote in *Sinn Fein*: "The performance of *An Naomh ar Iarraidh* gave one the impression that the play could never be better produced. It is out of the heart of childhood, and it has the child's tears, the child's faith, the child's revelation. In this performance there was a delight that must always be wanting in the great art of the theatre; the child actors brought in no conscious, no distracting personality. It was like the enacting of one of the religious songs of Connacht. It was Gaelic from the beautiful traditional hymn sung at the opening to the prayer that closes the play. Standish O'Grady's masque is really for the open air. The scene is nominally a hut, but the speeches and sentiments demand spaciousness; the plain with forest for a background. After childhood with its inner life, here was youth with its pride in conquest and deliverance. The language of *The Coming of Fionn* is noble, but it is not quite dramatic speech. In the production there was no professionalism, no elaborate illusion. It was one with all noble art, because it came out of a comradeship of interest and inspiration; the art was here not rootless, it came out of belief, work and aspiration."

In the notes which I prefixed to the programme of the plays I said that our plans included the enacting of a Pageant in the early summer and of a Miracle Play at Christmas. The early summer has come, and with it our Pageant. It deals with the Boy-Deeds of Cúchulainn, I have extracted the story and a great part of the dialogue from the *Táin*, merely modernising (but altering as little as possible) the magnificent phrase of the epic. I have kept close to the *Táin* even at the risk of missing what some people might call dramatic effect, but in this matter I have greater trust in the instinct of the unknown shapers of our epic than in the instinct of any modern. I claim for my version one merit which I claim also for my episode of the Boy-

Deeds in the *Táin*, namely, that it does not contain a single unnecessary speech, a single unnecessary word. If Conall Cearnach and Laoghaire Buadhach are silent figures in our Pageant, it is because they stand silent in the tale of events as told by the Ulster exiles over the camp-fire of Meadhbh and Aileall. For Feargus I invent two or three short speeches, but the only important departure (and these have a sufficiently obvious purpose) from the narrative of the *Táin* are in making Cúchulainn's demand for arms take place on the faithche of Eamhain Macha rather than in Conchubhar's sleeping-house, and in assigning to the Watchman the part played by Leabharcham in the epic. For everything else I have authority. Even the names of the boy-corps are not all fanciful, for around Follamhan, son of Conchubhar (he who was to perish at the head of the macradh in the Ford of Slaughter) I group on the playground of Eamhain the sons of Uisneach, of Feargus, and of Conall Cearnach, boys who must have been Cúchulainn's contemporaries in the boy-corps, though older than he. On how many of those radiant figures were dark fates to close in as the tragedy of Ulster unrolled!

The Chorus and the Song of the Sword have been set to music by Mr. MacDonnell, the latter to an arrangement of the well-known Smith song in the Petrie Collection, the former to an original air. I feel this music gives dignity to very common-place words. My friend Tadhg Ó Donnchadha has kindly checked over the verses in bad Rannaigheacht Bheag which I put into the mouths of the Chorus. Obligations of another sort I owe to my brother, who is responsible for the costumes, grouping and general production of the Pageant, and to my nephew, Mr. Alfred McGloughlin, for help in the same and other directions. Mr. McGloughlin's name does not figure among the School Staff, but he might truly be called a Member of the Staff without Portfolio. He is at our service whenever we want anything done which requires artistic insight and plastic dexterity of hand, be it the making of plans for an Aula Maxima or the construction of a chariot for Cúchulainn. It may be wondered why we have undertaken the comparatively ambitious project of a Cúchulainn Pageant so early in our career, so soon, too, after our St. Enda's Day Celebration. The reason is that we were anxious to crown our first year's work with something worthy and symbolic ; anxious to send our boys home with the knightly image of Cúchulainn in their hearts, and his knightly words ringing in their ears. They will leave St. Enda's under the spell of the magic of their most beloved hero, the Macaomh who is, after all, the greatest figure in the epic of their country, indeed, as I think, the greatest in the epic of the world. Whether the Pageant will be an entire success I cannot venture to prophesy, but I feel sure that our boys will do their best and that, if they do not render full justice to the great story, at least they will not spoil it. I feel sure, too, that Eamonn Bulfin will be duly beautiful and awful as Cathbhadh the Druid; that Denis Gwynn will be gallant and noble as Conchobar Mac Neasa, Conchobar, young and gracious, as yet unstained by the blood of the children of Uisneach; and that Frank Dowling will realise, in face and figure and manner, my own high ideal of the child, Cúchulainn; that, "small, dark, sad boy, comeliest of the boys of Éire," shy and modest in a boy's winning way, with a boy's aloofness and a boy's mystery, with a boy's grave earnestness broken ever and anon by a boy's irresponsible gaiety; a boy merely to all who looked upon him, and unsuspected for a hero save in his strange moments of exaltation, when the seven-fold splendours blazed in his eyes and the hero-light shone above his head.

AN MACAOMH DECEMBER 1909

As the Boy-Corps of Eamhain stands out as the idealization of the system, Cúchulainn stands out as the idealization of the child fostered under the system. And thus Cúchulainn describes his fostering: "Fionnchaomh nourished me at her breast; Feargus bore me on his knee; Conall was my companion-in-arms; Blai, the lord of lands, was my hospitaller; fair-speeched Scancha trained me in just judgment ; on the knee of Amhairgin the poet I learned poetry; Cathbhadh of the gentle face taught me druid lore; Conchobar kindled my boyish ambition. All the chariot-chiefs and kings and poets of Ulster have taken part in my bringing up/" Such was the education of Cúchulainn, the most perfect hero of the Gael. Cúchulainn may never have lived, and there may never have been a Boy-Corps at Eamhain; but the picture endures as the Gael's idealization of the kind of environment and the kind of fostering which go to the making of a perfect hero. The result of it all, the simplicity and the strength of true heroism, is compressed into a single sentence put into the mouth of the hero by the old shaper of the tale of Cúchulainn's Phantom Chariot: "I was a child with children; I was a man with men."

Civilization has taken such a queer turn that it might not be easy to restore the old Irish plan of education in all its details. Our heroes and seers and scholars would not be so willing to add a Boy-Corps or a Grianán to their establishments as were their prototypes in Ireland from time immemorial till the fall of the Gaelic polity. I can imagine how blue Dr. Hyde, Mr. Yeats, and Mr. MacNeill would look if their friends informed them that they were about to send them their children to be fostered. But, at least, we can bring the heroes and seers and scholars to the schools (as we do at Sgoil Éanna) and get them to talk to the children; and we can rise up against the system which tolerates as teachers the rejected of all other professions, rather than demanding for so priestlike an office the highest souls and the noblest intellects of the race. I think, too, that the little child-republics I have described, with their own laws and their own leaders, their life face to face with nature, their care for the body as well as for the mind, their fostering of individualities yet never at the expense of the commonwealth, ought to be taken as models for all our modern schools. But I must not be misunderstood. In pleading for an attractive school-life, I do not plead for making school-life one long grand picnic: I have no sympathy with sentimentalists who hold that we should surround children with an artificial happiness, shutting out from their ken pain and sorrow and retribution and the world's law of unending strife; the key-note of the school-life I desiderate is effort on the part of the child itself, struggle, self-sacrifice, self-discipline, for by these only does the soul rise to perfection. I believe in gentleness, but not in softness. I would not place too heavy a burden on young shoulders, but I would see that no one, boy or man, shirk the burden he is strong enough to bear.

The first number of *An Macaomh* appeared on the eve of our Cúchulainn Pageant and the Distribution of Prizes. The Pageant was a large undertaking, but we seem to have satisfied everyone except ourselves. We had over five hundred guests in our playing-field, including most of the people in Dublin who are interested in art and literature. I think the boyish freshness of our miniature Macradh, and especially the shy and comely grace of Frank Dowling as Cúchulainn, really pleased them. Mr. Colum wrote very generously of us in *Sinn Fein*, Mr. Ryan in the *Irish Nation*, and Mr. Bulfin in *An Claidheamh Soluis*.[2] The *Freeman's Journal*, in addition to giving a special report, honoured us with a leading article from the pen of Mr. Stephen MacKenna.

Mr. MacNeill distributed the prizes, and he, Mr. Bulfin, and Dr. Henry addressed the boys and our guests.[3] I have a grievance against the reporters for leaving before the speeches. They were only speeches at a school fete, but they contained things that were better worth recording than all the news that was in the newspapers the next day. I did not go beyond what I felt when, in tendering the speakers the thanks of the masters and the boys, I said that our year's work would have been sufficiently rewarded if it had received no other recompense than the high and noble things Mr. MacNeill had just spoken in praise of it.

Our plays this year will take place some-where between St. Brigid's Day and the beginning of Lent. They will consist of a Heroic Play in English and a Miracle Play in Irish. Mr. Colum is writing the English Play for us: its subject is the doom of Conaire Mór at Bruidhean Da Dearga. The Miracle Play will probably be the dramatized version of *Íosagán* which I print in this number of *An Macaomh*.

In writing the Cúchulainn Pageant I religiously followed the phraseology of the *Táin*. In *Íosagán* I have as religiously followed the phraseology of the children and old men in Iar-Connacht from whom I have learned the Irish I speak. I have put no word, no speech, into the mouths of my little boys which the real little boys of the parish I have in mind boys whom I know as well as my pupils at Sgoil Éanna would not use in the same circumstances. I have given their daily conversation, anglicisms, "vulgarisms/'" and all: if I gave anything else my picture would be a false one.

The story which I now dramatize has been described by an able but eccentric critic as a "standard of revolt." It was meant as a standard of revolt, but my critic must pardon me if I say that the standard is not the standard of impressionism. It is the standard of definite art form as opposed to the folk form. I may or may not be a good standard bearer, but at any rate the standard is raised and the writers of Irish are flocking to it. *Íosagán* is not a play for the ordinary theatres or for the ordinary players. It requires a certain atmosphere, and a certain attitude of mind on the part of the actors. It has in fact been written for performance in a particular place and by particular players. I know that in that place and by those players it will be treated with the reverence due to a prayer. In bringing the Child Jesus into the midst of a group of boys disputing about their games, or to the knee of an old man who sings nursery rhymes to children, I am imagining nothing improbable, nothing outside the bounds of the everyday experience of innocent little children and reverent-minded old men and women. I know a priest who believes that he was summoned to the death-bed of a parishioner by Our Lord in person; and there are many hundreds of people in the countryside I write of who know that on certain nights Mary and her Child walk through the villages and if the cottage doors be left open, enter and sit awhile at the firesides of the poor.

AN MACAOMH CHRISTMAS 1910

It seems a far cry now back to our plays of February last, on the little stage at Cullenswood House, and their subsequent performance in the Abbey Theatre. Mr. Colum's dramatization of one of the high tragedies of the Gael, *The Destruction of Da Derga's Hostel*, was in the mood of great antique art, the mood of Egyptian sculpture and dán díreach verse, solemn, uplifting, serenely sad like the vigil of those high ones who watch with pitying but unrelenting eyes the awful dooms and dolours of men. The other play, my dramatization of my own *Íosagán*, owed whatever beauty it had, a beauty altogether of interpretation, to the young actors who played it; and they did bring into it something of the beauty of their own fresh lives, the beauty of childhood, the beauty of boyhood. I fear that we shall find it difficult in the future to achieve anything finer in acting than was achieved by Sorley MacGarvey, Éamonn Bulfin, Desmond Ryan, and Denis Gwynn in *The Destruction of the Hostel*, and by Patrick Conroy and the whole group of children in *Íosagán*. And an almost higher achievement was the vast solemnity, the remote mysteriousness, put into the chant of the Three Red Pipers by Fred O'Doherty, John Dowling, and Milo MacGarry. We performed the plays three times in our theatre during February.* In April we repeated them at the Abbey with Dr. Hyde's *An Naomh ar Iarraidh* and Mr. O'Grady's *The Coming of Fionn*.

We brought the year to a close by going down to Cúchulainn's country and performing the Cúchulainn Pageant at the Castlebellingham Feis. I think that was the most spacious day in all our two years since we had come together to Sgoil Éanna. I shall remember long the march of the boys round the field in their heroic gear, with their spears, their swords, their hounds, their horses; the sun shining on comely fair heads and straight sturdy bare limbs ; the buoyant sense of youth and life and strength that were there. There was another march with our pipers and banners to the station; and then a march home through the lamplit streets of Dublin. It was our last march to the old Sgoil Éanna. 'We have a larger school now, in a worthier place; but the old place and the faces in that march (for some who marched that night have never since answered a rally of Sgoil Éanna and never will again as schoolboys) are often in my mind ; and sometimes I wonder whether, if ever I need them for any great service, they will rally, as many of them have promised to do, from wherever they may be, holding faith to the inspiration and the tradition I have tried to give them.'

* After we had sent out the invitations and received the answers, we realized that our theatre would not hold more than two-thirds of each evening's guests. We had consequently to enlarge the theatre by a half, a feat which we accomplished in three days.

AN MACAOMH MAY 1913

And I have to thank Mr. W. B. Yeats and his fellow-workers at the Abbey Theatre for a very great generosity a special performance which they arranged to give for us on the evening of May 17th. Mr. Yeats, in a lecture on Rabindranath Tagore, had spoken of Mr. Tagore's school for Indian boys as "the Indian St. Enda's". A friend of mine, interested by this, suggested that we should go to Mr. Yeats and ask him whether his Theatre could not do something to help St. Enda's. We had hardly time to frame our project in words when Mr. Yeats assented to it; and then he did a more generous thing still, for he offered to produce for the benefit of St. Enda's the play of Mr. Tagore's to the production of which he had been looking forward as to an important epoch in the life of the Abbey the first presentation to Europe of a poet who, he thinks, is possibly the greatest now living. And he invited me to produce a St. Enda's play along with Mr. Tagore's I understood then more clearly than ever that no one is so generous as a great artist; for a great artist is always giving gifts.

The play we decided to produce along with *The Post Office* was my morality, *An Rí*. We had enacted it during the previous summer, with much pageantry of horses and marchings, at a place in our grounds where an old castellated bridge, not unlike the entrance to a monastery, is thrown across a stream. Since that performance I had added some speeches with the object of slightly deepening the characterization; and our boys were already rehearsing it for indoor production. Of Mr. Tagore's play I knew nothing except what I had heard from Mr. Yeats, but, I saw that both of us had had in our minds the same image of a humble boy and of the pomp of death, and that my play would be as it were antiphonal to his. Since I have seen Mr. Tagore's manuscript I have realized that the two plays are more similar in theme than will be to his in the nature of an "amen"; for in our respective languages, he speaking in terms of Indian village life, and I in terms of an Irish saga, we have both expressed the same truth, that the highest thing anyone can do is to serve.

AN MACAOMH CHRISTMAS 1913

(…) the exhilaration of fighting has gone out of Ireland, and for the past decade most of us have been as Fionn was after his battles "in heaviness of depression and horror of self-questioning." Here at St. Enda's we have tried to keep before us the image of Fionn during his battles careless and laughing, with that gesture of the head, that gallant smiling gesture, which has been an eternal gesture in Irish history; it was most memorably made by Emmet when he mounted the scaffold in Thomas Street, smiling, he who had left so much, and most recently by those Three who died at Manchester. When people say that Ireland will be happy when her mills throb and her harbours swarm with shipping, they are talking as foolishly as if one were to say of a lost saint or of an unhappy lover: "That man will be happy again when he has a comfortable income." I know that Ireland will not be happy again until she recollects that old proud gesture of hers, and that laughing gesture of a young man that is going into battle or climbing to a gibbet."

What I have just written has reminded me of a dream I had nearly four years ago. I dreamt that I saw a pupil of mine, one of our boys at St. Enda's, standing alone upon a platform above a mighty sea of people; and I understood that he was about to die there for some august cause, Ireland's or another. He looked extraordinarily proud and joyous, lifting his head with a smile almost of amusement; I remember noticing his bare white throat and the hair on his forehead stirred by the wind, just as I had often noticed them on the hurling field. I felt an inexplicable exhilaration as I looked on him, and this exhilaration was heightened rather than diminished by my consciousness that the great silent crowd regarded the boy with pity and wonder rather than with approval as a fool who was throwing away his life rather than a martyr that was doing his duty. It would have been so easy to die before an applauding crowd or before a hostile crowd: but to die before that silent, unsympathetic crowd! I dreamt then that another of my pupils stepped upon the scaffold and embraced his comrade, and that then he tied a white bandage over the boy's eyes, as though he would resent the hangman doing him that kindly office. And this act seemed to me to symbolize an immense brotherly charity and loyalty, and to be the compensation to the boy that died for the indifference of the crowd.

This is the only really vivid dream I have ever had since I used to dream of hobgoblins when I was a child. I remember telling it to my boys at a school meeting a few days later, and their speculating as to which of them I had seen in my dream: a secret which I do not think I gave away. But what recurs to me now is that when I said that I could not wish for any of them a happier destiny than to die thus in the defence of some true thing, they did not seem in any way surprised, for it fitted in with all we had been teaching them at St. Enda's. I do not mean that we have ever carried on anything like a political or revolutionary propaganda among the boys, but simply that we have always allowed them to feel that no one can finely live who hoards life too jealously: that one must be generous in service, and withal joyous, accounting even supreme sacrifices slight. Mr. J. M. Barrie makes his Peter Pan say (and it is finely said) – "To die will be a very big adventure," but, I think, that in making my little boy in *An Rí* offer himself with the words "Let me do this little thing," I am nearer to the spirit of the heroes. (...)

Be certain that in political economy there is no Way of Life either for a man or for a people. Life for both is a matter, not of conflicting tariffs, but of conflicting powers of good and evil; and what have Ricardo and Malthus and Stuart Mill to teach about this? Ye men and peoples, burn your books on rent theories and land values and go back to your sagas. If you will not go back to your sagas, your sagas will come to you again in new guise: for they are terrible immortal things, not capable of being put down by respectable society or by political economy. The old truths will find new mouths, the old sorrows and ecstasies new interpretation. Beauty is the garment of truth, or perhaps we should put it that beauty is the substance in which truth bodies itself forth ; and then we can say that beauty, like matter, is indestructible, however it may change in form. When you think that you have excluded it by your brick walls it flows in upon you, multitudinous. I know not how the old beauty will come back for us in this country and century; through an Irish theatre perhaps, or through a new poetry welling up in Irish-speaking villages. But come back it will, and its coming will be as the coming of God's angel, when

"... seems another morn
Risen on mid-noon".

AN MACAOMH, Christmas 1909

'Pageants' — Stephen MacKenna

The pageant is coming back to the modern world. In England, in France, in Ireland people have rather suddenly seen that this mediaeval form has particular merits. It is a happy blend of many arts. It stands between the drama and the mere professional show, in a happy freedom of its own. It is less rigid in its intellectual demand than is the drama, which must always labour with a greater or less depth of psychology. Yet it, too, tells a human story, and can carry a great intensity of emotion. It gives far prettier pictures to the eye than any mere procession, more varied and blended colour of costume, and more of the natural grace of pose and action. It can use lyric poetry in choruses, or even in single singing as naturally as it can give march-music or the ornate prose of solemn discourses. [...]

A very large number of people will remain long under the impression of the new order of pageant as they saw and heard it yesterday at St. Enda's School in the inspiring presentation of the Boy-Deeds, or Youthful Exploits of Cúchulainn. St. Enda's is bilingual, but its magnificent youthful exploit of yesterday was unilingual, Irish. And of all the large audience stretched over the sunny pageant-field, all must have felt that here was at once a new form of art and a new reason for hope shown in the country. The story of Cúchulainn, in boy-deeds and hero-suffering alike, all the world knows to be beautiful. As Mr. Pearse rightly says in his "book", it is one of the very most moving of the epic stories of all literature. But here, as the first boyish triumphs were acted out before us, it took a new and closer meaning. With all the beauty of the sumptuous costumes, exquisite by the art of colour-blending as they are of themselves graceful in line and flow, there was the Irish itself, perfectly enunciated and modulated, or delightfully chanted, by fresh Irish children, who, ninety-four already, are growing up to be Irish, and talk Irish and think Irish, the new generation Gaelic in the grain. No one with one dash of the Celt but must have been deeply moved to hear the beautiful heroic story of Cúchulainn and his peers opened in the language that has not died in Ireland from the days of Cúchulainn himself and of Conor MacNessa and of the Red Branch; there was a magic in the old tongue telling the old tale: it seemed like a prophecy of hope for the Gael to hear the rich Irish from the boys on the hurling-field and in the hunting booths of the story and flowing freely from the lips of scores of the spectators gathered to hear the old Gaelic at a twentieth century pageant on the fringe of Dublin City. More than twenty times one thing was said at St. Enda's: "If only all

Dublin could have been compelled to be here!" And there is the force of the pageant. If there only could be such displays in every town of Ireland – as beautifully arranged and as defiantly and inspiringly Irish – the very nobility of the spectacle would first attract, and then the nobility of the ideal would work its way. The pageant educates while it delights. And it has the peculiar merit that, given good will, it can be made popular, open to all: it does not necessarily, as do other means of propaganda, mean doors only opened by money: a free field, the pleasant artistic service of managers and personages, a few plutocrats, perhaps, to pay scot and lot, and all the rest can come in freely, the more the merrier. It would not be possible everywhere to arrange a pageant so sumptuous, so perfect in every detail of story, language, costume, and conduct, as this of the Boyish Exploits of Cúchulainn. But mediaeval pageants must have had many a rustic roughness, many a naïve simplicity, many a droll breakdown: there is no very sound reason why in country Ireland we should make it a motto to do nothing unless we can be masters of a city-like perfection in everything we do. It would not be a bad thing if we could make ourselves a little mediaeval in spirit, that so we might make Cúchulainn and his like serve modern Ireland. It is extraordinary to think of the long time during which all this old beauty, with its modern use, lay locked up, away from the popular mind – the stories that are so healthful and so helpful and so delightful. They are not so far from us now as they were only a decade ago; it will be well for Ireland if a decade hence they furnish the main fund of the thought of every boy and girl in the land. They are as full of fragrance as a garden of apple-trees in bloom, and the people that walked in these pleasant places, from childhood onward, should grow up radiant with health and happy courage. It is tradition that makes a nation, and it is loyalty to some common fine ideals that makes a great nation; perhaps no people has a healthier ancient fund to draw on than we have in these hero-tales; it is a noble work to help to make the race owner again of its own best possessions, the memories of its old-time chivalry, recorded in beauty, and ringing Irish still after two thousand years.

NOTES

1 An Craoibhín's *An Naomh ar Iarraidh*: Douglas Hyde's *The Missing Saint*.
2 Mr Bulfin: William Bulfin, journalist and father of Éamonn Bulfin.
3 Dr. Henry: J.P. Henry (1862–1930), surgeon, Gaelic scholar and author of *An Modh Díreach*.

DÚNLAING ÓG AGUS AN LEANNÁN SÍ

Seo téacs an "dráma" Ghaelaigh a léiríodh le linn an tsosa idir *Íosagán* agus *The Master* san Irish Theatre i mBealtaine na bliana 1915 agus ar labhair an Piarsach faoi ar an ócáid chéanna. Ó *Irisleabhar na Gaeilge*, Deireadh Fómhair 1899, a tógadh an téacs agus mionleasuithe litrithe déanta air. (Fágadh leaganacha canúnacha.) Le Séamus Ó Fiannachta/ Séamus Dubh (an bailitheoir) an chéad nóta ina dhiaidh. Le heagarthóir *Irisleabhar na Gaeilge*, mar ar foilsíodh an blúire sa bhliain 1899, an ceann eile. Sa bhlúire drámata seo, atá suite an oíche roimh Chath Cluana Tarbh tugann leannán sí fáistine do Dhúnlaing go gcaillfear é sa chath. Is díol spéise an saghas friotail a úsáidtear i bhfáistine an leannáin sí: "Titfidh sibh uile go léir ar aon rian/ Is bog dearg 'bheidh an mhaigh amárach/ le bhur gcuid fola go morálach." Agus é ag trácht ar an amhrán "An Rós Geal Dubh"/"Róisín Dubh" sa phaimfléad *Ghosts*, ar chuir sé críoch leis ag deireadh na bliana céanna sin 1915, tharraing an Piarsach aird ar leith ar mhoitíf dhoirteadh na fola ar dhóigh leis bheith ina nóta coitianta i litríocht na Gaeilge.[1]

The following is the text of the dramatic fragment which was produced during the interval between *Íosagán* and *The Master* in the Irish Theatre in May 1915 and about which Pearse gave a lecture on the same occasion. The text, with some spelling amendments, is taken from *Irisleabhar na Gaeilge*, October, 1899. The first note afterward is by Séamus Ó Fiannachta/Séamus Fenton, the original collector, and the second by the editor of the *Gaelic Journal* where the fragment was published. The fragment includes a prophecy given to Dúnlaing on the eve of the Battle of Clontarf. Its imagery would have been of particular interest to Pearse who was to identify "blood-thirstiness" as a prevalent note in Gaelic literature in his pamphlet *Ghosts*, completed at the end of the same year: "Titfidh sibh uile go léir ar aon rian/Is bog dearg 'bheidh an mhaigh amárach/le bhur gcuid fola go morálach." ("You will all fall together/The plain will be soft and red tomorrow/Proudly with your blood").[2]

357

Blúire de dhráma Gaelach

[An oíche roimh Chath Cluana Tairbh. Dúnlaing Óg agus an tSíbhean, i. a leannán sí féin]

DÚNLAING ÓG A stór ghrianaigh,
Cad do dhorchaigh do shnó grách geal?
An le linn mise dul fé chath?

AN LEANNÁN SÍ Neosad duit gan mhoill
Caidé an fáth fé ndeara mo ghné dul díom,
Mar titfirse agus titfidh Brian
Titfidh sibh uile go léir ar aon rian
Is bog dearg 'bheidh an mhaigh amárach
le bhur gcuid fola go morálach.

DÚNLAING ÓG Má thitimidne, titfidh Gaeil
Beidh Gael ar an gcath 'na rí;
Ní chomhrófar go lá an bhráith
A dtitfidh lenár dhá láimh sa mhaigh.

LEANNÁN SÍ A Dhúnlaing, seachain an cath!
Gheobhair céad agus bliain do ré
Agus seachain cath an aonlae.

DÚNLAING ÓG Fear agus céad do chlannaibh Luirc
Tugadh Murchadh Mór thar cheann mo choirp
Agus tabharfadsa an corp séimh seang sin
Thar ceann mhic Ard-Rí Éireann.

LEANNÁN SÍ Tiocfaidh Pilib luachmhar na long
Agus Conchubhar na bhfonn bhfial:
Diadh maiseach Mac Sróil.
Ón namhaid riamh nachar thriall.

Seisear caogad do chlannaibh rí
Nach mbeidh aon ní díobh gan pheilm óir,
Luaramh agus gabháil tréan,
Claíomh géar agus culaith sróil.

DÚNLAING ÓG Tiocfaidh Donncha, dea-mhac Bhriain
Go mbeidh ina dhiaidh sin fiche céad
Dos na fearaibh dob áilne do Dhál gCais
Agus nach bhfilleadh aon fhear ó chéad,

LEANNÁN SÍ Seo duit an brat draíochta,
Agus cosnóidh sé tusa ó gach bascadh
Agus rian claímh dá dtiocfadh ortsa

DÚNLAING ÓG Slán agus beannacht leat.

Do chuaigh sé isteach sa chath maidin amárach Aoine an Chéasta an
lae sin: luigh sé isteach le Murchadh Mórach Briain ag gearradh na
nDubh-Lochlannach. Do chuala Murchadh Mórach Briain scriosbhuillí
Dhúnlaing. "Is ionadh mór liom" do ráidh Murchadh, "go gcloisim do
bhuillí, a Dhúnlaing, agus nach bhfeicim tú." "Ní bheidh an scamall
sin go brách orm," do ráidh Dúnlaing. Ní mó ná aga nuair a tháinig
Mac Rí Loclannaigh suas agus do bhain an ceann do Dhúnlaing. Ina
dhiaidh sin do bhain Murchadh an ceann do bheirt Mhac Rí Lochlann.
    Tháinig ansin Gruagach Oileáin na nÉan agus naonúr dearbh-
bhráithreach céile dó, chuireadar cath ar Mhurchadh. Chomh tiubh
agus 'bhaineadh sé an ceann díobh léimeadh arís an ceann ar an
gcolainn le geasaibh draíochta. Bhí seanbhean Éireannach ag
aoireacht linbh i gcúirt an Ghruagaigh: chonaic sí an cath ar siúl agus
na cinn ag léimeadh as na colannaibh. Chuaigh sí ag triall ar mhnaoi
an Ghruagaigh agus dúirt léi gurb olc an gnó bhí aici dhá dhéanamh
– óir b'í bean an Ghruagaigh bhí ag cur na ngeasa orthu- "Mar" ar
sise, "Is beag an meas tá ag an nGruagach ortsa, fad is maireann an
bhean so áirithe."
    Phrioc an t-éad bean an Ghruagaigh. D'oscail sí an doras thuaidh
– doras na draíochta. D'éirigh an coileán con bhí in aice na tine agus
chuir gloim as; do chualathas ar fud cúig cúige na hÉireann an ghloim,
mar bhí fhios ag an gcoileán go raibh an draíocht imithe díobh ar
oscailt an dorais.
    Fén an sin do thit an ceann don Ghruagach agus do na naonúr
Dubh-Lochlannach.
    Do ghléas sí suas a capall ansin agus ghluais sí go páirc an
bhuailthe. Chonaic sí Murchadh sínte sa pháirc. Do bhagair lámh
uirthi, teacht féna dhéin. Do tháinig sí agus d'fhiafraigh di caidé críoch
an Ghruagaigh. D'fhreagair sí,
    "Mar ghloim coileáin do chuala is mó".

*****

"Imigh go hobann," ar sé "agus tabhair dom deoch do thobar na h-íce. Agus inseod duit gan cháim bás do naonúr bráithreach i nDuirg Aoibhinn" (=Glas Naíon.)
Thug sí an deoch chuige, agus d'ól sé é agus dúirt,
Cá tír nó cá hoileán duit, nó cad í an áit as d'fhásais ?
Gur measa duit gloim coileáin con ná bás naonúr do chlainn do mháthar?
"Mise iníon Amhlaoibh Átha Cliath,
Marcach na dtriath ba ghéire lann;
Is mé bean Ghruagaigh Oileáin na nÉan,
Is dó gan bhréag rugas mo chlann."
(Five of us, "on Gaelic business bent," remained in Sneem a few days last August. During this time we saw a good deal of that fine old seanchaidhe, Seaghán Chróchain Uí Bheirn (…) He recited several poems, sang many songs, and told us many a scéal Fiannaíochta in Sheahan's Hotel. I wrote down a good many from him, including the above. He says the above is part of a drama that used to be acted dialogue-wise in his younger days. (…) SÉAMUS
The above fragment of a drama is interesting in view of Dr Hyde's statement at p. 55 in the Story of Early Gaelic Literature "In Ireland, on the other hand, the dramatic stage was never reached at all". (The occurrence of the metres so frequent in the Ossianic poems seems to point to its having been composed about three centuries ago – ED)

Irisleabhar na Gaeilge, Deireadh Fómhair 1899, Vol 10, p.18–20

FÉACH CHOMH MAITH/FURTHER READING

Séamus Fenton, *It All Happened*, M.H. Gill and Sons, 1948. (Ba é Séamus Fenton/Séamus Dubh an "Séamus" a luaitear thuas./Séamus Fenton is the "Séamus" mentioned above)
Seán Ó Morónaigh, eag., *Drámaíocht ó Dhúchas: ó bhéalaithris Thaidhg Uí Chonchubhair*, An Comhlachas Náisiúnta Drámaíochta, 2006. Tá tábhacht mhór ag baint leis an rianadh a dhéanann Ó Morónaigh ar fhréamha na dramaíochta dúchais. Ó Morónaigh's masterly research provides an important overview of the dramatic "agallamh" or dialogue poem in folk literature.
Meidhbhín Ní Úrdail, Cath Cluana Tarbh/The Battle of Clontarf, Irish Texts Society, Vol.64/Iml.64.

NOTES

1 Féach Róisín Ní Ghairbhí, "A people that did not exist? Reflections on some sources and contexts for Pearse's militant nationalism", in Ruán O'Donnell, ed., *The Impact of the 1916 Rising: Among the Nations*, Irish Academic Press, 2008, lgh. 161–86, go háirithe lgh.181–3.

2 See Róisín Ní Ghairbhí, "A people that did not exist? Reflections on some sources and contexts for Pearse's militant nationalism", in Ruán O'Donnell, ed., *The Impact of the 1916 Rising: Among the Nations*, Irish Academic Press, 2008, p.161–86, esp. p. 181–3.

'A FORGOTTEN PLAY BY PATRICK PEARSE'

THE IRISH PRESS, 8th JUNE 1953

For thirty years it lay in an Offaly farmhouse...Recently discovered it will this year be produced in Dublin. An unfinished play by Patrick Pearse which had lain forgotten for over thirty years in an Offaly farmhouse will be staged at this year's Oireachtas in Dublin. The play is "Eoghan Gabha" ("Owen the Blacksmith") and it was discovered, with other Pearse manuscripts, by Mr. Éamonn Bulfin at his home in Derrinlough, Birr.

The permission of Pearse's sister, Margaret, to stage the play was sought, and has been given; and it is hoped that The Runners, a Tullamore drama group, will shortly begin rehearsals of "Eoghan Gabha."

"Eoghan Gabha" will be produced by Mr. Noel McMahon, Dublin-born advertising display manager with the Tullamore firm of Williams, and The Runners will have the advice of a native Irish speaker, Mr. Donal O'Carroll, a teacher in Tullamore Technical School.

"It has been suggested that a conclusion should be written for this play," Mr. McMahon told I.N.A. "but that can be decided later on. The Runners will stage it in its present form as a tribute to the memory of Pearse, and the curtain will fall as the last words he wrote are spoken."

Whether "Eoghan Gabha" was interrupted by the Rising cannot be said for certain; but the man who has brought this fragment of literature back to the light is himself a romantic link with Patrick Pearse. For Éamonn Bulfin – son of William Bulfin, author of the classic "Rambles in Éirinn" – was one of Pearse's pupils at St. Enda's College and fought by his side during Easter Week.

FOR SAFE KEEPING

When the Rising came Éamonn Bulfin was appointed Staff Lieutenant at Pearse's Headquarters and was placed in command of the

Rathfarnham Volunteer Company. After the G.P.O. garrison had surrendered he was interned first in Frongoch and then in Durham Jail, and in 1919 was deported to the Argentine as an "undesirable alien".

He had been born in Buenos Aires, where his father was editor of the famous newspaper "The Southern Cross".

It was, however, soon after the Rising that the Pearse manuscripts first came into Éamonn Bulfin's possession. British troops were frequently raiding St. Enda's; and fearful lest the manuscripts should be destroyed, the patriot's mother sent word to Bulfin to take charge of them. He brought them to his home in Derrinlough; but soon afterwords he was arrested by the British in connection with the so-called German Plot.

Exiled to the Argentine in 1919, Mr. Bulfin was appointed representative of the Irish republic by the Dail. Even when he was conscripted into the Navy, he carried on his work, for his presence in the dock area was an invaluable link between the Irish in Buenos Aires, British Ports and the homeland.

When the late Laurence Ginnell became Ireland's Minister Plenipotentiary to the Argentine, Éamonn Bulfin was appointed Secretary to the diplomatic mission. The two men organised a Republican loan campaign; but the day before the loan was to be launched the Treaty was signed and they were called home.

MANUSCRIPTS FOUND

The Civil War was raging when Bulfin landed at Cobh; and in the years of stress and rebuilding that followed, the Pearse manuscripts lay forgotten and unread.

"Then within the last couple of years," says Mr. Bulfin, "I began a task that had been on my mind for a long time – the documentation of a mass of writings left me by my father when he died in 1910.

"Among these papers I found the original manuscript of 'Rambles in Éirinn' written in my father's copperplate hand. And beside it was another sheaf of notepaper covered with the neat backhand writing of Patrick Pearse."

It was then, as he turned the pages written by his old school master and friend, that the memory of Mrs. Pearse's message came home to Éamonn Bulfin. He laid his father's work aside; and as he read what Pearse had written he realised that he had discovered a piece of literary trove, the existence of which no one could have suspected.

"Eoghan Gabha", perhaps the most important of the manu-scripts, is written on both sides of notepaper headed "The Gaelic

363

League", 24 Upper O'Connell Street – Publication Committee, P. H. Pearse, B.L. Hon. Secretary.

Set in the time of Sarsfield, the play tells of an apprentice blacksmith, Colum Ó Ceallaigh, who falls in love with the daughter of his master, Eoghan Ó Grada. They plan to marry but the blacksmith forbids them when he learns that Colum is the son of a man one of whose kinsfolk slew his brother.

In the second act, Sarsfield himself comes to the forge and speaks to the smith, who is unaware of his real identity. With him is the apprentice – now a Jacobite soldier. At that point Pearse laid the play aside and never completed it.

QUESTION OF DATE

On other sheets of paper – some of them headed "An Claidheamh Soluis," the paper edited by Pearse – are a lullaby in English with an Irish Refrain; and two poems "The Keening of Mary" and "Keen for Fair-haired Donough" – the latter an English version of the well-known Irish Lament "Donnchadh Bán."

There is no date on the manuscripts to indicate when they were written: but Padraic Óg Ó Conaire; Head of the Dáil Translation Staff and a pupil of Pearse's at St. Enda's believes that "Eoghan Gabha", at least, was written between 1903–09.

This was the period when Pearse was secretary of the Gaelic League Publication Committee. The theory is strengthened by the fact that notepaper on which the play is written bears the printed date "190–".

Mr. Desmond Ryan, author of "The Man Called Pearse", and another past pupil of Saint Enda's says that the manuscripts form part of "quite a bit" of unfinished material left by Pearse. He points out that Pearse named specifically the works he wished to be republished or published. Apparently "Eoghan Gabha" was not included.

At the same time it is felt that the manuscripts now in Mr. Bulfin's possession should be given a more enduring form.

Mr. Ernest Blythe, Manager of the Abbey Theatre, comments: "This is surely a task for the Manuscripts Commission. 'Eoghan Gabha' – the only one of the manuscripts I have had the opportunity of reading – is typical of Pearse in many ways.

"The dialogue sparkles, the characters are well drawn and the Irish is faultless. It is, of course, only a fragment – but a very precious fragment."

OLD PLAYBILLS

And Dr. Richard Hayes, Director of the National Library, told the Irish News Agency: "This is a most welcome discovery, and – even in photostat – would be a rich addition to the Pearse letters and manuscripts already in our possession."

With the manuscripts are programmes and playbills, themselves of historical interest. One playbill was printed for a production in the old Irish Theatre in Hardwicke Street, Dublin, of Pearse's plays, "Íosagán" and "The Master".

The plays were staged by the boys of St. Enda's, the title role being taken by Diarmuid McGinley – President from 1943/46 of the Gaelic League.

In "The Master", the part of Ciaran was taken by Pearse himself; of Daire by Éamonn Bulfin, and of Ceallach by the late David Sears.

Another programme of a 1909 pageant, staged when St. Enda's was still in Oakley Road, lists the names of Denis Gwynn, Éamonn Bulfin and Desmond Ryan.

The idea of staging "Eoghan Gabha" at this year's Oireachtas first occurred to Father Joseph Hurley, S.J. of St. Stanislaus College, Tullamore. A close friend of Mr. Bulfin, Father Hurley is a well-known archaeologist and Gaelic scholar, and organised a section of a Tostal exhibition at Tullamore, in which some of the recently discovered Pearse and Bulfin manuscripts were shown. – I.N.A.

"OIREACHTAS LÁ NA NÓG PRIEST SAYS IRELAND NEEDS HER YOUTH" "PEARSE PLAY" *IRISH INDEPENDENT*, 28TH OCTOBER 1953

"Eoghan Gabha", Patrick Pearse's recently discovered play, received its first productin as part of the Oireachtas programme in the R.I.A.M theatre, Westland Row, last night.

Comhaltas Drámaíochta na Tulaigh Móire, a group from Tullamore, staged the play, which is set in a country village taken from the time of Sarsfield. The play was produced in the form in which it appears in the manuscript, with the sole addition of a prologue and epilogue taken from the well-known Irish poem "A Phádraig Sairséal, slán go dtí thú."

Theatrically, the play can give little satisfaction in this form, as it breaks off abruptly in the early stages of the second act leaving the audience completely at sea as to the manner in which the plot was intended to develop.

At the close of the performance a member of the company presented a bouquet to Senator Margaret Pearse, who attended the production.

SELECTED CAST LISTS

Editors' Note: Below we have included some of the extant information available concerning original cast lists. While this is not a complete list, it contains some fascinating information on the people included in Pearse's theatrical circle.

ÍOSAGÁN

Íosagán: Eunan MacGinley
Sean-Mhaitias: Pádraic Óg Ó Conaire

From information in Joseph Holloway's account of the play. Joseph Holloway Diaries, NLI / Ó dhialann Holloway, LNÉ.

MACGHNÍOMHARTHA CHÚCHULAINN

Cathréim trírannach arna tarraing ar Tháin Bó Cuailgne do Phádraic Mac Piarais. An fhoireann anseo síos:

An Cór: Buíon Bard agus Manach
(Chorus: Bards and Monks)
Conchubhar Mac Neasa, Rí Uladh: Donncha Mac Fhinn
(Conchubhar, Son of Neasa, King of Ulster: Denis Gwynn)
Feargus Mac Róigh: Peadar Ó Conchubhair
(Feargus, son of Roigh: Peter O'Connor)
Laochra den Chraobh Rua *(Heroes of the Red Branch)*
Conall Cearnach: Eoghan Mac Carthaigh
(Conall the Triumphant: Eugene McCarthy)
Laoghaire Buadhach: Micheál Ó Conchubhair
(Laoghaire the Victorious) Michael O'Connor
Laochra eile den Chraobh Rua *(Other heroes of the Red Branch)*
Ailfrid MacLochlainn *(Alfred McGloughlin)*
Domhnall Ó Conchubhair *(Donal O'Connor)*
Pádraig Ó Tuathaigh *(Patrick Tuohy)*

Seosamh Ó Clochartaigh *(Joseph Stone)*
Cathbhadh Draoi: Éamonn Builfin
(Cathbhadh the Druid: Éamonn Bulfin)
Follamhan Mac Conchubhair, i.Taoiseach na Macra: Adamhnán
Mac Fhionnlaoich
(Follamhan, son of Conchubhar, Chief of the Boy-Corps
Eunan MacGinley)
An macra ar cheana
(The Boy Corps, as follows)
Eoghan: Seán Paor *(Eoghan: John Power)*
Naoise: Hoirbeard Ó Buachallla *(Naoise: Herbert Buckley)*
Ainnle, i.Clann Uisnigh: Maitiú Ó Ceallaigh
(Ainnle, the children of Uisneach: Matthew O'Kelly)
Ardán: Seosamh Ó Buachalla *(Ardan: Joseph Buckley)*
Buadhach: Buadhach Ó Faoláin *(Buadhach: Victor Whelan)*
Diarmaid: Diarmaid Mac Carthaigh *(Diarmaid: Dermot MacCarthy)*
Feargus: Pádraic Mac Cathmhaoil *(Feargus: Patrick Campbell)*
Cathal: Cathal MacLochlainn *(Cathal: Charles McGloughlin)*
Conchubhar: Peadar MacFhionnbhairr *(Conchubhar: P.J. Gaynor)*
Conn: Lughaidh MacMaoláin *(Conn: Louis McMullen)*
Cairbre: Conchubhar Mac Fhionnlaoich *(Cairbre: Conor MacGinley)*
Coireall: Coireall Ó Broin *(Coireall: Cyril Byrne)*
Conall: Tomás Paor *(Conall: Thomas Power)*
Cormac: Seaghan Ó Cathail *(Cormac: John Cahill)*
Brian: Brian Mac Néill *(Brian: Brian MacNeill)*
Ruaidhrí: Horás Mac Eoinín *(Ruaidhrí: Horace Jennings)*
Art: Deasmhumha Mac Giolla Dhuibh *(Art: Desmond Black)*
Mathghamhain: Uaitéar Ó Cuirrín *(Mathghamhain: Walter Curran)*
Flann: Seaghan Mac Maoláin *(Flann: John McMullan)*
Fiacha: Seosamh Ó hEidhin *(Fiacha: Joseph Hynes)*
Seatanta Mac Sualtaimh, i.Cúchulainn: Proinsias Ó Dúnlaing
(Seatanta son of Sualtamh, afterward Cúchulainn: Frank Dowling)
Culann Ceárd i. Ceárd uasal d'Ultaibh: Pádraic Ó Conaire
(Culann the smith, a noble smith of Ulster: Patrick Conroy)
Céird eile *(Other smiths)*
Muiris Ó Fearchair *(Maurice Fearhar)*
Colm Ó Neachtain *(Colm Naughton)*
Eoin Mac Dhaibheach *(Eoin MacGavock)*
Iubhar Mac Riangabhra, ara Chonchubhair: Proinsias Ó Conghaile
(Iubhar son of Riangabhra, Conchubhar's charioteer: Frank Connolly)

Giollarnadh each agus gadhar *(Horse and dog gillies)*
Riobard Ó Ruaidhín *(Robert Ryan)*
Uilleoc Ó Mórdha *(Ulick Moore)*
Antoine MacEoinín *(Anthony Jennings)*
Fear iomchurtha sleighe Chonchubhair:
Breanndán Ó Seaghdha *(Brendan O'Shea)*
Fear iomchurtha sgéithe Chonchubhair:
Seosamh Ó Nualláin *(Joseph Nolan)*
Giollaí beaga *(Pages)*
Seaghan Ó Luachra (John Loughrey)
Domhnall Mac Carthaigh (Donal MacCarthy)
Antoine Mac Concoille (Anthony Woods)
Fear faire: Deasmhumha Ó Riain
(A watcher: Desmond Ryan)
Óglaigh *(Soldiers)*
Colm MacDomhnaill *(Colm MacDonnell)*
Risteard Bairéad *(Richard Barrett)*
Maolmhuire Mag Shearraigh *(Milo MacGarry)*
Gearóid Mac Eochadha *(Gerald Keogh)*
Deasmhumha Mac Daibhid *(Desmond Davitt)*
Micheál Ó Ceallaigh *(Michael O'Kelly)*
Bantracht *(Women)*
Máire Nic Mhaoláin *(Mary McMullan)*
Máire Bhreathnach *(May Walsh)*
Siubhán Nic Choluim *(Susan Colum)*
Eibhlín Ní Bhroin *(Eileen Byrne)*
Muriel Ní Luachra *(Muriel Loughrey)*
Iris Ní Eidhin *(Iris Hynes)*
Aos ceoil agus oirfidigh *(Musicians)*
Eoghan Laoide *(Owen Lloyd)*
Tomás Mac Domhnaill *(Thomas McDonell)*
Uilliam Mac Aindrias *(William McAndrews)*
Seaghan Ó Deoráin *(John Doran)*
Séamas Mac Einrí *(James Henry)*

Eolas ón gclár. Buíochas le Leabharlann Uí Ailín
Information from original programme, courtesy of Allen Library
Note: Desmond Ryan in A Story of a Success attributes costumes, grouping and general production to Willie Pearse and 'help in the same and other directions' to Alf Mac Lochalainn.[1]

AN PHÁIS/ PASSION PLAY

Nóta: *Níor tugadh ainmneacha ar an gclár mar gheall ar ábhar íogair an dráma ach is féidir cuid de na hainmneacha a aimsiú i bhfoinsí eile.*
Note: *The cast was not given on the programme because of the sensitive question of the religious matter depicted. However it is possible to reconstruct some of the cast from other sources.*

An Mhaighdean Muire *(the Virgin Mary)*: Mary Bulfin
Christ *(Críost)*: Thomas McDonnell
Píoláit *(Pilate)*: Willie Pearse
Barrabas: Mícheál Mac Ruaidhrí
Gadaithe *(Thieves)*: P.H. Pearse, Thomas MacDonagh
Ceol *(Music)*: Thomas McDonnell

FIONN, A DRAMATIC SPECTACLE

Characters (in the order of their entrance)
Cupbearers: Alfred Gaynor, Joseph McGilligan
Heroes: Tadhg Carleton, Eunan MacGinley, Thomas Butler,
Bernard Cooney, William Kenny
Chief Musician: Frederick Holden
Druid: Conor MacGinley
Art the Lonely: Joseph Sweeney
Goll Mac Morna: Mr William Pearse
Pages: Desmond Murphy, Owen Clarke
Fionn: David Sears
Lugh Lámhfhada: John Joyce
The Son of Míodhna: Fredk O'Doherty

Information from original programme. Courtesy of Pearse Museum/OPW with thanks to Brian Crowley.
Eolas ón gclár. Buíochas le Músaem na bPiarsach/OPW agus go háirithe Brian Crowley.

THE MASTER: A MIRACLE PLAY

The Irish Theatre, Hardwicke Street
Thursday, Friday and Saturday May 20th, 21st and 22nd
Translated by the Author from his Original Irish

Art: Eunan MacGinley
Breasal: Joseph Sweeny
Maine: Desmond Murphy
Ronan: Augustine Geary
Ceallach, Pupils of Ciaran: David Sears
Ciaran, a Teacher: William Pearse
Iollann Beag, a little Pupil of Ciaran's: Owen Clarke
A King's Messenger: Desmond Ryan
Daire, A King: Éamonn Bulfin
Michael: John Kilgallon

Place, a cloister in a wood.
The play is now produced for the first time.
The persons in both plays are named in the order of their entry.
The airs sung are by Thomas MacDonnell.

THE SINGER

Characters
Macdara, the Singer: Éamonn Bulfin
Colm, his brother: Eunan MacGinley
Maolsheachlainn, a Schoolmaster: Fintan Murphy
Cuimín Éanna: David Sears
Diarmuid of the Bridge: Conor MacGinley
Máire Ní Fhiannachta, Mother of Macdara:
Máire Nic Shiubhlaigh
Sighle: Miss Betty King[2]
A number of Insurgents

Eolas ón mbunchlár. Buíochas le Brian Crowley, Músaem na bPiarsach agus
an OPW as sinn a chur ar an eolas faoin gclár seo.
Information from original programme. Special thanks to Brian Crowley of the
Pearse Museum and OPW for bringing our attention to this programme.

NOTES

1 Desmond Ryan, *The Story of a Success*, p.20.
2 Note: Betty King was the stage name of Patricia 'Gypsy' Walker, the sister of Máire Nic Shiubhlaigh. Gypsy had acted with the Leinster Stage Society.

BIBLIOGRAPHY/ LEABHARLIOSTA

WRITINGS BY PEARSE/SCRÍBHINNÍ AN PHIARSAIGH

Mac Piarais, Pádraic, *Íosagán agus Scéalta Eile* (Baile Átha Cliath: Conradh na Gaeilge, 1907).

Mac Piarais, Pádraic, *An Mháthair agus Scéalta Eile* (Dundalk: Dún Dealgan Press, 1916).

Ó Buachalla, Séamus (ed.) *The Letters of P.H. Pearse* (London: Gerrards Cross/Colin Smythe, 1980).

Ó Buachalla, Séamus (ed.), *The Literary Writings of Patrick Pearse* (Dublin: Mercier Press, 1979).

Ó Buachalla, Séamus, (eag) *Na Scríbhinní Liteartha le Pádraic Mac Piarais, na Scríbhinní Gaeilge* (Dublin: Cló Mercier, 1979).

Ó Coigligh, Ciarán (eag.), *Filíocht Ghaeilge Phádraig Mhic Phiarais* (Baile Átha Cliath: An Clóchomhar, 1981).

Ó hÁinle, Cathal,(eag.), *Gearrscéalta an Phiarsaigh* (Baile Átha Cliath: Cló Thalbóid, 1979).

Pearse, Mary Brigid (ed.), *The Home-Life of Pádraig Pearse* (Dublin: Mercier Press, 1979, 1st pub. 1934).

Pearse, Patrick, *From a Hermitage* (Dublin: Irish Freedom Press, 1915)

Pearse, Patrick, *Three Lectures on Gaelic Topics* (Dublin: M.H. Gill and Son, 1898).

Pearse, Patrick, *Collected Works of Pádraic H. Pearse: Plays. Stories, Poems* (Dublin: Phoenix Publishing Co. Ltd., 1918).

Pearse, Patrick, (Desmond Ryan ed.), *The Story of a Success* (Dublin: Maunsel & Co., 1920).

Pearse, Patrick, *The Singer* (National Library of Ireland, MS 7389).

Pearse, Patrick, *An Rí / The King*, in *An Macaomh*, Vol. II No.2, May 1913.

Pearse, Patrick, *Owen*, in *Fianna*, December 1915 (TCD, Early Printed Books, IN 20.90&91 no.22).

Pearse, Patrick, *Íosagán* (Irish), in *An Macaomh*, Vol I. No. 2, Christmas 1909.

Pearse, Patrick, *Eoghan Gabha*, MS 15, 004, NLI.

Pearse, Patrick, *Macghníomhartha Chúchulainn*, *An Macaomh*, Meán-samhradh 1909, lgh.34- 46.

Ryan, Desmond, *Collected Works of P.H. Pearse: Plays, Stories, Poems* (Dublin: Maunsel and Co, c.1918).

Ryan, Desmond, *Collected Works of P.H. Pearse: Scríbhinní* (Dublin: Maunsel and Co, c.1918).

BIOGRAPHICAL SOURCES/FOINSÍ BEATHAISNÉISE

Augusteijn, Joost, *Patrick Pearse: The Making of a Revolutionary* (Basingstoke: Palgrave Macmillan, 2010).

Edwards, Ruth Dudley, *Patrick Pearse: The Triumph of Failure* (Dublin: Irish Academic Press, 2006 edition).

Le Roux, Louis, *Patrick H. Pearse* (Dublin: Talbot Press, 1932).

Murphy, Brian P., *Patrick Pearse and the Lost Republican Ideal* (Dublin: James Duffy, 1991).

Ó Buachalla, Séamus, *An Piarsach sa Bheilg. P.H Pearse in Belgium. P.H. Pearse in België*, (Dublin: An Gúm, 1998)

Pearse, Mary Brigid (ed.), *The Home-Life of Pádraig Pearse* (Dublin: Mercier Press, 1979, 1st pub. 1934).

Pearse, Patrick, Unpublished Biographical Fragment, Pearse Museum.

Ryan, Desmond, *Remembering Sion: A Chronicle of Storm and Quiet* (London: Arthur Barker, 1934)

Ryan, Desmond, *The Man Called Pearse* (Dublin: Maunsel and Co., 1919)

SELECTED READING/ROGHA LÉITHEOIREACHTA

Breathnach, Diarmuid agus Ní Mhurchú, Máire, Sraith *Beathaisnéis* (Baile Átha Cliath: An Clóchomhar, dátaí éagsúla) ar fáil ar líne ag www.ainm.ie.

Colum, Mary, *Life and the Dream* (London: Macmillan, 1947).

Crowley, Brian, "'His Father's Son": James and Patrick Pearse', *Folk Life: Journal of Ethnological Studies*, Vol. 43 2004–5, pp.71–88.

Deane, Seamus, *Celtic Revivals, Essays in Modern Irish Literature 1880–1980* (London: Faber & Faber, 1985).

Feeney, William, *Drama in Hardwicke St, A History of the Irish Theatre Company* (London and Toronto: Associated University Presses, 1984).

Higgins, Roisín and Uí Chollatáin, Regina (eds.), *The Life and After-life of P.H. Pearse* (Dublin: Irish Academic Press, 2009).

Hobson, Bulmer (ed.), *The Gate Theatre Dublin* (Dublin: Gate Theatre, 1934).

Hogan, Robert, with Richard Burnham and Daniel P. Poteet, *The Abbey Theatre, the Rise of the Realists, 1910–1915* (Dublin: Dolmen Press, 1978).

Kelly, James and Mac Murchaidh, Ciarán (eds.), *Irish and English: Essays on the Irish linguistic and cultural frontier, 1600–1900* (Dublin: Four Courts Press, 2012).

Matthews, P.J., *Revival: the Abbey Theatre, Sinn Féin, the Gaelic League and the Co-operative Movement* (Cork: Cork University Press, 2003).

Moran, James, *Four Irish Rebel Plays* (Dublin: Irish Academic Press, 2007).

Moran, James, *Staging the Rising: 1916 as Theatre* (Cork: Cork University Press, 2006)

Morris, Catherine, *Alice Milligan and the Irish Cultural Revival* (Dublin: Four Courts Press, 2012).

Murphy, Gerard, *Early Irish Lyrics* (Dublin: Four Courts Press, 1999).

Mac Congail, Nollaig agus Ní Mhuircheartaigh, Eadaoin, *Drámaí Thús na hAthbheochana* (Gaillimh: Arlen House, 2008).

Mac Lochlainn, Gearóid, *Ealaín na hAmharclainne* (Baile Átha Cliath: ClódhannaTeoranta, 1966).

McNulty, Eugene, *The Ulster Literary Theatre and the Northern Revival* (Cork: Cork University Press, 2008).

McNulty, Eugene, 'Breaking the Law: Patrick Pearse, cultural revival, and the site of sovereignty', *Journal of Postcolonial Writing*, Vol. 46 Issue 5 (Nov. 2010).

Ní Fhlathúin, M, 'The anti-colonial modernism of Patrick Pearse', in H. Booth and N. Rigby (eds.), *Modernism and Empire* (Manchester: Manchester University Press, 2000).

Ní Ghairbhí, Róisín, 'A People that did not Exist? Reflections on some Sources and Contexts for Patrick Pearse's Militant Nationalism', in O'Donnell, Ruán (ed.), *The Impact of the 1916 Rising* (Dublin: Irish Academic Press, 2008), pp.161–86.

Ní Ghairbhí, Róisín, 'The Battle before us now is a Battle of Words, Pearse and Postcolonial Theory' in Higgins, Roisín and Uí Chollatáin, Regina (eds.), *The Life and After-life of P.H. Pearse* (Dublin: Irish Academic Press, 2009), pp.156–67.

Nic Congail, Ríona, *Úna Ní Fhaircheallaigh agus an Fhís Útóipeach Ghaelach* (Gaillimh: Arlen House, 2010).

Nic Shiubhlaigh, Máire, *The Splendid Years* (Dublin: James Duffy and Company, 1955).

Ó Buachalla, Séamus, *A significant Irish educationalist: the educational writings of P. H. Pearse* (Dublin & Cork, Mercier Press, 1980).

Ó Brolachán, Honor, *Joseph Plunkett*, Sixteen Lives Series (Dublin: O'Brien Press 2012).

O'Donnell, Ruán (ed.), *The Impact of the 1916 Rising* (Dublin: Irish Academic Press, 2008).

O'Leary, Philip, *The Prose Literature of the Gaelic Revival: 1881–1921* (Pennsylvania State University Press, 1994).

Ó Morónaigh, Seán, *Agallaimh na hÉigse, Cíoradh agus Cnuasach* (Camus: An Comhlachas Náisiúnta Drámaíochta, dara heagrán, 2010).

Ó Morónaigh, Seán, *Drámaíocht ó Dhúchas, Ó Bhéalaithris Thaidhg Uí Chonchubhair* (Camus: An Comhlachas Náisiúnta Drámaíochta, 2005).

Ó Riain, Pádraic, *A Dictionary of Irish Saints* (Dublin: Four Courts Press, 2011).

Ó Siadhail, Pádraig, *Stair Dhrámaíocht na Gaeilge* (Conamara: Cló Iarchonnachta, 1993).

Sigerson, George, *Bards of the Gall and Gael examples of the poetic literature of Erinn; done into English after the metres and modes of the Gael by George Sigerson* (London, Dublin: T Fisher Unwin, 1907).

Sisson, Elaine, *Pearse's Patriots: St Enda's and the cult of boyhood* (Cork: Cork University Press, 2003).

Tagore, Rabindranath, *Collected Poems and Plays* (London: MacMillan, 1936).

Townsend, Charles, *Easter 1916: The Irish Rebellion* (London: Penguin Books, 2006).

Trotter, Mary, *Ireland's National Theaters* (Syracuse, NY: Syracuse University Press, 2001).

Uí Chollatáin, Regina, *An Claidheamh Soluis agus Fáinne an lae 1899–1932: Anailís ar phríomhnuachtán Gaeilge ré na hAthbheochana* (Baile Átha Cliath: Cois Life Teoranta, 2004).

Vandevelde, Karen, *The Alternative Dramatic Revival in Ireland* (Cambridge Station, CA: Academica Press, 2004).

Walsh, Brendan, *The Pedagogy of Protest: the educational thought and work of Patrick H. Pearse* (Oxford: Peter Lang, 2007).

Windisch, Ernst, *Die altirischeheldensage Táin bó Cúailnge, nach dem Buch von Leinster, in text und uebersetzung mit einer einleitung hrsg. von Ernst Windisch. Gedruckt mit unterstützung der Kgl. sächsischengesellschaft der wissenschaften* (Leipzig: S Hirzel, 1905).

Manuscripts and Printed Material/
Lámhscríbhinní agus Ábhar clóbhuailte

Joseph Holloway's Diaries, NLI
Pearse Papers, NLI
Photographs and printed material, Pearse Museum/OPW
Photographs and printed material, Allen Library
Fianna Magazine, Trinity College Library.

Newspapers, Journals, Magazines/
Nuachtáin agus Irisí

An Macaomh
An Claidheamh Soluis
An Sgoláire (the student magazine of St. Enda's)
Dublin Evening Mail
Irish Independent
Irish Press
Irish Times
Irisleabhar na Gaeilge
Our Boys
Samhain
The Irish Monthly

Web-based sources/Ón Idirlíon

www.ainm.ie This searchable database lists detailed biographies and works for hundreds of figures associated with the Irish language. It is based on the magisterial *Beathaisnéis* series of Diarmuid Breathnach and Máire Ní Mhurchú.

www.ucc.ie/celt Most of the published English language writings of Pearse, including his main political writings, are available on line here.

www.playography.ie While not exhaustive, the lists of plays which were produced professionally in Ireland that are provided in *The Irish Playography* and *Playography na Gaeilge* are a very useful resource.

OTHER SOURCES/FOINSÍ EILE

Interview with Alf and Fionnnuala Mac Lochlainn, October 2008
Interview with Mr. Dave Kenny, journalist, July 2012, regarding the
Walker family
Information from Róisín Ní Dhonnacha, Coláiste Mhuire gan Smál
on the Irish of North Conamara, especially regarding colloquialisms
in *Eoghan Gabha*.

INDEX